ORGANIZATIONS IN INDUSTRY

Strategy, Structure, and Selection

Edited by

GLENN R. CARROLL
MICHAEL T. HANNAN

OXFORD UNIVERSITY PRESS
1995

Oxford University Press

Oxford   New York
Athens   Auckland   Bankok   Bombay
Calcutta   Cape Town   Dar es Salaam   Delhi
Florence   Hong Kong   Istanbul   Karachi
Kuala Lumpur   Madras   Madrid   Melbourne
Mexico City   Nairobi   Paris   Singapore
Taipei   Tokyo   Toronto

and associated companies in
Berlin   Ibadan

Published by Oxford University Press, Inc.,
200 Madison Avenue, New York, New York 10016

Oxford is a registered trademark of Oxford University Press

Library of Congress Cataloging-in-Publication Data
Organizations in industry : strategy, structure, and selection /
edited by Glenn R. Carroll, Michael T. Hannan.
p. cm.   Includes bibliographical references and index.
ISBN 0-19-508309-1 (c.)—ISBN 0-19-508310-5 (p)
1. Industrial organization.   2. Organizational behavior.
3. Industrial sociology.   I. Carroll, Glenn R.
II. Hannan, Michael T.
HD31.0777   1995
302.3'5—dc20   94-9011

9 8 7 6 5 4 3 2 1

Printed in the United States of America
on acid free paper

To James S. Coleman

PREFACE

As its title suggests, this book discusses organizations. It differs from the hundreds of existing books on the topic by its pronounced attention to *empirical* issues. Except in the introductory chapters, the introductions to the major sections, and the concluding chapter, we and our coauthors examine the actual structure and evolution of organizations in many interesting industries. Each of these chapters focuses on a single industry and describes the organizational history of that industry. These discussions include developments from the origins of the industry to the near present and cover both existing organizations and those no longer in operation. The "industries" described include automobile manufacturing, biotechnology, financial services (credit unions and investment banks), health care (health maintenance organizations and medical diagnostic imaging producers), labor union organizing, microcomputer manufacturing, art museums, newspaper publishing, radio broadcasting, railroad transport, and telephony.

Why emphasize empirical phenomena? Mainly because we expect that this book will be used as a secondary or supplemental text for courses in organization design, organizational sociology, organizational theory, and strategic management. The primary readings or textbooks for these courses usually concentrate on conceptual issues and on abstract and general theories of organizations. This book should be seen as a companion to these texts, a down-to-earth fellow traveler for students to take with them as they learn to analyze formal organizations. Our experience in teaching such material is that students learn best when abstract ideas are presented with a healthy dose of concrete reality.

The uses we envision for the book require that its empirical materials be selective. We and our coauthors did not set out to write general histories of industries and their constituent organizations. Instead, we tried to write organizational analyses of the histories of industries—selective accounts of historical patterns and events that illustrate the operation and importance of organizational processes.

We believe that this approach has several advantages. First, and most obviously, it provides historical and institutional knowledge about particular industries. We think that obtaining such knowledge helps prepare one for a career in modern society, although there are usually too few opportunities to learn it in the typical social science or business curricula.

Second, the old social science adage—that the best insights arise from comparative analysis—applies to organizations and industries. Analyzing and comparing specific industries and their organizations provides potentially valuable insight into the social world. This insight often goes beyond what can be learned from intensive study of one kind of organization or one industry.

Third, we believe that a general lesson from the study of organizational histories is that purposive organizational change is exceptionally difficult. Many students fail to grasp this basic reality, perhaps because the popular literature on management often conveys the impression that organizational change is easy. Reading about the scores of well-equipped organizations that were unable to carry out apparently simple solutions to organizational problems provides a health reality check.

Fourth, a historical perspective on industry highlights the operation of selection processes among organizations. Few organizations manage to remain dominant in an industry for more than a few decades. Most fail shortly after birth. Reconciling these facts with common views of organizations as adaptive and flexible typically proves difficult, if not impossible. Attention to the historical development of industries forces one to confront the realities of selection. A second stage of learning involves understanding different types of selection processes and being able to recognize the various conditions that bring them on.

Many chapter authors employ a certain theoretical perspective. That perspective is known in the scholarly literature as *organizational ecology*. It emphasizes environmental selection as a mode of organizational change (in Chapter 2 we discuss this view at length). It contrasts with adaptation, the dominant view of organizational change. Because, until recently, most theories of organizational change have focused on adaptation rather than selection, little material pertinent to organizational ecology has made its way into textbooks. This is especially true for ancillary material such as cases and illustrations. We hope that this book will provide a remedy for instructors who see the value of problems and questions raised by ecological theory and who want to deal with them systematically in the classroom. Its purpose is not to proselytize for organizational ecology but instead to provide a level playing field for its discussion and application.

Not all of the chapter authors are organizational ecologists, even broadly defined. Each chapter author is an established and well-regarded researcher of organizations. He or she has conducted extensive scientific research on organizations in his or her chosen industry. The results of this research partly decide the focus of individual chapters. Some authors emphasize organizational strategy instead of selection. Others highlight aspects of organizational structure. Most chapters treat the interplay of organizational structures and strategies with processes of environmental selection. Therefore, we have chosen the subtitle: "Strategy, Structure, and Selection."

Because it relies on experts on organizations in diverse industries, we believe that the book presents deeper and wider instructional materials than is usual.

Most cases and illustrative descriptions that we are familiar with are written either by student case writers or by journalists. The scrutiny and judgment provided by respected organizational theorists surely make an important difference.

HOW WE ANALYZE THE ORGANIZATIONAL WORLD

A time-honored way to study business organizations develops lessons from the study of unusually successful organizations. This approach first identifies one or several highly successful businesses. Then it looks back into their histories to uncover the reasons for their good performance. This approach assumes that success of a particular organization can be traced in a simple way to its strategy and structure. To take one of many possible examples, consider the well-known book *In Search of Excellence* by Tom Peters and Robert Waterman.[1] These authors identified a set of forty "excellent" companies and explained the reasons behind the success of each. For instance, Peters and Waterman explain the success of Walt Disney Productions Inc. as a result of its organizational culture with its strong people-oriented service character. From the perspective of this approach, this conclusion seems reasonable, because this corporate culture is surely a hallmark of Disney. Despite the common sense appeal of this approach, it is seriously flawed and often leads to incorrect conclusions. Why? How could study of successful firms not help but be enlightening?

The problem with this approach lies in its logic of causal inference. There are two sides to the problem. By looking only at some successful firms and attributing their success to specific actions, one cannot be sure that other similar firms that did not undertake the same action performed less well. Indeed, there is no assurance that these firms did not actually outperform the chosen "excellent" firms. Similarly, one cannot be sure that other firms that took the same action experienced the kind of success observed in the local firm. It might be that the vast majority of firms with a particular characteristic did very poorly. Both points illustrate *sample selection bias,* meaning the sample units chosen for study contain an inherent bias, usually because they were chosen based on the outcome variable (e.g., firm performance). To make a case for causality, logic requires that evidence come from a research design that avoids (or at least minimizes) sample selection bias.

One sound way to avoid sample selection bias involves identifying a set of similar organizations (perhaps incumbents of a single industry) without regard to their success and then charting the actions and fates of the set's constituent organizations over time. The key is to include in the study group *all* similar organizations at a particular point in time or a random sample of such organizations. It is this feature that avoids the problem of sample selection bias. Analysis then consists of following prospectively the behaviors and performances

1. Peters, T., and R. H. Waterman. 1982. *In Search of Excellence*. New York: Harper & Row.

of all organizations. From this type of research design, one can calculate the overall success and failure rates of all firms undertaking any specific action, thus providing a sound evidentiary basis for causal inferences and for policy conclusions.

Some theoretical rationale is needed to guide decisions about which organizations are similar and thus should be grouped together in the comparison set. In organizational ecology, the *population* concept provides this rationale. As we explain in Chapter 2, an organizational population consists of all those organizations in a system with similar general form and environmental resource dependencies. We acknowledge that it is not always easy to decide definitively the boundaries of an organization population. Nonetheless, researchers have usually been able to choose boundaries of organizational populations in ways that generate meaningful dynamics. We are also confident that, no matter how difficult it might be to discern population boundaries, this approach to studying organizations has a sounder logical basis than using case studies of successful firms.

There is also usually another methodological advantage of analyzing organizations by studying complete populations (or random samples from populations). Organizational populations tend to be large, numbering in the hundreds, thousands, and often even higher figures. Sets of this size provide great statistical power and allow researchers to detect the operation of subtle processes. Large samples also allow systematic effects to be discerned when there is considerable randomness. When there are many potential factors affecting organizations and not all can be controlled explicitly, it often makes sense to treat them as random.

As the follow-up reports on Peters and Waterman's "excellent" companies show, organizational fortunes wax and wane over time. For instance, this list included Wang Laboratories, which is now in bankruptcy, and Atari, which has lost almost all of its market in computers and computer games. Fluctuations in viability occur frequently within short periods and almost certainly over long periods. Effective study of organization population dynamics usually requires information on the *full history* of the population, dating from its inception. Identifying a population's starting point can be a tricky matter, but it is important because much evidence in hand suggests that organizational evolution is *path dependent,* which means that prior events and actions affect current behavior. Path dependence in organizational evolution can sometimes involve the lingering effects of the industry's social conditions when an organization starts.[2]

Even if data on the earliest history cannot be recovered, observing organizational populations over long periods yields other benefits. One of these is an ability to overcome the *presentist fallacy,* the unconscious assumption that the way the world looks today is much like it has always looked and will continue

---

2. Ignoring the initial or early history of a population gives a truncated observation window and creates the technical problem known as *left truncation*. Missing the early history often makes it hard to detect some processes that have long-run effects on the evolution of an organizational population.

to look. When stated explicitly, this assumption seems rightfully absurd and few would admit to holding it. Yet when people think of organizations and industries, they are frequently trapped cognitively by the present. They can rarely remember organizations that were once dominant but have declined or disappeared. Moreover, they tend to think that the largest and most successful organizations of the moment will retain their power and importance for a very long time. For instance, when the ecological perspective on organizations initially appeared in the mid-1970s, critics such as Charles Perrow[3] were quick to claim that it was a theory applicable only to small organizations. Large and powerful organizations such as General Motors, IBM, and the Bank of America could control their environments and therefore were immune from selection processes, Perrow argued. Less than twenty years later, the speciousness of these claims jumps off the page, as many previously dominant firms have failed or are in the process of doing so. The particular examples cited by Perrow have each faced very rough seas in recent years; they can now hardly be regarded as indomitable organizations. History abounds with examples of fallen organizations that once seemed unassailable.

Knowledge of an industry's history sensitizes us to the likelihood of major organizational events. Because history is typically filled with many bizarre and forgotten cases, it also expands awareness of the many diverse organizational arrangements possible to accomplish certain tasks. Such awareness is often useful in evaluating contemporary claims of novelty and innovation and in designing organizations. In our view, this last function of historical knowledge—alerting one to the diversity of organizational forms appearing in an industry—is especially important. The central questions of organizational evolution concern changes in a population's *diversity* over time. The orienting question posed by Hannan and Freeman[4]—Why are there so many different kinds of organizations?—remains as salient as ever because efforts to answer this question might unlock many basic mysteries of organizational life. Such efforts will also illuminate many debates about the relative roles of adaptive and selectional processes of change. At a more microscopic level, the research agenda suggested by this question directs attention to processes of organizational initiation, growth, decline, merger, and failure. Primarily for this reason, many chapter authors show data of this kind and discuss the results of sophisticated technical studies of these processes.

Another major reason for focusing on the so-called vital events (organizational founding and mortality) is that these are readily *observable* organizational phenomena. In general, the research strategy we advocate, which forms the basis for many chapters on specific industries, involves concentrating on features of organizational populations that can be easily observed. This research strategy differs notably from that of most other attempts to explain the organizational world. For the most part, other theories of organizations ac-

3. Perrow, C. 1986. *Complex Organizations: A Critical Essay* (Third Edition). Glencoe IL: Scott Foresman.
4. Hannan, M. T., and J. Freeman. 1977. "The Population Ecology of Organizations," *American Journal of Sociology* 82:929–64.

count for outcomes as consequences of difficult-to-observe features of organizations such as organizational culture and transaction costs. Because it is costly and difficult to obtain comparable measurements on many organizations over time, theories that emphasize the operation of subtle features are rarely tested comparatively. As a result, progress in testing such theories lags far behind theoretical developments and elaborations. By contrast, the research strategy we advocate often requires only the *counting* of various organizational phenomena (even if this counting is very comprehensive in terms of history and the population). The strategy's simplicity allows meaningful comparison over very long periods of time and across populations of extremely dissimilar types of organizations, as the chapters on industries make clear.

This approach has its costs. In return for the ability to explain organizational changes over long periods of time and to secure robust empirical findings, it overlooks much micro-level detail. At present, we are comfortable with this situation, because this approach addresses issues that have long been neglected by organizational researchers and because there is no shortage of other studies focused more closely on fine-grained aspects of organizations. As this approach develops further, it might be prudent to incorporate more microscopic concerns. We feel that it is most important now to work on the topic of greatest promise—the big picture of long-term organizational change.

A NOTE ON STYLE

To make this book as accessible as possible, we have asked the contributors to minimize their use of citations and references in the main text of their chapters. Instead, we have encouraged them to list all relevant background and scientific literature at the end of their chapters in a separate section. We trust that the scholars on whose work we draw—and without which this book would not be possible—will understand this convention and not be offended by fewer appearances of their names. We have also asked the chapter authors to avoid using the advanced technical material that many of them employ in their scientific work. Our goal here is to reach a broad audience.

ACKNOWLEDGMENTS

A number of colleagues, friends, and students helped make this a better book. At Berkeley, Amrei Kieschke typed many drafts in her usual punctual and accurate way. Gwen Cheeseburg managed the often confusing correspondence between the editors and the contributors. Doctoral students Lyda Bigelow, Marc-David Seidel, Albert Teo, and Lucia Tsai gave insightful comments on an earlier version of much of the book, as did Visiting Scholar Marianne Nordli Hansen. At Stanford, Bill Barnett, Susan Olzak, and Joel Podolny provided incisive critiques of the theoretical chapters. Graduate students Elizabeth Dundon, Morten Hansen, Young Kim, Jesper Sørensen, and John Torres helped us review chapters and prepare comments for contributors.

Financial assistance for some tasks of preparing this book came from the Institute of Industrial Relations at Berkeley and the Graduate School of Business at Stanford. Hannan also was supported by National Science Foundation Grants SES-9123708 and SES-9247842.

Berkeley, Calif. G. R. C.
Portola Valley, Calif. M. T. H.
May 1994

CONTENTS

CONTRIBUTORS

Philip Anderson is associate professor of business administration at the Amos Tuck School of Business, Dartmouth College. His undergraduate degree in agricultural economics is from the University of California at Davis; his Ph.D. in management of organizations is from Columbia University. His research interests include processes of technical evolution, managing during industrial transformations, firm reorganization, and competitive strategy. Professor Anderson's work has appeared in *Administrative Science Quarterly,* the *Academy of Management Journal,* and a number of other publications. He is also the coauthor of *Inside the Kaisha: Understanding the Enigma of Japanese Business Organization,* forthcoming from Harvard Business School Press.

William P. Barnett is associate professor of strategic management at the Graduate School of Business, Stanford University. In 1988, he received the Ph.D. in business administration from the University of California at Berkeley. Barnett studies competition within and among organizations. His published work appears in various book chapters as well as *Administrative Science Quarterly, Journal of Law, Economics, and Organization,* and *Industrial and Corporate Change.* This research examines processes of labor mobility, and of organizational founding, growth, change, and failure—emphasizing how these processes are affected by competition and mutualism. Most recently, Barnett is studying how strategic behavior affects organizational and industrial evolution, including studies of research and development consortia and of American banks.

David Barron is university lecturer in the School of Management Studies, Oxford University, and a Fellow of Jesus College. He obtained the Ph.D. in sociology from Cornell University in 1992. Barron's main interests lie in the sociology of organizations and economic sociology. He is currently developing a cross-national comparison of change in financial institutions.

Judith R. Blau is professor of sociology at the University of North Carolina at Chapel Hill. Her work on social networks, organizations, and the sociology of culture is published in articles in *Administrative Science Quarterly, American Journal of Sociology,* and *American Sociological Review.* Recent books are *Social Contracts and Economic Markets* (Plenum, 1993), and *Social Roles and Social Institutions: Essays in Honor of Rose Laub Coser,* which is co-edited with Norman Goodman (Westview, 1991). Blau's most recent research involves collaborative studies with Kenneth C. Land on organizations and social change.

Glenn R. Carroll is an organizational sociologist who currently holds the Paul J. Cortese Chair in Management at the University of California at Berkeley's Haas School of Business. His previous books include *Dynamics of Organizational Populations* (1992, with M. T. Hannan) and *Publish and Perish: The Organizational Ecology of Newspaper Industries* (1987).

Frank Dobbin studies public policy, organizational practices, and the intersection of the two. His *Forging Industrial Policy: The United States, Britain, and France in the Railway Age* (Cambridge University Press, 1994) charts the emergence of modern industrial policy styles through the history of railroad policy. Recent articles examine the evolution of national industrial policies, organizational responses to industrial policy, and the rise of personnel policies designed to promote equal opportunity in employment.

John Freeman is the Helzel Professor of Enterpreneurship and Innovation at the Haas School of Business, University of California at Berkeley. His research is on the population ecology of organizations with special interest on the effects of changing technology on such populations. With Michael T. Hannan, he published *Organizational Ecology* in 1989.

Michael T. Hannan is professor of sociology at Stanford University and professor of organizational behavior and human resources at Stanford's Graduate School of Business. He was formerly Henry Scarborough Professor of Social Sciences at Cornell University. He is the author of *Aggregation and Disaggregation in the Social Sciences* (1991) and coauthor of *Social Dynamics: Models and Methods* (1984), *Organizational Ecology* (1989), and *Dynamics of Organizational Populations* (1992).

Ralph Hybels is a Ph.D. candidate at the New York School of Industrial and Labor Relations at Cornell University. His dissertation explores the theory of density-dependent selection in organizational ecology by examining the role of the business press in the processes by which organizational forms in biotechnology are legitimated.

Huseyin Leblebici is professor of organizational behavior in the department of business administration, University of Illinois. His current research interests include the evolution and institutionalization of transactional patterns in service organizations, particularly in the legal and financial services industries. He is also conducting research on the generative processes of organizational forms. He received the Ph.D. in business administration from the University of Illinois at Urbana-Champaign.

Will Mitchell is associate professor of corporate strategy at the University of Michigan School of Business Administration. He earned the Ph.D. degree at the School of Business Administration of the University of California at Berkeley and the B.B.A. at Simon Fraser University in Canada. His research interests address factors affecting firm survival, particularly issues concerning business strategy in environments of rapid technological change.

Joel Podolny is assistant professor of organizational behavior and Fletcher Jones Faculty Scholar for 1993–94 in the Graduate School of Business at Stanford University. His current work draws from the research areas of social networks, economic sociology, and complex organizations.

Allan Ryan is an assistant professor of organizational analysis in the Faculty of Business at the University of Alberta. He is currently conducting research on the role that financial markets have played in the creation and development of American biotechnology firms.

David Strang is assistant professor of sociology at Cornell University. His main research interests concern the development of institutional analyses of change in organizational populations and in state policies. Much of his present organizational research examines the emergence of health maintenance organizations. These studies have focused on interactions in the founding dynamics of different types of HMOs, and on the generation of public policy toward health maintenance organizations.

Anand Swaminathan is assistant professor of corporate strategy at the School of Business Administration, The University of Michigan, Ann Arbor. His research interests include organizational ecology, entrepreneurship, buyer-supplier relationships, social movement organizations, and the analysis of career histories. He is currently working on the evolution of specialist organizations in the brewing and wine industries. With James B. Wade, he is investigating the growth and decline of the Women's Christian Temperance Union and the effect of Prohibition on the American brewing industry. He received the Ph.D. in business administration from the Haas School of Business, University of California at Berkeley.

I

THEORETICAL ISSUES IN STUDYING ORGANIZATIONS

In *An Evolutionary Theory of Economic Change,* economists Richard Nelson and Sidney Winter (1982) proclaim that, "Theorists should strive to speak the truth but not the whole truth." Their reasoning is that if a "theory" were to tell the whole truth about a phenomenon—meaning that it addressed and explained virtually every known characteristic—then it would be a description, not a theory. It would likely be long, detailed, and very concrete; it would likely not be applicable to any other phenomena or situations due to its devotion to the particular of a single case. Theory, by contrast, intentionally abstracts and generalizes. Theory focuses on some dimensions of a phenomenon and deliberately ignores many others. A good theory is simple and elegant but also explains the essence of a phenomenon (the *truth*). A good theory is also very general in that it can be applied usefully to many different contexts and many other phenomena. Theories are compared with each other in terms of accuracy, parsimony, and explanatory power.

Social science theories are not nearly as advanced as the theories of, say, physics. However, social science theories do have value in that they often illuminate things about the social world that were previously unknown or misunderstood. Organizational theory refers to the set of theories that attempt to explain the processes and outcomes of formal organizations. This set of theories is commonly distinguished further by theoretical perspective, a designation that indicates similarity in assumptions, chosen problems, and general orientation. The field of organizational studies contains a healthy number of competing perspectives, including contingency theory, resource dependence theory, transaction costs theory, institutional theory, and organizational ecology.

This book draws most heavily from organizational ecology, although many other theoretical ideas are also used. In this section we introduce and explain some theoretical issues involved in studying organizations. Chapter 1 provides a general treatment. It explains the rationale for developing a separate theory of organizations. It also compares and contrasts explanations of some specific industry trends using organizational theory and more conventional ideas.

Chapter 2 concentrates an organizational ecology. We introduce and explain this perspective explicitly and in some detail, because the chapter authors do not. It is more economical to have a common introduction to the theory. This does not mean that the chapters do not use the ecological perspective and its theories in their accounts of industries. Instead, their use of theory is mainly implicit. It is implicit in the ways they look at their industries, the problems they choose to highlight, the data they use to understand their industries, and the explanations they offer for why the industries developed as they did.

BIBLIOGRAPHY

Nelson, R. P., and S. G. Winter. 1982. *An Evolutionary Theory of Economic Change.* Cambridge, MA: Harvard University Press.

1

Focus on Industry: The Organizational Lens

GLENN R. CARROLL AND MICHAEL T. HANNAN

A theory is like a lens: looking through one provides a view of things that are not ordinarily seen. Changing the lens causes things to be seen in a different way. Similarly, using different theories makes different phenomena become salient. We designed this book to examine a variety of modern industries through a different, and perhaps unfamiliar, lens: organizational theory.

WHY ORGANIZATIONAL THEORY?

In *Bureaucracy,* political scientist James Q. Wilson claims that only two kinds of people deny the importance of organizations: economists and everyone else. Wilson bases his claim about economists on the paramount explanatory importance that economic theory places on individuals and their goal-oriented actions. For everyone else, Wilson blames the common sense view that an organization is only as good as the people in it. Both views assume that there is not much more to an organization than its individual members. If so, then there is little need for a special theory of organizations. The social sciences already contain many theories of individual action, and these should suffice to explain organizational life.

Without denying the importance of individuals, we and many other behaviorally oriented social scientists contend that there is much more to organizations than their members and that these other things are often critical to understanding organizations. We base our position on two general claims. First, organizational structure shapes performance and life chances of organizations. Second, dynamics of organizational populations also shape outcomes.

ORGANIZATIONAL STRUCTURE MATTERS

To comprehend the importance of organizational structure, consider a key decision in universities: promotion to tenure for professors. The assistant professor position is a probationary one. In most universities, the longest a person can remain an assistant professor is seven or eight years. At the end of this period, an "up or out" decision must be made. The up option involves granting the faculty member lifetime tenure, which is essentially lifetime employment security at the university (barring rare cases of moral transgression or severe budgetary crisis). Obtaining tenure is equivalent to receiving a thirty- or forty-year guaranteed labor contract for most candidates, the total value of which runs into the millions of dollars. For obvious reasons, universities take these decisions very seriously.

Universities differ in how they conduct tenure reviews and in the criteria and standards they apply. However, in most universities (and especially in the most highly regarded ones) tenure rests upon an evaluation of a professor's research record. The candid opinions of outside experts are solicited, and an internal faculty committee is usually formed to make a detailed and exhaustive assessment of the candidate's work. Once this information is compiled, it is reported to a larger group of faculty members who usually meet to discuss the merits of the case. They then vote yea or nay (in a recommendation to university officials). Along with appropriate documenting materials, a report of this meeting is then forwarded to higher levels in the university, where additional reviews are conducted and a final decision is rendered.

Consider hypothetical cases at a major public university and at a major private university, with the candidate having a very strong record in each case. Let the faculty members voting at the two places also be the same; so obviously they make the same individual evaluations, and it leads to the same vote tally at each university. Let the vote be 80 percent in favor of granting tenure and 20 percent against.

What is the final decision on the assistant professor's lifetime employment contract? If all that mattered were the preferences of individual faculty members, then the disposition of the case would be similar at the two universities. However, it is our guess, based on years of experience with such cases, that the assistant professor would receive tenure at the public university and would be denied tenure at the private university.

The public/private distinction between universities is a *structural* difference, and, in this instance, it explains a very important outcome. However, this distinction is also a crude one that represents at a global level many important underlying structural differences between public and private universities. If we could go deeper into the two universities, then we would likely see many specific structural differences. For instance, faculty personnel rules at public universities tend to be written in ways that place a premium on fairness and equity. At private universities, the rules tend to be written with less such emphasis and more emphasis on excellence. One reason the rules contain different inherent biases might be that private universities typically have stronger central administration than public universities, where faculty governance often plays a central role. Another reason might be that private universities need to be more fiscally conservative. Unlike public universities that have the massive financial backing of the state, they have no guarantor of last resort in times of financial crisis.

Universities also differ in how they design the tenure review process, and several elements in the resulting decision-making structure can affect the outcome. For instance, in some universities the internal review is conducted with a "Chinese wall" between it and the written opinions of the outside experts, a situation where one's general stature in his or her field of research is less likely to affect voting. At some universities, all tenured faculty in a department vote on each tenure case, whereas at others, a select group of faculty (say, full professors) vote and, at others, only appointed members of a small personnel committee vote. Universities also vary in how many different committees review the case or get consulted in the process. Each of these structural factors can account for the outcome in a particular case.

As the example illustrates, the specifics of each organization's structure matter. So too do their general structural features, which often have predictable effects. Much organizational theory consists of identifying and analyzing abstract characteristics of decision making and other organizational structures. Theorists typically scrutinize an organization's division of labor (the allocation of tasks), authority system, bases of grouping activities, incentive system, information flows, and relationships with the environment. Organizations are often characterized in terms of their complexity, levels of formalization, and degrees of centralization.

Organizational structure gives an organization a *life of its own,* one that is independent of its specific participants. The structure of an organization can be designed and used to produce outcomes that are intended. For instance, some large diversified corporations have adopted a divisionalized structure to ensure that adequate attention gets directed to its specific lines of business as well as to long-range corporate planning and finances. Other firms needing more integration or a project orientation have adopted a matrix structure. However, organizational structures often generate *unintended effects.* These can be detrimental, as when obsequiousness, political infighting, excessive paperwork, and delays occur. Or they can be beneficial, as when employees identify strongly with a firm or when the grouping together of two disparate activities induces an otherwise unconsidered innovation.

Organizations frequently resist change and persist in character and structure well beyond the involvement of any one individual or even a generation of individuals. Many observers have been surprised in returning to their old organization to find that although the names and faces have changed, the way of life inside the organization has not. Why? What makes organizations so inertial? Sociologists have identified a variety of forces favoring the status quo, including norms, political interests, sunk investments, and external relationships. Although conventional wisdom suggests that inertia, the antithesis of adaptability, is a negative characteristic of organizations, some organization theorists point to its benefits (as discussed in Chapter 2).

ORGANIZATIONAL POPULATION DYNAMICS MATTER

Formal organizations are ubiquitous. During their lives, most individuals are born in hospitals, taught in schools, employed by corporations, safeguarded and sometimes conscripted by governmental agencies, and buried or cremated by funeral service firms. We keep our money, our prisoners, our children, and our elderly in specialized formal organizations devoted to these purposes. Our recreation and leisure time activities are managed by an industry of specialized firms. Both individuals and groups insure themselves against potential disaster of all kinds through specialized companies that rationalize the uncertain future. Adult members of society are connected, at virtually any age, to scores of formal organizations; they also regularly purchase products and services from hundreds or even thousands of them.

Collective actions—the decisions and events that affect the lives of many in a single stroke—occur almost exclusively within formal organizational structures that have been delegated the authority to act on behalf of many. Organized military forces recruit and train younger members of society with the intention of providing security. Trade and commerce are organized and regulated by governmental agencies, international organizations, and large corporations. Political ideas get transformed into political movements when an organizational structure develops around them. Once developed, political organizations tend to define issues and select candidates by their own criteria. In doing so, they often respond to the logic of campaigning and the media rather than to the original political goals of their founders or followers.

Despite society's great experience with formal organizations, intuition about them is notably limited. For instance, few citizens know much about the number of organizations in their society or the prevalence of organizations in various sectors of the economy. Nor do they know the sizes of organizations in an industry compared with each other or how most organizational phenomena have changed over time. At most, people can sometimes give aggregate numbers of specific highly visible markets, e.g., the Big 3 in automobile production. Or, from those with knowledge of economic and census data, one might get aggregate measures of production, employment, sales, and the like.

Nearly all market-based measures of aggregate economic performance lump together the performances of all or many organizations in a market. By doing so, these measures obscure differences among organizations and they downplay the distinctiveness of formal organizations. Although this practice might be appropriate for some purposes, it presents a highly limited view of economy and society. Moreover, this view has become increasingly less relevant during the twentieth century. For several reasons, we believe that the distinctiveness of formal organizations needs to be recognized in analysis and incorporated into appropriate measures.

For one thing, the law recognizes the distinctiveness of formal organizations. Most modern legal systems consider organizations as entities unto themselves, corporate actors with identities transcending those of their owners and participants. The law recognizes organizations as persons. As with real persons, each is regarded as possessing certain rights (albeit rights different from those given to humans). Among other things, the holding of rights means that organizations cannot easily be melded into other organizations, if they decide not to be.

Every organization maintains a separate internal authority system that allows it to make many independent decisions. Granted, laws sometimes prescribe and proscribe certain behaviors. However, these tend to be about broad social issues such as equal opportunity, health and safety, and fair competition. Such laws usually are designed to protect individual human rights or to ensure socially desirable outcomes, e.g., competition among firms in an industry. They also typically apply to all relevant organizations evenly. Distinctiveness is thus muted in only a few specific decision areas. More commonly the legal system steadfastly refuses to intervene in internal organizational disputes (e.g., disputes about the transfer prices that divisions use in transacting with each other), though it routinely mediates similar disputes between independent organizations. Although social scientists emphasize the external constraints on organizational authority, the authority vested in organizational decision makers is, typically, final.

Autonomous decision making within organizations makes it extraordinarily unlikely that any two organizations experience the same sequence of decisions and consequent actions. Decisions build upon each other. (In technical language, the decision stream is path dependent.) So two organizations facing apparently the same decision problem might act differently. Chance factors also affect organizations differently, introducing more heterogeneity into the decision process. Therefore, each organization is, in effect, a unique social experiment.

Much change in the organizational world also results from unique, single events experienced by specific organizations. The start of a single organization, for instance, creates jobs, including positions of authority. The demise of an organization eliminates jobs, sometimes thousands of them.

Recognizing the distinctiveness of formal organizations might seem to undermine the value of general organization theory, which often treats all kinds of organizations as similar. In our view, however, distinctiveness simply calls for a particular kind of general organization theory, one relying on population dynamics. Such theory is sensitive to distinctiveness, because an organizational population's characteristics include by definition the characteristics of every organization it contains. That is, when assessing an organizational population, it is important to know, first, how many organizations it includes and, second, how the relevant characteristics are distributed among them. So, for instance, we think it matters whether the workers in an industry (say, steel) are organized into one large union or into many smaller ones. We also think that the number of organizations in a population matters even when the market shares or concentration levels of the largest organizations are the same. Why?

Our view rests on three general observations. First, organizational action usually involves problems of *collective rationality* rather than individual rationality. Collective rationality refers to situations involving multiple actors where actions are highly contingent on the past and anticipated actions of other actors. In contemplating a new diversification move, for example, it matters greatly to a firm whether other competitors already operate in the target area of the diversified activities. It also matters whether other firms are likely to follow the focal firm in its diversification efforts.

Second, the organizational *diversity* of a population and a society is very important. It is related to the capacity of the population to innovate to its ability to perform well in heterogeneous environments, and to its adaptiveness in responding to uncertainty. The more diverse the population, the more likely that organizational structures exist that can deal effectively with unexpected environmental events.

Third, few organizations manage to remain dominant over long periods of time. Thus the *evolutionary potential* of any group of organizations to initiate or to profit from environmental change cannot be ignored. Views of organizations that focus only on the largest organizations or that look only at a short period cannot easily appreciate the evolutionary importance of certain groups of organizations.

To see the importance of organizational population dynamics, consider again the case of tenure for faculty in universities. When told about this unusual institution described above, many people react by questioning the rationality of the practice of tenure. Given all the privileges granted to professors, why is it necessary to also give them lifetime job security? After all, there would likely be no shortage of applicants for university faculty positions if they did not include tenure.

Tenure originated decades ago as a way to ensure faculty freedom of speech and to guard against their unwarranted dismissal for political reasons. It still serves that function today, but the rationale is less compelling than it was previously; other guarantees of free speech exist. Today tenure is mainly an employment benefit, one that is awarded based on competence, hard work, and promise. Like any group of workers, professors vigilantly fight to protect this established benefit, both individually and through professional associations.

Critics of the university occasionally propose to do away with tenure. Despite the great operational flexibility this would allow, few administrators take the idea seriously. Why? The realities of labor law mean that the proposal could probably only be carried out for new faculty, thus creating two classes of faculty within the university. A larger obstacle is created by institutional processes within the population of universities. Tenure is a taken-for-granted (or institutionalized) part of faculty life. If one university were to eliminate tenure, then it might still be able to hire faculty. However, we suggest, it would suffer greatly in the competition for highly talented faculty. The better universities set the norms for the entire university realm. No university could maintain its high status if faced with such a market disadvantage; status depends on hiring and retaining the best faculty. Most good universities find it difficult enough to compete on a level playing field for top university faculty. Few less prestigious universities wish to risk the censure by their competitors that would likely accompany a decision to abolish tenure.

Yet universities do differ widely in their criteria and standards for tenure. Some emphasize teaching more than research; some require one to be a world leader in his or her field, while others seek only certified competence. These differences impart great diversity to the university population, a diversity that allows more Americans to attend universities than is possible in most countries and that allows the university sector to respond flexibly to various public shifts in mood for more back-to-basics education or more basic science. As these different themes get played out in enrollments and donations, the status orderings of universities occasionally change, thus showing what we call evolutionary potential. Tenure works for the university whose status has risen in such contexts by making it more likely that the university can retain the faculty upon which its identity rests.

At least two other more specific aspects of population dynamics affect how universities think about tenure: time of founding and structure of competition. Like all organizations, universities are imbued with many social characteristics of their era of initiation. Recently founded universities (age compared with others) are more likely, we suggest, to incorporate modern labor contracts, i.e., faculty employment without tenure. Specialist universities such as the Thunderbird School of Management of Glendale, Arizona, which compete primarily with universities within their niche, likely have a wider range of faculty employment contracts, including many without tenure.

The example illustrates several important general dimensions of organizational population dynamics: number of organizations (what we call *density*), organizational diversity, relative age distribution, and level of competition. In the following chapters, authors will rely on these and other population variables (such as the number of start-ups or dissolution in a period) to describe and interpret the organizational histories of their industries. All these variables implicitly recognize the distinctiveness of organizations in that they are based in some way on accounts or measures of each organization in a population.

The most controversial aspect of this approach is that it often counts large and small organizations with equal weight. It is important to recognize that such procedures do not assume that large and small organizations are generally equal in their effects on other organizations or on society. However, they clearly are not. We contend that large and small organizations are only equal in certain ways that are specifically laid out in arguments about organizational population dynamics.

SOME ILLUSTRATIVE EXAMPLES

Brief consideration of some concrete cases might help clarify the difference between explanations based on organization theory and those based on other forms of reasoning.

Microbreweries and Brewpubs
During the 1980s, new, small brewers appeared in Oregon and California. These brewers made and sold traditional ales and beers, beverages carrying the image of being local and "hand crafted." The appeal of these drinks was for many something like an antidote to mass society and its methods of mass production.

Microbrewed beers and brewpubs now number in the hundreds nationwide and have a loyal, highly visible, and growing following.

Why did microbreweries and brewpubs become so popular in the 1980s? Conventional wisdom explains their rise as a result of changing tastes. As the lifestyles of Americans changed over the last twenty years, so too did their eating and drinking habits. The smaller and less familial households of the baby boom generation prompted a "culinary revolution" in parts of America. Along with increased sophistication about food came an interest in wine and eventually a curiosity about various malt beverages, which included ales, porters, and stouts. The microbreweries and brewpubs sprang up in response, according to this explanation.

Viewed from an organizational perspective, the rise of microbreweries and brewpubs is the seemingly paradoxical result of opportunities created by high concentration in the brewing industry. When large generalist[1] producers compete in a market, they attempt to differentiate themselves by making different products and cultivating different images. There are few opportunities for small specialist producers in such a crowded and heterogeneous market. However, when only a few generalist producers compete in a market, each typically produces for as many consumers as possible, which means their products and images are often not highly differentiated. Opportunities exist in such a market for small specialist producers who make appeals to peripheral market segments.

In effect, market resources have been partitioned into two segments: one dominated by mass producer generalists, the other populated by small specialist producers. Such processes have been observed in the industries of newspaper publishing, book publishing, and music recording. The irony about brewing is that the specialist producers—microbreweries and brewpubs—supply types of products that disappeared from the market in the late nineteenth century due to their perceived crudeness and inferior quality. The modern taste for these beverages did not so much cause the microbrewery movement as result from it. Through clubs, festivals, newsletters, and good ole bar talk, microbrewers have helped create and define the tastes for their products.

Home Delivery Food Services
One innovative organizational form that appeared in America at the start of the twentieth century was the home delivery food service. Delivering prepared meals to the home was the natural outgrowth of earlier experiments with communal and cooperative kitchen experiments, which had been rejected by American families, mainly because they lacked privacy and individuality. Home delivery food service solved the privacy problem while still freeing upper middle-class families from the need for servants. Responding to this seemingly lucrative opportunity and aided by the newly available automobile, food delivery services sprang up at locations throughout the country. A typical service provided full three-course meals prepared with a variety of foods, and changed its menu daily. At the time, prospects for this service looked almost limitless, and organizers were optimistic about its future.

With the luxury of hindsight, we know now that food delivery operators should not have felt so rosy. Within only several years, most home deliverers of food would be out of business. The organizational form was not only virtually eliminated from American society; it was also erased from the memory of the American public. Why? What caused this apparently promising form's demise? The social historian Harvey Levenstein (1988), who has studied the history of American eating practices, contends that the problem was economical in nature. Compared with the other available alternatives for regular family eating, home delivery of meals was simply too costly.

Levenstein's argument about food delivery services is an example of a general *logic of retrospective rationality* commonly applied to the rise and fall of organizational populations. According to this logic, the emergence and spread of an organizational form show that the form was efficient and the demise of organizational form reveals that it was inefficient. In other words, this logic accounts for the existence (and prevalence) of an organizational population retrospectively. It relies on a strong assumption that differences in efficiency govern success and failure of different organizational forms.

A different type of explanation, drawn from organizational theory, recognizes that growth of organizational populations often involves positive feedback or self-reinforcement. That is, the mechanisms of growth often stimulate further growth in a population of organizations. A variety of such mechanisms have been identified, including the social legitimation of the organizational form, the development of a market of sufficient size, the emergence of supporting institutions, collective gains in efficiency from learning by doing, and changes in consumer tastes and habits. Positive feedback in organizational population growth is important for analyzing cooperation between organizational forms. It can give rise to path dependence in the competitive process. In the case of competing organizational forms, path dependence can affect competitive outcomes. For instance, it can cause an inherently less efficient organizational form to propel itself to a population size sufficient to prevent its displacement by a newly emerging organizational form with superior inherent efficiency. In other words, an advantage in numbers or prevalence can allow an organizational population to overcome a disadvantage in operational ability or efficiency. Such an outcome is path dependent: without the prior history of population growth the more efficient organizational form would proliferate and come to dominate.

Stories about path dependence ought to be read as cautionary tales. They point to the potential dangers of relying on the logic of retrospective rationality to explain the disappearance of organizational forms such as the home delivery food service. Studies of path-dependent phenomena show that events or fluctuations occurring early in the evolutionary process, often simply random in nature, can shape subsequent developments. That is, a few early chance occurrences get the process moving in one direction or another. For the case of home delivery food service, many early entrepreneurial successes might have led to a different fate for this organizational population. A greater early presence of food service delivery organizations might have been sufficient to develop a stronger market, to reduce costs, and to prompt families to think of and use the service for its provision of meals.

The Swiss Watch Industry

In the period immediately following World War II, the firms comprising the Swiss watch industry dominated world markets. Nearly nine of every ten watches produced throughout the world in 1945 were made by a Swiss firm. The Swiss watch industry employed over 70,000 persons in the mid-1950s, and it contained over 2,300 firms. By the 1980s, the Swiss watch industry was a ghost of its glorious past. Fewer than one in seven watches was manufactured by a Swiss firm. The largest watchmaking enterprises in the world in 1980 were centered in Japan (Hattori-Seiko) and the United States (Timex). By 1984, Swiss industry employment had contracted to about 31,000 persons, and the number of operating firms had dwindled to 632.

What happened? What prompted the death of over 1,600 firms? Conventional explanations of business failure focus on the managers of firms. For instance, Dun and Bradstreet Inc., which records failures and publishes information about them in its annual *Failure Record,* claims that well over 90 percent of all American business failures can be accounted for by managerial deficiencies. Of these, about half are held to be the result of "inappropriate managerial experience"; the other half are regarded as the simple consequence of "managerial incompetence."

An organizationally informed alternative explanation begins by taking note of the technological changes that have occurred in the modern watch industry. Until about 1950, the industry was dominated by mechanical watches using pinlever and jewel-lever technologies. Small Swiss firms, which employed highly skilled craftsmen, produced an overwhelming number of these watches. Between 1950 and 1970, large American firms began to take over the market by producing watches made with new electric and tuning fork technologies and selling them through their own distribution and retail networks. As quartz watch technology appeared in the 1970s, large vertically integrated Japanese firms took the dominant position in the industry. Few of the Swiss firms producing mechanical watches could adapt effectively to the new technologies and the market conditions they created. In the world watch industry, technological changes ushered in new organizational competitors and eliminated old ones.

Does a firm's inability to incorporate new technologies signify the incompetence of its management? Not necessarily. In the watch industry in particular, the new technologies did not initially seem to be viable. Swiss firms faced a decision whether to invest in improvements in the well-established technologies upon which their success was built or to invest in a highly uncertain new technology. In this case, it is hard to criticize managers for taking the conservative route, especially when the more adventurous route would render the firm's current competencies obsolete. Moreover, Swiss firms were often doing better with the old technology than even rosy projections could envision them doing with a new technology. In short, prior success by a firm with a given technology often creates great inertia. Managers find themselves in what has been called a "competency trap."

Life Insurance Companies

The notion of insuring a life financially against the possibility of death is a modern one. Until 1850, very few life insurance companies operated in America. Death was considered one of those natural or divine phenomena over which men and women had little control and little ability to manage. Planning for someone's death and arranging to receive money in the case of someone's death struck many as a callous, even immoral, act.

The life insurance industry started growing significantly in the last half of the nineteenth century, and then really came into its own in the first quarter of the twentieth century. Whereas few persons carried some form of life insurance in the early 1800s, by 1925 the number had jumped dramatically. Many early life insurance contracts provided for only enough remuneration to cover burial costs. Eventually, the idea of life insurance expanded to include compensation for loss to the aggrieved. By the mid-twentieth century, it was commonplace to think of life insurance as a requirement to protect one's family against the vagaries of the future. Those without life insurance were considered irresponsible.

A tremendous expansion in the organizational base of the life insurance industry occurred between 1900 and 1930. At the turn of the century, fewer than 50 life insurance companies operated throughout the nation. By 1930, the number had increased ninefold: almost 450 life insurance firms could be found in the United States.

What brought on this development? Why did life insurance companies proliferate as they did? Conventional answers to these questions usually look to the specifics of the historical period in question. They search for other patterns, trends, or developments that might account for the rise of the life insurance industry. For example, an economically minded answer might recognize the rapidly increasing wealth and affluence of Americans in this era. As incomes surpass the sheer provision of material needs, tastes can be expected to expand to include not only luxury goods but also less attainable items, such as immortality. By this argument, the demand for life insurance reflects the insatiable and economically irrational desire for immortality. A more rational economic explanation might point out that, as incomes rose in this period, the projected career financial loss from an untimely death rocketed upward. Thus it became more sensible to try to protect one's family from such an occurrence.

Conventional sociological explanations for the rise of the life insurance industry follow a similar logic. But they focus on non-economic trends such as the increased rationalization of many aspects of life in this period or the continued secularization of society (Zelizer 1979). According to these views, the newfound popularity of life insurance simply reflected larger trends in society, away from traditional authority and social structures, including the church. Other arguments of this kind might relate the spread of life insurance to the breakdown of the extended family (which had historically taken care of aggrieved families) or to the individualistic nature of institutions developing in the United States at the time.

An alternative, organizationally based explanation for the growth of the American life insurance industry recognizes that the pattern of slow and then rapid organizational population growth applies to many diverse organizational forms and industries. The theory focuses on *density,* defined as the number of organizations in a population. According to the density model of organizational evolution (explained in detail in Section III), when an organizational form appears initially, its novelty and unproven reliability slow its acceptance by authorities, lenders, suppliers, clients, and potential employees. As the form spreads and density grows, these barriers break down, and the organizational form becomes socially accepted or legitimated. At some point, the legitimation process is essentially completed, and further increases in the form's prevalence or density do not affect legitimation. However, competition is now likely to be affected by greater density. According to the model, initial increases in the density of an organizational population have little impact on competition. However, after a certain population threshold is reached, increases in density intensify competition dramatically.

Organizations and Career Success
Organizations also affect the lives of their members. Consider how organizational structure and organizational population dynamics shape careers. Organizational theorists emphasize that opportunities vary among industries, firms, and occupations. Future opportunities depend on explicit promotion practices. However, they also depend on demographic factors such as growth rate of firm, industry, or occupation, and age distribution of the labor force in place. Rigorous analysis shows that opportunity structure often has more telling effects than most individual-level attributes in propelling careers onward and upward. Yet, people making career decisions usually fail to give such matters significant weight.

Organizational population dynamics also greatly affect careers. When an organization fails, many jobs are eliminated at once, including many important positions of authority. Conversely, organizational start-ups signify newly created jobs and authority positions. Organizational growth and decline also open and close many jobs. How important are these processes? The relevant data are crude, but estimates suggest that between 8 percent and 15 percent of all employed persons in the United States change jobs in a given year as a result of a job being eliminated or newly created. This is a surprisingly high proportion, considering that only about 20 percent of the labor force changes jobs for any reason in a typical year.

OVERVIEW

An organizational perspective on industry thus lets us see different answers to common questions. We wrote this book with our contributing colleagues to help students use organizational theory on their own. We expect that readers will have read or will be reading concurrently a basic text or set of readings in organizational theory, one that contains mainly abstract ideas, arguments, and models. Our purpose here is not to replicate this material but to teach by example. As the Preface indicated, most of the chapters that follow treat specific industries such as automobile manufacturing. They are written by organizational theorists who have studied their respective industries at length. Often, the chapter authors have made important social scientific discoveries about their industry. The chapter authors have drawn on their knowledge and expertise to write historical industry overviews, wide-angle views of their industry, and its development as seen through the organizational lens. The "industries" covered include automobile manufacturing, biotechnology, financial services (credit unions and investment banks), health care (health maintenance organizations and medical diagnostic imaging producers), labor unions, minicomputer manufacturing, art museums, newspaper publishing, radio broadcasting, railroad transport, and telephony.

The few other chapters in the book are those we the editors wrote to provide some theoretical guidance for interpreting the material in the industry chapters. The most extensive of these is the next chapter where we lay out many general ideas about organizations used in the book. This conceptually difficult chapter is essential reading. It describes in detail the nature of the lens of organizational ecology. We expect that some readers will find parts of it too abstract at first reading. However, we hope that reading the chapters on industries will make clear the value of the theoretical chapter. After reading about the industries and attempting to understand their histories, these theoretical materials can aid in drawing generalizations. We also think the theory chapter aids in comparing and contrasting different industries.

Following Chapter 2, we have divided the book into sections based on the primary theory applicable to the industry chapters each contains. These theories are: Environmental Selection (Section II); Density-Dependent Evolution (Section III); Resource Partitioning (Section IV); and Segregating Processes in Organizational Communities (Section V). At the beginning of each section, we provide a brief description of the theory and its applicability. Chapter authors focus on the histories of their industries, the empirical material. A final section reviews the industry analyses and discusses briefly some managerial implications.

NOTE

1. Chapter 2 discusses more rigorously the distinction between specialist and generalist organizational forms.

BIBLIOGRAPHY

Dun and Bradstreet, Inc. Various Years. *The Failure Record*. New York: Dun and Bradstreet.
Levenstein, H. 1988. *Revolution at the Table*. New York: Oxford University Press.
Wilson, J. Q. 1989. *Bureaucracy*. New York: Basic Books.
Zelizer, Viviana. 1979. *Morals and Markets: The Development of Life Insurance in the United States*. New York: Columbia University Press.

RECOMMENDED READING

For further reading about the perspective of organizational theory:
Allison, G. 1971. *Essence of Decision: Explaining the Cuban Missile Crisis.* Boston: Little Brown.
Wilson, J. Q. 1989. *Bureaucracy.* New York: Basic Books.

For a basic textbook in organizational theory:
Scott, W. R. 1992. *Organizations: Rational, Natural and Open Systems,* 3rd ed. Englewood Cliffs, NJ: Prentice-Hall.

For an overview of contemporary organizational theory and research:
Aldrich, H., and P. V. Marsden. 1988. "Environments and Organizations." In N. Smelser (ed.), *Handbook of Sociology.* Beverly Hills: Sage, pp. 361–92.

For an illustrative case:
"Note on the Watch Industries in Switzerland, Japan, and the United States." *Harvard Business School Case,* 9-373-090. September 1976.
"Hattori-Seiko and the World Watch Industry in 1980." *Harvard Business School Case,* 9-385-300. March 1987.
"The Swiss Watch Industry, 1981–1985." *Harvard Business School Case,* 9-387-033. 1986.
"Message and Muscle: An Interview with Swatch Titan Nicholas Hayek." *Harvard Business Review* (March–April 1993):99–110.

2

An Introduction to Organizational Ecology

MICHAEL T. HANNAN AND GLENN R. CARROLL

This chapter introduces the theoretical approach called organizational ecology.[1] Our discussion (coupled with the more detailed material in the section introductions) has two main goals. One is to provide background for understanding the accounts of the evolution of the industries covered in the book. We also want to make clear that the arguments developed in the book come from a systematic perspective. Knowledge of the approach, its assumptions, propositions, and models, helps make sense of the developments in these industries. More important, it eases application of the ideas and general patterns to other contexts.

The field of organizational studies contains several vigorous theoretical perspectives. We concentrate on organizational ecology, the approach used predominantly by the authors in this book. We explain the perspective explicitly and in some detail, because the chapter authors do not. Instead, they use theory largely implicitly in how they look at their industries, the problems they highlight, the data they present, and the explanations they offer.

Chapter 1 briefly introduced the ecological perspective. This chapter gives more details. We concentrate on the assumptions about organizations, environments, and organizational change that motivate the perspective. Introductions to the main sections of the book discuss particular theories and models that inform the substantive chapters.

WHY DO ORGANIZATIONS PROLIFERATE?

Theoretical perspectives on organizations differ in what they view as their most interesting and important properties. The most basic theories try to explain why organizations have become so numerous and so powerful. Explanations of organizational ubiquity build on assumptions about the distinctive properties and competencies of formal organizations.

Social scientists distinguish *collective actors* (sometimes called corporate actors) from individual persons. Examples of corporate actors include families, clubs, gangs, communities, social and political movements, nation-states, and international federations. Like individual persons, collectives possess the capacity for unitary action. For instance, a family can decide to migrate, a club or a gang can admit or exclude members, a community can vote to merge with another, a social movement can hold a demonstration, a nation can wage war, and an international body can vote sanctions against a nation. In such cases, the decision binds all of the members of the collective. Moreover, the decisions can rarely be attributed to one member. Social scientists like to think of collective actors as having "lives of their own," meaning that their behaviors cannot be reduced to the behaviors of their members. Commonly, collectives have a legal standing as autonomous actors—they have rights and can incur obligations.

Organizations represent a special type of collective actor. Like other collective actors, organizations can take unitary action and can control collective resources. However, unlike families, communities, and nation-states, organizations claim to fulfill *specific and limited goals*. If successful, they receive public legitimation and social support as agents for accomplishing these stated goals. Leaders or members can undermine public goals by manipulating organizations to serve private goals and organizations often pursue goals other than their public goals. Nonetheless, organizations gain resources and support from society based on their claims to pursue specific, limited goals. So, for example, automobile manufacturing firms gain resources (capital, workers, and so forth) based on their claims to seek profits by manufacturing automobiles, a product enhancing society's transportation capabilities. Universities garner public funds and private contributions with the claim to create knowledge and to disseminate it through teaching and publication. Guerrilla armies recruit soldiers and financial support for the express purposes of promoting certain interests and, often, overthrowing a political regime.

The concept of organization connotes *planned durability*. Founders and members usually design firms and associations to last indefinitely. Of course, organizations do not live forever—most live only a very short time. Yet, people make investments in the expectation that organizations will persist. Intended durability distinguishes organizations from transitory collective structures such as teams put together to handle a disaster or a task force designed for a specific, time-limited project (e.g., the multinational military task force created by the United Nations to invade Iraq in 1991).

Planned durability implies important social characteristics. Think about what it takes to build a permanent structure. Scarce resources must be raised and committed for the long term. Organization builders must accumulate capital (or credit), commitment of potential members, entrepreneurial skills, and legitimacy. Once invested in an organization, resources are difficult to extricate. Although physical assets and even a name can be sold, most resources invested in an organization dissipate when an organization falls apart. Creditors usually regard themselves as fortunate to receive a few cents on the dollar.

The idea of building a durable structure also weakens the link between particular individuals and the organization. For an organization to last, it must design structures and procedures that outlast the participation of any person or group of persons. German sociologist Max Weber, the founder of organization theory, made this feature the centerpiece of his analysis of the bureaucratic form of organizing. He argued that the most important result of the invention of this organizational form was that it allowed for the first time the design of durable structures that depend weakly on the social characteristics of the person holding office. The principle of making weak links between personal attributes and positions in organizations spread widely. Nearly all organizations in contemporary societies possess structures that reflect this principle.

Organizations deplete resources in simply maintaining their structures. Indeed, the costs of overhead in an organization are high compared with the amount of work, especially compared to nonorganizational alternatives. Much overhead involves the costs of administration.

For instance, recent studies attribute 25 percent of the total costs of American hospitals to administration. That is, for every three dollars spent on patient care, one dollar gets spent on administration. Put differently, the same procedure costs much more when done in a hospital than when performed by an individual physician in his or her office. Universities conduct extensive studies to calculate the indirect costs (overhead) on research conducted by faculty. Indirect costs include portions of the salaries of university administrators, accountants, personnel officers, and other university staff, along with some costs of libraries, computing services, utilities, police and fire protection, and so forth. At private universities like Stanford, accounting studies suggest that the true overhead rate runs about 75 percent. That is, for every dollar spent on direct costs of research (such as paying the salaries of researchers and assistants, buying specialized equipment and supplies, and so forth), the university expends 75 cents to support the research indirectly. Some indirect costs such as utilities would be incurred even if the research were done outside the university. However, a great fraction of the overhead comes from the costs of simply running the organization (administration in the broad sense). In contemporary American firms, we see the overhead most obviously in the many layers of middle management.

Overhead costs make it very costly to rely on durable organizations as a way to get things done. Nonetheless, modern societies and economies contain millions of firms, associations, bureaucracies, and so forth. It is difficult to think of any realm of social action in which organizations do not figure as key actors. Such observations raise the fundamental question: *Why do people agree so often to commit scarce resources to such expensive solutions to collective action problems?* New institutional economists explain the ubiquity of firms as a consequence of commonplace failures of markets to function efficiently. That is, they argue that firms arise to fill the gaps created by market failure. Specifically, Oliver Williamson (1985) contends that organizations function more efficiently than markets in certain situations, namely when transactions must be completed in the face of opportunism (actors will disguise their true intentions and take unfair advantage when possible), when the failure is uncertain, and when entering a transaction limits the number of potential bargaining partners in the future (thereby allowing partners to take unfair advantage).

Although few sociologists think that organizations arise mainly in response to market failures, many of them contend that organizations have advantages in coordinating complex tasks. Like the new institutional economics, these arguments are based on efficiency considerations. Efficiency arguments for the ubiquity of organizations seem plausible. Yet, many organizational analysts express skepticism. They do so because much research raises doubt that organizations use resources more efficiently than other kinds of social actors. For instance, firsthand observers rarely conclude that organizations minimize the costs of completing transactions. Instead, they document a strong tendency for organizations to become "ends in themselves," which means that leaders and members give heavy weight to preserving the organization even at the expense of failing to meet the espoused goals.

Consider the common treatment of whistleblowers, those members who are brave enough to reveal malfeasance and waste in their organizations. One might think that managers or leaders would praise and reward informants for identifying problems that need fixing or waste that could be cut, allowing the organization to better meet its goals. However, this almost never happens. Whistleblowers typically face ostracism for failing to act as team players. They often lose their jobs or find themselves shunted to less desirable jobs. Researchers also document a systematic tendency for organizations to accumulate personnel and to create elaborate structures (e.g., levels of hierarchy) that go far beyond the technical demands of work. In these varied ways, real organizations appear to function to make life easy for their members instead of maximizing their public goals.

Efficiency-based accounts have difficulty explaining why so many organizations do simple tasks that involve low levels of coordination. For instance, much of the work of public bureaucracies involves routine processing of standardized forms, such as applications for drivers' licenses. In contrast, collections of skilled persons collaborating in ad hoc groups (perhaps involved in formal contracts) can often do quite complex tasks. Consider, for example, the team of doctors and other professionals who come together for a surgical operation. Moreover, ad hoc collections of organizations also undertake projects as complicated as those done within any organization, such as the military campaign referred to earlier in this chapter.

What alternative arguments can explain the ubiquity of organizations? Ecologists have emphasized two other specific characteristics of formal organizations. One is *reliability,* by which we mean the capacity to achieve low variance in the quality of performance, including its timeliness. Organizations on average can generate actions with smaller variations in quality than can other kinds of collectives. Given uncertainty about the future, potential members, investors, and clients might value reliability more than efficiency. That is, rational actors might be willing to pay a high price for the certainty that a product or service of a minimum quality will be available when needed. Therefore, they prefer to transact with organizations.

Consumers in modern societies prefer organizations as transaction partners, because they regard them as reliable. Large purchases and potentially risky purchases usually take place with established firms rather than with individuals. For instance, few persons buy or sell a house without the involvement of real estate agencies, though it is entirely possible to conduct the transaction individually and save a significant amount of money. Similarly, when renting a car in a developing country, many Americans opt for the more expensive services of large international car rental firms (and use the additional organizational support of an international credit card company) to ensure that a car will be available when promised and to avoid making deposits with firms of unknown reliability.

The second key advantage is *accountability,* the ability to construct rational accounts for organizational action. What sociologists call norms of rationality prevail in modern societies. All social actors, individual and collective, experience pressure to cast decisions in terms of connections between means and ends. Actions appear more valid if they are justified as stemming from a rational account that ties means to ends. It no longer suffices to provide traditional justifications, claiming that one acts a certain way because he or she has always acted this way. Justifications of rational action tend to emphasize use of appropriate procedures, in part because they are observable. Procedural rationality means showing that actions follow the appropriate procedures rather than that they meet an objective. The strength of norms of procedural rationality can be appreciated by considering the many cases in which employees receive reprimands for failing to follow procedures, even when their deviation from the rules improved the organization's performance.

Formal organizations have unequaled capacities to make procedurally rational accounts. The plethora of information that they collect and file means that they can document how resources have been used. They can produce a "paper trail" that satisfies accepted accounting practice. They can also reconstruct the sequences of decisions, rules, and actions that produced an outcome. When outcomes look distorted compared with claimed goals (e.g., the high levels of compensation for executives of nonprofit corporations or of chief executive officers [CEOs] of unprofitable firms), organizations can claim that codified rules and procedures were employed to produce rational allocations of resources and appropriate organizational actions. In a world that increasingly favors procedural rationality, this ability gives organizations a great advantage over other actors.

Current theory and research suggest that testing for accountability is especially important during the start-up phase. Potential members demand assurance that their investments of time and commitment will not be wasted. That is, they want assurances of durability. When joining means becoming an employee, people want guarantees that careers will be managed in some rational way. Potential investors or supporters also assess accountability. For instance, the profession of public accountancy arose in the United States in response to the desires of British investors in American railroads for assurances that their investments were being managed in appropriate ways (Chandler 1977). Demands for procedural rationality in this narrow sense have become both widespread and intense.

Pressures for accountability work intensely when (1) organizations produce symbolic or information-loaded products such as education, (2) substantial risk exists, as in medical care, (3) the organization and its employees (or clients) typically form long-term relations, and (4) the organization has ostensibly political purposes.

Two trends in contemporary American society also heighten demands for accountability. The first is the tendency to litigate disputes. When conflicts are brought into the legal system, the importance of documenting procedures and actions increases greatly. The second source is the growing pressures for formal equality with a diverse work force. Employers must document that decisions about hiring, firing, and promotion heed widely accepted standards, that is, they are procedurally rational.

WHY ARE THERE SO MANY KINDS OF ORGANIZATIONS?

As we reviewed above, efficiency, reliability, and accountability can explain the proliferation of durable, special-purpose organizations. But what should these corporate actors look like? One can imagine a world in which all kinds of transactions get done by a single, all-encompassing organization or by many smaller organizations with identical structures and different tasks. Such a system would be characterized by complete homogeneity (absence of diversity). The chapters in this book on specific industries make clear that this is not so. Contemporary societies possess enormous diversity of organizations. We see organizations with one or a few members and others with millions of members. Some organizations have finely elaborated structures, complete with organization charts and detailed job designs. Others have fluid job assignment and consensual decision making. Some have broad missions, for example, firms that operate in many industries and in many countries; others have narrow objectives. Organizational diversity refers to the distribution of organizations over such distinctions. If all or most organizations in a system have the same form (e.g., they all have similar designs, types of authority, and so forth), diversity is low. If, on the other hand, many examples of each of the possible forms exist, diversity is high.

Organizational diversity varies widely among countries. The United States stands out as extremely diverse; the Soviet Union, before the collapse of state socialism, stood at the other pole. We also see great variation among industries and over the history of industries, as the rest of this book shows. Any good theory of organizations should be able to explain differences in levels of diversity among systems and changes in diversity within systems.

Organizational diversity rises and falls in several ways. First, there are the consequences of *transformations* by existing organizations. Strategic responses of managers and leaders to changing environmental conditions can yield new designs, thereby increasing diversity. Gannett Newspapers' launching of the nationally oriented *USA Today* is an instance of such change. Transformations can also lower diversity. For instance, the American system of higher education once contained a great many single-sex colleges in addition to many other coeducational ones. Most of the single-sex colleges have gone coeducational, thereby lowering diversity. In these cases, changes in diversity reflect efforts at adaptation by existing organizations.

Diversity can decline due to *imitation* of successful organizations. One can argue that the wholesale switch toward coeducation was an example of such imitation. Perhaps a better example is the trend of American manufacturing firms adopting Japanese organizational structures (e.g., flat hierarchies, quality control circles) and practices of lean production. This trend has lowered diversity within the worldwide system of automobile manufacturing (even German firms have started adopting these practices). Homogenizing tendencies also reflect the spread of fads from schools of management or from professional societies (DiMaggio and Powell 1983).

Transformation and imitation are both examples of *adaptation processes* of individual organizations. In these and all adaptation processes, individual organizations are seen as changing in response to changes in environments, technologies, or other conditions. Most discussions of organizational change presume the individual organizational level of analysis and employ the imagery of adaptation.

Alternatively, organizational diversity can increase or decrease due to *selection processes*.[2] Selection refers to change in the composition of a set of organizations from differential replacement of one form by another. One organizational form comes to dominate because more such organizations arise and fewer fail than is the case for some alternative form. For instance, the trend toward coeducational higher education partly reflects selection processes: few single-sex colleges have been founded in recent years and many have failed.

Observed change in organizational diversity over a period of time usually reflects a mix of the three processes. Some organizations successfully build innovative structures, some organizations copy others, new kinds of organizations arise, and some existing organizations disappear. What of the mix? Most writing and research on organizations emphasize transformation and imitation as the motors of change in the world of organizations. That is, such analysis assumes, usually tacitly, that the most prevalent and most important fraction of the mix involves adaptive actions by existing organizations. Organizational ecology argues the opposite case: that few organizations succeed at transformation and imitation and that selection serves as the driving force of long-term change. This position is only tenable if organizations exhibit great inertia in their structures over time.

STRUCTURAL INERTIA

To claim that organizations have great inertia is not to imply that leaders do not try to adapt to changing environments. They clearly do. As we see it, the real issue is whether organizations can *accurately and consistently time* their reorganizations to match variations in unpredictable, turbulent environments. A reasonable depiction of the adaptation problem facing organizations involves two elements. First, organizations frequently cannot make good forecasts about future states of the environment. Second, they cannot have much confidence that designed modifications will have their intended effects (whether the cure will be worse than the disease). If this characterization is accurate, efforts at adaptation should be essentially random with respect to the future.

Does the possibility that organizations can imitate "best practice" undermine these arguments? Ready examples of success must surely help to overcome internal resistance to change. However, a different constraint blocks widespread imitation. Much organizational knowledge is tacit. It is neither written into procedures nor coded into technology. Consequently only the most concrete features of technique can be easily copied and incorporated into ongoing organizations.

Moreover, actions by others limit imitative adaptation. Although it might be in the interests of leaders of many organizations to adopt a certain strategy, the environmental carrying capacity for organizations with that strategy is often quite limited. Only a few can succeed in exploiting such a strategy. Those in the vanguard (and perhaps those who trail the vanguard closely) have decided advantages in such cases. Imitation does not help other organizations to improve their fortunes.

History readily illustrates the difficulties of adaptation. Few organizations achieve either great longevity or great social power, and virtually none achieves both. In other words, few organizations succeed in solving their adaptive problems for very long in a turbulent world.

Why are organizations so inertial? Some inertial constraints arise internally. Investments in plant, equipment, and specialized personnel cannot be easily transferred to other tasks and functions. Decision makers also face constraints on the information they receive. Research on flows of information in organizations reveals that leaders fail to receive anything close to full information on activities within the organization and in the relevant environment. Nobel laureate Kenneth Arrow (1974, p. 49), in an essay on the information economics of organization, argued that, "The combination of uncertainty, indivisibility, and capital intensity associated with information channels and their use imply (a) that the actual structure and behavior of an organization may depend heavily upon random events, in other words on history, and (b) the very pursuit of efficiency might lead to rigidity and unresponsiveness to further change."

Internal politics encourage inertia. Attempts at transformation usually upset political equilibria, because such change requires that resources be reallocated. For example, consider what happens when a manufacturing firm attempts to shift from a strategy of designing state-of-the-art products and seeking markets for them (a product-driven strategy) to a strategy of building what customers want (a market-driven strategy). Such a change lowers the political clout of the engineering units and increases the power of marketing. Changes in salaries and other internally allocated resources ordinarily follow. In general, some subunits will gain and others will lose when an organization makes a fundamental change. Thus, some portions of the organization (often a majority) have an interest in opposing any proposed reorganization. Strong resistance can block reorganization completely. Even weak resistance can greatly slow processes of adjustment. Reorganization likely yields generalized benefits—those that benefit the organization as a whole. Moreover, such benefits take some (often considerable) time to be realized. Any negative political response can generate short-run political costs high enough to cause decision makers to forgo a planned reorganization.

According to recent research in psychology, people give greater weight to potential losses than to equally likely potential gains in making decisions (Kahneman, Slovic, and Tversky 1982). That is, the disutility of a loss of a given size is greater than the utility associated with a gain of the same size, which suggests that leaders and members in subunits facing losses with change will tend to oppose it more vigorously than those who stand to gain will support it.

Perhaps the most powerful break on radical transformations comes from tacit social agreements about what actions are sensible and proper. Sociologists have documented a tendency for operating procedures and task allocations to become infused with social value—they become understood as the "right" ways of doing things in an organization. If such a process takes hold, the costs of transformation increase greatly. Normative understandings provide legitimate justifications beyond self-interest for those who wish to oppose reorganization. Instead of defending self-interest, members and subunits often achieve the same purpose by defending tradition.

Social psychologists argue that people rely on schemas (highly simplified cognitive maps) in making sense of their environments. Schemas limit both the amount of variety that people can perceive and the range of responses they consider. If these arguments are correct, they presumably apply to people acting as agents of organizations. As long as organizational decision makers rely unwittingly on schemas, organizations will tend to remain close to their roots. This is because strong schemas preclude serious consideration of many novel responses to threats and opportunities in the environment.

External pressures also generate inertia. Getting timely information about relevant environments entails costs, especially in turbulent situations where it has most value. In addition, personnel tend to specialize in using certain information channels even when other, perhaps newer, channels would provide better information. Such specialization limits the range of information about the environment that organizations can obtain and process.

Environments also impose *legitimacy constraints* on what are the "right" or appropriate types of activities for a given kind of organization. As with any asset, legitimacy sustains flows of resources from the environment. Adaptive change that violates legitimacy incurs costs. For instance, American business schools must operate MBA programs to be considered "real" business schools by alumni, the press, and outside donors. Although it might make sense (in terms of internal considerations) for a given school to drop its MBA program, the costs imposed by the environment of doing so would be enormous—the school could lose accreditation, faculty, students, and donations. Generally speaking, the likelihood that adjustments will compromise legitimacy discourages efforts at fundamental transformation.

Inertia also derives from the very characteristics that make organizations favored as solutions to collective action problems. Reliability and accountability depend on reproducing structure with high fidelity over time. Yet, high reproducibility of structure means that organizational structures resist transformation. As noted above, this means that some aspects of structure can be transformed only slowly and at considerable cost, because many resources must be applied to produce the result. Such structures have a deadweight quality: responses to environmental variations trail events at considerable distance. Lags in response often last longer than typical environmental fluctuations and longer than the attention spans of managers and outside authorities. Thus, inertia often blocks transformation completely.

To understand better our arguments about organizational inertia, consider the case of General Motors. Formed in 1908 by William C. Durant, General Motors initially operated as a holding company. It combined as many as twenty-five automobile manufacturers in the period up to 1916. By 1918, General Motors had adopted a divisionalized structure. It organized divisions for its Buick, Cadillac, Chevrolet, Oakland, and Oldsmobile automobiles. General Motors sold 344,000 automobiles in 1919, which represented about 20 percent of the American market.

Economic historian Alfred Chandler (1962) argues that the divisionalized organizational form and the resulting economies of administration and scale allowed General Motors to eventually dominate the American and world markets (see Chapter 10). By the mid-1960s, General Motors retained the divisional structure, but its size had expanded dramatically. The company sold over four million new cars in the United States, for a market share of nearly 50 percent. It also had very substantial overseas sales and operations. By this time, General Motors looked so different from its earlier manifestations that it seems to contradict our claims that organizations can rarely transform themselves. How can cases like this be reconciled with inertia arguments?

Perhaps General Motors poses an exception to the inertia argument. The history of the auto industry suggests that this might be so. As is shown in Chapter 10, the early history of the industry contained thousands of automobile producers and would-be producers. The vast majority of these enterprises could not cope with market and technological changes and were driven out of business, often before they really got started.

Despite the temptation to regard General Motors as a case of successful adaptation, we think it would be a mistake to do so. The theory of structural inertia concerns a specific kind of transformation. As impressive as these changes are, they do not qualify as highly relevant. The theory of structural inertia holds that the constraints on change operate most intensely on *core* features. It also holds that attempted changes in core features generate the greatest risks. In our view, General Motors has experienced few, if any, transformations in its core (based on the divisional structure) since 1916. Indeed,

General Motors' inability to adjust accounts for its great difficulty in responding to the challenge of Japanese automakers, whose core features differ in some important ways.

What do we mean by the core features? The logic of identifying the core hinges first on an understanding of the interrelations of the elements of the structure. The more extensive are the other adjustments in the organization that would be required to reform a particular element, the more core-like is the element. Organizational characteristics can be ordered, at least roughly, by the extensiveness of other smaller adjustments they would prompt and this ordering ranks features by their "coreness." So, for example, for a firm to switch its marketing strategy usually entails fewer other changes than for it to enter new product markets (unrelated to its current products). Radical change in products usually requires new capital, new manufacturing capabilities, changed marketing, and the like.

Another important dimension of core reorganization concerns how much of a departure the intended new state of affairs represents compared to the old way of doing business. Redesigns that extend or refine the existing method of operations are less fundamental than those that branch out into unrelated activities. For instance, saving and loan institutions that responded to deregulation by entering consumer-based lending markets outside of their traditional market in residential mortgages undertook less radical change than those that entered such activities as property development.

Michael T. Hannan and John Freeman (1989) proposed a more specific list of generic core organizational features. Each entails extensive adjustments, if tinkered with, and each can be assessed in terms of relatedness. Their four core features are

1. The *mission*. What are the basic public goals of the organization? Does it produce automobiles (as with General Motors)? Or does it tend to the spiritual needs of its members (as with the Roman Catholic Church)? Imagine the changes required if General Motors were to attempt the unthinkable change of switching its goals to be similar to the Catholic Church.

2. The *form of authority*. Is organizational authority grounded in rules or on expertise? Are rules formally defined and written, or are they normatively defined? Does authority emanate from a single charismatic leader, or is it rooted in a set of responsibilities attached explicitly to positions?

3. The *basic technology*. How are the outputs of the organization produced? Think about the difficulties involved in switching to an alternative production system. As the Swiss watch industry (discussed in Chapter 1) illustrates, what seems simple in retrospect often escapes contemporaries.

4. The general *marketing strategy*. How are the outputs sold or distributed? Is the firm's appeal to a mass market or to a specialized market segment? Much tacit organizational knowledge is involved in every successful marketing strategy.

Features that do not qualify as belonging to the core are usually called *peripheral* features (see Scott 1992). Examples of peripheral features include the number of levels in an organizational hierarchy, accounting methods, and joint ventures with other organizations. Organizations modify peripheral features

regularly, and these adjustments often yield benefits. We think that much organizational theory concerns these sorts of adjustments and ignores core transformations, which differ qualitatively. Indeed, much of the debate over the
adaptability of organizations can be resolved by invoking this distinction.

According to the theory of structural inertia, organizations sometimes try to
change their core features but rarely succeed. Moreover, the theory also maintains that attempts at transformation in the core increase the probability of
failure of an organization, robbing it of much of its accumulated competitive
advantage. Adaptive changes usually involve a shift in competitive posture,
which means that, whatever the other advantages of the modifications, the re-
formed organization will have less relevant experience than most of its new
rivals. It might also encounter retaliation from the new rivals whose turf has
been invaded. Moreover, it might be weakened by the costs of overcoming
entry barriers such as capital expenditure required for competitive reposition-
ing.

Empirical research supports the theory in the limited tests that have been
conducted so far. In Chapter 13, William Barnett discusses one test from his
studies of the telephone industry.

In recent years, some firms have recognized the difficulty of transforming
core structures and have tried a different strategy. They have tried to innovate
by constructing freestanding new organizations within the firm. Often firms
locate these new structures far from their corporate headquarters. The reasoning behind this strategy accepts the inevitability of strong inertia within existing
organizations. Instead of taking the risk and incurring the costs of transforming
the original structures, they create new and highly autonomous organizational
structures to undertake bold and radical new strategic ventures. For example,
IBM entered the personal computer business by starting a new organization,
far from the stultifying atmosphere of its headquarters. (Chapter 3 discusses
this case in detail.) When Gannett Newspapers' management set out to create
the national newspaper *USA Today,* it created a new structure, which was initially hidden from the staffs of its many local newspapers. General Motors developed a similar isolated organization to produce its Saturn model.

The practice seems to show the potential for success, as the examples illustrate. Nonetheless, even in these cases, insiders report that envy and political
infighting from the rest of the organization sometimes run rampant. Given the
legal authority of the "parent" firms, the new and successful substructure
might be reined in, starved off, or folded back into the parent. If so, then decentralized core changes of this kind might simply show some delay in the time
between initial enactment and the period of precariousness.

FORMS, POPULATIONS, AND COMMUNITIES
OF ORGANIZATIONS

Emphasizing the strength of inertial forces within organizations affects how we
view change generally within the world of organizations. Most research on or-

ganizations formulates arguments from the perspective of a single organization. If we are correct about the strength of inertia, then much can be learned from a broader focus. Our broader focus considers *sets of organizations* facing similar environments. This view allows us to consider systematically some important forces shaping the organizational world that cannot be seen at the organizational level, for example, variations over time and place in the rate at which new organizations come forth.

We favor a broader focus for a second reason: it sheds light on the ways in which environments shape organizations. *The environment of each organization consists mainly of other organizations.* These include the governments that claim jurisdiction over their activities, schools that prepare cohorts of potential recruits, firms that supply technical, material, and symbolic inputs, organizations that produce similar products and services, and those that purchase or use the products and services. Change in the environment of an organization usually means changes in the composition or activities of other organizations and organizational populations. The dynamics of the organizational world cannot be understood well from analysis of any single organization, because the dynamics of sets of like organizations are usually linked (and each is part of the other's environment). Therefore, we favor analysis of the relevant interacting sets of organizations.

The basic concept for considering sets of organizations is the *organizational form*. Form serves as the organizational ecologist's analogue to the biological ecologist's species. Form summarizes the core properties that make a set of organizations ecologically similar. Thus organizations with the same form depend in a common way on the material and social environment. A set of organizations possesses the same form in this sense if environmental changes affect them similarly.

In the treatments of particular industries in this book, forms are defined in ways that fit the histories. So, for instance, labor unions distinguish between the craft form (which organizes workers by occupation or craft) and the industrial form (which organizes workers by place of employment). Breweries are distinguished by the mass-production form (which uses modern production techniques and mass marketing), the microbrewery (which uses craft production techniques and world-of-mouth marketing), and the brewpub (which uses craft production and point-of-sale marketing), and so forth.

Organizational populations are specific time-and-space instances of organizational forms. That is, an organizational population consists of the set of organizations with a particular form within a (bounded) social system. A public bureaucracy and an investment bank are examples of organizational forms. The set of public bureaucracies in Japan during 1946–93 and the set of investment banks in the United States during the same period are examples of interesting organizational populations.

Organizational populations resemble industries in many respects. Due to the common usage of the term *industry,* in this book we have often used population and industry almost interchangeably. However, the distinction does matter in social science theory and research. As we understand the work of industrial organization economists, they typically begin to delimit industries by analyzing consumer choices in a market. For instance, they consider the substitutability of various products and define industries to include close substitutes. This approach allows a researcher to identify direct competitors and to assess the strength of that competition.

Organizational ecologists typically begin from a different vantage point, that of the production system. They examine the *potentially* competing firms in a market and then assess their legal, institutional, and structural differences to identify populations of organizations. Organizational ecologists view the market as a socially constructed phenomenon. They estimate models to find empirically the presence or absence of competition between firms and groups of like firms. Instead of beginning the analysis by excluding firms assumed to be outside the market (as does industry in the usage of the economics of industrial organization), ecologists begin by identifying the population of all potential competitors and then make the observed relationships in a market a primary object of analysis. The power of models based on the population perspective comes from their ability to explain how industries evolve to the point where their segments or submarkets appear distinct (often despite contemporaneous similarity in function, e.g., modern beer brewing).

Organizational community refers to the broader set of organizational populations whose interactions have a systemic character, often caused by functional differentiation. Some analysts refer to such communities as organizational fields or as societal sectors. A typical community of organizations in industrial settings consists of populations of supplier firms, populations of consumer firms (in the case of intermediate product markets), populations of labor unions, populations of regulatory agencies, industry associations, and so forth.

These concepts have important methodological implications for viewing and analyzing the organizational world. There is an indisputable, though often overlooked, danger in generalizing from a few well-known success stories to broad classes of organizations. To avoid the selection bias entailed in analyzing only successful cases, ecologists analyze processes of change in *entire* populations or communities of organizations. They focus on the changing makeup of these sets rather than on changes in the behavior of (possibly unrepresentative) individual organizations. In this book, introductions to major sections and chapters on particular industries provide detailed and concrete illustrations of the power of this approach.

To highlight selection processes, ecologists address questions of change in the organizational world by analyzing the so-called vital rates of organizational populations. The vital rates are the *rate of founding, rate of transformation,* and *rate of mortality.* In analyzing these vital rates, ecologists focus on the effects of larger social, economic, and political systems.

Ecologists also emphasize the dynamics that take place within and between organizational populations. The overriding image in such analyses is one of *competition.* Individual organizations possess the capacity to grow when resources to support growth are available. Numbers of organizations also grow under conditions of abundance, as entrepreneurs move to take advantage of opportunities. Both kinds of growth—in scale of individual organizations and in numbers of organizations—can eventually deplete any finite resource. If at least some relevant resources are finite, organizations compete for resources. Such competition controls selection. Intense competition reduces the rate at which individual organizations grow and the rate at which new organizations enter an arena. It also increases the chances that extant organizations will fail. In other words, a focus on selection leads to an emphasis on competition as a key driving force. Many chapters in this book discuss ecological ideas about competition in the organizational world. Often, specific models of competition that have been developed within the ecological perspective are used. We explain and review these in the introductions to the major sections of the book.

NOTES

1. We appreciate the helpful comments of Bill Barnett, Susan Olzak, and Joel Podolny on an earlier version of this chapter. Barnett's students in a Stanford MBA class on business strategy also provided helpful comments.

2. The distinction between adaptation and selection sometimes gets confused because selection can be viewed as adaptation at the population level. However, the confusion is only terminological: once the level of analysis is fixed, the differences between the two processes are clear. For instance, the Swiss watch industry example discussed in Chapter 1 might be viewed as adaptation by the world watch industry, but it is obvious that Swiss watch companies could not adapt and thus were subject to selection pressures.

BIBLIOGRAPHY

Arrow, Kenneth J. 1974. *The Limits of Organization*. New York: Norton.

Chandler, Alfred D. 1962. *Strategy and Structure*. Boston: MIT Press.

Chandler, Alfred D. 1977. *The Visible Hand*. Cambridge, MA: Harvard University Press.

DiMaggio, Paul J., and Walter W. Powell. 1983. "The Iron Cage Revisited: Institutional Isomorphism and Collective Rationality in Organizational Fields." *American Sociological Review* 48:147–60.

Hannan, Michael T., and John Freeman. 1989. *Organizational Ecology*. Cambridge, MA: Harvard University Press.

Kahneman, D., P. Slovic, and A. Tversky. 1982. *Judgment Under Uncertainty: Heuristics and Biases*. Cambridge, MA: Cambridge University Press.

Scott, W. Richard. 1992. *Organizations: Rational, Natural, and Social Systems*, 3rd ed. Englewood Cliffs, NJ: Prentice-Hall.

Williamson, Oliver E. 1985. *The Economic Institutions of Capitalism*. New York: Free Press.

II
ENVIRONMENTAL SELECTION

Ecological theory emphasizes environmental selection. When stated in its simplest terms, the theory of environmental selection explains the rise and fall of populations of organizations by the variations in abundance of the environmental resources on which they depend. This means relating variations in environmental conditions to (1) the rate at which new organizations arise, (2) rates of growth and decline of individual organizations, and (3) rates of organizational mortality.

According to ecological theory, new organizations and organizational forms spring from the environment. The environment also sets the conditions under which organizations operate and survive. Organizational environments consist of the resources (capital, knowledge, personnel, equipment, customers, etc.) needed to build and sustain organizations. They also include the other organizations that hold many of these resources and those that potentially represent competitors.

Theorists have characterized organizational environments in a multitude of ways, as for example, placid or turbulent, resource abundant or scarce, competitive or opportunity laden. Most of these characterizations are developed in the context of a specific theory of organizational change or effectiveness. Instead of reviewing these theories here, we explain the general approaches that ecologists use to understand environments. We focus on environments of organizational populations rather than communities, because that is the focus of most theory and research.

The concept of *niche* provides a general way to express effects of environmental variations and competition on the growth rates of organizational populations (Hannan and Freeman 1989). It also provides a way to formalize ideas about competition. The *fundamental niche* of a population consists of the set of all environmental conditions in which the population can grow or at least sustain its numbers. Thus the fundamental niche of an organizational form consists of the social, economic, and political conditions that can sustain the functioning of organizations that embody a particular form. For instance, the modern form of corporation (as distinct from, say, the family firm) depends on a legal system that defines property rights and upholds contracts, as well as a political system that enforces these legal rules. Thus, the niche of the modern corporate business firm is defined partly in these specific legal and political terms.

Suppose that two organizational populations rely on different resources and are affected by different social and political institutions. Then we would say that their fundamental niches do not intersect. The ecological similarity of two or more kinds of organizations can be defined in terms of the degree of intersection of their fundamental niches. In general, the potential for two populations to compete is proportional to the intersection of their fundamental niches. Two populations compete if and only if their fundamental niches intersect.

The presence of a competing population reduces the range of conditions in which a population can be sustained. The term *realized niche* refers to the restricted environmental space in which a population can be sustained even in the presence of competing populations of organizations. The realized niche is a subset of the fundamental niche, and it is substantially smaller than the fundamental niche in most realistic cases.

Except in the highly unusual case of a population isolated from all competitors, only the realized niche can be observed. Suppose that a pair of populations competes for a resource and that one of them can exclude the other from the full range of overlap of their fundamental niches. Then, the realized niche of the stronger competitor coincides with the fundamental niche. But, the realized niche of the weaker competitor is smaller than its fundamental niche. Interestingly, the two populations will not be observed to compete in this case. That is, the two realized niches will not intersect. More generally, the absence of an observed niche intersection does not imply two organizational populations do not compete.

Detailing the niche of an organizational form requires intensive analysis of its natural history. Learning about the social, economic, and political conditions required to sustain a form of organization involves study of historical instances of the organizational form and the functioning of organizations that embody it. Thus analysis of an organizational population begins by identifying the resources that sustain it. The next step includes quantifying the relevant resources and examining how they change over time.

The resource levels at any point in time set the *carrying capacity* or equilibrium size for the organizational population. If competition from other forms of organization is weak, then the population can be expected (eventually) to obtain a size roughly near its carrying capacity. And, changes over time in the resource levels reflect themselves in changes in the size and distribution of the organizational population. Because organization building is often a slow and difficult process, however, populations are frequently at sizes much lower than the carrying capacity. In other words, there is a lag between the realized size of a population and its possible sustainable size, a lag resulting from the time and effort required to assemble organizations and their supporting institutions.

Fast food restaurants can be used to illustrate the theory of environmental selection. The story is well known. The modern form of the fast food restaurant appeared in the United States after World War II. The population of fast food chains expanded quickly to cover most of the country and now many parts of the world. Fortunes were made as entrepreneurs refined and developed the form, branching out from the original hamburger menu to nearly all sorts of food. In the last decade or so, the growth of this population has slowed and perhaps even reversed.

Which environmental resources support this population? In the United States beginning in the mid-1950s, the economy entered a sustained expansion and the baby boom also caused the number of young consumers to begin to grow rapidly. Moreover, the population was simultaneously becoming more dispersed and more interconnected through developing transportation and communication networks. All this led to a faster-paced society and, when coupled with a traditionally practical view of food, set the stage for a type of restaurant that served a few simple items in an expeditious manner.

The abundance of inexpensive supplies such as beef, bread, and potatoes spurred on development of the form, as did the availability of low-cost teenage labor. American families, whose incomes were rising, found a new lifestyle in eating out without great cost and with food that appealed strongly to their children. The simple and readily transportable organizational form used by this population also meant that it could proliferate rapidly, bringing the population close to its huge carrying capacity in only a matter of several decades. This growth has slowed in recent years due to declines in the size of the teenage population, the rising cost of supplies (especially beef), the scarcity of cheap labor, and the increased nutritional health consciousness of Americans.

The preceding story about fast food restaurants uses for its explanation only the environmental resources that support the organizational population. That is, it uses the idea of the potential niche. The most glaring omission in this kind of environmental selection explanation is that it does not consider competing organizational forms. The realized niche describes the resource space of a population after competition has been considered. Another example illustrates this difference.

In Chapter 1, we describe briefly transformations that have occurred in the world watch industry. Recall that this industry experienced massive selection due to technological changes. When electric and tuning fork technologies replaced pin lever and jewel lever technologies, American firms with integrated distribution systems made market inroads on the small specialized firms of Swiss craftsmen. However, when quartz watch technology appeared in the 1970s, large vertically integrated Japanese firms took the dominant position in the industry.

Is this account an application of environmental selection theory? The basic technological changes were exogenous to the organizational populations, and the different organizational forms depended on different technologies. Therefore, a case can be made that the selection was environmental. Such an explanation misses an important part of the history: the competition between organizational forms. Assume for the moment that the technological change was endogenous, that it was a product of the organizational populations (the assumption is justified in the sense that the application-specific elements of the technology were not developed outside the industry). The first question to ask now is, did the other environmental resources on which the watch industry depends change? To some small extent they no doubt did; as watches became cheaper, there were more potential customers and sales could be expected to climb. However, the basic market resource was still the adult population of the modern world, and most people still did not feel that they needed more than a couple of functioning watches.

What happened in this industry was, we think, less a result of changes in the potential niche of any organizational form than of competition among organizational forms. That the new technologies changed the nature of competition is, of course, central to the analysis. Yet, the new technologies did not change enormously the total potential niche. If the Swiss firms could have adapted in sufficient time, we doubt they would have disappeared. The theoretical difference between this account of the rise of Japanese watchmakers and the one given for the emergence of American fast food restaurants is that competition is the motor of change, not environmental resource expansion.

This section contains historical accounts of organizations in industries that emphasize the causal importance of three different kinds of environments. In Philip Anderson's account of organizational change in the microcomputer industry (Chapter 3), the key environmental events involve *technical change*. Frank Dobbin's treatment of the railroad industry (Chapter 4) points to the role of *governmental regulation* in shaping the population of firms. Finally, Judith Blau's discussion of change in the population of American art museums (Chapter 5) illustrates the power of *cultural change* in affecting organizational evolution. We think that comparing these very different industries and their different dimensions of environment provides an appreciation of the richness of the imagery of environmental selection.

BIBLIOGRAPHY

Hannan, M. T., and J. Freeman. 1989. *Organizational Ecology.* Cambridge, MA: Harvard
    University Press (paperback edition 1993).

3

Microcomputer Manufacturers

PHILIP ANDERSON

In 1976, the only microcomputers in the world processed data eight bits at a time, held fewer than four typewritten pages in memory, typically stored data on cassette tapes, and only executed programs written by their owners—which could not run on any other microcomputer. The number of microcomputer producers could be counted on one's fingers. Fewer than twenty years later, manufacturing of these devices is a great worldwide industry, whose technology has advanced almost inconceivably from those pioneering days. Hundreds of organizations make personal computers (PCs) and workstations based on microprocessors. In the face of dramatic technical progress and spiraling demand, how has the population of organizations making microcomputers evolved to its present state?

A BRIEF HISTORY OF THE MICROCOMPUTER INDUSTRY

The Origins
In the beginning, there was the Altair.

Not really, of course. Pinpointing the birth of an industry is difficult, for most innovations have precursors and near-neighbors. The first microcomputer represented an evolutionary branching, not wholly new, but enough of a departure to signal the emergence of a new organizational population. To understand why the Altair inaugurated a revolution, we need to understand what distinguishes microcomputers from any other type of computer.

From the time the first commercially sold computer, the Sperry Univac, appeared in 1952, computer manufacturers were above all *architects* of data processing systems. The heart of a computer is its central processing unit, the element that performs logical and mathematical calculations. The manufacturer specified the set of instructions a computer understood and how the central processing unit would act on those instructions. One could not produce a computer without designing its logical architecture.

In 1969, one could not produce a calculating machine without designing a *set* of complex circuits. Lacking the know-how to build a calculator architecture, a Japanese firm commissioned the American semiconductor manufacturer Intel to produce a *chip set,* a group of semiconductors, for its newest calculating machine. Instead, Intel designed the first microprocessor, a single chip containing all the logic circuitry of a calculator's central processing unit. A year after Intel's microprocessor was first offered for sale in 1971, Texas Instruments introduced the first single chip that held all the elements of a computer—not just the processor but also input/output and memory circuits. The era of the hand-held electronic calculator had dawned, and a new generation of semiconductor manufacturers specializing in microprocessors was born.

This breakthrough in chip design made possible computers distinct from their predecessors because a microprocessor defines the computer's fundamental *logical* architecture. Designing a computer around a microprocessor is not a trivial exercise, and microcomputer manufacturers make critical design choices that differentiate one machine from another. Yet the fundamental logic of the machine—its instruction set and how it treats instructions—is dictated by the semiconductor manufacturer that produces the microprocessor. All firms that build machines around the popular Intel "iAPX" chip family, for example, accept common constraints on the way data are processed in their products. Before the microprocessor, the essence of what it meant to be a computer manufacturer was that a firm designed its own core logic as well as the complex architecture surrounding the central processing unit. Historically, microcomputers have been much less expensive than machines that do not employ microprocessors, but price is not the principal reason why microcomputer manufacturers are an identifiable population within the larger computer industry complex. The architectural issue explains why microcomputer manufacturers are affected similarly by changes in the environment affecting the manufacturers of other computers in different ways.

The potential for evolutionary branching in the computer industry was established by the semiconductor manufacturers' breakthroughs, but the leap from microprocessor to microcomputer was not immediate. Intel improved its original 4-bit 4004 chip, producing the 8008 in 1972. This was an 8-bit chip, and a schematic drawing with a parts list for a microcomputer based on the 8008 was published in *Radio Electronics Magazine* in July 1974. Yet the 8008 lacked certain vital functions, and its successor, the Intel 8080, became the processing heart of the first microcomputer. Although several engineers may have designed and sold individual computers based on the 8080 in 1974, the first microcomputer offered for broad commercial sale debuted on the cover of the January 1975 issue of *Popular Electronics.*

Its name was the Altair, and it was offered for sale by a firm named Micro Instrumentation and Telemetry Systems (MITS). MITS was not founded for the purpose of producing a microcomputer. Originating in a garage as a seller of mail-order equipment for airplane and rocket hobbyists, MITS branched into electronic components and was the first American firm to sell calculator kits. Rapid price cutting in the hand-held calculator market drove MITS deeply into debt, and its founder decided to build computer hobby kits as a way out of the morass.

To understand why the Altair represented a departure and why it is empirically sound to think of microcomputer manufacturers as a distinct population, it is necessary to distinguish these devices from their near-relatives. Calculators are obviously related to microcomputers, but a calculator is not a general-purpose machine—for example, it cannot perform word processing. Neither is a dedicated word processor a general-purpose machine, though the word-processing typewriter market pioneered in 1964 by IBM was revolutionized the year after the Altair debuted through Wang Laboratories' introduction of computing technology. Similarly, "intelligent terminals," introduced in 1970, developed a huge market, but their capabilities were restricted to off-loading certain communications functions from the central computers to which they were connected. The Altair, for all its limitations, was an authentic general-purpose computer.

For a period of time, MITS and the Altair stood alone. From today's vantage point, burdened by knowledge of the way this industry actually developed, it is difficult to realize how many evolutionary roads were not taken. MITS might have become an industrial giant; in fact, it became one of the first computer firms to fail, sold in 1977 to a disk drive manufacturer that quickly discontinued the Altair product line. Calculator producers such as Texas Instruments or Casio might have become dominant in microcomputers. Leading terminal manufacturers such as Televideo, or word-processing leaders such as Wang or Lanier, might have built on their know-how to crowd rivals from the microcomputer arena. A small firm named Atari, founded in 1972 to make video games, had already introduced a home game machine and was on the verge of its spectacular rise and fall; neither it nor other firms making dedicated game machines had much impact on microcomputers. Successful forward integration by microprocessor manufacturers (e.g., Intel, Motorola) or backward integration by software developers (e.g., Microsoft, Lotus) might have altered the resource space. A number of retailers (e.g., Computerland/Imsai) and firms that made peripheral components (e.g., Epson) have attempted microcomputer manufacture without conspicuous success. As it happens, the ecological history of the population of microcomputer manufacturers became principally the story of a struggle between organizations founded by entrepreneurs for the express purpose of manufacturing microcomputers, and organizations branching into microcomputers from other areas of the computer industry.

The Early Years
The notion that the personal computer revolution was pioneered by fanatical entrepreneurs who founded companies by building a PC in a garage has entered industrial folklore. In the earliest days, anyone who could create a working microcomputer found a ready pool of demand among hobbyists. The critical organizing resource appeared to be skilled design labor. It is possible to identify

one or two engineers behind every early microcomputer, and a number of pioneering firms failed simply because their machines broke down in use. Yet surprisingly few enterprises fit the Apple Computer mold—a firm founded for the express purpose of building a personal computer. The earliest rivals of MITS typically were founded for another purpose and gravitated toward computer manufacturing. Predominant were electronic hobby kit builders (e.g., South West Technical Products, Ohio Scientific, Heath) and firms originally founded to build circuit boards for other microcomputers (e.g., Cromemco, Processor Technology, Vector Graphics, and Morrow Designs).

There were few hardware standards for machines built in the 1970s, and the purchasers of a given machine tended to form a closed community, unable to use hardware or software fashioned for other models. Yet even at this early date, the microcomputer world was roughly divided into two camps. One employed microprocessors based on Intel's architecture, although the most popular machines were designed around the Z80 chip from Zilog, an enhancement of the Intel 8080. The other used the MOS Technology 6502, a microprocessor patterned after the Motorola M6800 chip.

These two architectures diverged so much that software tended to be developed for one or the other; converting programs to run on both was notoriously difficult. In the Intel/Zilog domain, one of the first operating systems designed for microprocessors became ubiquitous: Control Program for Microcomputers (CP/M) from Digital Research. Programs written for an 8080/Z80 machine with CP/M would necessarily run on another machine with the same chip and operating system, but it was reasonably easy for a programmer to create versions of the same basic code that took into account individual machine idiosyncrasies. In the MOS/Motorola arena, manufacturers tended to employ proprietary operating systems. As a result, the great majority of firms founded between 1976 and 1981 were built around the combination of an Intel or Zilog chip and CP/M. Organizations used this architecture because a cheap, reliable operating system was available for it. Software developers wrote CP/M programs because a lot of organizations were building CP/M computers. Buyers flocked to CP/M computers because there was a good deal of software available for them.

However, this circular process took time. Before CP/M became widespread enough to become the dominant choice of firm organizers, two enterprises achieved extraordinary success with the MOS 6502 architecture. The first was Apple Computer, which entered the market in 1976. The second was Commodore Business Machines. Through vastly different strategies, each created a unique niche for itself.

Much has been written about the spectacular rise of Apple, and many factors have been credited for its early success. Apple produced one of the first microcomputers that could display color graphics. One of its founders devised an elegant controller that enabled users to work with relatively inexpensive floppy disks at a time when many other machines used cassette tapes for storage. The company's flair for evangelistic marketing has become legendary. Apple as an organization was not built by its young founders, but by a smart, veteran top management team recruited from first-rank Silicon Valley semiconductor manufacturers.

Yet two structural factors must not be overlooked. First, a dozen small start-up firms entered the market in 1976 along with Apple, building computers around the 6502. Only Apple succeeded. Apple's sensational growth depended on crowding out a number of rivals from a resource space that ultimately supported only one flourishing enterprise. (Atari achieved some success with two 6502-based computers, but remained a minor factor in the industry.) Second, Apple's success was directly related to the state of the industry at the time of its founding. Absent a group of competitors sharing a common standard, Apple was able to grow using a proprietary operating system. In a world of incompatible machines, Apple received a tremendous boost when a newly invented software application, the spreadsheet, was designed to execute on an Apple II. Introduced in 1979, Visicalc would only run on Apple's hardware, and it was this spreadsheet more than any other single factor that propelled Apple into the industry's top rank, breaking out of the pure hobbyist market.

Commodore was the other enterprise to succeed with the 6502 architecture, employing a completely different strategy. To this day Commodore remains the only example of a microprocessor manufacturer successfully integrating into the personal computer industry. Commodore Business Machines was founded in 1954 as a typewriter repair shop. By the early 1970s, it had become a major calculator manufacturer, but like MITS, it was virtually driven out of that business by the price wars of the early 1970s.

Consequently, Commodore decided to purchase one of its chip suppliers, MOS Technology, the developer of the 6502 microprocessor. MOS sold a hobbyist kit computer, the KIM-1, and Commodore elected to push 6502 sales by designing very low-cost computers for the mass market. From the introduction of the PET in 1977 through its later models, the VIC-20 and the model 64, Commodore became the major force in the low-priced home-computer market. Commodore was also the first American microcomputer maker to emphasize export sales, and for a time it completely dominated the European market. No 6502 manufacturer could compete with Commodore's prices, and by 1980 this arena was controlled by Apple in the higher price range, and Commodore at the lower end.

The third dominant firm of the 1970s employed the Z80 microprocessor, but did not employ CP/M. It was the Tandy Corporation, which had been founded in 1927 as a leather business but moved into electronics retailing in 1962 by purchasing a small chain of electronics stores called Radio Shack. Tandy added hundreds of retail electronics stores, and by the dawn of the microcomputer era, it was the dominant force in that distribution channel. Tandy's first computer, the TRS-80, was introduced in August 1977 with a proprietary operating system, TRS-DOS. Like Commodore, Tandy sacrificed computing power to achieve low prices, but principally it became one of the three largest microcomputer makers because it had stores everywhere. Tandy sold *reliability*. Its machine was technically inferior to many other Z80 designs, but the buyer knew where to get local service and advice. TRS-80s were being sold all over the United States at a time when computer distribution was basically a local or regional business, further reassuring the customer that there would be a large pool of users to attract software developers. With Radio Shack behind it, the

TRS-80 appeared to be a computer with a future in an era when buying a computer meant placing a wager on the ability of its manufacturer to survive.

By the dawn of the IBM-compatible era, considerable evolution had already taken place in the nascent industry. Three dominant firms had arisen, each with its own proprietary operating system. The principal challenge to them was a host of smaller enterprises employing the Z80 architecture and CP/M operating system. Thousands of programs existed for CP/M machines, and firms entering this segment accounted for the great majority of new organizing activity. Already, most of the firms that had pioneered the microcomputer business had exited or failed; the size of the total population kept growing because a large number of firms were entering the Z80-CP/M market.

Before the IBM PC appeared in 1981, a handful of industrial giants had produced small, desktop computers. Digital Equipment Corporation, IBM, NCR, NEC, Olivetti, Wang, and Xerox all produced machines with proprietary processors selling for between $10,000 and $20,000 at a time when an Apple II system typically cost $2,000–$3,000. Only Xerox and Panasonic (Matsushita) employed nonproprietary microprocessors, but their machines were still priced over $10,000. There simply was not a niche in the microcomputer industry for computers at such price points, and these large enterprises exerted little pressure on the microcomputer population.

Before 1981, only two major companies made serious attempts to produce microcomputers. Texas Instruments introduced a machine in 1980 employing its own 16-bit microprocessor. It was reasonably powerful and priced at $450 to reach the mass home computer market. The system employed proprietary cartridges, and TI was caught in a pricing war with Commodore, whose machines used inexpensive disk drives. Texas Instruments abandoned the home computer market in 1983. Like Digital and IBM, Hewlett-Packard introduced an expensive desktop computer in the mid-1970s, but in 1980 it placed a $4,000 microcomputer on the market, the HP 85. This model enjoyed some popularity among business users, but at a time when the CP/M standard was becoming entrenched, HP's proprietary design did not have enough appeal to launch the company into the front ranks. When the IBM PC arrived on the scene, its principal rivals were far smaller than those it encountered in other arenas.

The Triumph of the IBM PC Architecture
The debut of the IBM PC in August 1981 is the watershed event in the evolutionary history of the microcomputer industry. This machine was advanced for its time but was not at the cutting edge of technology. Rather, the IBM PC defined a dominant design, an industry standard that laid the basic configuration of what a personal computer would be for years to come. It brought an end to the era in which firms could succeed with idiosyncratic and proprietary designs (with one exception, the Apple Macintosh). It created an institutional environment that supported not only explosive growth in market demand but a tidal wave of organizing activity. It choked off the fastest-growing segment of the industry, the 8-bit CP/M market, leading to the demise of dozens of firms. It altered the dynamics of complementary industries, such as semiconductor

manufacture, peripheral component manufacture, and software production. The IBM PC is the most important microcomputer ever introduced, not because of its technical impact but because it permanently altered the organizational landscape for microcomputer manufacturers.

Technically, the most important contribution of the IBM PC was that it changed the industry's center of gravity from 8-bit to 16-bit computing. IBM chose to employ the Intel 8088 microprocessor, a chip that handled 16-bit instructions and addresses. Sixteen-bit computers are faster than 8-bit computers, but more importantly, they can access much more main memory. The range of addresses a computer can access goes up exponentially with instruction size; doubling the length of an instruction from 8 bits to 16 bits increased a microcomputer's main memory capacity from 64,000 bytes to over one million bytes. In reality, the improvement was somewhat less dramatic; Apple invented a technique that effectively doubled the Apple II's capacity to 128,000 bytes while IBM artificially limited the maximum memory size of its PC to 64,000 bytes. But the additional memory made possible a new generation of software too complex to run within the 64K limit of most 8-bit computers. One of the first programs to take full advantage of this new capability was Lotus 1-2-3, an enhanced spreadsheet program that was far faster than Visicalc and allowed the construction of much larger spreadsheets. As Visicalc had been the pivotal application turbocharging Apple's sales, Lotus 1-2-3 became the program that spelled the end of 8-bit computing.

The 8088 was not Intel's most advanced chip. Another member of Intel's "iAPX" family, the 8086, was a pure 16-bit chip; the 8088 was a hybrid that processed 16-bit instructions and addresses internally, but moved them into and out of the microprocessor in 8-bit chunks. Several 8086 computers were on the market when IBM introduced its PC; their principal shortcoming was that they could not run most of the software that had been developed for 8-bit machines. The iAPX 16-bit chips, including the 8088, were not backward compatible with Intel's 8-bit 8080 series of microprocessors. IBM chose the 8088 because it was much easier to convert 8-bit software to run on the hybrid chip than to rewrite an application for a pure 16-bit machine.

Easing the conversion path from 8-bit to 16-bit applications took on additional importance because IBM was unable to use the standard CP/M operating system. Digital Research, the maker of CP/M, refused to write a 16-bit version of its operating system within IBM's deadline, so IBM turned to Microsoft to implement a new 16-bit operating system. Crucially, IBM allowed Microsoft to sell a version of the disk operating system (DOS) to other computer manufacturers; IBM's version would be called PC-DOS, while other versions would be called MS-DOS.

Allowing the licensing of its operating system was part of IBM's most critical strategic choice: unlike any other machine ever made by IBM, the PC was to feature an *open architecture*. Virtually every component was made by subcontractors, not by IBM. It was possible to copy the PC's *bus,* the main electrical path connecting the microprocessor to everything else. The PC was designed to accept five *expansion cards,* circuit boards that would add features to the basic machine such as extra memory, printer and video connections, or devices to send and receive data over telephone lines. Opening the bus meant that cards designed for the IBM PC would work in other machines employing the same architecture.

The only part of the machine that IBM kept proprietary was a piece of the operating system governing basic input/output operations. IBM placed its basic input/output system (BIOS) in a special chip that it copyrighted. For a crucial few years, this one decision dramatically affected the life chances of other organizations. It was possible for other firms to copy IBM's general design, use the same microprocessor and operating system, yet not necessarily run programs designed for the IBM PC due to BIOS incompatibility. (In this critical period, the acid test for many a putative clone was whether it could run Microsoft's airplane flying simulation.)

The ecological impact of the IBM PC was profound. First, the vast majority of firms making 8-bit microcomputers did not survive the transition. Some attempted to produce IBM-compatible machines, while others tried to improve 8-bit designs or slash their prices; in either case, the rapidity with which the environment changed to the 16-bit/MS-DOS standard overwhelmed them. The new standard emerged on the backs of firms that had not made significant microcomputers before.

Second, the three previously dominant firms were supplanted as IBM's most significant rivals, though none actually exited the industry until Tandy sold its manufacturing operations in 1993. Commodore continued its mass-market low-price strategy throughout the mid-1980s. In unit volume, the Commodore 64 became the most popular computer ever made. However, its price was so low that Commodore's market share in dollars was not especially significant. Commodore 64s were used principally as game machines, and the rise of Nintendo in the mid-1980s drove them out of the marketplace rapidly. Commodore attempted to revolutionize the industry in the mid-1980s by introducing the Amiga, a computer with spectacular graphics. The Amiga was completely incompatible with the IBM standard, and became a marginal product.

Tandy slowly changed over to production of IBM-compatible machines, but its role in the industry shrank dramatically. Tandy appears to have fallen victim to the type of competency trap discussed in Chapter 1. The firm continued selling only through Radio Shack stores and carrying only its own computers in Radio Shack stores, despite the evolution of the industry's distribution channels. Since most customers preferred to shop in stores that offered wider variety or seek rock-bottom prices through mail order, Tandy's distribution strategy gradually become more of a millstone than an advantage.

Apple's response to the sea change in its environment was in retrospect the most successful. The company's survival was seriously in doubt by 1985; the Apple II continued to be the firm's cash cow, and a strong faction with the firm was committed to defending it in the face of superior technology. Buoyed by a huge existing software base and deep penetration into the secondary school market, the Apple II continued to sell well through the mid-1980s, but as the graphics performance of IBM-compatible machines improved, Apple II sales plummeted despite the firm's attempts to revive the line by introducing a 16-bit successor, the Apple II GS.

Apple survived because it was able to introduce a radically different machine, and had the resources to survive a disastrous beginning to its transformation. Blending original technology with innovations pioneered but never commercialized by Xerox, Apple introduced the Lisa in 1983. Based on the Motorola 68000, a microprocessor processing 32 bits internally with 16-bit input/output, it incorporated an advanced graphical interface, but its $10,000 price spelled failure. It was succeeded in early 1984 by another 68000-based machine with similar graphical capabilities, the Macintosh. As Apple II sales wound down, the Macintosh maintained Apple's status as a leader in the industry, though the IBM-compatible market was far larger. As with the Apple II and IBM PC, its success depended on a particular application; to Apple's surprise, the Macintosh tapped a sizable market segment that wanted a computer suitable for desktop publishing.

The third principal impact of the IBM PC's emergence was the establishment of a resource space that could support new organizational entrants into the industry, the clone manufacturers. IBM's open architecture and relatively high prices provided breathing room for rival organizations. The most significant of these was an entrepreneurial start-up specifically founded to produce a portable IBM-compatible computer. Compaq Corporation successfully engineered an alternative to IBM's copyrighted BIOS, and it became the fastest-growing start-up in the history of American enterprise on the strength of its reputation for 100% IBM compatibility. During a critical window in 1982 when IBM was unable to fill the demand for its PC—which exceeded internal sales forecasts by 800% and more—Compaqs were in stock and performed reliably. On the strength of its remarkable start, Compaq added desktop machines to its initial line of portables and became a strong second in the industry.

IBM did not sell dazzling technology or efficiency; it sold reliability and accountability. The world's largest computer maker stood behind the PC; it could be relied on to offer service and support, provide an upgrade path over time, and deliver an ever-wider base of users to attract third-party software and hardware developers. IBM promised durability; it was inconceivable that the firm would go out of business or exit computer manufacture. IBM meant professionalism, rationality, and accountability, from its carefully crafted documentation to its extensive public-relations efforts explaining where PCs fit into the grand overall IBM vision of computing. Clone manufacturers borrowed legitimacy from IBM and in turn enhanced IBM's own legitimacy. There would be software, peripherals, distribution channels, and millions of users for 8088/MS-DOS computers thanks to IBM, and because dozens of enterprises were imitating the IBM architecture, there would be price competition and a fresh flow of ideas in the MS-DOS world for the foreseeable future.

The fourth ecological impact of the IBM PC was that it virtually mandated the entry of IBM's chief rivals from other computer segments into the microcomputer arena. Firms such as Digital Equipment, Hewlett-Packard, Wang, Sperry, Burroughs, Data General, NEC, and Fujitsu concluded that they too needed an Intel/MS-DOS computer in their product lines to match IBM. Each of these organizations stumbled in its first attempts, typically by sacrificing IBM compatibility for performance superior to IBM's PC. However, all have stayed in the industry as a matter of competitive necessity, and their presence has complicated patterns of competition in the industry by introducing linkages between microcomputers and other computing devices. A firm such as Compaq does not need to worry how its microcomputer pricing will affect its minicomputer sales, whether its microcomputers will supplant its computer terminals, whether its Intel-architecture microcomputers can work with other logical computing architectures it has developed, and whether a competitive move in microcomputers will spark unwanted retaliation in another industry; for firms with broad lines of computing equipment, such considerations are often paramount.

Technologically, the triumph of the IBM PC ushered in an era of relative stability. In March 1983, IBM introduced its second model, the XT, which included a 10-megabyte fixed disk for mass storage. Since fixed disks were widely available from third parties, other firms quickly countered; principally, the innovation enabled software companies to offer more complex programs that would not fit easily onto a floppy disk. In 1984, IBM introduced the PC AT, featuring the Intel 80286 microprocessor, a 16-bit chip approximately five times faster than the 8088. The AT was an evolutionary advance that nonetheless allowed even more powerful and complex software to run at acceptable speeds on a microcomputer. (In 1983, IBM also began marketing a stripped-down home computer at a relatively low price, but for a host of reasons the PCjr failed and does not appear to have made much of an impact.)

The true significance of these evolutionary advances lay in their effects on industry pricing. IBM maintained a price umbrella, charging a premium for its perceived quality and reliability that allowed clone manufacturers to make reasonable profits despite undercutting IBM's prices. The price of 8088 PCs had been drifting down from IBM's original $2,880 benchmark, and the XT, which debuted at $4,995, created a new price umbrella. Two market segments emerged, one for low-priced PCs and one for expensive XTs. As both sets of prices glided downward, the debut of the AT at the price of $5,795 provided yet another umbrella, and a further division of the market into inexpensive PCs, middle-range XTs, and expensive ATs.

It was not difficult for firms that produced 8088 computers to make the transformation to the 80286, and most companies that survived the increased crowding in the clone market were technically able to produce both low-end and higher-end IBM-compatible machines. By 1983, however, IBM had expanded its capacity to the point of being able to meet its own demand, and a number of clone manufacturers whose existence had depended on shortages exited the industry. The population grew nonetheless as two different types of firms entered the market. One typically entered with 8088 machines at very low prices. The other entered with an 80286 computer priced slightly under the AT. It was relatively rare for such entrants to diversify their product lines; companies with high-end and low-end products tended to be those that had entered before the

AT appeared, supporting both an original 8088 machine and a follow-on computer designed to compete with the AT.

The most significant technical advance during the PC era was the 1984 introduction of successful substitutes for IBM's BIOS chips. Two semiconductor companies legally reverse-engineered IBM's copyrighted code, and their chips rapidly appeared in every Intel/DOS machine. One hundred percent IBM compatibility could now be taken for granted. The institutional impact was huge—it was no longer necessary to demonstrate reliability for each individual computer model. The ability of a new clone computer to run the vast library of software developed for MS-DOS was assumed, effectively lending IBM's legitimacy to small, young companies. Legitimation is usually an expensive hurdle for new enterprises; as the PC evolved, legitimacy increasingly began to flow from adhering to recognized standards.

One other critically important trend was the increasing legitimation of mail-order sales. The industry had been pioneered by mail-order distribution but as the market broadened beyond hobbyists and incompatibility reigned, having a local dealer for support assumed increasing importance. The availability of BIOS chips ensuring IBM compatibility removed one major objection to buying through the mail. The proliferation of magazines reviewing computer products and certifying the quality of a mail-order firm's service greatly enhanced confidence in mail order. Downward pressure on prices encouraged consumers to bargain hunt, and the best bargains were usually found via mail order. The legitimation of mail-order distribution removed one of the principal barriers to entry: the fact that computer store chains were reluctant to carry more than three or four nationally distributed brands. Starting in the mid-1980s, a number of small start-ups dedicated to inexpensive yet technologically competitive PCs experienced much more rapid growth than the industry as a whole. One of them, Dell Computer, counted among the largest firms in the industry by 1990.

The 32-Bit Era and IBM's Loss of Control

From the time the PC was introduced, it was clear that the next significant technological advance would be the transition from 16-bit to 32-bit microprocessors. Thirty-two-bit microprocessors would increase maximum addressable main memory from 1 million bytes to 4 billion bytes, allowing larger, more complex software to run without swapping programs and data between main memory and disk storage. They also were significantly faster and made multitasking—running several programs at once—much more feasible, given the right software.

Semiconductor manufacturers produced the first 32-bit microprocessors in the early 1980s, and their appearance sparked the emergence of a new niche in the computer industry. A start-up enterprise named Apollo introduced the first workstation in 1981. Workstations were much more powerful than personal computers, carried five-figure price tags, and typically featured expensive add-on hardware designed to optimize their ability to display computer graphics in motion. The initial market for them was in computer-aided design, computer-aided engineering, and simulation, tasks that had been performed on graphics terminals attached to central minicomputers or microcomputers. Workstations were almost always connected to a computer network, and eventually Unix, an operating system designed for networking, became dominant in this segment.

Workstations are technically microcomputers, but until quite recently, they occupied a price/performance position that overlapped very little with that of personal computers. Consequently, from an ecological point of view, it is inappropriate to treat PC and workstation manufacture as a single form. Historically, the ecological interaction between these two machine classes has been of the type treated in Section V of this book, in which two or more subpopulations exert *aggregate* influences on each other's life chances. Present trends suggest that within a very few years the workstation and personal computer niches will overlap quite substantially, but for the purposes of this chapter, the transition from 16- to 32-bit microcomputers does not start with the emergence of workstations.

In the mainstream PC market, although the transition to 32-bit computing seemed technically inevitable years before it occurred, the way in which *organizations* brought it about had profound ecological consequences. The IBM PC architecture had acquired such momentum that the primary requisite for a 32-bit system was backward compatibility. Users wanted assurance that their huge investments in 16-bit PC hardware and software would not be obsolesced.

IBM's attempt to change the competitive structure of the industry was formally announced in April 1987, but was widely understood in 1986. IBM chose to produce a new line of microcomputers called the Personal System 2 (PS/2) to distinguish them from the original PCs. The top of the PS/2 line would employ Intel's 32-bit 80386 and would run all programs designed for the PC architecture. However, the PS/2 line would employ a proprietary bus called the Micro Channel, which meant that the hundreds of thousands of expansion cards designed to plug into the original PC bus would not work with the PS/2. The Micro Channel was designed for expansion cards with more local intelligence, which could offload certain data transfer tasks from the main processor and thus speed up the performance of the microcomputer system. IBM's rivals could produce clone computers, but they could not match the performance of IBM's systems as a whole if the most advanced expansion cards and software routines to take advantage of them would only work with the patented Micro Channel.

In conjunction with the unveiling of the PS/2, IBM and Microsoft announced that they were working on the successor to the MS-DOS operating system, which would be compatible with the existing base of DOS applications. To be called OS/2, it would incorporate a Macintosh-like graphical interface and would take advantage of the multitasking potential built into 32-bit chips. The IBM version of the graphical interface would contain proprietary features that Microsoft could not license to clone manufacturers.

It is obvious today that IBM's strategy failed to change the nature of competition in microcomputers. That failure is rooted in the type of forces described in Chapter 2. Inertia plays a large role, but too many observers have confused inertia with sloth. OS/2 suffered from a critical flaw in its conception: IBM managers decreed that it had to run on an 80286 chip. IBM had sold thousands of ATs to customers who paid a premium for them because IBM provided rationality and accountability, not just hardware. Thanks to this commitment, not stupidity or lethargy, IBM felt it needed to include 80286 owners in the OS/2 vision. The 80286 processed 32-bit data internally and had been designed by Intel to run in a "protected mode" that permitted multitasking. However, designing a multitasking operating system to work at reasonable speeds on an 80286 proved to be a nightmare. Largely as a consequence, OS/2 was severely delayed and proved slow and unwieldy upon its introduction.

The Micro Channel strategy failed because the market had grown beyond the need for IBM to legitimate the PC architecture. Compaq understood this, and in a bold stroke it introduced an 80386 computer in September 1986. It was considerably faster than an AT-class machine, it accepted standard PC expansion cards, and of course it could run the existing base of MS-DOS software. Until this point, IBM had defined the moment when the industry would move to the next level of technology, popularizing fixed disk drives with the XT and the 80286 processor with the AT. Now, there were enough customers demanding faster PC-compatible machines, and enough clone manufacturers capable of creating momentum behind a new generation of semiconductors to legitimate a standard without IBM. Compaq succeeded because the PC standard had taken on a life of its own thanks to the growth of demand and population density.

A group of nine important IBM-compatible manufacturers defined an alternative to the Micro Channel. The 16-bit AT bus was enshrined as the industry standard architecture, while a new bus capable of accepting both 16-bit and 32-bit expansion cards was established as the extended industry standard architecture (EISA). Lotus, Intel, and Microsoft established a standard for extended memory that allowed programs to access more main memory than the artificial 640,000 byte limit IBM had imposed on MS-DOS. The way was opened for machines that could take advantage of 32-bit speed, while promising that when true 32-bit multitasking operating systems arrived, the owner would not be burdened with an obsolescent computer.

The immediate ecological consequence was that a new wave of manufacturers entered computer manufacture, producing 80386 machines. Meanwhile, the price of 80286-class microcomputers was driven down dramatically, and entry-level 8088 machines soon fell to levels characteristic of home computers, hastening the rapid demise of the low-priced 8-bit computer market. As with the AT, two classes of new entrants emerged: firms offering very low-priced 8088 or 80286 machines, and those selling 80386 machines toward the bottom of the premium price range. Incumbent firms that survived generally offered a range of machines at different price/performance points.

The more subtle impact of Compaq's move was a shift in the locus of innovation from IBM to the semiconductor manufacturers, principally Intel. Intel had introduced the 8088 chip in 1978, three years before the IBM PC appeared. The 80286 debuted in 1982, two years before the AT, and the 80386 in 1985, one year before Compaq pioneered it and two years before IBM adopted it. IBM did produce the first microcomputer to incorporate Intel's next chip, the 80486—but this time, the new machine appeared as soon as Intel made the 80486 available in production quantities (in October 1989). The first microcomputers with the next generation of Intel microprocessor, the Pentium, debuted while Intel was still ironing out defects before ramping the chip up to full production (in May 1993). No longer did IBM define when the industry would move to a new generation of microprocessors: the time between one generation and the next now would be driven by the semiconductor firms' design cycles.

The 80486 was an evolutionary advance that principally improved on the speed of the 80386 by integrating several previously separate chips on the processor and running at higher clock speeds. Because the 80486 was a natural extension of the 80386, incumbent firms with 80386 machines adopted it very rapidly, leading once again to a segmentation of the market into premium (80486), mid-priced (80386), and economy (80286) systems. However, another new development bifurcated the high-end 80486 market. By the late 1980s, it was increasingly common for computers to connect to a central microcomputer via a local area network (LAN). The server typically contained large databases that could be accessed by any of the machines networked to it. This *client-server* architecture created a demand for very fast machines with large disk drives to act as the network hub. For the first time in this industry, a class of machines was being sold as something other than a *personal* computer. The first wave of 80486 machines appears to have been sold more to the server market than the desktop market. Reliability was overwhelmingly important in this market, since so many machines depended on the network; consequently, far fewer start-up enterprises entered the industry with an 80486 machine than had entered as a result of the move to the 80386.

The history of the microcomputer industry illustrates many of the themes outlined in Chapter 2 and the introduction to this section. The story of the industry is not one of gradual adaptation by its early pioneers; the first generation of PC manufacturers was decimated by IBM's entry into the marketplace, and the dominant enterprises were unable to retain the early leadership they had established. Superior technology did not of itself determine success or failure; rather, legitimation, standardization, and compatibility played critical roles. The emergence of a standard ended an era in which idiosyncrasy and proprietary technology was a viable strategy, but greatly expanded the carrying capacity of the industry, both by catalyzing a dramatic increase in sales and by providing legitimacy for start-up enterprises, especially after achieving 100 percent IBM compatibility became technically simple. The greatest burst of organizing activity resulted from Compaq's demonstration that IBM's leadership was no longer required to maintain a standard.

The hallmark of organizational ecology is that it studies the transformation of populations in a rigorous, quantitative way. Having established the background, it is now appropriate to ask what empirical analyses of this industry tell us about environmental selection under conditions of rapid technological change.

SELECTIVE FORCES IN THE EVOLUTION
OF THE INDUSTRY

At the outset of this chapter, we asked how the population of organizations evolved from the crude technology of 1976 to the powerful servers of the early 1990s. A fundamental question in organizational ecology is whether changes in organizational features over time reflect changes in existing organizations or changes at the population level.

Figure 3-1 shows the number of entries, exits, and the population size of the industry from 1976 to 1991. (The data for this figure and the analyses reported in this section were collected by the leading research firm in this area, International Data Corporation.) It is immediately apparent that the majority of firms that have made computers have enjoyed relatively brief life spans. A common pattern observed in many studies is that a population size reaches a peak in its early maturity and then gradually declines. The microcomputer industry has not yet reached this point, but the majority of firms that have ever manufactured a microcomputer have lasted fewer than five years. A minority of firms making microcomputers in 1980 survived to 1985; a minority of firms making microcomputers in 1985 survived to 1990. The membership of the industry in the early 1990s was vastly different from what it was in the mid-1980s or the early 1980s.

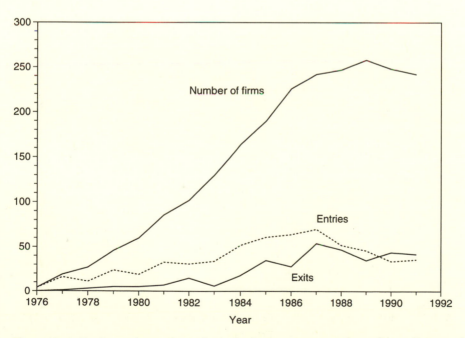

Figure 3–1 Entries, exits, and number of microcomputer producer firms. (*Source:* Author's analysis of data provided by International Data Corporation.)

Figure 3-2 plots the transformation of the industry from the vantage point of 1990. The graph shows the percentage of industry sales accounted for by firms that entered the industry in a given year. The general message is clear: few of the computers sold in 1990 were made by firms that entered the industry before 1980 (most of these were Apples), and an important fraction of the computers sold in 1990 were made by firms that entered the industry since 1985. Adaptation and selection have both occurred; clearly, a significant proportion of modern computers are sold by firms that have weathered technology and market shifts over the years, but the change to the modern era has also been due in large measure to the introduction of computers by firms that replaced early computer makers eliminated in the struggle for survival.

Change in this industry has occurred to a large extent because firms that made one kind of computer (e.g., Z80 CP/M machines) went out of business and other firms entered the industry making different kinds of computers. For this reason, organizational ecologists are interested in the forces that influence the rate of entries and exits. If entries and exits were completely random, selection would have no direction. It is when certain environmental conditions facilitate foundings or failures that selective forces produce an evolutionary transformation. Table 3-1 summarizes the results of an empirical analysis of factors linked to entries and exits in microcomputers.

Organizational ecology has linked rates of entry into a population to the population's size and the rate of recent entry in ways described more fully elsewhere in this book. In the microcomputer industry, a pattern often found in

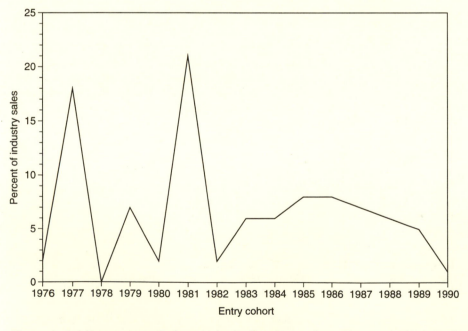

Figure 3–2 Microcomputer industry sales by firm entry cohort. (*Source:* Author's analysis of data provided by International Data Corporation.)

Table 3-1 Factors influencing entry and exit rates in the microcomputer industry

Factor	Effect on entry rate	Effect on exit rate
Population size	Positive	Negative
Square of population size	Not significant	Positive
Entries previous year	Positive	Not significant
Square of entries previous year	Negative	Not significant
Time since introduction of new technology generation[a]	Positive	Positive
Square of time since introduction of new technology generation[a]	Negative	Not significant
Industry demand	Not significant	Not significant
Industry concentration	Not significant	Not significant
Demand uncertainty	Not significant	Positive

[a]For exit rates, this clock is reset to zero for a firm when it adopts the new technology generation.

other industries prevails: the rate of entry increases with population size. The more firms there are in the industry, the more organizing templates there are for entrants to imitate. (In many populations, this is true only up to a certain point, at which there are so many firms that entrants seem to be discouraged by the crowding. The microcomputer industry does not appear to have reached that point yet, but may in the future.) The number of entries in the previous year has a curvilinear effect often found in other industries. Up to a point, the more firms that enter one year, the more are attracted the next. Yet past a certain point, more firms entering in one year will depress the rate of entry the following year.

Controlling for other factors, the introduction of a new generation of technology seems to affect entry rates via a type of clock. The appearance of a new generation of microprocessor does not in itself set off a wave of organizing activity, but if we imagine a clock that starts ticking when a new generation is introduced, we see that the founding rate first increases, then decreases with the time elapsed from the first introduction. A new technological generation appears to open a window for entry, but as time passes the window closes.

Equally interesting is an array of factors *not* related to the founding rate. Industry demand and concentration are not linked to founding rates, holding other things equal. This is a common finding of ecological studies and an interesting one: sales increases do not per se increase organizing activity, and the degree to which a few powerful firms control sales does not depress organizing activity. (Other effects of concentration are discussed in Section IV.) Rather, entry in this industry is a function of population dynamics and the appearance of successive technology generations.

Organizational ecologists have also studied factors that relate to the hazard rate, the limit of the probability that a firm will exit the industry given that it has survived to a given point in time. The effect of density is discussed in detail in Section III of this book. The microcomputer industry exhibits a characteristic pattern: up to a point, the more firms there are in an industry, the lower the exit rate, but past that point, greater density leads to a higher exit rate. Ecologists have also studied the linkage between a firm's longevity and the probability of exiting, and here as in many industries, an organization's hazard rate decreases the longer it has survived since its entry.

Technology affects mortality patterns in an interesting way. The appearance of a new technology does not in itself set off a massive wave of exits. Rather, the emergence of a new generation starts a clock for each firm using the previous generation of technology. The longer the period that elapses before the firm adopts the new technology, the greater the firm's probability of exiting. If and when a firm does make the transition to a new generation, the clock ceases to be a factor until the next round of technological advance. This general finding suggests, for instance, that it was not the triumph of 16-bit technology per se that led to the disappearance of the Z80 CP/M pioneers, but rather their inertia, reflected in an inability to adopt the new technology quickly, that spelled their doom.

Again, demand and concentration have no relationship to mortality rates holding other things constant. However, uncertainty does seem to affect mortality rates. If we define uncertainty as the inability to project the future from the past, we find that the more demand in a given year deviates from the historical trend, the higher the hazard rate. Firms seem able to cope with different levels of demand; it is sudden, unpredictable *fluctuations* in demand that increase the chances of exit.

ORGANIZATIONAL ADAPTATION: IBM AND DIGITAL EQUIPMENT

As discussed in Chapter 2, organizations do change (although they seldom change *form*) and executives do seek to adapt to changing environments. Inertia is a relative thing; the fundamental question is whether organizations can change as rapidly as their environments can. When they cannot, aggregate population change tends to reflect the exit of incumbent firms and their replacement by firms with different strategies, unconstrained by prior commitments.

However, a fundamental insight of organizational ecology is that processes involving selection can usually be recast at a higher level of analysis as adaptation processes. In an industry that transforms as rapidly as this one, firms often adapt and survive through a process of destruction and re-creation within firm boundaries. Very little organizational ecology research has looked inside the firm to examine the equivalent of foundings and failures among *subunits*. An examination of two computer industry giants' experience in microcomputers sheds light on the nature of adaptation in complex organizations under conditions of rapid technological change.

IBM

As noted earlier, IBM was not the first large firm that attempted to enter the microcomputer industry, and IBM's first attempts to introduce a personal computer were considered a failure. The genesis of the IBM PC was top management's decision to establish an independent business unit (IBU) within IBM whose mission was the development of an inexpensive microcomputer. Project Chess was one of seven such ventures chartered by the corporate management committee, and its head reported personally to IBM's CEO, then John Opel. Opel's backing kept the project from being destroyed by the firm's internal politics, and IBM executives have noted that the IBM PC was made possible only by, in essence, founding a new organization within IBM.

However, the PC's unexpected success meant that IBM had to draw it back under the corporate umbrella and coordinate its actions with those of other computer lines affected by PC sales. Accordingly, the IBU was folded into a larger entity in August 1983, the Entry Systems Division. This unit was given control not only of PCs but also of the System-23 Datamaster minicomputer, the Displaywriter word processor, and two smaller systems, the 5520 and 5280. In essence the PC operation was swallowed up by giving its head, Philip Estridge, control of a larger, diversified division of which PCs were only a subunit.

In 1985, the Entry Systems Division was brought even further into the corporate family. IBM's central marketing organization was given control of all retailing and channel relationships, and the division's administration and management were moved to New Jersey, close to corporate headquarters but far from the product development and manufacturing operations in Florida. At the same time, Estridge was replaced by William Lowe. This arrangement lasted through 1988, when the Entry Systems Division was split into two units, one for workstations and one for PCs. Lowe left IBM to work for Xerox, and James Cannavino took over the PC Division. Under this arrangement, Cannavino's strategy was subject to the approval of a PC executive board consisting of marketing and development executives from around the globe.

By 1992, IBM had been under severe pressure for several years, suffering declining market share because of its inability to reach rapidly enough to the changing marketplace. IBM's response was to disband the Entry Systems Division, and return to the independent business unit concept. In June 1992, IBM formed a wholly owned subsidiary to sell IBM PCs in Europe made by one of its clone competitors under the brand name Ambra. IBM essentially spun off its own clone manufacturer to compete with other clones in the low-price segment. In September, IBM formed the IBM Personal Computer Company, an autonomous operation charged with full responsibility for IBM's personal computer operations. This organization was given the authority to market computers directly through mail order, bypassing IBM's distribution channels if it chose, and to buy components anywhere, bypassing other IBM units if it desired. IBM had come full circle, concluding that a personal computer business could survive within the corporation only if it were practically an independent venture.

Digital Equipment

Although Digital Equipment Corporation (DEC) had reduced its PDP-11 minicomputer to a single-board chip set by the mid-1970s, it lagged behind in microcomputers because of its heritage and the convictions of its CEO, Ken Olsen. Digital had pioneered the minicomputer market, and many thought it inevitable that DEC would come to dominate microcomputers. However, Olsen saw microcomputers as toys and believed computer users were best served by sharing time on a central computer, not by owning their own machine. He had built Digital on two principles: never compete on price, and always have the highest quality. PCs seemed cheap and shoddy to him.

Additionally Digital's organization and culture depended on an intensely political process by which fiercely independent units had to reach a consensus to act. Dozens of microcomputers were in development throughout Digital, but none made it to the marketplace because each division manager coveted the PC market for himself; achieving consensus was impossible. Consequently, the inventor of Visicalc, a former DEC programmer, became frustrated with DEC's lack of interest in selling him an "intelligent terminal" and borrowed a colleague's Apple II to develop the first spreadsheet, catapulting Apple to the top of the microcomputer industry.

In 1980, Olsen decided to build a microcomputer his way—competing on technical superiority and not price—that would revolutionize and from his point of view legitimize the industry. The DEC Professional would be highly ergonomic with advanced networking features, superior graphics, and a multitasking operating system, and would be based on DEC's highly successful PDP-11 architecture. However, with the introduction of the IBM Personal Computer, Olsen also approved a completely incompatible alternative, the DEC Rainbow. Based on an Intel processor like IBM's, the Rainbow would run either CP/M or MS-DOS—but was not IBM compatible and would not run IBM PC software. At the same time, Olsen sanctioned the introduction of a dedicated word processor with some PC-like features, the DECmate II. Predictably, corporate infighting delayed all three machines and forced design compromises, the rival teams sabotaged each other's efforts to attract third-party developers, each claiming that the other projects had no legitimacy within Digital and would be terminated before reaching the marketplace.

Olsen introduced all three machines in May 1982. DEC was in the uncomfortable position of sponsoring three entries into the microcomputer arena that were incompatible with each other and with the solidifying IBM standard. Little software was written for the Professional, since the PDP-11 architecture was proprietary. The DECmate II word processor was followed by the DECmate III, but was never successfully sold as a more general-purpose machine. The Rainbow suffered from a lack of software due to its inability to run IBM-compatible packages, and was an insignificant factor in the PC market. Consequently, in May 1984, Digital merged the three businesses into one PC unit and in 1985 it terminated both the Rainbow and the Professional.

Olsen has often been criticized for Digital's failure to create a successful IBM-compatible machine, but a deeper analysis sheds light on the difference between inertial commitment and lethargy. As a corporation, DEC was highly successful in the mid-1980s pursuing the VAX strategy—it had a line of computers ranging from workstations to near-mainframes all running the same software on the same operating system employing the VAX minicomputer architecture. At a time when IBM offered a half-dozen incompatible lines that could barely communicate with one another, DEC seemed to offer a seamless networking solution. PC compatibles diluted the fundamental DEC message, of a unified, networked family of computers. DEC's commitment to this strategy led to its most profitable years, but also undermined its ability to compete in microcomputers. In 1985, Digital offered a VAX-on-a-chip workstation that fit the strategy well, and the company established a significant presence in the workstation arena. DEC failed in microcomputing, but for precisely the same reasons that drove its success in the minicomputer arena.

In September 1986, Digital introduced its first IBM-compatible machine, an AT-class microcomputer called the VAXmate. Priced far above the usual AT price range, it featured a built-in ability to network with a VAX. However, it appeared just as Compaq propelled high-end microcomputing into the 32-bit generation. Digital missed the entire 80386 generation by offering only an expensive 80286 machine with networking capabilities that few wanted.

With the failure of the VAXmate, Digital essentially exited the microcomputer market for two years, becoming an original equipment manufacturer instead of a true PC maker. In January 1989, it debuted a series of 80386 machines at last—but they were made by Tandy, and were simply sold with the Digital nameplate. New server class 80486 machines were introduced in 1990 and 1991, but they were made by Tandy or Intel for DEC. Only in 1992 did Digital reenter microcomputer manufacture with its new low-profile line replacing the Tandy- and Intel-built machines.

After years of failure, Digital reached the same conclusion as IBM: personal computers could survive only as an autonomous unit within the broader corporation. Olsen stepped down in mid-1992, and his successor reorganized the company. Of significant importance in the reorganization was the establishment of a separate business unit for personal computers, headed by an outsider who formerly ran the Zenith microcomputer business. The PC unit was permitted to compete or contract with other DEC subunits as it saw fit.

Thus, at both IBM and Digital Equipment, the painful process of adaptation consisted largely of foundings and failures at the subunit level. IBM's original PC business was absorbed into a diversified entity and gradually stripped of autonomy, until IBM found it necessary to launch a new and independent entity to cope with change too rapid for the parent corporation to handle. Digital spawned three separate PC businesses, which were merged together into a unit that abandoned the original product lines and launched a fourth unsuccessfully. After exiting manufacture, DEC reentered, like IBM, forming a semiautonomous unit to cope with the microcomputer industry's rapid pace of change. The Digital and IBM stories illustrate two key insights of organizational ecology: that inertia must be defined relative to the pace of environmental change, and that adaptation processes can mask what amount to selection processes at a lower level of analysis.

CONCLUSION

In the absence of significant regulatory or social pressures, evolution in microcomputers has been driven largely by technological change. The consequence of a very rapidly shifting environment has been a transformation of the population largely through selective forces. Although some firms have survived this transformation, adaptation has reflected significant selective pressures at the subunit level. The industry's future promises more turmoil as the workstation and personal computer markets converge. Its history suggests that its shape at the end of the 1990s will reflect selective forces hinging on population dynamics and the impact of successive technical generations.

BIBLIOGRAPHY

Chposky, James, and Ted Leonsis. 1988. *Blue Magic: The People, Power and Politics Behind the IBM Personal Computer*. New York: Facts on File Publications.

Freiberger, Paul, and Michael Swaine. 1984. *Fire in the Valley: The Making of the Personal Computer*. Berkeley: Osborne/McGraw Hill.

Levering, Robert, Michael Katz, and Milton Moskowitz. 1984. *The Computer Entrepreneurs*. New York: New American Library.

Pearson, Jamie Parker. 1992. *Digital at Work: Snapshots from the First Thirty-five Years*. Burlington, MA: Digital Press.

Rifkin, Glenn, and George Harrar. 1990. *The Ultimate Entrepreneur: The Story of Ken Olsen and Digital Equipment Corporation*. Rocklin, CA: Prima Publishing & Communication.

Rose, Frank. 1989. *West of Eden: The End of Innocence at Apple Computer*. New York: Penguin Books.

Veit, Stan. 1993. *Stan Veit's History of the Personal Computer*. Asheville, NC: WorldComm.

Young, Jeffrey S. 1988. *Steve Jobs: The Journey Is the Reward*. Glenview, IL: Scott, Foresman.

4

Railroads

FRANK DOBBIN

In the United States, local, state, and federal governments played central roles in the evolution of the railway industry. Although the industry evolved incrementally in terms of track mileage, passenger and freight traffic, and capitalization, it changed dramatically at several points in terms of strategy, selection, and structure in the wake of major shifts in public policy. As a result, analysts have organized railway history into several, discrete periods marked by changes in public policy that brought about sea changes in the industry. Of course, public policies were responsive to the industry's economic peculiarities, such as capital intensity and asset specificity, and the problems and evils that policymakers perceived in those peculiarities.

This chapter focuses on business strategy, industry structure, and selection mechanisms between 1825 and 1990. The main environmental changes during this period were generated by the interaction between the industry's economic characteristics and public policy. Whereas the organizational environment is conceived as the market in most of the chapters in this book, in this chapter it is conceived as government regulation and public policy. In such heavily regulated industries as the railroads, the state is a particularly salient part of the environment. For instance, in some periods American policy made the rail industry exceptionally cooperative and in others it produced cutthroat competition. Public policy generated very different kinds of environments over time— different kinds of markets, in effect.

This chapter underscores the special role of public policy in the rail industry, but it also points to the broader importance of public policy in creating the organizational environment. Whereas some of the policies that governed the rail industry were unique, a number now govern most U.S. industries. Antitrust law is a prime example. Organization theorists typically set aside public policy in examining the environment, on the principle that today most industries operate in similar public policy environments. This chapter highlights the

importance of today's public policy regime by contrasting it with previous regimes. It also provides clues to the early evolution of other industries, such as
banking, canals, and insurance, that were influenced, like railroads, by policy
regimes favoring public capitalization and private cartels.

Several of the industry's economic characteristics proved important in the
evolution of the policy environment and the industry. First, railroads produce
large *secondary economic returns*—in terms of the promotion of commerce,
agriculture, and manufacturing—relative to their *primary returns,* i.e., corporate profits. These large secondary returns produced atypical motives among
railroad promoters. Second, a high *fixed cost–variable cost ratio* encouraged
railroads to maximize business by slashing prices to just above operating costs.
This had important implications for selection in the industry. Third, almost all
railroads held *service monopolies* between certain points and competed with
other roads between other points, which encouraged them to charge high rates
where they faced no rivals and low rates on competitive routes to maximize
business. Fourth, the industry was characterized by *small numbers of competitors* on each route, which encouraged railroads to try to control competition
through cartels, pools, joint stockholding, leasing of competitors, predatory
pricing to bankrupt competitors, acquisitions, and mergers. Finally, *asset specificity,* or the impossibility of transferring capital invested in railroads to other
uses, meant that railroads would often continue to operate even when they
were losing money. These peculiar economic characteristics interacted with
public policy to shape the industry's environment.

Between 1825 and 1990, U.S. railroads were governed by five different policy
regimes. In each period public policies determined how strategy, structure, and
selection would operate (see Table 4-1). In the first period, between 1830 and
1869, public capitalization led to thousands of railroad foundings across the
United States. The industry was divided between intercity trunk lines and small
independent spur railroads, and the two groups were highly mutualistic. Small
lines financed in anticipation of demand by eager governments often failed.
Next, between 1870 and 1889, state governments controlled rates to prevent
inequities, with the effect of stimulating competition and later spawning cartels.
Competition led to the failure and acquisition of many railroads, and created
marked resource partitioning because specialist lines with noncompetitive
routes had much greater chances for survival than did generalist lines with
competitive routes.

In the third period, between 1890 and 1919, anticartel and antitrust legislation
undermined price-fixing and caused railroads to engage in predatory pricing.
One result was unprecedented numbers of failures and acquisitions. Fourth,
between 1920 and 1965, Congress tried to both sustain price competition and
prevent the abandonment of service on unprofitable routes. Many railroads
could not offer competitive prices when they were forced to serve unprofitable
locations, and these railroads often failed—to be acquired by their competitors.
Everywhere, holding companies and rate associations produced surreptitious
cartels to dampen rate competition and stabilize existing firms. Finally, after
1966, Congress nationalized certain portions of the industry, and deregulated

Table 4–1 Strategy, structure, and selection in the railroad industry

Period	Principal policies	Strategy	Structure	Selection
Period 1 1830–1869	Public capitalization	Foundings financed for secondary returns Uncompetitive	Intercity trunk RRs and small spur RRs	Lines capitalized to create demand fail Mutualism
Period 2 1870–1889	Rate regulation Weakly pro-cartel	Cutthroat competition then cartels	Regional networks compiled from failed RRs	Competitive lines fail Resource partitioning
Period 3 1890–1919	Anticartel and antitrust	Rate discrimination and mergers	Mergers create huge railroads	Independent lines fail; some merge; others are acquired
Period 4 1920–1965	Anticartel and antimerger Rate and abandonment regulation	Holding companies and rate associations	Large surreptitious cartels	RRs cannot cut losing routes and fail Many acquisitions, few mergers
Period 5 1966–1993	Partial nationalization Deregulation of mergers, abandonments, rates	Active competition among independents	State-run sector and consolidated private RRs	Most lines merge or are acquired

prices, abandonments, and mergers. The result was a flurry of acquisitions and the abandonment of large segments of little-used track.

What caused these policy changes? Most analysts link U.S. rail policies to the nation's longstanding suspicion of the concentration of economic power in the state or in private hands. For instance, states amended their constitutions to outlaw the public capitalization schemes that were popular before 1870 because the schemes gave public officials excessive power that resulted in corruption. Later, Congress outlawed the price-fixing practices that were popular in the 1870s and 1880s because price-fixing gave private railways excessive power that resulted in unfair rates.

The origins of American rail policy are the subject of a voluminous literature that we cannot do justice to here, but this much is clear: policy changes were not direct responses to the economic evolution of the industry, for other countries that faced substantially similar economic issues adopted entirely different policies. While the United States was outlawing cartels, Britain was making them legal. While the United States was preventing mergers, France was merging private firms into a single national monopoly.

PUBLIC CAPITALIZATION, 1830–1869

British engineers had experimented for a decade with different steam locomotive designs before George Stephenson introduced his "Rocket" in 1829, the first truly practicable engine. The success of the Rocket gave impetus to the railway industry in Britain and the United States alike. In the United States, state and local governments offered generous financial inducements to private rail promoters, in the form of bond guarantees, stock subscriptions, and land grants. Governments helped to capitalize private railroads because they were eager to reap the secondary economic benefits that railroads were expected to bring—growth in agricultural exports, in demand for manufactured goods, and in commercial activity of all sorts.

Merchants, manufacturers, and farmers lobbied in town meetings and state houses for public aid to railways, and one result was that railways were often built in the hope that they would create their own demand. For instance, the promoters of the New York and Oswego Midland proposed to build a major line through the state of New York. They collected promises of capital in the amount of $5.7 million from fifty towns scattered across the state, and built a zigzagging line that connected these towns, but that did not serve a single major city. The N.Y.&O.M. never did generate sufficient demand, but many small railroads, such as the Salem and Lowell in Massachusetts that opened in 1850 to connect the mill town of Lowell with the port at Salem, generated more than adequate demand.

Between 1830 and 1870, state and local governments invested huge sums in railway construction. In the 1830s and 1840s, state governments provided fully 40 percent of the capital used to build railroads, and estimates put public capitalization before the Civil War at somewhere between one fourth and one half of the cost of building railroads. In these years, state governments practiced "rivalistic state mercantilism" (Scheiber 1981, p. 131) with the aim of winning the lion's share of the nation's transport and commerce. They made large public investments in canals, turnpikes, banks, and manufacturing establishments as well.

Early experiments with public funding of railroads generated untold corruption that garnered support for the doctrine of laissez faire, but in the early years governments had no compunctions about investing in private enterprises. On the contrary, governments acted as public entrepreneurs: "The elected official replaced the individual enterpriser as the key figure in the release of capitalist energy; the public treasury, rather than private saving, became the major source of venture capital; and community purpose outweighed personal ambition in the selection of large goals for local economies" (Lively 1955, p. 81). In those years, "No ambitious town could stand idly by and see a new railroad go to a rival place. There was no option but to vote bonds" (Ripley 1912, p. 38).

Public Capitalization and Foundings

As a result of the general enthusiasm for railroads created by Stephenson's new locomotive, combined with activism among state and local governments, foundings took off in the 1830s and 1840s. National railway statistics were not gathered until the Interstate Commerce Commission was established in 1887; thus we must rely on the comprehensive data collected for Massachusetts during this period, which is representative of the national trend. Fortuitously, the rail industry was highly localized in this early period and thus the state was the effective boundary of the population. By the time the population boundary was expanded by the construction of interstate lines and by the technical integration of different railroads, national data were collected. Thus we turn to U.S. data in the last three periods.

The number of charters granted by the Commonwealth rose from three in the 1820s to thirty-four in the 1830s to a peak of seventy-eight in the 1840s. This activity was stimulated, in part, by Britain's contemporaneous "railway mania" and in particular by the availability of capital in London money markets, which stimulated American state and local governments to issue bonds in British sterling and offer them to London investors. The American railway mania was a classic case of a process Michael Hannan theorized in 1986, in which early foundings and technological innovations create legitimacy for a new type of organization and attract substantial resources for foundings.

In this early period, both public and private investors put money into railroads based not on rational calculations of *primary* returns—the potential profitability of the enterprises—but on calculations of *secondary* returns. Then between 1862 and 1871, Congress passed land grant bills in aid of four transcontinental railroads in the hope of producing secondary benefits. The land grants were expected to open up trade to the West and stimulate growth. Federal and earlier state land grants provided rights-of-way and huge checkerboard tracts of land—ten to forty miles wide—alongside the routes. Federal grants were designed to spur rail construction while evading constitutional restrictions on federal investment in private enterprises. The whole purpose of the land grants was to enable railroads to recoup construction costs by selling off the land. Like state and local capitalization schemes, federal land grants were designed to speed the construction of railroads that would create demand, rather than to fulfil existing demand. In all, federal and state governmènts gave over 140 million acres to railroads (Haney 1908, p. 6).

The land grant legislation produced only a handful of foundings, but the transcontinental lines generated scores of new branch lines on the basis of the industry's natural mutualism. As William Barnett and colleagues have argued, in mutualistic industries, such as the telephone and rail industries, the existence of large firms that serve huge networks has a positive effect on the survival chances of small firms, for they enable smaller firms to make connections with the large networks (Barnett and Carroll 1987; Barnett and Amburgey 1990). Thus in the rail industry, once a trunk line was built, entrepreneurs could connect a minor city with the rest of the world simply by building a connecting spur line. For instance, after the east-west Boston and Worcester Railroad connected Worcester with rail and sea routes in Boston, a spur line from Worcester northward to Fitchburg was built to give the latter town access to the entire network.

Public Capitalization and Failures
Failures were quite common among early American railroads, in part because railroads were capitalized by governments in anticipation of demand. In Britain, transport demand was great on many routes by 1830 and governments provided no capital to railroads; hence most railroads were built to compete for the traffic that canals and turnpikes were serving. By contrast, even in the relatively settled state of Massachusetts, many railroads were built to generate demand, and many failed to do so. As early as the 1840s, Massachusetts saw forty-nine railroad failures. Many railroads failed after winning charters—which they needed to expropriate private lands—but before opening for business, because they never collected sufficient capital. Many others failed after completing construction when their receipts proved inadequate to meet their operating expenses. This evidence reinforces the finding of David Tucker and colleagues (1988) that government subsidies may increase both foundings and failures in an industry. Government capitalization may increase foundings by increasing the pool of available resources, but it may lead to an increase in subsequent failures by artificially inflating foundings.

In sum, due to the availability of public financial backing during this first period, railroad founding *strategy* was based less on the expected profitability of a railroad than on the secondary economic benefits the railroad was expected to return to a community. Investors, particularly governments, paid little heed to whether their investments would turn a profit—they were concerned exclusively with the benefits that would accrue to their regions. In this period, railroads gained tremendous legitimacy from the early successes of British locomotives and from the British railway mania. The effects of public capitalization are visible in Figure 4-1, which shows large numbers of total foundings in the 1830s and 1840s when demand was still very low.

Figure 4–1 Decennial totals of entries and exits of railroads in Massachusetts. (*Source:* Author's analysis of data from Massachusetts Railroad Commissioners.)

Industry *structure* was characterized by a proliferation of small branch lines and a small number of longer lines that served major cities. In Massachusetts, by 1870 a handful of trunk lines such as the Boston and Lowell, the Boston and Maine, the Boston and Providence, and the Boston and Worcester, had spawned over forty operating secondary lines to provide connecting service to smaller towns, such as Framingham, Harvard, Pittsfield, and Stoughton. In between these lines were lines such as the Fall River and the Salem and Lowell, which primarily gave medium-sized cities access to ports.

At the beginning of the period there was virtually no competition among railroads, because most held service monopolies, and hence there was little reason for railroads to combine or try to fix prices. As a result, railroads had unitary structures, in that they owned single stretches of track without tributaries, for most of the period. By 1870, none of Massachusetts' trunk lines had acquired secondary lines. Mergers were rare, and railroads seldom sought to expand—railroaders established new firms rather than increasing the size of the railroads they already controlled. Thus Figure 4-2 shows that as late as 1870, the average Massachusetts railroad operated less than forty miles of track.

Selection was little influenced by competition before 1870. Most railroads, large and small alike, held exclusive routes and faced no competitors. Failure much more often resulted from public investment in ill-conceived lines, which produced large numbers of precompletion failures among publicly capitalized railroads. Moreover, while many operating firms found that they could not

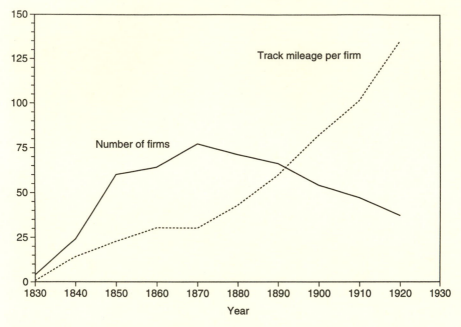

Figure 4–2 Massachusetts railroad population. (*Source:* Author's analysis of data from Massachusetts Railroad Commissioners.)

meet their capital obligations, relatively few of those firms closed down because asset specificity removed the incentive to liquidate. Figure 4-1 shows an especially high number of failures in the decade ending in 1850.

The period of public capitalization came to an end in the early 1870s as a result of widespread corruption and graft in the administration of public aid. Many governments had been defrauded by railway promoters who used creative accounting dodges to transfer public monies to themselves. As a result, governments found themselves responsible for paying off large public debts. Over a dozen state governments and scores of cities and towns defaulted on their commitments to railway investors. In response, most state and local governments swore off providing future aid to railroads. By 1870, fourteen states had actually passed constitutional amendments prohibiting public investments in private enterprises. Then in 1871, when it came to light that railwaymen had bribed eighteen senators and congressmen to vote for generous aid to the first transcontinental railroad, Congress foreswore further land grant aid.

RATE REGULATION, 1870–1889

The environment changed dramatically at the beginning of the 1870s as a result of one functional change in the operation of the industry and one broad shift in policy. The functional change followed successful efforts to establish physical connections between railroads, to set uniform operating procedures, and to standardize rail gauge and other technologies. In short order, the rail network became integrated so that trains could continue from the track owned by one company to the track owned by another, facilitating through traffic and making it possible to string short railroads together for long-distance service. Competition was enlivened, which brought efforts by railroads to escape competitive pricing through rate discrimination—irregular rate structures that were deemed unfair. The policy shift occurred when state governments responded by regulating rates to address perceived inequities. Regulation produced unforeseen price competition, which led to an unprecedented series of mergers and acquisitions and also a move toward cartelization that briefly altered the nature of selection pressures.

This period also saw the emergence of what Glenn Carroll (1985) has called "resource partitioning" (see Section IV of this book). The trunk lines, which acted as generalist organizations and typically competed with other trunk lines, engaged in active price competition that led to failures and increased concentration. By contrast, small, specialist, spur lines that connected minor cities with trunk lines typically faced no competition from generalists. In effect, rich niches appeared for specialist lines, niches that were safe from predatory price competition.

Antidiscrimination Law

Most railroads hold service monopolies to some destinations along their routes and face competition on others. The typical railroad connects two terminal cities that are served by other roads, such as Indianapolis and Cincinnati, and has depots in a number of small towns that are not, such as Oxford, Ohio. This railroad was forced to charge competitive prices for Indianapolis-Cincinnati service, but could charge whatever the traffic would bear between Oxford and Cincinnati. The industry's high fixed costs encouraged railroads to set rates just above variable costs on competitive routes, and the result was dualistic rate structures. Railroads offered lower prices for long-distance competitive service (e.g., Indianapolis-Cincinnati) than for short-distance, uncompetitive service *over the same track* (e.g., Oxford-Cincinnati). This practice became known as local rate discrimination and it was much vilified by the National Grange of the Patrons of Husbandry (est. 1867), a group comprised of farmers and ranchers who transported produce and livestock from isolated rural communities to urban markets. State governments established regulatory commissions to prevent local rate discrimination against isolated towns, and personal rate discrimination against particular customers. All six New England states had established such commissions by 1870, and by 1887 twenty-five states had installed commissions.

Many state commissions failed to end rate discrimination, but commissions in key states with substantial rail traffic, such as Massachusetts and Illinois, did succeed. The new short haul–long haul regulations prevented railroads from charging higher rates for short-distance transport than they charged for long-distance transport on the same route. These regulations undermined the dualistic pricing strategy by forcing railroads that charged cutthroat rates on their competitive routes to charge equal or lower rates on shorter noncompetitive routes. Between 1869 and 1875, aggressive price competition in conjunction with these antidiscrimination rules caused unprecedented failure rates, particularly in the East. In Massachusetts there were forty-one failures between 1870 and 1875. These changes stimulated railroads to look for ways to control competition in the industry.

Rate Regulation, Bankruptcy Law, and Selection
Rate regulation, in the form of antidiscrimination legislation, undermined the prevailing pricing strategy that railroads depended on to sustain profitability, that of charging high rates on noncompetitive routes to offset low rates on competitive routes. This posed a particular problem because railroads faced significant asset specificity, which made it impossible for rail operators to shut down and reinvest their capital elsewhere. Railroads' investments in rights-of-way, buildings, and track were extremely high, and these resources could not be converted to other uses. As a result, railroads that faced financial failure due to their inability to meet capital obligations did not encounter the same kinds of selection pressures found in other industries.

First, the nontransferability of railroad assets meant that railroads would often continue to operate despite the fact that they lost money. Investors in troubled railways had little to gain by demanding the liquidation of assets and distribution of receipts to shareholders. Early bankruptcy laws that allowed companies to continue to operate in receivership were a prime cause here—if bankruptcy laws had been such that financial failure led to abandonment of service, lines that lost money would have exited the industry.

Second, asset specificity meant that railroads that *did* go bankrupt were often purchased by new investors for a fraction of their original capital cost. Financial failure sometimes meant death for a particular operating company, but it seldom meant permanent abandonment of service. New owners, relieved of debt service, could often operate a railroad profitably. This practice remained common in subsequent periods. Between 1900 and 1920, for instance, every charter granted in Massachusetts went to a new company that had assumed the operation of a failed line.

These two practices—operating at a loss and operating with capital obligations wiped out—led to a two-tiered rail system. The first tier was comprised of railroads with massive original capital obligations that they actively tried to pay off, and the second tier was comprised of railroads that had either given up hope of amortizing debt or had been relieved of capital obligations through bankruptcy. Now lines with heavy capital obligations competed with railroads that sought to cover operating expenses alone, which led to a spate of financial failures among otherwise healthy railroads. Paradoxically, railroads that had been financially mismanaged early on, and had undergone bankruptcy, were in a better position to compete than lines that had been well managed and had remained solvent.

Price competition heated up after the Civil War, in part because new railway construction increased the number of competitive routes. Figure 4-3 shows that track mileage increased by nearly 50 percent during the 1860s, and then nearly doubled in the 1870s. In Massachusetts, railway failures exceeded foundings for the first time in the decade that ended in 1880 (see Figure 4-1).

Cartel Policy and Business Strategy

With dualistic rate structures outlawed, and with failures abounding, state and federal governments encouraged the creation of rail cartels and pools. Cartels fixed transport prices and pools fixed prices and apportioned traffic or profits among different railroads. In 1866, Congress passed legislation that would allow railroads to share rolling stock and track to facilitate traffic pooling and collaboration. In 1875, the Massachusetts Board of Railroad Commissioners argued that, "An open and reasonable [cartel] would probably be found far less fruitful in abuses than a secret and irresponsible one. One or the other must exist under the circumstances of the case" (p. 41). In 1878, the board held that, "Uncontrolled competition is but one phase in railroad development and must result in some form of regulated combination"—in other words, collaborative price setting was inevitable (Massachusetts Board of Railroad Commissioners 1878, p. 80).

Railroad freight agents met regularly, and in full view of the public, to set rates on competitive routes. Under long haul–short haul legislation, railroads could charge high rates for short routes so long as they charged high rates for longer routes as well; thus by buoying prices on competitive routes these rate associations solved the problem posed by the legislation. During the 1870s,

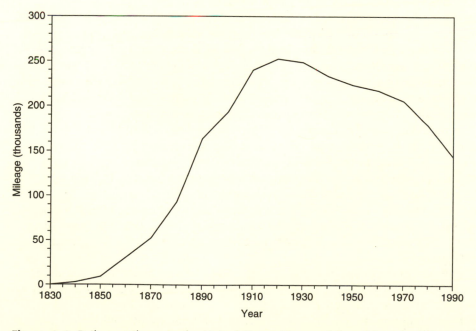

Figure 4–3 Railway mileage in the United States. (*Source:* Adapted from Locklin 1954, U.S. Bureau of the Census 1975, and U.S. Treasury Department 1992.)

Albert Fink, who had started his career as an engineer for the Baltimore and Ohio and had become a manager of the Louisville and Nashville Railroad, established the Eastern Trunk Line Association to set rates and allocate traffic for East-West interstate railroads. The idea was to stabilize the industry and prevent rate wars by making pricing and service agreements that would be beneficial to all members. During the reign of the cartel, between the mid-1870s and the mid-1880s, competitive pressures on railroads abated. Massachusetts recorded only ten failures between 1876 and 1880, down from forty-one in the first half of the decade (Dobbin and Dowd 1992).

However, these pools did not last, because while state and federal legislatures generally favored them in the 1870s, the courts would not enforce pooling contracts, which they deemed to conflict with common-law doctrine against "restraints of trade." Voluntary participation in pools was perfectly legal before the passage of the Sherman Act and establishment of the Interstate Commerce Commission at the end of the 1880s, but the courts would not hold railroads to agreements they wished to break, and would not compel participation in pools. Thus by 1884 the Eastern Trunk Line agreement lay in shambles. Subsequent efforts to create stable regional cartels during the 1880s almost invariably fell apart when one railroad broke ranks. In Britain, by contrast, pooling and cartels emerged in a wide range of industries in the last three decades of the nineteenth century. Parliament took a benign view of pools, and agreed to enforce voluntary pooling agreements. Consequently, British pools worked where American pools failed.

Regulation, Cartel Policy, and System Building
In the 1870s and 1880s, when state-level rate regulation stripped railways of the capacity to sustain income by charging exorbitant rates on monopoly routes, and when federal case law prevented them from making dependable price-fixing agreements, many railroads suffered severe financial losses and were acquired by large networks. New York investors put together huge railway systems through mergers, leasing arrangements, and joint stockholding agreements. *System building* became a popular business strategy.

In the late 1860s, Jay Gould, the "Mephistopheles of Wall Street," sought to put together an interregional rail system that would give the Erie control over a number of lines in the Midwest, and his efforts stimulated the Pennsylvania to take preemptive action to control roads serving Chicago, Indianapolis, St. Louis, Cleveland, Toledo, Michigan's peninsula, Erie, Pittsburgh, and other major midwestern cities by 1876. By 1880, Gould was buying stock in a number of lines, including the Wabash, the Lackawanna, the Central of New Jersey, and the Boston, New York, and Erie, to put together a huge transcontinental network.

The earliest network-building strategy had been to make local acquisitions to dominate rail transport in one area, thereby creating regional networks of competing lines that were owned by a single company. Gould revolutionized network building by acquiring interregional railroads that could allow him to provide long-distance through-service between regions. In the railway industry this sort of end-to-end consolidation of railroads amounted to vertical integration, because inputs were the goods transferred *from* connecting lines and outputs were the goods transferred *to* connecting lines. Gould reasoned that with exclusive service on particular midwestern and western routes, he would have a virtual monopoly on all western traffic that originated, or terminated, in the East.

Soon other network builders followed the same strategy, and the result was a rise in huge, integrated, railway systems during the 1880s. By the early 1890s, the Pennsylvania had nearly 8,000 miles of track, the New York Central had over 6,000 miles, and nine other railroads had between 5,000 and 10,000 miles of track. Figure 4-4 shows this change. In 1870 there was only one U.S. railroad operating over 1,000 miles of track, and by 1890 there were forty such railroads. Integration was achieved through formal mergers, but also through trusts, holding companies, joint stockholding agreements, and leasing arrangements.

In sum, government regulation of railway rates altered the nature of the industry markedly in this second period. The industry's high fixed costs, asset specificity, and small numbers of competitors made truly competitive pricing difficult to sustain. The early *strategy* that railroads adopted, of dualistic rate structures that took advantage of exclusive routes while drawing business on competitive routes, was undermined in the early 1870s by state-level rate regulation. One popular new strategy was price fixing. However when the courts refused to enforce price-fixing agreements, railroads turned to the strategy of system building to evade rate wars and monopolize long-distance service.

Industry *structure* changed noticeably over these years. Many small railroads failed and were bought up by trunk lines. In 1870, the Boston and Maine

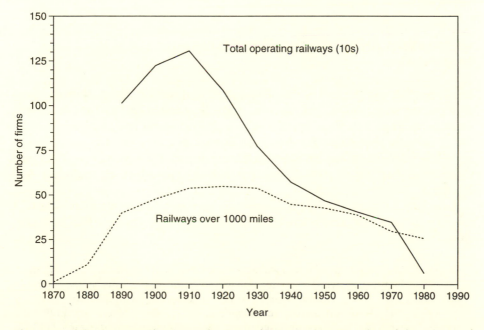

Figure 4–4 Operating railways in the United States. (*Source:* Adapted from Kennedy 1991, and Moody's Investor Service 1992.)

owned but three short branches it had built itself, but by 1890 it had acquired full or partial interest in twenty-one other railroads. In turn, a number of trunk lines were acquired, in part or in full, by Jay Gould and other system builders. Many other railroads did not formally merge, but came under the control of larger regional roads like the Boston and Maine via leases. The industry had consisted of hundreds of small one-line railroads and a few regional trunk lines in 1870 and by 1890 it contained an increasing number of interregional trunk lines that controlled branch lines and parallel lines (those that served the same endpoints). Figure 4-1 shows that between 1870 and 1890 the number of railroads in Massachusetts declined for the first time, and that the average length of railroads nearly doubled.

Industry structure was also changed by the completion of the transcontinental lines built with land grants. From the inauguration of the Union Pacific and Central Pacific lines in 1869, connecting Sacramento with Chicago, rail service west of Chicago was opened and new secondary lines began to be planned and built. In part as a result of the opening of trunk-line service to the West, total rail mileage in the United States increased rapidly between 1870 and 1890 (see Figure 4-3).

Selection varied widely across this brief period. In the first half of the 1870s, rate wars put many small railroads out of business. Figure 4-1 shows especially high numbers of failures in the decade that ended in 1880. Between the mid-1870s and the mid-1880s, there was a bit of a respite due to the success of the pools at preventing rate competition, but by the end of that period most pools had fallen apart and many small railroads sought the protection of larger regional partners.

ANTICARTEL AND ANTITRUST LEGISLATION, 1890–1919

Between 1870 and the end of the 1880s, state and federal law made some popular pricing strategies illegal, such as rate discrimination, and made others, such as pooling, difficult to sustain. But in 1887, federal law changed dramatically, virtually requiring all railroads to engage in active price competition. It would be a decade before the Supreme Court declared the core of the Interstate Commerce Act constitutional, but the subsequent effect on railroads was dramatic.

American concern with the monopolistic powers of railways increased with the rise of huge, integrated railways in the 1880s. As Thomas McCraw concludes:

> In the minds of many members of the generation that came to maturity during the 1880s and 1890s, the huge new companies we now call center firms seemed somehow unnatural . . . the consequences of some evil tampering with the natural order of things. They were not merely economic freaks but also sinister new political forces—powers that had to be opposed in the name of American democracy. (1984, p. 77)

Congress spent much of the 1880s debating legislation to contain these powers. What was needed, according to railway customers ranging from eastern oilmen to midwestern merchants to southern farmers, was a regulatory power at the federal level that would establish ground rules for operation and put an end to various restraints of trade practiced by the railroads, including price fixing and rate discrimination. The Act to Regulate Interstate Commerce made pooling and rate discrimination illegal and established the Interstate Commerce Commission (ICC) to adjudicate complaints.

The Pooling Prohibition, Discrimination, and Mergers
A number of states had outlawed price discrimination in the 1870s, but public policy had generally been neutral toward cartels and pools before 1887. Although pooling contracts were not legally enforceable because they constituted restraints of trade, voluntary participation in pools that fixed prices and apportioned traffic and profits was perfectly legal. Thus before 1887, pool organizers such as Albert Fink lobbied Congress in the hope of making the agreements legally enforceable.

Although the 1887 act outlawed pooling, the ICC's powers were decimated by early Supreme Court decisions and the commissioners found it difficult to enforce the act before 1897. Despite the fact that new federal legislation was weakly enforced at first, it helped to generate selection pressures akin to those that had been in operation between 1869 and 1875, before pooling and price fixing became widespread. There were strong pressures for price competition, which produced an incentive to win business and increase revenues by means other than rate reductions.

Local rate discrimination was one strategy railroads pursued in response to the changed environment. The rate discrimination clause of the 1887 act was weakly worded, and rate inequities were increasingly difficult to detect as the national network became more dense and as routing became more complex. Thus many railroads practiced discrimination without being detected between 1887 and 1910, when federal regulation of discrimination was reinforced by new legislation.

Personal rate discrimination was a second common business strategy. Railroads gave special advantages to particular shippers in order to win their exclusive business. Sometimes they did this surreptitiously by giving rebates, in cash or in kind. In turn, the shipper might be able to corner the local market due to unusually low shipping costs, and the railroad would end up with the business of the monopoly firm in the field. A case in Galveston, Texas, in 1908 exemplifies the problem. Only two storage facilities for cotton seed existed in Galveston, which was a port for international shipping. The Southern Pacific owned one of those facilities, and gave highly preferential storage rates to a single cotton shipper. Hence other cotton seed shippers were driven out of the market because they could not offer competitive prices. The Southern Pacific thereby gained a virtual monopoly in the transport of cotton seed by giving one shipper a clandestine shipping rebate. This strategy came to prevail as a way to win market share and escape cutthroat price competition, though it was by no means new. Standard Oil had been party to many rebate schemes in the early 1870s, and was eventually prosecuted for its participation.

Mergers were the final strategy that was popularized to circumvent anti-pooling legislation. The paradox of both the Sherman Antitrust Act and the Act to Regulate Interstate Commerce was that by preventing cartelization, they encouraged mergers: "While cartels were illegal, . . . mergers that created monopolies or near monopolies . . . were not illegal, even if they were intended to restrain trade" (Fligstein 1990, p. 35). The economy-wide turn-of-the-century merger movement was spawned in part by the Sherman Act, which outlawed trusts and other restraints of trade and made horizontal integration among competing firms the only dependable strategy for dampening price competition.

Railway mergers, in particular, were also stimulated by the Act to Regulate Interstate Commerce. When the Supreme Court upheld the Interstate Commerce and Sherman acts in the trans-Missouri case in 1897, railway managers came to accept that they would not be able to revert to cartelization and turned, en masse, to mergers to control prices. Mergers skyrocketed, as we see in Figure 4-5. During the mid-1890s, 30 to 40 railroads merged each year, but suddenly in 1897 the number rose to nearly 80 and in 1900 it increased to nearly 130. Between 1897 and 1904, some 700 American railway companies were merged, and by 1910, 54 companies controlled more than two thirds of the nation's railroad mileage (Ripley 1915, pp. 458–60).

ICC Enforcement and the Holding Company Strategy

The Progressive Era produced a series of bills that enhanced the ICC's capacity to undermine rate discrimination. The Hepburn Act (1906) empowered the ICC to prevent personal discrimination and to establish maximum rates, the Mann-Elkins Act (1910) expanded the ICC's authority over local rate discrimination and gave it veto power over proposed rate changes, and the Railroad Valuation Act (1913) improved the ICC's ability to evaluate rates.

Local and personal rate discrimination became much harder to carry out, and railroads initially responded by merging to quell competition. However, the government soon began to enforce the restraint of trade provision of the antitrust law by preventing mergers. In 1909, the government denied the proposed Burlington–Great Northern Pacific merger, which led railroads increasingly to combine by establishing *holding companies* to buy the stock of other railroads. Between 1917 and 1920, the federal government took temporary control over the nation's railroads as part of the war mobilization effort, but in 1920 private ownership was restored and a new set of regulatory mechanisms was put into place.

In sum, organizational *strategy* changed significantly again as a result of policy changes. The Interstate Commerce Act, when it was finally enforced, prohibited both discrimination and pooling and stimulated mergers and the use of holding companies to quell predatory price competition. Figure 4-5 shows a large increase in mergers beginning in 1897, when the Supreme Court upheld the Interstate Commerce Act and the Sherman Antitrust Act as they applied to railroads.

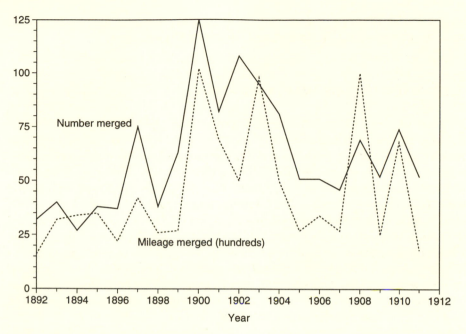

Figure 4–5 Railway mergers in the United States. (*Source:* Adapted from Ripley 1912.)

Industry *structure* changed significantly around the beginning of the twentieth century, as mergers reached an all-time high. Now railroaders began to believe that huge, interregional networks had the best chances of survival. Hence firms that faced significant competition were likely to merge. The industry became increasingly divided into generalist organizations serving important intercity routes and noncompetitive specialist lines that served remote destinations or relatively minor cities. The population size rose through much of the period, but by 1920 it had begun to decline (see Figure 4-4). More importantly, average route mileage rose 45 percent between 1890 and 1920 despite the fact that spur lines were still being founded in much of the country. National data on holding companies are not available; however, in Massachusetts, the thirty-eight railroads that survived to 1920 were controlled by just eleven independent companies.

With the disappearance of pooling, *selection* pressures changed markedly. New federal policies led railroaders to believe that only one firm could survive in any particular intercity market. While subsequent federal policies would prevent mergers from eliminating competition, the immediate result was that railroads practiced predatory pricing in the belief that if they could not kill off their competitors, they would perish themselves. Thus mergers and acquisitions increased because the threat of imminent failure increased. In Figure 4-4 this situation is obscured between 1897, when the Court upheld anticartel and antitrust law, and 1910, by the fact that new railroads continued to be founded; however, the effect is clear between 1910 and 1920, when the number of operating railroads declined by over 200. Unfortunately, national data on foundings were not published by the Interstate Commerce Commission.

THE POLICY TUG-OF-WAR, 1920–1965

Between 1920 and 1965, U.S. rail policy upheld the conflicting goals of fostering price competition in the industry and sustaining service on every stretch of track ever built. To add to the confusion, Congress also sought to regulate rates in the rail industry to ensure "fair" competition between railroads, road transport, and air transport. The idea was to keep all forms of transport alive and viable for all possible routes. The contradiction between the goal of preserving price competition and the goal of sustaining service to all rail destinations led to a series of disarticulated policies and to great instability in the industry. The problem resulted from industry overcapacity. Federal law required railroads to be competitive, but prevented them from abandoning unprofitable stretches of track to reduce costs. The situation was exacerbated by economic crises that threatened the industry during the 1930s, at the end of the 1940s, at the end of the 1950s, and again at the end of the 1960s.

After the industry was run under strict state control during the Great War, private control was restored in 1920. In the same year the Transportation Act granted the ICC wide-ranging control over construction, abandonment of track, rates, competition, and mergers. In practice, the legislation enforced price competition while preventing firms from closing down lines that lost money—or merging where overcapacity created losses.

Between 1920 and 1965, Congress vacillated between seeking to stabilize the industry by quelling competition and seeking to protect consumers by stimulating competition. The Hoch-Smith Resolution of 1925 gave the ICC expanded investigatory powers over rate inequities to ensure that competitive rates were offered on all routes. Then the Emergency Transportation Act of 1933 gave the railroads temporary power to act cooperatively during the Great Depression. The temporary Railroad Adjustments Act of 1939 and the permanent Railroad Modification Act of 1940 gave the ICC the power to help faltering railroads survive by modifying the terms of their bonds. But then the Transportation Act of 1940, in the wake of federal regulation of motor and air transport in the late 1930s, sought to equalize and stimulate competition among different forms of transport. The Transportation Act of 1958 aimed to remedy some of these contradictions but it did not fully deregulate the industry and its ultimate effects were modest.

Antimerger Policy and Anticompetitive Strategies

Antitrust law and interstate commerce legislation combined to keep price competition alive in the industry. Between 1909 and 1956, the ICC prevented most mergers among healthy rivals. Managers responded with new kinds of associational strategies designed to quash competition. Railroads frequently used *holding companies* and *stock acquisitions* to combine. For instance, the Van Sweringens put together a group of eastern railroads that included the Chesapeake and Ohio; the Pere Marquette; the New York, Chicago, and Saint Louis; the Wheeling and Lake Erie; the Chicago and Eastern Illinois; and westward, the Missouri Pacific. During the 1920s, many railroads bought large stakes in competing railroads. The Baltimore and Ohio, after being severed from the Pennsylvania under antitrust law, acquired an interest in six different railroads to control competition.

Nonetheless, *acquisition* continued to be the preferred strategy for avoiding competition. Because the ICC had a mandate to sustain service on all of the nation's railroads, it generally supported applications by strong railroads to acquire faltering lines. Formal integration thus occurred most often during periods of financial decline, and generally involved acquisitions rather than mergers. One result of the ICC's reluctance to allow mergers between still-healthy lines was that large segments of the industry were on the brink of insolvency for much of the period. Acquisitions peaked during the Depression, despite Roosevelt's suspension of antitrust policy and support for industry cooperation. Between 1929 and 1932, gross revenues declined by one half. Between 1928 and 1940, one third of America's 849 railroads disappeared (Moody's Investor Service 1992, p. a33). The ICC made every effort to broker an acquisition for each bankrupt line, in keeping with the policy of preventing the abandonment of track; however, these arrangements often had the effect of saddling a healthy company with routes that lost money.

There were very few new firms founded after 1920, and very few firms failed without being acquired; Figure 4-4 charts the number of railway firms over time and captures the pattern of consolidation in the industry. There was a steady decline in the number of firms operating the nation's rail routes between 1910 and 1970. What the decennial data do not show is the flurry of consolidations that occurred during each economic crisis, for instance, the population of railroads declined by 140, or 17 percent, between the beginning of 1929 and the end of 1932 (Moody's Investor Service 1992, p. a33).

A third business strategy was participation in the regional *rate association*. Rate associations were independent bodies that brought together the traffic chiefs of regional railroads to review proposed changes in charges and conditions of transport. Proposed changes were made known to shippers and carriers, who could then express their opinions to the associations. The courts had held that members must be able to set rates independently if they chose to, but the associations provided a way to preclude rate wars and protect revenues. The Justice Department considered these associations to violate antitrust law; however, by stabilizing the industry they made most shippers, carriers, and railroads happy and thus they engendered little opposition. In 1948, railways, regulatory agencies, and rail customers joined forces to pass the Reed-Bulwinkle Act, which legalized rate associations. The associations did not exactly fix prices, and they did not exactly preclude competition, but they did serve as a brake on incipient rate wars that might otherwise have thrown even more railroads into bankruptcy.

The Regulation of Track Abandonment

In 1920, Congress gave the ICC the authority to prevent railroads from abandoning service on existing routes. Precedent for such intervention in the operations of private firms came from the tradition of common carrier regulation. In return for charters granting service monopolies, public carriers were required to provide transport on the routes for which they held charters. This doctrine remained largely intact until 1976, and in conjunction with the industry's asset specificity, which continued to prevent the liquidation of capital, it severely constrained business strategy. Railroads were enjoined from eliminating unprofitable services except where all affected parties concurred in the abandonment. The ICC permitted the abandonment of only 25 percent (63,332 miles) of U.S. railroad track between 1920, when competition from road and air transport began in earnest, and 1969 (Keeler 1983, p. 38). By preventing the abandonment of unprofitable routes, the ICC prevented firms from adopting efficient structures that would allow them to offer truly competitive prices.

The Regulation of Competing Forms of Transport

Federal regulation of competition among air, road, and rail transport pushed railroads in yet another direction strategically. From 1940 the Interstate Commerce Commission held authority to regulate rates in the rail industry to preserve healthy competition among railroads, trucks, buses, and planes. This included the capacity to set *minimum* rates, so as to prevent prices that would drive competing forms from the market. While the legislation was successful in preventing predatory, below-cost rate setting, it had the effect of interfering with active price competition.

Of course, it is difficult to accurately estimate the importance of rate regulation and abandonment regulation on the railways' competitive position vis-à-vis other forms of transport. Some argue that public subsidies for airport and highway construction are to blame for the decline of the railroads. In any event, the railroads lost substantial ground to other sectors. Before 1920, railways had provided virtually all intercity passenger transport, and by 1950, when reliable comparative statistics became available, railroads were providing only 6 percent of intercity passenger transport and private automobiles were providing 86 percent (U.S. Bureau of the Census 1975, p. 707). Freight transport succumbed somewhat later, and to a lesser extent, than passenger transport, but railways nonetheless lost market share in freight as well.

Railroad foundings and new construction also came to a virtual halt after about 1920. During the 1910s, system builders continued to lay down new track to complete their networks, even when other roads already served the routes. Federal pro-competition policy was part of the cause. Continued construction produced substantial overcapacity, and there was increasing talk of the redundancy of routes in the U.S. rail network. Railway foundings and new construction slowed to a crawl after 1920, in part due to competition from road transport and in part due to previous overbuilding. In the forty years after World War II, there was not a single new railroad founded in the United States.

In sum, business *strategy* was increasingly politicized between 1920 and 1965, because railroad profitability and survival were so dependent on public policy. The railroads came to support federal regulation of road, rail, and air rates because it buoyed their prices and prevented cutthroat competition. Once road transport became a viable source of competition, federal minimum rates became essential to sustaining profitability because federally set rates were based on a "fair rate of return" calculus that took railroads' required operation of unprofitable lines into account. Federal minimum rates for both trains and trucks could thus shield railroads that were handicapped by unprofitable routes from all-out price competition.

The *structure* of the industry changed as well. Rate bureaus created regional integration of a weak sort, and acquisitions of failing lines by healthy railroads led to greater consolidation. Because Washington remained committed to the principle of competition, however, end-to-end combinations that did not extinguish competition were favored over combinations between railroads that competed directly. The industry gradually became more concentrated between 1920 and 1965, as Figure 4-4 shows. The average railroad more than doubled in size.

Selection worked against railroads that had a preponderance of unprofitable routes on which they were not able to suspend service. The acquisitions that resulted from these failures produced an increasing number of exclusive rail routes. In the quarter-century after World War II, nearly one-half of *rail* freight traffic in the East was removed from competition as a result of acquisitions (Healy 1985, p. 247). Competition from other forms of transport became increasingly important in these years. Despite the fact that aggregate demand for freight service grew, rail's proportion of freight business declined significantly. Passenger service suffered even more. The number of freight cars in service declined by less than one half between 1920 and 1970, while the number of passenger cars declined by over four fifths.

A comparison with Britain illustrates the effects of American policy. While Parliament had ruled against proposed mergers as early as 1872, it had also made cartels legally enforceable in most cases. Antimerger and pro-cartel policies, taken together, led British railroads not to seek mergers but to "rely on less formal and often less stable methods of regulating competition between themselves, such as . . . pricing and pooling agreements" (Channon 1983, p. 59). While policy in both countries discouraged mergers, Britain's pro-cartel policies permitted even small railroads to stabilize prices and thereby escape bankruptcy. The result, in Britain, was a fairly stable level of industry concentration between 1870 and 1921, when the government reorganized the industry into regional monopolies. By contrast, well into the twentieth century the U.S. antimerger stance continued to prevent mergers among healthy companies, while the U.S. anticartel stance made price stabilization through associations difficult and contributed to a high rate of failure.

PARTIAL NATIONALIZATION AND DEREGULATION, 1966–1993

The Department of Transportation, founded in 1966, responded to a rail crisis in the latter half of the 1960s by orchestrating federal takeovers of intercity passenger rail service and of Northeast freight service, and by deregulating much of the rest of the industry to permit reorganization.

Partial Nationalization: Amtrak and Conrail

Increased competition from trucking caused rail's proportion of the nation's freight traffic to decline from 69 percent in 1945 to only 40 percent in 1970. In 1968, the two competing railroads that served Chicago and the Northeast were on the verge of being unable to sustain operations, and the Pennsylvania and New York Central Railroads were merged into a single company, the Penn Central. Federal approval for the merger reversed the longstanding policy of disallowing mergers that would undermine competition. Two years later, Penn Central was hemorrhaging badly and passenger losses throughout the country were putting railroads at risk of bankruptcy. Nationally, passenger services had lost money in every year since the end of World War II, and by 1970 the railroads were providing less than 1 percent of intercity passenger service (Itzkoff 1985, pp. 14–15; U.S. Bureau of the Census 1975, p. 707). Current losses in freight made passenger losses insupportable, and Congress responded by establishing the National Railroad Passenger Corporation, known as Amtrak, which began service in 1971 under a federal board of directors. In the Northeast, Amtrak took over key segments of track on the Boston-Washington corridor, but throughout most of the country it operated passenger service on privately held track. Then in 1973, Congress passed the Regional Rail Reorganization (3R) Act, establishing an agency to plan the reorganization and public takeover of freight railroads in the Northeast under Conrail.

The creation of Amtrak left regional railroads in business, but gave the federal government responsibility for its unprofitable passenger services. Conrail, which began operating in 1976, combined the operations of the Penn Central and five other railroads in the Northeast and created unified, publicly owned freight service for much of the region. Conrail only reduced the number of operating railroads by five, yet the rate of exits roughly doubled between the last half of the 1960s and the first half of the 1970s as a result of the growth of truck transport and a general economic crisis in the industry (Moody's Investor Service 1992, p. a33).

The decisions to create Amtrak and Conrail seemed to reflect Congress's recognition that the railway industry was naturally monopolistic. These particular strategies, however, departed markedly from what other countries had done when they had come to that realization. Both France and Britain had used public policy to create private regional monopolies, in 1852 and 1921 respectively. And both later created unified, nationalized, rail systems, in 1937 and 1947 respectively. Throughout the world, national governments had responded to the unique economic characteristics of the rail industry by setting rates for monopolistic private railroads, and later by nationalizing railroads. Congress has not yet fully embraced these solutions; and American policy swung away from public control after 1975.

Deregulation of Mergers, Abandonments, and Rates

After 1975, Washington sought to undo the federal regulations that had for so long tied the hands of railroad operators. The Railroad Revitalization and Regulatory Reform (4R) Act removed obstacles to mergers, abandonments, and competitive pricing. The main short-run effect of this legislation was to increase merger activity. Since the beginning of the century, federal antitrust law and railroad regulation law had discouraged combinations. By altering this stand, the 4R Act permitted roads to achieve long-desired consolidation. Moreover, by facilitating the abandonment of track, the 4R Act made it possible for newly merged railways to eliminate regional overcapacity, which produced an added incentive to merge. Competing railroads could now merge and abandon one set of tracks to reduce overhead. The results were dramatic. In one year the number of operating railroads in the United States declined from 320 to 59 (Moody's Investor Service 1992, p. a33). The industry responded to the legislation by lobbying for further deregulation.

The initial deregulation had been part of an economy-wide movement that took form under the Ford administration. The trend continued under the Reagan administration in the 1980s; however, proposals to extricate the state from governance of the railways met with mixed success. The Staggers Act, which was designed to loosen controls on managerial decisions, was signed by Jimmy Carter in 1980. Railroads had favored rate regulation so long as the main effect was to sustain *minimum* rates, but once the 4R Act eliminated the rate floor, railroads had lobbied for further deregulation to eliminate the ceiling. The Staggers Act removed *maximum* rates on the majority of routes and sped up regulatory decisions over proposed rate changes.

Yet when the Reagan administration sought to further reduce the government role in railroads by ending public subsidies to Amtrak, Congress objected on the grounds that Amtrak would quickly fall into bankruptcy and discontinue intercity passenger service. When Reagan proposed the sale of Conrail to the Norfolk Southern Railroad, the Justice Department objected on the grounds that the acquisition would violate antitrust law.

In sum, *strategy* between 1965 and 1975 was highly politicized in large measure because regulation narrowly constrained traditional business strategy. Railroads lobbied for federal rules governing rail, air, and road transport. After the passage of the 4R Act in 1976, which eliminated minimum prices that had buoyed revenues, railroads lobbied for further deregulation so that they could compete aggressively for business. They subsequently sought mergers that would enable them to increase the efficiency of their holdings, and this is evident in Figure 4-4, which shows a rapid reduction in the number of operating railways during the 1970s. The effect of the deregulation of track abandonment can be seen in Figure 4-3: total rail mileage was reduced more between 1970 and 1990 than in the preceding fifty years.

The *structure* of the industry changed dramatically with the establishment of Amtrak, which decoupled passenger and freight transport by forming a federally governed passenger service monopoly. With the establishment of Conrail, a federally governed railroad came to dominate freight services on the dense network of lines in the Northeast. Industry structure changed dramatically again in the aftermath of the 4R Act, which removed most obstacles to mergers and produced a spate of consolidations. Almost overnight, the number of operating railroads was reduced by a factor of five and average operating mileage rose accordingly.

Selection also changed radically as a result of deregulation of the industry.

Throughout most of the century, railroads failed due to overcapacity that resulted from federal legislation preventing them from merging and from closing redundant routes. After 1976, railroads' hands were not tied by federal policy, and thus they could try to avoid negative selection not merely by lobbying for federal regulations that would advantage them, but also by pursuing more rational management practices.

CONCLUSION

Public policy had dramatic effects on strategy, structure, and selection in the rail industry, and those effects are best seen across a long historical time frame. The policies we take for granted today that fall under the general rubric of *antitrust* appeared in the middle of the rail industry's history. Rail history suggests that those policies did not always have the effects they are thought to have, of sustaining natural competitive conditions and efficiency. They frequently had the opposite effects. The anticartel and antitrust legislation passed at the end of the 1880s, designed to sustain competition, actually led to a wave of mergers that extinguished much competition in the industry. The antimerger policy in effect after 1920 actually prevented lines from merging to reduce inefficient overcapacity in the industry, and produced unnecessary bankruptcies and inflated rates. This evidence points to the pitfalls of presuming that public policy has neutral effects on strategy, structure, and selection. Analysts typically hold public policy constant in examining the evolution of organizations and industries, accurately presuming that many of today's industries grew under a fairly stable set of industrial policies, at least in the United States. However, consistency in the public policy environment across time should not obscure the important role that policy plays in constituting the environment.

Even before competition heated up in the industry, public policy had palpable effects on foundings and failures. During the "railway mania" of the 1840s and 1850s, entrepreneurs responded to the availability of public capital by founding hundreds of railroads. As a result, rail foundings were not stimulated by entrepreneurial interest in the industry so much as by the interest of governments in promoting economic growth. One result was that foundings and failures alike were very high, as is evident in Figure 4-1, in part because governments paid little attention to potential profitability and in part because entrepreneurs were often motivated by the hope of skimming off public funds rather than by potential profits. Mutualism had a palpable effect as small spur lines were spawned by the publicly financed construction of large trunk lines.

Then between 1870 and 1889, the policy environment changed. Public capitalization ended and state governments began to regulate unfair rates—with the effect of stimulating rate competition. Competition had played little role in failures in the previous period, but now cutthroat pricing bankrupted scores of railroads, leading first to a series of acquisitions and next to price-fixing arrangements. Weak government enforcement of cartels soon thwarted price fixing and unleashed rate wars. Resource partitioning was evident in the 1870s and 1880s, as large railroads faced tremendous competitive pressures and small specialists serving exclusive routes were shielded from competition.

With the passage of the Interstate Commerce Act in 1887 and the Sherman Antitrust Act in 1890, cartels, pools, rate discrimination, and trusts were finally outlawed, and once the Supreme Court upheld these laws in 1897, the industry underwent an unprecedented wave of mergers. Now that existing means for controlling predatory pricing were illegal, many railroads saw little choice but to merge with their competitors. Then when the government began to prevent anticompetitive mergers, railroads turned to holding companies to dampen competition.

After the Great War, policy changed again. The government assumed the power to prevent mergers, to prevent firms from abandoning track, and to regulate rates. Between 1920 and 1965, federal policy vacillated between the goal of promoting stability and the goal of promoting competition, and the result was great instability in the industry. Some policies prevented railroads from offering competitive prices. Others buoyed rail prices. Still others prevented mergers that would achieve efficiency until one partner was virtually bankrupt.

After 1965, federal policy moved away from regulation and toward nationalization. Passenger rail service was divorced from freight service and nationalized. Freight service in the Northeast was brought under federal control. However, subsequent deregulation gave remaining private railroads greater authority to reorganize by merging and abandoning unprofitable routes, and the result was a restructuring of the industry into a smaller number of large, and much leaner, railroads.

Many of the competitive forces that operate in other industries were evident in the rail industry, but in a number of cases those forces were overshadowed by public policy. In the early period, railroads won tremendous legitimacy as a result of locomotive demonstrations and government backing, and this spawned a great many foundings. But public capitalization created significant overcapacity in the industry and the antiabandonment policy in effect after 1920 prevented the industry from achieving its ideal size in terms of trackage: for many years the industry exceeded the market's carrying capacity due to these policies. Competition clearly led to a decline in the number of railroads in the United States during the twentieth century. But early pro-cartel policies prevented competition from causing firms to fail, and later price supports had the same effect: failures were dampened by public policy in 1870–1889 and 1920–1965.

Public policy has traditionally been viewed as a force that can either interfere with the operation of natural market mechanisms or reinforce those mechanisms. In this chapter we have seen that public policies largely create the conditions for competition in the first place. In the rail industry, policies established the rules of the game and altered those rules markedly at several historical junctures.

NOTE

Thanks to Timothy Dowd for research assistance.

BIBLIOGRAPHY

Adams, Charles Francis, Jr. 1893. *Railroads: Their Origin and Problems*, rev. ed. New York: Putnam.

Armitage, Susan. 1969. *The Politics of Decontrol of Industry: Britain and the United States*. London: Weidenfeld and Nicolson.

Barnett, William P., and Terry Amburgey. 1990. "Do Larger Organizations Generate Stronger Competition?" In Jitendra Singh (ed.), *Organizational Evolution: New Directions*, Newbury Park, CA: Sage. pp. 78–102.

Barnett, William P., and Glenn R. Carroll. 1987. "Competition and Mutualism Among Early Telephone Companies." *Administrative Science Quarterly* 32:400–21.

Bernstein, Marver H. 1955. *Regulating Business by Independent Commission*. Princeton, NJ: Princeton University Press.

Bruchey, Stuart. 1990. *Enterprise: The Dynamic Economy of a Free People*. Cambridge, MA: Harvard University Press.

Carroll, Glenn R. 1985. "Concentration and Specialization: Dynamics of Niche Width in Populations of Organizations." *American Journal of Sociology* 90:1262–93.

Chalmers, David M. 1976. *Neither Socialism Nor Monopoly: Theodore Roosevelt and the Decision to Regulate the Railroads*. Philadelphia: Lippincott.

Chandler, Alfred D., Jr. 1956. *Henry Varnum Poor: Business Editor, Analyst, and Reformer*. Cambridge, MA: Harvard University Press.

Chandler, Alfred D., Jr. 1977. *The Visible Hand: The Managerial Revolution in American Business*. Cambridge, MA: Harvard University Press.

Channon, Geoffrey. 1983. "A. D. Chandler's 'Visible Hand' in Transport History." *The Journal of Transport History*. Third Series 2:53–64.

Cleveland, Frederick, and Fred Powell. 1909. *Railroad Promotion and Capitalization in the United States*. New York: Longmans, Green, and Co.

Dobbin, Frank. 1994. *Forging Industrial Policy: The United States, Britain, and France in the Railway Age*. New York: Cambridge University Press.

Dobbin, Frank, and Timothy Dowd. 1992. "Public Policy Regimes, Market Dynamics, and Business Strategy: Railway Foundings in Massachusetts, 1825–1922." Unpublished manuscript. Princeton University, Department of Sociology.

Dunlavy, Colleen. 1991. "Mirror Images: Political Structure and Early Railroad Policy in the United States and Prussia." *Studies in American Political Development* 5:1–35.

Dunlavy, Colleen. 1993. *Politics and Industrialization: Early Railroads in the United States and Prussia*. Princeton, NJ: Princeton University Press.

Fisher, Charles E. 1947. *Whistler's Railroad: The Western Railroad of Massachusetts*. Bulletin No. 69. Boston: The Railway and Locomotive Historical Society.

Fligstein, Neil. 1990. *The Transformation of Corporate Control*. Cambridge, MA: Harvard University Press.

Goodrich, Carter. 1960. *Government Promotion of American Canals and Railroads 1800–1890*. New York: Columbia University Press.

Goodrich, Carter. 1968. "State In, State Out—A Pattern of Development Policy." *Journal of Economic Issues* 30:365–83.

Haney, Lewis Henry. 1908. *A Congressional History of Railways in the United States to 1850*. University of Wisconsin Bulletin 211. Madison: University of Wisconsin Press.

Hannan, Michael T. 1986. *A Model of Competitive and Institutional Processes in Organizational Ecology*. Technical Report 86-13. Ithaca, NY: Cornell University Department of Sociology.

Hannan, Michael T., and John Freeman. 1989. *Organizational Ecology*. Cambridge, MA: Harvard University Press.

Healy, Kent. 1985. *Performance of the U.S. Railroads Since World War II*. New York: Vantage.

Heydinger, Earl L. 1954. "The English Influence on American Railroads." *Railway and Locomotive History Bulletin* 91:7–45.

Hollingsworth, J. Rogers. 1991. "The Logic of Coordinating American Manufacturing Sectors." In John L. Campbell, J. Rogers Hollingsworth, and Leon N. Lindberg (eds.), *Governance of the American Economy*. New York: Cambridge University Press, pp. 35–74.

Itzkoff, Donald M. 1985. *Off the Track: The Decline of the Intercity Passenger Train in the United States*. Westport, CT: Greenwood.

Keeler, Theodore E. 1983. *Railroads, Freight, and Public Policy*. Washington, DC: Brookings.

Kennedy, Robert Dawson, Jr. 1991. "The Statist Evolution of Rail Governance in the United States, 1830–1986." In John L. Campbell, J. Rogers Hollingsworth, and Leon N. Lindberg (eds.), *Governance of the American Economy*. New York: Cambridge University Press, pp. 138–81.

Kolko, Gabriel. 1965. *Railroads and Regulation 1877–1916*. Princeton, NJ: Princeton University Press.

Levin, Richard. 1981. "Regulation, Barriers to Exit, and Investment Behavior of Railroads." In *Studies in Public Regulation*. Cambridge, MA: MIT Press, pp. 181–224.

Lipset, Seymour Martin. 1963. *The First New Nation: The United States in Historical and Comparative Perspective*. New York: Norton.

Lively, Robert A. 1955. "The American System: A Review Article." *The Business History Review* 29:81–96.

Locklin, David. 1954. *Economics of Transportation*, 4th ed. Homewood IL: Irwin.

Massachusetts Board of Railroad Commissioners. 1870–1879. *Annual Report of the Railroad Commissioners*. Boston: Commonwealth of Massachusetts.

McCraw, Thomas K. 1984. *Prophets of Regulation*. Cambridge, MA: Harvard University Press.

Moody's Investor Service. 1992. *Moody's Transportation Manual*. New York: Moody's.

Ripley, William Z. 1912. *Railroads, Rates and Regulation*. New York: Longman's Green.

Ripley, William Z. 1915. *Railroads, Finance and Organization*. New York: Longman's Green.

Scheiber, Harry N. 1981. "Regulation, Property Rights, and Definition of 'the Market': Law and the American Economy." *The Journal of Economic History* 41:103–9.

Shonfield, Alfred. 1965. *Modern Capitalism*. London: Oxford University Press.

Skowronek, Stephen. 1982. *Building a New American State: The Expansion of National Administrative Capacities: 1877–1920*. New York: Cambridge University Press.

Solo, Robert. 1974. *The Political Authority and the Market System*. Cincinnati: South-Western.

Stone, Richard D. 1991. *The Interstate Commerce Commission and the Railroad Industry: A History of Regulatory Policy*. New York: Praeger.

Tucker, David J., Jitendra Singh, Agnes G. Meinhard, and Robert J. House. 1988. "Ecological and Institutional Sources of Change in Organizational Populations." In Glenn R. Carroll (ed.), *Ecological Models of Organizations*. Cambridge, MA: Ballinger.

U.S. Bureau of the Census. 1975. *Historical Statistics of the United States: Colonial Times to 1970.* Part 2. Washington, DC: Government Printing Office.

U.S. Treasury Department. 1992. Statistical Abstract of the United States. Washington, DC: Government Printing Office.

Wilcox, Clair. 1960. *Public Policies Toward Business,* rev. ed. Homewood, IL: Irwin.

5

Art Museums

JUDITH R. BLAU

The public art museum is an organizational form that enjoys a privileged position in contemporary society. Any museum of note is a mecca for tourists, and even a small museum is a source of pride for a city and its residents. It is a symbol of distinction and mark of taste. A museum's art objects are so valued that they are described as being "priceless." Every country boasts about its major museums because they help to define the national heritage and are integral to a people's awareness of their cultural attainments, historical past, and sense of worth.

This feeling suggests that museums epitomize the taken-for-granted character that is central to organizational ecology theory. The legitimacy of the canon of High Art, in fact, is cast in terms that go beyond this taken-for-granted character; works of art are revered and sacralized. For this reason, public museums that display art collections are fairly rugged organizations. Once founded, their survival is virtually guaranteed. Competition pressures are minimal, and given the high start-up costs, notably acquiring a collection, museums manage to secure operating costs to maintain that collection. There are other reasons for the adaptability of the organizational form: there are no wide margins for improvements in efficiency, and museums have been nearly impervious to technological innovations. Because of increasing levels of education, larger and larger segments of the population have acquired the taste for art. As a result, the niche for art museums appears to be an ever-expanding one.

Yet in the 1980s and 1990s, artists, philosophers of art, collectors, curators, and critics began to challenge the taken-for-granted definition of art. For example, the questions, "Who defines art?" and "What is art?" open the realm of possibilities to include graffiti works, comic strips, neon lights, "found objects," industrial products, polemical pieces, explicitly "ugly" works, and objects made by a computer. To give an example of the problematic nature of art in the 1990s, I briefly describe a work by Fred Wilson. He is considered to be a major contemporary artist, and was selected to represent the United States at the 1992 Biennale. His works are exhibited at many American museums. At one exhibit in 1991 at the Smithsonian Museum he engaged two Mexican actors as part of a performance exhibit. The actors put themselves in a gilded cage that he designed and that was placed in the rotunda of the Smithsonian. Inside the cage, the Mexican performers wore masks and colorful Guatemalan garments, but carried leather briefcases. Typing on computers, they drank Coca-Cola and ate bananas. As museum goers flocked around them, they stopped their computer "work" and reached out of the cage to beg ("dinero, dinero"), indicating to those that had cameras that for a bit more "dinero" they would be happy to pose: "Pho-to, pho-to, pho-to" (*Art Papers* 1993).

It is often said that the line between popular culture and High Art is becoming increasingly blurred,[1] but Wilson's exhibit (and others like it) raises questions about both the nature of art and the relationship of art to politics and to contemporary culture. The master canon of High Art is under attack. So far, the museum as an organizational form has not been jeopardized—that is, existing ones have accommodated themselves to these transformations in art—although there is evidence of a slowing rate of new museum foundings. In this chapter I examine the history of the museum as an organizational form, the great importance of aesthetic theory (which is the ideational environment for the art museum), and the perception that art is a public good.

SOURCES OF LEGITIMACY

In organizational theory legitimacy is all important as an explanation for the emergence and persistence of an organizational form. It signals that the form is institutionalized and has a taken-for-grantedness (Hannan and Freeman 1989). Museums depend on two sources for their legitimacy: the social construction of High Art, and a political-legal framework that recognizes the importance of public goods.

This abstract conception of social construction that underlies High Art is especially powerful for understanding cultural organizations because their sheer existence lies outside of practicality. And, powerful institutional actors have vested interests in the social construction. These include social and economic elites, members of the academy, and producers of culture. Museums cannot be understood independently of artworks—or, more precisely, the evaluations of experts and collectors—and in this way the social construction of what is art legitimizes the museum as an organizational form. A social construction, thus, effects the ways in which museums can exploit resources, and, likewise, how museums are exploited as a resource in their own right.

Stated differently, the source of legitimacy for the museum form is fundamentally related to the distinction between Popular Culture and High Culture. However, these terms trivialize what we historically have come to consider a truly moral distinction. Instead, what is involved is nonart versus art, or, to put a metaphysical spin on it, *Überfluss*—the superfluous and unauthentic—versus *Erlebnis*—the profound and life-changing. Thus, on the one hand, the social construction distinguishes between television soap operas, popular magazines, and rock music, and, on the other, ballet, poetry, and chamber music. The social construction, however, is challenged on many fronts: "cross-over" music; the recognition of superior visual and technical qualities in the commercial arts; the impact of the traditions embodied in the "serious" arts on commercial undertakings; and the authentication of previously unrecognized or autonomous art traditions (such as folk and urban black art).

The arts are also increasingly commentaries on social life, and directly confront issues relating to economic justice, abortion, ethnicity, race, religion, and gender politics. An example from literature, Salman Rushdie's *The Satanic Verses* provides a dramatic example of the contentiousness of art and also the power of art in the contemporary world. While many critics have defended *The Satanic Verses* as a brilliant novel and major literary achievement, Rushdie's novel was banned by many countries with substantial Muslim populations and a death decree was issued against him. The point was early made by Plato that art can be morally and politically subversive, but I shall describe how this potential of art was virtually ignored within the Western tradition, from the period of the Enlightenment to contemporary times.

Aside from aesthetic evaluations, the conception of public goods also plays an important legitimizing function for art museums. The organization and economics of art museums cannot be understood independently of the definition of public goods, but this definition changes over time and varies among different countries. In contemporary European countries, the arts (museums, orchestras, dance companies) are subsidized at fairly high levels. Although prevailing levels of subsidization are not as high in the United States compared to European nations, there is also a conception in the United States that the arts (like education and health care) must be, at least in part, supported by government agencies because they contribute to the public welfare and are not self-supporting.

In the arts, this conception encounters difficulties when some segments of the community defend a work on the basis of artistic criteria, while others denounce it on political, social, or religious grounds. Since the 1970s, there have been increasing numbers of encounters between government officials and artists that hinge on the question of the public interest, and hence, the nature of art as a public good. Just to give one example, a sculpture commissioned in 1986 for the San Diego court house depicted an immigration officer searching an undocumented Mexican worker. Descriptions suggest that it was provocative because of its sympathetic portrayal of the Mexican—atop a donkey cart—and the unsympathetic portrayal of the immigration officer. It was challenged by the San Diego Chamber of Commerce and subsequently removed (Dubin 1992, p. 75). Thus, quite aside from the aesthetic merits of artwork, questions are raised about underwriting the costs of something that is made for public display when it is critical of the underwriters, or, raises uncomfortable political questions. What is, in other words, the public interest?

Both conceptions—High Art and public goods—evolved within the social and economic context of the nineteenth century, and in the twentieth century there were expanding resources for cultural organizations, including a growing mass audience, schools of art, and a market for collectors and patrons. However, the last decades have posed challenges to the legitimacy of the concept of artworks as well as to the idea that art is a public good, and resources for art have been jeopardized by competing claims on economic resources. The implications of this argument are examined with historical data on art museums.

THE ENVIRONMENTAL NICHE

Urban places have an unusual capacity to foster artistic inventiveness, create art markets, generate audiences, and attract tourists. As Bourdieu and Darbel (1990) note in a survey of museums and art attendance in five countries, Paris is exceptional in its number of museums and strikingly high rate of museum attendance. The authors attribute this interest to the exceptional tastes and cultivated dispositions of Parisians. However, such tastes and dispositions are difficult to distinguish from more global characteristics of cities such as sheer population size, location, and urban resources (Blau 1989). For example, Paris is an old city and the capital of a prosperous nation and formerly the seat of kings and center for vast religious undertakings. These days, Paris attracts huge numbers of tourists, many (if not most) of whom visit its museums. This, in turn, encourages the city to devote more resources to its museum industry.

To make this point that large places become museum centers, which increases the likelihood of these places supporting even more museums, Table 5-1 provides a partial list of art museums located in one square-mile of the U.S. capital. Because Washington, D.C., itself has one of the highest unemployment rates and highest school dropout rates in the nation, it is difficult to attribute Washington's prominence as a museum center to the unique artistic interests of resident Washingtonians. Rather, art museums have a special symbolic importance in national capitals. These capitals provide the suitable distinguished environment for art, and because art itself is bestowed with legitimacy of a high order, it serves its nation's capital. Thus art has moral and political importance, in addition to its aesthetic significance.

It is often assumed that there are a few major cities that dominate over all others in their cultural resources, including the visual arts. In one sense this is true. The prestige and sizes of museums in Washington, D.C., New York City, and Chicago are incomparable. Yet we find that cities of all sizes located throughout the United States have acquired their own art museums. It is frequently the case that a museum is established by a local affluent family that has collected works of art, then willed it to the city or local college, which seeks funding through government and foundation sources, and then ultimately incorporates the museum as a nonprofit enterprise. When we examine a cross-section of medium to large U.S. cities by the number of art museums each has and the city's population, it is evident that population is a good predictor of the number of museums a city supports. Population is a proxy for urban resources and for demand (potential visitors). Figure 5-1 is a plot of logged number of art

Table 5–1 Major art museums in downtown Washington, by year of founding

1783	Anderson House. Works from the revolutionary war period.
1792	White House. Nineteenth- and twentieth-century American and French collections.
1793	Capitol. Art and sculpture in the Old Senate Chambers, President's Room, and the Old Supreme Court.
1846	National Museum of American Art. Large collection of American art.
1869	Corcoran Gallery. American art and European Old Masters.
1891	Dumbarton Oaks. Pre-Columbian art.
1906	Freer Gallery. Oriental collection and American art influenced by Far Eastern traditions.
1918	Phillips Collection. French Impressionists, American Modernists.
1937	National Gallery of Art. European and American works, twelfth century to the present.
1957	B'nai B'rith Klutznick Museum. Jewish ceremonial and folk art.
1961	Diplomatic Reception Rooms of the State Department. Eighteenth- and nineteenth-century American art and furniture.
1962	National Portrait Gallery. Paintings, sculptures, photographs.
1964	National Museum of African Art. Traditional art of the sub-Sahara.
1966	Hirshhorn Museum. Nineteenth- and twentieth-century art.
1972	Renwick Gallery. American crafts and decorative arts.
1976	Art Museum of the Americas. Twentieth-century Latin American art.
1981	National Museum of Women in the Arts. Works by female artists, sixteenth through twentieth centuries.
1982	Arthur N. Sackler Gallery. Asian art.

Sources: Artwise Washington DC: The Museum Map (Streetwise Maps Inc., 1991); American Association of Museums, *Official Museum Directory* (Chicago: National Register Publishing, 1992).

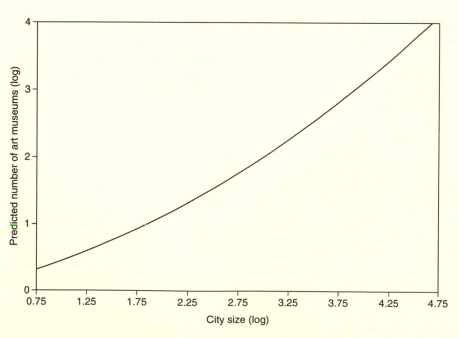

Figure 5–1 Art museums by city size. (*Source:* Author's analysis.)

museums by logged population for the largest 125 U.S. metropolitan places—that is, all places with at least a quarter of a million people.

It is clear that the relationship is not linear, but rather that population size has a multiplier effect on the number of art museums. This is also the case for other types of elite culture suppliers, such as theater companies, opera companies, and symphonies. That is, New York City, Chicago, and Los Angeles have more art museums and symphony orchestras than they "deserve" given the sizes of their populations, whereas Akron, Lansing, and Milwaukee have somewhat fewer. This analysis suggests that niche crowding can be beneficial. The largest American cities and also the nation's capital (which has a population about half that of Chicago) provide rich environments for art museums. However, the graph indicates that there are no real monopolies, that is, cities of all sizes acquire art museums and there is a rough correspondence between population size and the numbers of museums.

ORGANIZATIONAL DYNAMICS OVER TIME

Early Beginnings

The cultural retardedness of Americans is often exaggerated. It is true that in the early decades of the nineteenth century, American audiences were largely ignorant, if not contemptuous, of European art. The combined historical experiences of the revolution and the Puritan tradition set Americans against art that was associated with aristocracy and Catholicism. Furthermore, while Americans were preoccupied with nation building during the eighteenth and nineteenth centuries, the elites of Europe, along with churches, continued to amass and consolidate their great art collections. However, these were privately owned, and except for religious art, not in the public domain. The very concept of public art was hatched on August 10 1793, when the doors of the Louvre were thrown open to the public, precisely one year to the day after the monarchy was overthrown.

However, the Louvre was a precocious beginning, and it was not until later in the nineteenth century that most of today's most prestigious museums were established: London's National Gallery (1832), Victoria and Albert (1851), and the Tate (1897); The Prado in Spain (1819); Moscow's Hermitage (1852); and Holland's Rijksmuseum (1885). Others were not open to the public until the twentieth century, such as Florence's Pitti Palace in 1919 and the Pinacoteca Nazionale in Sienna in 1915. The institutionalization of public art occurred in the United States following the Civil War, about in synch with the patterns in European countries, even in the absence of a long tradition of elite and religious patronage. Boston's Museum of Fine Arts and New York's Metropolitan Museum opened in the early 1870s, Chicago's Art Institute in 1879. Of course, art museums that specialize in "modern art" rather than collections of "old masters" are creations of the twentieth century. Although the Pompidou in Paris, New York's Museum of Modern Art, and the Pasadena Museum of Modern Art have different sorts of works compared with, say, the Metropolitan Museum or the Tate, they differ in insignificant ways from their older counterparts with respect to administration, educational programs, fund-raising efforts, and so forth. The organizational form has not changed much since the Louvre opened in 1793.

Art Museum Foundings in the United States

Figure 5-2 is a plot of the foundings of all existing art museums in the United States from 1810 to 1992. Owing to the initial large investments in the building and collection, a museum rarely closes. Thus, the plot includes virtually all of the art museums that were ever founded. It is evident that the rate of founding has accelerated over time. As already mentioned, the idea of the art museum was slow to catch on. Virtually all of the antebellum public museums were affiliated with colleges: the Mead Art Center in Amherst (1821), the Museum of Art at Bowdoin (1811), and the Trumbull Gallery at Yale (1832). After the Civil War, there was a slow but steady increase in the number of new museums. After around 1900, it is evident that the number of annual foundings accelerated over time. This is understandable given the increasing support for culture.

After 1930, there are three notable declines in annual foundings. The first occurred during the 1940s, when public resources were deployed in the war effort. The second dip in the early 1970s was short-lived and, relative to the one in the 1940s, not very pronounced. This decline is probably related to the consequences of expansion in the early to mid-1960s in the ensuing context of an uncertain economic and funding environment of the late 1960s. However, the founding rate plummeted in the late 1970s, and in the 1980s through the early 1990s it exhibits an unusual pattern of general decline, with an occasional "boom" year and subsequent "bust" year. On the basis of the pattern observed after about 1978, it would be difficult to predict a trend for the last years of the twentieth century and the beginning of the twenty-first century.

A statistical analysis of the periodization of the founding rate trajectory reported in Figure 5-2 indicates organizational dynamics that are fairly consistent with social historical accounts of museums in the United States (Blau 1991). Figure 5-2 and Table 5-2 provide a broad summary of the points I make in this chapter.

Nineteenth Century

As subsequently interpreted, Section I, Article 8 of the Constitution protects the proprietary rights of the artist, but does little for the arts. However, President John Quincy Adams called for "laws promoting . . . the cultivation and encouragement of the mechanic and of the elegant arts, the advancement of literature" (quoted in Cummings 1991, p. 33). The early results were nothing but disastrous. The first official commissions by Congress, notably John Trumbull's paintings for the Capitol rotunda and the centennial sculpture of George Washington by Horatio Greenough, aroused such controversy—justifiable in the views of contemporary art historians—that the federal government withdrew from patronage for the remainder of the century.

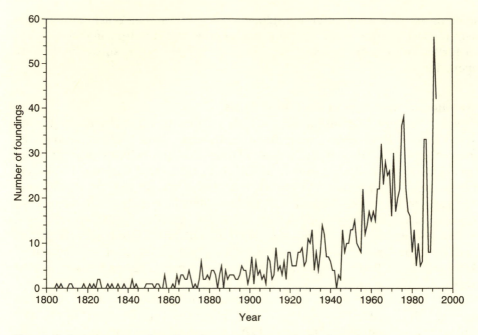

Figure 5–2 Art museum foundings by year. (*Source:* Author's analysis.)

As a result, artists banded together to form associations and turned to wealthy elites for support. Increasingly, elites (not artists) played the predominant role in mobilizing civic leaders in museum-building efforts in the postbellum period. Extant documents reflect complex motivations (DiMaggio 1987). One was philanthropic and civil pride. Another was fostered by the prestige or the cultural capital (Bourdieu 1984) that has historically accompanied patronage of the arts. Still another was confounded with the new nationalistic spirit, which fostered both the promotion of American arts and competition with European countries to acquire collections of the established and respectable masters as well as, somewhat later, works in "experimental" styles, such as paintings by the French Impressionists.

As far as the general public was concerned, there was no clear distinction between popular and high culture. While most Americans in the nineteenth century, according to Levine (1988), loved and recited Shakespeare and attended the public theaters in which minstrels and Italian opera were presented together, there was little interest in the visual arts. This was in part due to the religious sentiments that were widespread in evangelical and Puritan America. However, thanks to P. T. Barnum and the "dime circus," the American public was introduced to artworks. Classical sculptures and landscapes mingled with wax works, live entertainment, and flea circuses in what have been called the earliest form of the American museum (Meyer 1979).

Paradoxically, increasing affluence and increasing economic inequalities appear to have both played a role in stimulating museum building and creating

Table 5–2 Museum environments by period

Historical epoch	Cultural definition	Social and economic dynamics	Organizational mandate	Organizational leaders	Funding sources
19th century until 1900	Preservation	Inequalities/increasing affluence	Social control/edification	Elites	Economic elites
Early 20th century 1900–1930	Sublime/moral	Increasing educational attainments	Art is educational	Curators	Economic elites
1930–1960	High Art and Popular Art separate/Avant-Garde	Cosmopolitan public	Art is public good	Curators/educators/administrators	Museum members/public
Arts boom 1960–1980	Blur High Art and Popular Art	Art is legitimate	Translate to public	Arts critics	Federal government: NEA
Post-1980	Politicization of art	Recession/finance capitalism	Fund-raising	Financial experts	States/earned income

public interest in the arts. Industrial development in the last decades of the nineteenth century was accompanied by high rates of immigration, disruptive social change and poverty, exploitation of workers, appalling industrial conditions, and a high degree of residential segregation that reflected ethnic antagonisms. Estimates for northern U.S. cities suggest that around 1870, the top one-tenth of one percent had between 15 percent to 24 percent of the wealth (Gallman 1969). It is generally agreed that a major motivation to endow cities with cultural enterprises was to preserve the symbolic boundaries between the small elite and the growing masses. But this aim could not be achieved without demonstrating to the masses what these nuanced boundaries meant. In the Progressive Era at the end of the century, social control and social amelioration were inexorably intertwined. Moreover, in the context of inequality (sustained through high rates of immigration), educational levels were rising as were incomes. Wages (in real dollars) increased about 50 percent between 1860 and 1890 (Long 1960).

It is important to add that the volunteerism that was initially fueled by religion increasingly played an important role in promoting a climate within the nonprofit sector for the support of the arts. Thus, while wealthy elites provided essential financial resources, members of the growing middle class provided their free and paid time to museums (as well as to libraries, hospitals, social services agencies). Besides, they were on their way to becoming members of eager audiences.

As Figure 5-2 indicates, the trajectory of annual foundings is initially virtually flat. As already described, during the early decades of the century small museums were founded by colleges, and it was not until the postbellum period that many of America's most notable museums were established. In these postbellum decades the founding rate accelerated. The first row of Table 5-2 summarizes these social and organizational patterns that prevailed during this period. It should be emphasized that what we consider to be the very essence of artistic endeavors—creativity—was still not fully accepted by the elites that sponsored High Art. And, in fact, many of America's famous nineteenth-century painters—Mary Cassatt, John Singer Sargent, and James Whistler—studied and worked in Europe in the absence of support in the United States for their innovative work. The United States was not yet a major player in the art world.

Early Twentieth Century: The Emergence of a Middle Class
Given the considerable economic inequalities and high rates of immigration, it is surprising that instead of increasing polarization, a genuine shared culture was shaped by what Blumin (1989) terms the "middlin' folk." From the congeries of occupations that comprised the growing urban middle class emerged a lifestyle, set of behavioral codes, and social conventions that helped to shape cultural tastes. Part of the explanation for the expansion of middle-class culture was an improved standard of living and the availability of new consumer goods. This situation created rising expectations and an eagerness to participate in urban culture, and these were matched by an expansion in cultural opportunities. The other part of the explanation relates to the relative ease with which

new immigrants and their children could adopt the cultural codes of urban na-
tives. These cultural codes were not so old or codified that they defied imitation. A modest civic life, void of aristocratic conditions, contributed substantially to the success of middle-class culture.

As Kammen describes, "[Conditions] in America meant that indications of
inequality would be less visible than in Europe" (1980, p. 277). A main mechanism was the proliferation of middle-class institutions that were widely accessible to the rich and poor, and the high—and often realistic expectations—for
mobility, if not for oneself, then at least for one's children. Yet part of this story
is that without aristocratic traditions, urban elites were eager to justify themselves to the masses. Notwithstanding conspicuous violations, notably in large
cities, a deep-rooted commitment to simplicity in American life was linked to
highly practical lifestyles and modesty of consumption. The fact that pragma-
tism and democratic values pervaded education as well contributed to the ease
of access of people with humble origins to middle-class status. Under these
conditions there was an increasing finessing of class lines in terms of residence,
lifestyle, and affiliations, which meant an expanding interest in culture and the
arts.

However, both in European countries and in the United States the line between popular, vernacular culture and that of high culture grew increasingly
rigid. While vaudeville, sports, and other amusements were tamed and pressed
into service to provide forms of entertainment, the arts were increasingly defined in loftier terms. While High Art was bracketed, consumerism was linked
with leisure by means of the department store, vaudeville, public theaters,
newspapers, city parks, spectator sports, city festivals, traveling exhibits, and,
later, the radio and the cinema. Overproduction and the ready availability of
inexpensive clothing and housewares were especially important in contributing
to a middle-class lifestyle.

Nevertheless, a growing distrust of popular culture began to surface during
this period. Intellectuals, such as Oswald Spengler (1926/1928), were appalled
by "massification" just as the nineteenth-century elites had been contemptuous
of saloons, vaudeville, and other forms of working-class entertainment. This
feeling helped to further elevate the elite or traditional arts. However, this period is also critical in that it anticipates the later acceptance of what became
the avant-garde. While undoubtedly most art lovers during these initial decades
of the twentieth century anticipated each museum visit to be an encounter with
the beautiful and sublime, a few attended art galleries that were launching exhibits that museums would accept only later, in the 1940s. It was in these galleries that the provocative, banal, and atrociously "ugly" works were viewed
and discussed by the discerning few.

As Figure 5-2 indicates, there was a fairly steady increase in the number of
art museum foundings during this period. The second row in Table 5-2 summarizes the discussion of this epoch, and also draws attention to the organizational features of the art museum. These museums were still almost totally
dependent on wealthy families and whatever support could be obtained from
local governments. However, a form of indirect national support was enacted
by Congress. The 1918 Federal Inheritance Tax provided for the inclusion of

the arts as a deductible contribution, and therefore provided museums with an indirect federal subsidy. The increasing complexities of acquisition and collection management are reflected in the growing importance of the professional curator.

The 1930s Through the 1950s

With the exception of the war years, this period was one of extraordinary growth in the numbers of art museums. Important programs of the New Deal provided work for artists, and, although arts institutions were not supported, these federal programs may have indirectly offset the effects of the Depression on museum foundings (Figure 5-2).

The postwar period (like that between 1900 and 1930) was one of continued economic prosperity, and a dramatic increase in school enrollments had implications for a growing interest in the arts. Many of the immigrants who arrived during and after the war were especially well educated, and a sufficient number of them had been involved in artistic and literary circles in European countries, which had a profound effect on American artists, collectors, gallery owners, and, ultimately, the public. It was during this period that the United States became an important contender, if not the main leader, in modern art. Abstract Expressionism appeared in the late 1940s and American artists—Robert Motherwell, Willem De Kooning, Barnett Newman, Jackson Pollack—became household names. On an unprecedented scale, American learned the historical landmarks of Western art, the way to "look at" a painting, and gave themselves over to be educated in the traditional canon of High Art.

This was also the period in which the line between High Art and Popular Art was greatly reinforced. The expanded mandate of museums included new professional roles, including arts administrators, an educational staff, librarians, and archivists. Not only was this a response to the growing public interest in art, but also a strategy to attract more museum members and philanthropists, for even with the support of private foundations, funding problems reached critical levels.

It was during this period that High Art was linked with the public goods argument. It was initially John Dewey (1958 [1934]), famous philosopher and leading school reformer, who defended art as being educational and, by implication, worthy of national support. Yet there was widespread ambivalence about this position, which, in large part, can be traced to fear of public influence in the arts. After all, the masses, it was noted, valued kitsch over art, entertainment over the sublime. For this reason, some leaders of the museum movement expressed the position that the arts should remain in the domain of the nonprofit sector and rejected the idea of federal support for museums. Such a position was not inconsistent with the programs of the New Deal that supported artists rather than art organizations. For example, one publication of the American Association for Adult Education warned against federal support of the arts that "would make our treasures a weapon of politics" and "create dependence on the masses" (Adam 1937, p. 23). Such arguments as these continue to play a role in shaping subsequent legislation for the National Endowment for the Arts. Yet, what chiefly shaped arts organizations during this period was not so much this contention as to whether art was a public good or not, but rather the emergence of the avant-garde (Table 5-2).

The Arts Boom of the 1960s Through the 1970s

It was only with the advent of the "Great Society" programs and the administrations of Kennedy and Johnson that the arts were fully joined with the conception of public goods, and the rhetoric that motivated social programs also fueled the arguments for establishing the National Endowment for the Arts (NEA). Kennedy moved cautiously in view of considerable political opposition, but finally in 1965, legislation for both NEA and the National Endowment for the Humanities passed, though funding remained small until after the end of the Vietnam War. It was under the presidencies of Nixon, Ford, and Carter that arts subsidies programs flourished.

The legislation that was passed in 1965 was in formal terms very similar to that of other social programs; notably, it required state involvement and stressed block grants over direct subsidization. However, ambivalence about an arts program led to a far greater emphasis on the catalytic role of the NEA compared with its counterparts mandated to provide social programs. Earned income, foundation and corporate support, indirect support through tax policies, and federal and local funds constituted the complex mix of financial support for museums through the 1970s.

Post-1980

Following the long postwar boom from 1945, the recession that began in 1973 and from which the country never fully recovered (Harrison and Bluestone 1990) was one that probably had more devastating effects on the art world than most institutional sectors, owing to its special vulnerabilities. Structural changes in the economy hurt the middle class more than the rich, and it was, after all, the middle class on whom artists and museums had become especially dependent. Concerns with poverty, and inequalities between women and men, and between blacks and whites, certainly are evident in artists' manifestos and in their works.

The period of about 1980 through 1992, as indicated in Figure 5-2, was a tumultuous one. I trace these altercations to an economic downturn and also to the increasing ambivalence (if not hostility) expressed by public officials about the trends in art. Moreover, there was a new political philosophy in the 1980s that emphasized privatization, and this entailed a devolution of funding for many programs. Moreover, the 1980s were also accompanied by the downscaling of major corporations, declining profits, and huge deficits, which in turn had great consequences for corporate philanthropy (Parker 1991).

Beginning with the Bush administration, NEA appropriations were slashed and states were asked to share a greater load of the fiscal responsibilities for the arts. To illustrate, in 1979 NEA funds were approximately 80 percent more than state appropriations, whereas in 1989, state appropriations were approximately 60 percent more than NEA funds. Indirect federal subsidies that had traditionally been the rationale for individual charitable deductions to the arts were dramatically reduced by the 1986 tax law (Weil 1991). In short, the message to arts organizations was that they were to turn to individual subscribers for their support. The concept of art as a public good was under serious attack.

While there is no indication that museum attendance has declined (Blau and Quets 1989), and, in fact, earned income has increased for museums (DiMaggio 1991a), the economic environment for museums, beginning in the 1980s, has been highly uncertain. As Table 5-2 indicates, fund-raising problems have created new administrative burdens for museum staff. At the same time, art itself is in a stage of transformation, and the political dimension of aesthetics has become especially salient.

AESTHETICS AND THE ART MUSEUM

Artworks as a Social Construction

How does the conception of art become widely accepted? One useful way of viewing legitimation is as an institutional process of labeling. Such labels, writ large or small, are then deployed in everyday life to make distinctions that apply to concrete practices and to real things (Becker 1974). Labeling art by aesthetic evaluations and distinguishing art from nonart is relatively recent. Before public art museums, we can assume that private patrons collected art objects for their beauty or because they were canonical with courtly and churchly traditions. They were produced and enjoyed as part of daily social practice and amusement, or were the means of enforcing religious beliefs and dignifying political power. Craft and art were indistinguishable, and so joined provided a suitable medium for the expression of political, religious, and, social values. This was the case even in the Renaissance—both in Italy and Holland—as patron and artist worked in close cooperation and celebrated artworks that reflected common values of state, church, commerce, empire, and natural beauty.

It was Immanuel Kant who in the late eighteenth century formalized the Western concept of aesthetics. As the illuminary of the German Enlightenment, Kant's position was that something has artistic beauty if it is a beautiful representation of a thing. Kantian aesthetics joined art with beauty, and bracketed them together as something special that reflects the finality, purposiveness, and order of things. Art possesses moral significance. The Kantian world of taste is one in which we all agree about what is beautiful. He wrote, "The beautiful is the symbol of the morally good, and only in this light . . . does it give pleasure with a claim to the agreement of every one else" (Kant 1952 [1790], p. 353).

Aside from the complexities of aesthetic theory that slowly penetrated into the thinking of European philosophers and the lives of European elites, the consequences of making the distinction in the first place are profound. For the purposes here, two Kantian precepts are important. The first is that the judgments about art are universal; that is, we all agree about artistic qualities; there is no relativism or skepticism in matters of taste. Second, by assuming that art is sublime and not at all practical, then art exists in an autonomous sphere. That is to say, that art exists for its own sake (Gadamer 1986); art is distinct from politics (Koselleck 1988); and art is an autonomous symbol system that has "import," not meaning—in the sense that theory and knowledge have meaning (Langer 1957). In other words, we just enjoy art for its intrinsic pleasure, beauty, and delight. This is what is morally good about art. Again to oversimplify a bit, two traditions would draw on Kantian aesthetics in seeming contradiction with one another. One is the modernist tradition and the other is the avant-garde.

The Modernist Tradition

As direct descendants of the Enlightenment, Modernists self-consciously traced a canon of beauty through Western art, from Greek and Roman ideals, to the art of the Middle Ages, through the Renaissance and Baroque styles, and then to nineteenth-century landscapes and genre paintings. This tradition informs the core collection of major European and American art museums. Such a collection defines the canon of High Art and rests on authoritative judgments about beauty, technique, and a sense of historical continuity.

In the nineteenth century, authentication techniques supplemented aesthetic theory to establish the principle that artworks were educational. Works from all continents of the world were collected, classified, tamed, and decontextualized. The authentication of artworks also purged the unchaste and the vulgar.

Moreover, this conception of art is important for understanding how it can be said that politics are divorced from art and that those trained in aesthetics are the ones who make artistic evaluations. It follows from this conception that if there was going to be High Art enveloped within an institutional context, the residue, Popular Art, is something else and exists outside the realm of genuine art and aesthetic evaluations.

The implications of presentation and labeling art in museums were not questioned by an aesthetic philosophy of the nineteenth century, nor even in the early decades of the twentieth century (for which avant-garde works were described in neo-Kantian terms of expression and genius). But to anticipate what is now widely considered to be the death of the avant-garde, the museum idea was under attack as early as the mid-1960s.

Contemporary aesthetic theorists now interpret modernism as a denial of hegemonic conceptions that were inherent in the nineteenth century—that is, for example, ideas about the superiority of colonial nations, ideas about the proper place of women and of people of color. It was acknowledged that there had been a failure to recognize diverse national traditions, and a wedding of the interests of powerful nations to their artistic traditions. This modern tradition in art is compared by Arthur Danto (1985, p. 18) to the proverbial pedestal upon which Western males put their women:

> It was a bold and finally successful strategy, leaving serious artists to suppose it their task to make beauty; so the metaphysical pedestal upon which art gets put

[the museum] is a political translocation as savage as that which turned women
into ladies, placing them into parlours doing things that seemed like purposive
labour without specific purpose.

Within this modern tradition, an expression surfaced in the mid-1800s, *l'art
pour l'art*. What it essentially meant was that art exists for the sake of art, and
it is the artist (not the expert or the public) that must be the judge of art because
he (or she) possesses unique creative insight, intuition, and skills. It was then
that a new view of the artist emerged: eccentric, estranged, if not deranged.
This then was the beginning of a side tradition in aesthetics, the view that art
is alienated or is autonomous from society (see Wolff 1983).

The Avant-Garde

From their very early origins avant-gardists made it a special point to explain
that their work altered conventional style without tampering with art as a distinct (and moral) category (see Baudelaire 1979 [1846]). Painters drew attention
to their own commitments to "meaning" (Klee 1964 [1898/1918]) to "latent
truths" and "pure art" (Kandinsky 1947). The avant-garde was an reinterpre-
tation within Kantian aesthetics; instead of expressing a historical manifest
destiny, artworks embodied the artist's creative vision, which viewers could
discover. From a sociological perspective, a convincing explanation of the success of the French Impressionists, probably the most significant avant-gardist
movement in the nineteenth century, is provided by White and White (1965).
They show how the modernist tradition collapsed in Paris as the result of structural reasons. There were too many artists applying to study in the over-
crowded academy, insufficient numbers of buyers and patrons, and a boring
uniformity in late nineteenth-century art style.

At the turn of the twentieth century, an avant-garde had emerged that was
explicitly antibourgeois, anticanon, but, nevertheless, not antiart. A useful
marker for American audiences was Duchamp's cubist painting, *Nude Descending a Stair Case,* exhibited in New York City in 1912. It was followed in
1917 by *The Fountain,* his famous autographed urinal. While the urinal appeared to be an assault on the very concept of art, Duchamp noted that because
photographs could reproduce visual images, artists would have to explore new
realms of expression (Shapiro 1976, p. 92). Duchamp's works were not completely revolutionary either. His precursors included the Spanish painter, Francisco Goya, and the Impressionists (as earlier, Manet's painting of contemporary, dressed males accompanying nude women for a picnic had shocked
Parisians). The Post-Impressionists (such as Gauguin and Van Gogh) and, in
very important ways, Picasso, also helped to prepare the battlefields, and in
early decades of the century there was a rapid succession of avant-garde movements, or "ism" movements—Dadaism, Cubism, Futurism, Surrealism—and
later—Expressionism, Photorealism, Minimalism.

The End of the Avant-Garde/Modernism

The point is made by contemporary philosophers of art (e.g., Bürger 1992;
Danto 1985; Ventós 1980) that the avant-garde that emerged in Europe in all of

the arts posed no great threat to the status quo. It was not an art of the street or of politics in any important sense and its qualities of interiority, isolation, and self-reference rendered it impotent to seriously challenge Modernist ideals. A consensus had emerged in the late 1960s that the avant-garde involved merely a formal revolution within Modernism. Art critic Harold Rosenberg (1967) observed that as early as the 1940s the significant reason the American museum existed was to display the works of the avant-gardists, and successive art movements played out logical contrapuntal queries within the framework of the dynamic that was Modernism. He noted, "In the ideologies of recent art movements art-historical reasoning has been offered as a substitute for consciousness of history. In this parody of vanguardism, which revives the academic idea of art as a separate 'realm,' art can make revolutionary strides without causing a ripple in the streets or in the mind of a collector" (p. 91).

Yet the philosophical tide was turning. Adorno (1982 [1967], p. 173) writes: "The German word *museal* [museumlike] has unpleasant overtones. It describes objects to which the observer no longer has a vital relationship and which are in the process of dying. They owe their preservation more to historical respect than to the needs of the present. Museum and mausoleum are connected by more than phonetic association. Museums are the family sepulchres of works of art." There were other critics. The practice of institutional labeling, Herbert Marcuse observed, purges history and art of consciousness of evil. He describes the location of the famous Prado collection of paintings by Goya. His paintings that depict the brutality, stupidity, and horror of imperial wars were hung by museum curators next to the portraits of the very kings who instigated the wars and presided over the terror. "The immediate response, not psychologically or physiologically sublimated (vomiting, weeping, furor, etc.), is transformed into esthetic experience" (quoted in Ventós 1980, p. 45).

In the 1960s, anti–status quo and politicized art began to emerge. Early signs included artists wrapping museums in canvas, exhibits of graffiti in New York's SoHo galleries, Happenings, and artworks that self-destructed. Increasingly, critics tracked the commingling of street works with art-art, commercial art with art-art, and political art with art-art. Certainly, the lines between commerce, politics, and art were blurring in the late 1970s. Various manifestos reveal the betrayal of the avant-gardist position: "Main Street is alright" (Venturi 1966); "Imagination without skill gives us modern art" (Stoppard 1973); "No more narrative . . . subject . . . object . . . no more representation" (Owens 1983, p. 66).

Under scrutiny is the very idea of the museum, which is challenged by antimodernist currents. Art, it is said, may not prevail. It is not different from everyday praxis (Habermas, 1983); it will not survive the contemporary assault on Western metaphysics (Jameson 1991, p. 27); it will be replaced by endless reproduction (Benjamin 1969); it is the trivialization of ideology (Eagleton 1991, p. 168), and the denial of contradictions (Foster 1985).

Others argue that art has been replaced by "identity politics" and absorbed into political culture as statements about race, gender, and ethnicity. In the late 1980s, works by feminists, homosexuals, and blacks challenged the public on new grounds. As Dubin (1992, p. 5) states, contemporary artists fiddled with what many hold to be "natural categories," such as "the chaste and polluted, masculine and feminine, in and out, public and private." Art critics mused in deprecating tones: "Art Is Only When" (Goodman 1978); "The Museum Is Dead" (Crimp 1983); "Metaphysics Is Dead" (Dziemidok 1985); "Epistemology Is Dead" (Vattimo 1985); "The Audience Is Dead" (Gopnik 1992).

THE GOOD OF ART

If Kant refused to wed the arts to specific practical purposes, his contemporaries spelled out the connection very clearly. The good of a nation is promoted by the arts, Adam Smith wrote, because they aid in developing the "general probity of manners," and "by encouraging poetry, music, dancing, dramatic representations and exhibitions," the state can combat the "vices of levity that arise from great prosperity" (1937 [1776], pp. 746, 748). Kant's French contemporaries were thinking pretty much along the same lines: "The task of the fine arts . . ., is to ornament, not only, as some unjustly claim, to give us a merely outward pleasure in attendant attractions, but above all to give our mind and hearts a refined attitude and a nobler character by means of the gentle impression of what is beautiful, harmonious, and charming" (d'Alembert 1992 [1751] pp. 75–76).

It is important to recognize the role of Platonic writings in Enlightenment philosophy; Kant's separation of art from everyday life helped at once to underline and disguise Plato's conception that art is something that is inherently dangerous. In Platonic metaphysics, philosophers possessed understanding and craftworkers possessed practical knowledge, whereas artists simply imitated, and what they imitated they could not understand. Thus, the arts are subversive and must be sanitized—even censored—to serve the interests of philosophy and politics. Danto (1985, p. 14) summarizes: "It is as though Platonic metaphysics was generated in order to define a place for art from which it is then a matter of cosmic guarantee that nothing can be made to happen." Thus the Platonic conception of art as mere reflection and imitation joined Kant's idea of art as beauty.

Thus endowed with practicality or utility, the arts were pressed into service by elites, governments, and the bourgeois as a public good that along with education instills discipline and proper attitudes. But art served this purpose so long as it was sanitized, labeled, and seemingly segregated from the realms of the practical—it could not be commonplace—and from the political—it could not be subversive. Because aesthetic theories of the nineteenth century eliminated the mythic, the sensual, and the polemical potential of art, pedagogical theory could deploy the arts for the purposes of cultivating sensibilities and edification.

One side of the argument, therefore, is that the avant-garde (High Art) is rendered powerless owing to its institutional context. That is, a photograph of refugees, or an ironic representation of the American flag, is art so long as it is placed in a museum. The social, ethical, and political intentions of the artist who paints the flag are thus undermined once the work is positioned in the museum. It is not what the artwork *is* but *where* it is that makes the difference. According to Bürger (1992, p. 10), "What distinguishes the uncoupling of art from the realm of instrumental reason and daily sensuality is exactly what presses art into the markets and dependence on anonymous public." Thus, the once-radical claim of the autonomy of art and art's liberation from social context set artistic production precisely in the marketplace, and hence became subordinate to capitalism, politics, and consumerism.

WHO PAYS THE PIPER: ART AS A PUBLIC GOOD

It was in the context of modernism and avant-gardism that enabling legislation for the National Endowment for the Arts was passed. It was in the context of privatization policies and devolution of federal programs to the states and the private sector that avant-gardism and modernism were challenged. Policies of privatization and devolution themselves raise interesting questions about the locus of authority for purposes of evaluation, of defining what is in the public interest, and of adjudication (Blau 1993). Specific examples clarify the nature of these difficulties (see Dubin 1992).

Richard Serra installed his *Tilted Arc* in 1981 in New York City's Foley Square. It was a curved 120-foot-long sculpture commissioned by the General Service Administration (GSA) with the approval and support of the NEA. After it was installed, however, there was protracted and acrimonious debate involving the artist and members of the arts community, who defended the aesthetic merits of the sculpture; many workers in the local buildings, who claimed it obstructed the plaza; and the GSA, which argued in the end that it could be used as a staging platform by terrorists. In 1989, storms of protest broke out over the Andres Serrano exhibit (that included images of a crucifix immersed in urine) and the Robert Mapplethorpe exhibit (photographs with themes involving interracial sex and homosexuality). The latter two cases technically involved First Amendment issues, but they also raised fundamental questions about public support for the arts in instances in which the classical canon appeared to be under attack.

What is a public good? In traditional economics, the definition rests on the classic position laid out by Samuelson (1954) that emphasizes indivisibility and nonexclusivity. That is, people can consume so long as there is no subtraction from any other individual's consumption. Thus roads and clean air lie within the realm of public goods. The arts have not been so straightforward. Some have argued that arts are not a public good because educated elites benefit at the expense of the poor who are also taxed (e.g., Banfield 1984). But in fact there are very few goods that exhibit the intrinsic characteristics of indivisibility and nonexclusivity (including clean air).

A more flexible definition of a public good recognizes that markets are abysmally poor in providing particular kinds of goods and in these instances they can be protected either in the not-for-profit sector or the public sector, or a combination of the two (Hansmann 1987). In this view, competitive markets are appropriate when resources are the only constraints on choices. However, this view is being challenged as economists observe that there are differences in capabilities to acquire resources, which justifies expanding the domain of public goods (Sen 1992). The basic underpinning of this argument is that public goods are essentially what people are observed to demand outside markets—that is, within the political arena. There is nothing intrinsic in a good to make it public or private, or that it must be supplied in the nonprofit sector.

Consumption is one aspect of the public goods argument. Production is another. The works of artists, inventors, and scientists (e.g., medical researchers) are caught in the calculus of public goods in interesting but different ways. If it is established that the products they create are ones that people value and the society needs, they are placed on the public goods agenda. But that also means that artists, inventors, and scientists ask for financial security, protection from pressure of the competitive marketplace, and (as in the Serra case, for example) protection from the vagaries of public opinion. There are many interesting issues that follow: the question of secrecy in scientific research; the presumption that high financial rewards corrupt altruistic and professional work, the problem of proprietary rights over scientific and creative products. One anomaly in the arts is that while there are laws (however cumbersome and ineffectual) to protect the artists' proprietary rights, and museum collections are maintained (at least in part) by public funding, individual artworks are bought and sold in a private market that is intensely competitive. The astronomically high prices of artworks belie their public character and continue to threaten the integrity of museum collections, as deacquisitioning is a survival strategy in bad times.

In the next section I briefly refer to how social movements put art on the public goods agenda and the implications this has had for the organization and administration of museums. There are paradoxical contradictions between the public goods conception of art and the aesthetic conceptions of artworks. As already discussed, the metaphysical project was successful because it bracketed art as being quite out of the ordinary, but also as being potentially subversive and politically dangerous. The increasing détente between popular and elite culture adds immeasurably to the complexities of these issues.

ORGANIZATIONS, MARKETS, AND SPONSORS

Social and Economic Elites

As Miller (1966) points out, the motivations of philanthropic elites in the nineteenth century were explicitly cast in the language of social control as their communities were threatened by volatile social change. Continuing into the twentieth century, the arts proved useful as an instrument of social control as they had been fully legitimized as being outside the realms of politics and practical life.

Recently the development of interest in high culture has been explained in terms of *cultural capital*—the promotion of and legitimation of activities to unify a social arrangement in the interest of elites and to establish inaccessible codes that would enable elites to maintain power but simultaneously create elusive envy on the part of the subordinated classes (Bourdieu 1984; DiMaggio 1991b).

The concept of cultural capital helps social scientists to organize a large body of research findings that show that well-educated and affluent individuals are more likely to attend museums and buy art, thus setting cultural boundaries between themselves and others (Robinson, Halford, and Triplett 1985).[2] Distinctions in cultural taste become attached to status and to specific social institutions, and thus regulate the rules whereby other inequalities are magnified. In this sense, Lamont and Fournier (1992, p. 3) refer to culture as a form of domination.

The institutions that the elites create and organize play an important role in explaining the nuances of cultural and social domination (Bottomore 1964). This is because the public provision of culture is accompanied by the rhetoric of education and enlightenment. We have only to recall the views of Adam Smith on this point.

Art Markets

Public collections disguise the market character of art. While art lovers and speculators have always mingled, it was only with the maturing of the American avant-garde that prices reached sensational new levels. In the late 1960s, given the scarcity of old masters, works by contemporary painters did spectacularly well in auctions. There are two views about the unrealities of prices for paintings in the 1970s and 1980s. From a purely behavioralist perspective, participation in art markets has been fueled by prospects of economic gain in a highly lucrative market. The high prices at auction houses are attributed by some (see Cantor 1991) to "new collectors"—the newly rich without philanthropic instincts and little knowledge of the arts. This unflattering view of the collector as a pure speculator appears to be partly true. The crash of art pieces in 1990 was in large part due to the withdrawal of the Japanese from London and New York auctions following the highly publicized fraudulent use of thousands of paintings to launder funds in the Tokyo real estate markets (Watson 1992).

From another point of view, genuine difficulties of evaluation have accelerated the speculative nature of art. In the absence of clear-cut standards of evaluation and given the rapid change of styles, buyers can preempt the critic's role by establishing the value of an artist's work by what they are willing to pay (Moulin 1987).

The Administration Model of Nonprofit Organizations

Distinctive organizational features of museums are a function of an attempt to further goals that are not always in synch with one another—preservation, collection of contemporary works, satisfying elite and public sponsors, and education (see Rubenstein 1991).

The transition at the end of the nineteenth century from patron control to standardization by a corps of professionals and bureaucrats was relatively swift

(DiMaggio 1987). With the emergence of avant-garde movements, the priority of preservation gave way to that of collecting new works, and artworks by contemporary American and European painters and sculptors were increasingly attractive. Curatorial positions were staffed by academic PhDs, but around the 1930s—with the increasing emphasis on the role of the arts in education, and the role of education in appreciating the arts (Dewey 1958 [1934]; Reed 1966 [1936])—the new profession of the museum educator emerged. As Zolberg observes, "The curator is the advocate of the artwork" whereas the "museum educator is the advocate of the public" (1986, p. 194). It was the post–World War II years in which art criticism and art history became vital intellectual forces in American universities, training students who would participate in the "arts boom" of the 1960s and 1970s.

By the 1970s, given a growing mass audience and the complexities of funding, administrative problems mushroomed, creating tensions among the divergent goals of museums—that of education, that of maintaining artworks, that of collecting new works, and fund-raising. This was the decade in which another profession, the museum arts administrator, became increasingly important (Zolberg 1986; Peterson 1986). Curators themselves divided into two camps: those who oversaw the preservation of the museums' collection and those who aligned themselves with art critics and artists to keep apace with new developments.

Of course, the arts of the 1970s—photorealism, conceptual art, pattern painting, minimalism, environmental art, and neo-expressionism—did not exactly "speak for themselves" and museum staffs launched educational programs to deal with disparate audiences—the new aficionados and the old-timers. A typical blockbuster exhibit was accompanied by taped tours for the former and special lectures by distinguished scholars for the latter. Expensive books were targeted somewhere in the middle.

Museums in the Corporate World

The increasing dependence of museums on corporate sponsors during the 1980s has been widely discussed. Martorella (1990) reports the growing importance of corporate collectors for shaping trends and fashions in the art world as their decisions about what to buy richochet through the markets comprised of dealers, private collectors, and museum curators. The arts are an effective, subtle, marketing tool. They buy goodwill. Additionally, it has been easy to make the link between artistic freedom and market freedom. Drawing from his interviews with senior managers in large corporations, Useem (1984, p. 124) notes that the arts are viewed within business circles as another technique to reduce employee alienation and to help workers see the connection between freedom in commerce and cultural endeavors. His respondents (top-level executives) explain that the arts help to "promote a culture conducive to the prosperity of free enterprise," and "help to postpone the revolution" because they contribute to the "flourishing of society" (Useem 1984, pp. 124–25).

But the arts and business are thrown together in yet another way. Nonprofit museums have increasingly employed private-sector strategies to deal with environmental uncertainties. As the prices for artworks rose on the auction block and public financial support declined, museums increasingly deacquisitioned from their core collections to buy new works or to pay for day-to-day operations. Other private-sector techniques—raising revenues from published books, restaurants, gift stores, and catalogs—help to bring in small change. Other techniques raise more substantial funds. Air rights enabled the Museum of Modern Art to build a profitable residential tower, and the Los Angeles Symphony owns the Hollywood Bowl, making it possible to subsidize its classical music concerts with popular performances.

The conception of professional educator and keeper of the public treasure is hard to sustain in the face of building financial pressures and the difficulties of enhancing the collection. The "blockbuster" approach used in the 1980s brought in huge crowds, but created tensions within the ranks of curators, and between curators and administrators. Referring to the recent practices of the Guggenheim administration as a "franchise directorship," Richardson (1992) describes the survival strategy as one of deacquisitioning art while acquisitioning museums. The Guggenheim's expansion plans are in various stages of completion: the newly renovated "headquarters"; the Soho branch; a museum in North Adams, Massachusetts; the former "Art of This Century" collection in Venice; an underground museum in Salzburg; a museum in Bilbao; and Dogana di Mare, another Venice project.

Richardson cites the Guggenheim director, Thomas Krens, as saying artworks are "assets that have to be maximized," while Richardson contends that instead they have become the museum's "junk bonds." The point is not an assessment of the survival strategies museum directors currently use, but to suggest that these strategies are strikingly different from those used in the past. They reflect an awareness of a growing mass audience as well as an adaptation of private-sector techniques to nonprofit-sector organizations in the face of new economic and political contingencies.

DISCUSSION

The transformation of the relations among art museums, the public, commerce, the mass media, and politics occurred within an economic context of decline. Having successfully achieved formal recognition of their rights to public entitlements and an informal understanding about being beneficiaries of corporate munificence, museums faced serious economic problems at the end of the 1980s. The public goods issue was again in contention; museums were threatened by the decline of middle-class audiences; cities were losing population at an accelerating rate; sources of revenues were highly uncertain; and no one seemed to know what art was anymore.

During the 1900s, increasing numbers of different types of institutions were defined as providing public goods. Some were better protected than others. Hospitals, libraries, parks, social services, and universities relied on a mix of government, foundation, and private support, but these institutions were largely protected from market forces. There has been, however, considerable contention about the merits of public support for the arts, and museums have had to make the case that art is meritorious. Moreover, the defense of art as autonomous accompanies the argument that art deserves certain privileges and protections.

Yet, on a speculative note, it is possible to discern major transformations in society that will impact on museums. There are obvious signs that the boundaries between High Art and Popular Art are being questioned. In addition, people are becoming cynical about "authoritative" culture of all kinds. On the basis of results of a recent arts survey, Elihu Katz (personal communication) of Hebrew University suggests that there appears to be heightened interest in local and participatory leisure and a disillusionment with culture that is prescriptive or dominating. The implications are that community and amateur leisure—including sports as well as the arts—would prevail over leisure forms devised by professionals. There are also fundamental changes in telecommunications that will facilitate the trend toward participatory leisure. With the increasing dispersion of consumers that accompanies deindustrialization and the advances in computer technology, David Harvey (1989, p. 47) argues that there may be no point to the museum.

Social scientists have urged us to see that changes in institutional legitimacy and the environment have important consequences for organizations (Hannan and Freeman 1989). Such changes are not random, but rather relate to fundamental changes in the economy and in the cultural climate. For example, Hirschman (1982) argues that epochs in which values of privacy prevail are succeeded by epochs in which a spirit of publicness dominates. I have argued in this chapter that fundamental changes in philosophy in the late eighteenth century have had continuing significance for the museum as an organizational form, the way it was exploited by social elites and by educators, and the role it played in shaping the tastes and identities of members of the American middle class.

The fundamental contradictions within Western aesthetics, namely, that artworks are both subversive (Plato) and sublime (Kant), have had far-reaching consequences in the nineteenth and twentieth centuries. These days art is increasingly being defined by philosophers as "mere culture," while artists are breaking down the barriers between artist, artwork, and audience, between what is political and nonpolitical, and between what is historical and what is contemporary. What might be suggested is that after two hundred years, the taken-for-granted status of art is now a matter of reexamination and debate.

NOTES

Research support from the National Science Foundation (SES-8611999; SES-9108923) is gratefully acknowledged. For their assistance with data analysis, I thank Walter Davis and Elizabeth Pressler-Marshall. Extremely helpful comments and suggestions were made by Judith Balfe, Peter Blau, Hannah Bruckner, and Rekha Mirchandani.

1. Throughout this chapter there are references to High Art and High Culture, Popular Art and Popular Culture. Highbrow and lowbrow is a roughly comparable distinction. Because the argument is that the boundary between them is increasingly difficult to define, it can be said that, conventionally, the former is rooted in traditional aesthetics and is situated in art contexts (e.g., the museum) and is usually sponsored by nonprofit organizations. Popular art and culture are vernacular, and often supported by the profit-making sector (e.g., television, professional sports, and film).

2. Conclusions about the composition of the art public are somewhat different when social context is taken into account. Individual attendance is higher in places with little inequality (Blau and Quets 1989), and the individual's likelihood of attendance not only depends on the person's own educational level but also on the overall educational level in the place where the individual lives (Blau 1988). In other words, many of the empirical results dealing with the role of cultural capital are difficult to replicate when individuals' attributes are contextualized.

BIBLIOGRAPHY

Adam, T. R. 1937. *The Civic Value of Museums*. New York: American Association for Adult Education.

Adorno, Theodor W. 1982. (1967). "Valéry Proust Museum." In *Prisms*. Translated by Samuel and Shierry Weber. London: Neville Spearman, pp. 173–86.

American Museum Association. Various Years. *Official Museum Directory*. Chicago: National Register Publishing Co.

Art Papers. 1993. "Constructing the Spectacle of Culture in Museums" (excerpts from lectures given by Fred Wilson and Ivan Karp at the Atlanta College of Art, Fall 1992) 17(May/June):2–9.

Banfield, Edward C. 1984. *The Democratic Muse*. New York: Basic Books.

Baudelaire, Charles. 1979 (1846). "The Museum of Classics at the Bazaar Bonne Nouvelle in the Galerie des Beaux-Arts, Boulevard Bonne Nouvelle, 22." In Elizabeth Gilmore Holt (ed)., *The Triumph of Art for the Public*. Garden City, NY: Doubleday, pp. 454–60.

Becker, Howard S. 1974. "Art as Collective Action." *American Sociological Review* 39:767–76.

Benjamin, Walter. 1969. *Illuminations*. Translated by Harry Zohn. New York: Schocken.

Blau, Judith R. 1988. "The Context of Art Attendance." *Social Science Quarterly* 69:930–41.

Blau, Judith R. 1989. *The Shape of Culture*. A Rose Monograph of the American Sociological Association. Cambridge, MA: Cambridge University Press.

Blau, Judith R. 1991. "Disjunctive History of U.S. Museums, 1869–1980." *Social Forces* 70:87–106.

Blau, Judith R. 1993. *Social Contracts and Economic Markets*. New York: Plenum.

Blau, Judith R., and Gail Quets, with Peter M. Blau. 1989. *Cultural Life in City and Region*. Akron, OH: Center for Urban Studies.

Blumin, Stuart M. 1989. *The Emergence of the Middle Class*. Cambridge, MA: Cambridge University Press.

Bottomore, T. B. 1964. *Elites and Society*. Harmondsworth: Penguin.

Bourdieu, Pierre. 1984. *Distinction*. Translated by Richard Nice. Cambridge, MA: Harvard University Press.

Bourdieu, Pierre, and Alain Darbel, with Dominique Shnapper. 1990. *The Love of Art.* Translated by Caroline Beattie and Nick Merriman. Stanford: Stanford University Press.

Bürger, Peter. 1992. "Problems in the Functional Transformation of Art and Literature During the Translation from Feudal to Bourgeois Society." In Peter Bürger and Christa Bürger (eds.), *The Institutions of Art.* Translated by Loren Kruger and Intro. by Russell A. Berman. Lincoln: University of Nebraska Press, pp. 69–88.

Cantor, Jay E. 1991. "The Museum's Collection." In Martin Feldstein (ed.), *The Economics of Art Museums.* Chicago: University of Chicago Press, pp. 17–22.

Crimp, Douglas. 1983. "On the Museum's Ruins." In Hal Foster (ed.), *The Anti-Aesthetic.* Port Townsend, WA: Bay Press, pp. 43–56.

Cummings, Milton C. 1991. "Government and the Arts." In Stephen Benedict (ed.), *Public Money and the Muse.* New York: W. W. Norton, pp. 31–79.

d'Alembert, J. Le Rond. 1992 (1751). "Discours préliminaire." Excerpt from Encyclopédie. In Peter Bürger and Christa Bürger (eds.), *The Institutions of Art.* Lincoln: University of Nebraska Press, pp. 72–76.

Danto, Arthur C. 1985. "The Philosophical Disenfranchisement of Art." In Peter J. McCormick (ed)., *The Reasons of Art/L'Art a ses raisons.* Ottawa: University of Ottawa Press, pp. 11–22.

Dewey, John. 1958 (1934). *Art as Experience.* New York: Capricorn.

DiMaggio, Paul J. 1982. "Cultural Entrepreneurship in Nineteenth-Century Boston." *Media, Culture and Society* 4:33–50.

DiMaggio, Paul J. 1987. "Nonprofit Organizations in the Production and Distribution of Culture." In Walter W. Powell (ed.), *The Nonprofit Sector.* New Haven, CT: Yale University Press, pp. 195–220.

DiMaggio, Paul J. 1991a. "Decentralization of Arts Funding from the Federal Government to the States." In Stephen Benedict (ed.), *Public Money and the Muse.* New York: W. W. Norton, pp. 216–54.

DiMaggio, Paul J. 1991b. "Social Structure, Institutions, and Capital Goods." In Pierre Bourdieu and James S. Coleman (eds.), *Social Theory for a Changing Society.* Boulder, CO: Westview Press, pp. 133–55.

Dubin, Steven C. 1992. *Arresting Images.* London: Routledge.

Dziemidok, Bohdan. 1985. On Aesthetic and Artistic Evaluations of the Work of Art. In Peter J. McCormick (ed.), *The Reasons of Art/L'Art a ses raisons.* Ottawa: University of Ottawa Press, pp. 295–306.

Eagleton, Terry. 1991. *Ideology.* London: Verso.

Feldstein, Martin, ed. 1991. *The Economics of Art Museums.* Chicago: University of Chicago Press.

Foster, Hal. 1985. *Recordings.* Port Townsend, WA: Bay Press.

Gadamer, Hans-Georg. 1986. *The Relevance of the Beautiful and Other Essays.* Translated by Nicholas Walker. Cambridge, MA: Cambridge University Press.

Gallman, Robert E. 1969. "Trends in the Size Distribution of Wealth in the Nineteenth Century." In L. Soltow (ed.), *Six Papers on the Size Distribution of Wealth and Income.* New York: National Bureau of Economic Research, pp. 1–24.

Goodman, Nelson. 1978. *Ways of World-Making.* Indianapolis: Hackett.

Gopnik, Adam. 1992. "The Death of an Audience." *The New Yorker* 68(October 5):141–6.

Habermas, Jürgen. 1983. "Modernity—An Incomplete Project." In Hal Foster (ed.), *The Anti-Aesthetic.* Port Townsend, WA: Bay Press, pp. 3–15.

Hannan, Michael T., and John Freeman. 1989. *Organizational Ecology.* Cambridge, MA: Harvard University.

Hansmann, Henry. 1987. "Economic Theories of Nonprofit Organization." In Walter W. Powell (ed.), *The Nonprofit Sector*. New Haven, CT: Yale University Press, pp. 27–42.

Harrison, Bennett, and Barry Bluestone. 1990. *The Great U-Turn*, rev. ed. New York: Basic Books.

Harvey, David. 1989. *The Condition of Postmodernity*. Oxford: Basil Blackwood.

Hirschman, Albert O. 1982. *Shifting Involvements*. Princeton, NJ: Princeton University Press.

Huyssen, Andreas. 1986. *After the Great Divide*. Bloomington: Indiana University Press.

Impey, Oliver, and Arthur MacGregor, eds. 1985. *The Origins of Museums*. Oxford: Clarendon Press.

Jameson, Frederic. 1991. *Postmodernism, or The Cultural Logic of Late Capitalism*. Durham, NC: Duke University Press.

Kammen, Michael. 1980. *People of Paradox, 2nd ed*. New York: Oxford University Press.

Kandinsky, Wassily. 1947. *Concerning the Spiritual in Art*. Translated by Michael Sadleir. New York: George Wittenborn.

Kant, Immanuel. 1952 (1790). *Critique of Judgment*. Translated by James Creed Meredith. Oxford: Clarendon Press.

Karp, Ivan, Christine Mullen Kreamer, and Steven D. Levine. 1992. *Museums and Communities*. Washington, DC: Smithsonian Institution Press.

Klee, Paul. 1964 (1898/1918). *The Diaries of Paul Klee*. Berkeley: University of California Press.

Koselleck, Reinhart. 1988. *Critique and Crisis*. Cambridge, MA: MIT Press.

Krauss, Rosalind E. 1986. *The Originality of the Avant-Garde and Other Modernist Myths*. Cambridge, MA: MIT Press.

Lamont, Michèle, and Marcel Fournier. 1992. "Introduction." In M. Lamont and M. Fournier (eds.), *Cultivating Differences*. Chicago: University of Chicago Press, pp. 1–17.

Langer, Suzanne K. 1957. *Problems of Art*. New York: Charles Scribner's.

Levine, Lawrence W. 1988. *Highbrow/Lowbrow*. Cambridge, MA: Harvard University Press.

Long, Clarence D. 1960. *Wages and Earnings in the United States, 1860–1890*. Princeton, NJ: Princeton University Press and the National Bureau of Economic Research.

Lowry, W. McNeil, ed. 1984. *The Arts and Public Policy in the United States*. Englewood Cliffs, NJ: Prentice-Hall.

Martorella, Rosanne. 1990. *Corporate Art*. New Brunswick, NJ: Rutgers University Press.

Meyer, Karl E. 1979. *The Art Museum*. New York: William Morrow.

Miller, Lillian B. 1966. *Patrons and Patriotism*. Chicago: University of Chicago Press.

Minihan, Janet. 1977. *The Nationalization of Culture*. New York: New York University Press.

Moulin, Raymonde. 1987. *The French Art Market*. New Brunswick, NJ: Rutgers University Press.

Owens, Craig. 1983. "The Discourse of Others." In Hal Foster (ed.), *The Anti-Aesthetic*. Port Townsend, WA: Bay Press, pp. 57–82.

Parker, Harry S., III. 1991. "Museum Finances." In Martin Feldstein (ed.), *The Economics of Art Museums*. Chicago: University of Chicago Press, pp. 61–73.

Pelles, Geraldine. 1963. *Art, Artists and Society*. Englewood Cliffs, NJ: Prentice-Hall.

Peterson, Richard A. 1986. "From Impresario to Arts Administrator." In Paul J. Di-
Maggio (ed). *Nonprofit Enterprise in the Arts*. New York: Oxford University
Press, pp. 161–83.
Peterson, Richard A., and David G. Berger. 1975. "Cycles in Symbol Production."
American Sociological Review 40:158–73.
Reed, Herbert. 1966 (1936). "Preface to the 1936 Edition." *Art and Society*. New York:
Schocken.
Richardson, John. 1992. "Go Go Guggenheim." *The New York Review of Books* 39(July
16):18–22.
Robinson, J. P., T. Halford, and T. A. Triplett 1985. *Public Participation in the Arts*.
College Park: University of Maryland.
Rosenberg, Harold. 1967. "Collective, Ideological, Combative." In Thomas B. Hess
and John Ashbery (eds.), *Avant-Garde Art*. London: Collier-Macmillan, pp.
81–92.
Rubenstein, Neil. 1991. "Museum Finances." In Martin Feldstein (ed.), *The Economics
of Art Museums*. Chicago: University of Chicago Press, pp. 73–85.
Rushdie, Salman. 1988. *The Satanic Verses*. London: Viking.
Samuelson, Paul A. 1954. "The Pure Theory of Public Expenditures." *The Review of
Economics and Statistics* 37:350–56.
Sen, Amartya. 1992. *Inequality Reexamined*. Cambridge, MA: Harvard University
Press.
Shapiro, Theda. 1976. *Painters and Politics*. New York: Elsevier.
Sinden, John A., and Albert C. Worrell. 1979. *Unpriced Values*. New York: Wiley.
Smith, Adam. 1937 (1776). *An Inquiry into the Nature and Causes of the Wealth of
Nations*. Edited, with an Introduction, by Edwin Cannan. New York: Modern
Library.
Spengler, Oswald. 1980 (1926/1928). *The Decline of the West* (2 vols.). Translated by
Charles Francis Atkinson. New York: Knopf.
Stoppard, Tom. 1973. *Artist Descending a Staircase and Where Are They Now?* Lon-
don: Faber.
Taylor, Joshua C. 1976. *America as Art*. New York: Harper & Row.
Useem, Michael. 1984. *The Inner Circle*. New York: Oxford University Press.
Vattimo, Gianni. 1985. "Aesthetics and the End of Epistemology." In Peter J. Mc-
Cormick (ed.), *The Reasons of Art/L'Art a ses raisons*. Ottawa: University of
Ottawa Press, pp. 287–95.
Ventós, Xavier Rubert de. 1980. *Heresies of Modern Art*. New York: Columbia Uni-
versity Press.
Venturi, Robert. 1966. *Complexity and Contradiction in Architecture*. Garden City, NY:
Doubleday.
Watson, Peter. 1992. *From Manet to Manhattan*. New York: Random House.
Weil, Stephen E. 1991. "Tax Policy and Private Giving." In Stephen Benedict (ed.),
Public Money and the Muse. New York: Norton, pp. 153–81.
White, Harrison, and Cynthia White. 1965. *Canvases and Careers*. New York: Wiley.
Wolff, Janet. 1983. *Aesthetics and the Sociology of Art*. London: George Allen &
Unwin.
Zolberg, Vera L. 1986. "Tensions and Mission in American Art Museums." In Paul J.
DiMaggio (ed.), *Nonprofit Enterprise in the Arts*. New York: Oxford University
Press, pp. 184–98.

III

DENSITY-DEPENDENT EVOLUTION

A major model of organizational ecology explains long-term organizational evolution as the consequence of the opposing force of two sociological processes: legitimation and competition. *Legitimation* of an organizational population means that its organizational form gets the status of a "taken-for-granted" solution to given problems of collective action. That is, the organizational form is accepted and used for a particular activity without much thought or debate. *Competition* refers to constraints arising from the joint dependence of multiple organizations on the same set of finite resources. One central idea of the theory is that both legitimation and competition are affected by *density*, defined as the number of organizations in the population. Another central idea is that the vital rates of an organizational population—rates of start-up and mortality—vary as functions of legitimation and competition (see Hannan and Carroll 1992 for a detailed technical discussion).

COMPETITION AND VITAL RATES

Intense competition within an organizational population depresses rates of entrepreneurial activity and rates of organization founding. As competition intensifies, more of the resources needed to build and maintain organizations have already been claimed by other organizations. Intense competition exhausts supplies of potential organizers, members, patrons, and resources; fewer resources go unclaimed, and markets are packed tightly. Because environmental conditions set a finite carrying capacity, more competitors means that the potential gains from starting an organization will be smaller. Rational persons with the knowledge and skills to build organizations might hesitate to make attempts in densely populated environments and so look for better opportunities. Such a process contributes to a negative relationship between competition and the rate of start-up. Capital markets and other macrostructures often reinforce this tendency. For example, big-time investors typically avoid participating in highly competitive markets such as the restaurant industry. Moreover, professional associations and government agencies often try to restrict entry under intense competition. All these forces imply that the start-up rate is inversely proportional to the intensity of competition.

Other forces cause competition to increase the rate of organizational mortality. Organizations must maintain flows of resources from the environment to keep structures intact. As competition intensifies, sustaining the flows of these resources becomes problematic for many, if not all, organizations in a population. Therefore, intense diffuse competition lowers the life chances of new organizations and those of existing ones by complicating the task of maintaining a flow of essential resources. In other words, when competition is already intense, further growth increases disbanding rates, after controlling for the environmental conditions that affect carrying capacities. Thus the mortality rate of organizations in a population is directly proportional to the intensity of competition within the population at the time. In other words, this is an effect of contemporaneous competition.

LEGITIMATION AND VITAL RATES

A taken-for-granted social form is readily visualized by potential organizers; one with dubious or unknown standing is not. The strength of norms endorsing rational organization as the appropriate vehicle for attaining collective goals affects the ease of starting organizations. When those who control resources take the organizational form for granted, the capacity to mobilize potential members and resources increases greatly. Reducing the need for such justifications lowers the cost of organizing. Thus the founding rate is directly proportional to the legitimation of the organizational form at that time.

The link between legitimation and organizational mortality is straightforward. Legitimation eases the problem of maintaining flows of resources from the environment and enhances the ability of organizations to fend off challenges. The mortality in an organizational population is inversely proportional to the legitimation of this organizational form at that time.

DENSITY, COMPETITION, AND LEGITIMATION

Consider the relationship between organizational density and competition. Intensity of competition depends on both the degree of intersection of fundamental niches and the numbers of competitors involved. Even when two populations in the same system have intersecting fundamental niches, they do not compete intensely if their numbers are very small compared with the abundance of resources. That is, organizational density, resource abundance, and competition are tightly connected. Growth in organizational density compared with carrying capacity increases both direct competition between pairs of organizations within a population and diffuse competition among all or many of them. Individual organizations can easily avoid direct competition with others for members and scarce resources when density is low compared with the abundance of resources. As density grows, the number of potential competitors grows. This makes avoidance more difficult, as can easily be seen by noting that, as density increases linearly, the complexity of the potential net of competition increases geometrically.

Elementary considerations of congestion suggest that growing density intensifies competition at an increasing rate. In other words, variations near high density have more impact on strength of competition than do variations in the lower range. When numbers are few, an increase in the population size by a single organization increases the frequency and strength of competitive interactions slightly, if at all. However, when density is high compared with the carrying capacity, the presence of another organization greatly increases the competition. Looked at from the viewpoint of the actions of a single organization, fashioning a strategy that works against all (or most) competitors becomes extraordinarily difficult when very many pairwise interactions must be considered simultaneously. So we argue that the intensity of contemporaneous competition increases with density at an increasing rate.

Now consider the process by which organizations gain legitimation or taken-for-granted status. It encompasses at least two kinds of activity. One is collective action by members of the population to define, explain, and codify the organizational form, and to repulse claims and attacks by rival populations. The second is collective learning by which effective routines and social structures become collectively fine-tuned, codified, and promulgated.

Intensity of both kinds of activities depends on organizational density. In the case of collective action, low density hampers attempts to protect and defend the claims of a population or of some of its members. Growth in numbers of organizations gives force to claims of institutional standing and provides economies of scale in political and legal actions. The capacity for collective action rises at least proportionately with density, and the process is no doubt self-reinforcing, at least initially. When founders organize collectively and form mutual benefit societies and trade associations, new entrepreneurs are enticed to enter the market. Those who do enter find that the association and its members provide useful guidance and assistance.

Extreme rarity of a form poses serious problems of legitimation. If almost no instances of a form exist, it can hardly be taken as the natural way to achieve some collective end. On the other hand, once a form becomes common it seems unlikely that increases in numbers will greatly affect its degree of social acceptance. In other words, legitimation responds to variations in density in the lower range, but the effect has a ceiling. The ceiling might be interpreted as the point at which the relative percentage of natural persons who take the form for granted reaches a sufficiently high level to make a normative prescription. That is, at this point further increases in the percentage of persons who take the form for granted do not affect its cultural standing. By this argument, legitimation increases density at a decreasing rate.

Putting together the various arguments involves recognizing that at low density the legitimation process dominates; at high density, competition prevails. The combined effect of these two processes yields the core empirical predictions of the theory of density-dependent legitimation and competition:

1. Density dependence in founding rates is nonmonotonic in the general shape of an inverted U.
2. Density dependence in mortality rates is nonmonotonic in the general shape of a U.

Empirical research on a variety of organizational populations supports the theory. The expected empirical relationships between density and start-ups and deaths have been discovered in studies of labor unions, breweries, newspapers, banks, life insurance companies, telephone companies, and cooperatives.

HISTORICAL IMPRINTING OF ORGANIZATIONAL STRUCTURE

Organizations and organizational forms often reflect the social conditions prevailing at birth (Stinchcombe 1965). Starting an organization involves acquiring environmental resources; and choice of initial resources often unwittingly establishes practices and structures that persist throughout the life of the organization. For instance, most college fraternities were established in three waves: a first wave occurring between 1840 and 1850, a second wave between 1865 and 1870, and a third wave in the early 1900s. The cultural character of these fraternities still reflects the social conditions surrounding their establishment. The first wave was largely elitist and situated in Northern liberal arts colleges; the second wave was Southern; and the third wave was composed of nonexclusionary "antifraternity" fraternities. So knowing the date of birth of an organization sometimes enables one to better understand certain features of that organization.

Organizational forms also display historical imprinting, but of a more basic kind. Sociologist Arthur Stinchcombe (1965) showed that the period in which an industry was established corresponded closely to the general occupational distribution of organizations in the industry. For instance, industries emerging before the modern factory (e.g., agriculture, retail trade, construction, hotels, logging, wholesale trade, printing, and publishing) use disproportionately high levels of unpaid family workers, have greater proportions of self-employed, and fewer clerical workers. Industries founded in the railroad age have greater proportions of clerical workers, and those founded in the modern era contain more staff and professional positions. When some organizational forms become recognized as "the way to do business" within a particular industry, later entrants to the industry tend to copy the basic features of the form established early. So knowing the date of establishment of a firm's industry allows one to anticipate features of the firm's organizational form.

DENSITY DELAY

A different kind of historical imprint placed on organizations stems from the competitive conditions at the time of establishment. The imprinting in this process is not on the structure of the organization or its basic form but on its survival chances (more precisely, on its *lifetime mortality schedule*). In particular, the number of organizations operating in an industry at the time of start-up has a persisting positive effect on the organization's probability of death (or, conversely, a negative effect on life expectancy). The greater the number of organizations present at its start, the higher an organization's lifetime mortality risks. Because density is defined as the number of organizations present in a population, and because the effect of density when an organization starts can be experienced at any point in an organization's life, this imprinting process is known as *density delay*.

Why does density delay occur? Why might intense competition at start-up have long-term effects on the mortality rates of "mature" organizations? Two general arguments have been put forth. The first concerns a liability of resource scarcity. Intense competition at start-up creates conditions of resource scarcity. When resources are scarce, new organizations that cannot shift quickly from start-up mode to full-scale operation face strong selection pressures. Those that do survive the start-up period likely do not have the slack to allow fine-tuning of routines. Staff members in such organizations have little motivation to invest heavily in the organization-specific skills that enable routines to be reproduced regularly.

We believe that an organization has great difficulty recovering fully from such deprived initial organizing. Inertia presumably occurs here as it does in all organizations. Moreover, attempts at redesigning the organization usually entail mortality risks. If so, then cohorts of organizations experiencing intense competition at founding are inferior competitors at every age.

A second argument predicting the density delay effect concerns *tight niche packing*, or market crowding. With intense competition, resources get exploited thoroughly. Newly established organizations often suffer reputational and other disadvantages compared with established competitors. Thus they are often pushed to the peripheries or margins of markets and resource distributions. Even if organizations succeed at creating structures and routines well suited to these regions of resource space, operation in such regions is likely to be precarious. Attempting to shift toward the center of the market or resource distribution at a later age also entails reorganization risks. So the organizations pushed to the fringe of the industry by initially intense competition are likely to exhibit higher mortality rates at all ages.

Competition is usually thought to be a contemporaneous phenomenon with swift effects: inferior firms are quickly abandoned by customers, investors, and employees. The density delay arguments are thus counterintuitive to many. Yet ample empirical evidence documents the strength and robustness of density delay effects. Scientific studies of many types of organizational populations have reported the predicted relationship between mortality and density at start-up. Very few disconfirming findings have been reported.

This section contains several chapters that emphasize the role of density-dependent selection in shaping organizational populations in industries. Chapter 6 summarizes the original test of the theory of density dependence. This was Hannan and Freeman's (1987, 1988) study of American labor unions during 1836–1985. David Barron's (Chapter 7) analysis of a form of financial institution, credit unions, also highlights the operation of density-dependent growth. David Strang's (Chapter 8) discussion of health maintenance organizations describes how different types of organizations using the HMO form compete via density dependence. This section also presents (Chapter 9) a summary of early ecological studies of newspaper populations. Finally, we describe an application of the density framework to the worldwide automobile manufacturing industry (Chapter 10).

BIBLIOGRAPHY

Hannan, M. T., and G. R. Carroll. 1992. *Dynamics of Organizational Populations: Density, Legitimation, and Competition.* New York: Oxford University Press.

Hannan, M. T., and J. Freeman. 1987. "The Ecology of Organizational Founding: American Labor Unions, 1836–1985." *American Journal of Sociology* 92:910–43.

Hannan, M. T., and J. Freeman. 1988. "The Ecology of Organizational Mortality: American Labor Unions, 1836–1985." *American Journal of Sociology* 94:22–52.

Stinchcombe, A. L. 1965. "Social Structure and Organizations." In J. G. March (ed.), *Handbook of Organizations.* Chicago: Rand McNally, pp. 153–93.

6

Labor Unions

MICHAEL T. HANNAN

This chapter applies the principle of density-dependent organizational evolution to labor unions. Specifically, we consider change in the population of American labor unions over its full history, 1836–1991. We first explain what legitimation and competition (the two main processes in the theory) have meant concretely in this case. Then we discuss the results of empirical studies of the relationship between density and the rate of organizational founding and the rate of organizational mortality.

Unions are especially interesting to organizational analysts because they began as *social movement organizations*. This beginning means that they have combined elements of social movement organization (with its focus on recruiting members and taking visible mass actions, such as demonstrations, marches, sitdown strikes, and so forth) with elements of bureaucracy (with hierarchies of authority, rules of procedure, fixed offices, and so forth). Unlike all of the kinds of organizations considered in this book except art museums, labor unions are not-for-profit organizations, i.e., voluntary associations. Organizational ecologists apply their theories and models to all kinds of organizational populations to find out whether their arguments are truly general. This chapter thus applies the theory of density dependence to a kind of voluntary association. The remaining chapters in this section discuss parallel applications to populations of various kinds of business firms.

Labor unions also have special interest for students of organizations because they set out to affect *employment relations*. By employment relation, we mean the social and contractual ties between employees and employers, the ties that determine compensation, security of employment, and control over the details of work. These ties have great importance both for the careers of individuals and for the structures of power and inequality in society. In this sense, unions stood (and stand) at a key juncture in the social and economic structure of society. Because of their location in the structure, unions contended for power with employers and other established interests in society. Tracing the changing fortunes of unions provides insight into the transformations of the larger social and economic structures.

The contentious history of the labor union movement provides an important research advantage. Because many were adversarial and sometimes radical organizations, the formation of national labor unions, no matter how small, apparently seldom escaped notice. Therefore, studies of national labor unions can avoid the problem of bias due to sampling old and long-lived organizations, which is noted in Chapter 1. That is, the archival record contains information on many small unions with short lifetimes (often less than a year).

OVERVIEW OF THE EVOLUTION OF AMERICAN UNION ORGANIZATION

Labor unions have succeeded in shaping American employment relations in dramatic ways. Many features of employment relations that Americans now take for granted—eight-hour days and overtime pay, paid vacation, seniority rights, insurance and pensions tied to jobs—resulted from hard-fought victories of labor unions and the larger labor movement. Not only was the movement powerful collectively, but individual unions gained millions of members and possessed the capacity to disrupt huge sectors of the economy. However, union membership and the influence of unions have declined sharply in recent years. Each year since 1957 has seen a decline in the proportion of the civilian labor force belonging to unions. The union movement now seems to be a spent force.

Understanding the rise of unions to power and influence and their subsequent decline requires attention to a broad range of topics. These include national politics and developments in national and international economic and industrial organization. This chapter does not attempt such a broad-ranging analysis. Instead, it explores the possibility that purely organizational processes have shaped the growth and contraction of the population of labor unions.

A labor union is a special kind of organization: an association of employees, usually voluntary, with the stated goal of improving working conditions and compensation. In addition, a union is characterized by a specific form of collective action: the strike (threatening to withhold labor collectively). The specific goal of improving working conditions distinguishes unions from worker political movements (such as socialist parties) and from utopian movements. Reliance on the strike distinguishes unions from employee associations, such as company-sponsored unions and mutual benefit or benevolent associations of workers.

This chapter concentrates on *national* unions. To understand the ecology of national unions, it is helpful to place them in evolutionary perspective. Unions of national scale evolved from combinations of unions operating on a local scale. The earliest American unions, called trade societies, enrolled journeymen workers in a single craft in a single city. This form of organization was narrow in areal scope and breadth of jurisdiction. This narrow scope reflected the organization of work at the time: cities and their hinterlands were the main units of production and exchange, and work was divided among trades or crafts. The first trade society, the Federal Society of Journeymen Cordwainers (a cordwainer was a shoemaker) was founded in Philadelphia in 1794.

Next, trade societies in a city formed federations to increase their bargaining power with firms that employed workers from several crafts (e.g., building contractors employed workers from all of the so-called building trades). The first, the Mechanics Union of Trade Associations, began in Philadelphia in 1827. It included carpenters, painters, bricklayers, and glaziers. The New York Trades Society covered fifty-two crafts by 1836 (before disbanding the next year).

The completion of the Erie Canal and the growth of railways (see Chapter 4) eroded the boundaries around urban and regional labor markets. Migrating craftsmen posed a major obstacle to successful union organization at the city level because an employer could respond to a strike by recruiting migrating craftsmen. As long as labor organization took place at the city level, craftsmen from one city did not owe allegiance to strike actions by a union in another. Unions responded to this threat by holding meetings to coordinate actions among unions in the same trade in multiple cities to attempt to obtain mutual recognition of picket lines.

Beginning in 1836, informal coordination was replaced by national unions. Although these new unions started as federations of local unions, they were national unions in the sense that they claimed jurisdiction over all workers in a trade in the country. The first national union was the Society of Cordwainers, founded in 1836 by a convention of representatives of trade societies of shoemakers from sixteen cities. The same year saw the beginning of the Society of Journeymen House Carpenters and the National Typographic Society (a union of typesetters). National craft unions founded during the 1840s and 1850s included the National Union of Carpet Weavers, the Glass Blowers League, the Journeymen Stonecutters Association, the United Hatters, and the National Union of Blacksmiths and Machinists.

These early unions were examples of one of the two main forms of union organization in the United States: *craft unionism*. The craft union form has its roots in the guild. It consists of journeymen craftsmen organized collectively for controlling conditions of work. Craft unions tried to regulate the entry of new members into the trade as well as their training (through formal apprenticeship). A key feature of the craft form is that workers at a work site were typically organized into several different unions. That is, the craft form defines a target membership by occupation rather than by firm or industry. The craft form, defined this way, has not been restricted to the highest skill levels; semi-skilled and unskilled workers often formed narrowly defined unions in industries dominated by the craft form of organization (e.g., unskilled laborers in the building trades were organized by the Union of Hodcarriers and Building Laborers, and longshoremen were organized by the National Longshoremen's Union.

Early craft unions were specialized organizations. They initially organized narrowly to target a specific occupational group: shoemakers or machinists, for instance. However, narrow craft unionism frequently did not fit the changing environment well, specifically the changing nature of industrial organization. Throughout the nineteenth century, industrial production grew in scale and became increasingly mechanized. Semiskilled and unskilled jobs proliferated, as technical innovations replaced some kinds of skilled workers and the scale of enterprise grew. Moreover, technical change kept redefining the set of relevant jobs, by eliminating some steps in a production process, combining others, and creating still others. As these trends became pronounced, it became clear to union organizers that many craft unions, by focusing on single narrowly defined crafts, were too specialized. Therefore, unions began to organize on a broader scale, by incorporating more diverse kinds of workers. This broadening came about in several ways.

One kind retained the basic principle of organizing workers by craft but included several crafts in the jurisdiction. For instance, the International Association of Journeymen Plumbers, Steamfitters, and Gas Fitters was founded to organize all craftsmen in the "pipe trades." Some multicraft unions were created by mergers among narrow craft unions. Often these mergers involved unions whose members worked at the same sites (meaning that a strike by one union would stop work for the others), working with substitutable processes or materials (e.g., painters and wallpaperers), or working along a vertical flow of work (e.g., warehousemen and longshoremen). For instance, the Window Glass Cutters League merged with the Window Glass Flatteners Association.

Multicraft unions also resulted from efforts of narrow craft unions to expand their jurisdictions. The most famous example concerns the United Brotherhood of Carpenters and Joiners (UBC), which began in 1888 when the Brotherhood of Carpenters and Joiners absorbed the United Order of Carpenters. In 1901, the UBC expanded its jurisdiction to cover "all that's made of wood," later extended to "or that was ever made of wood." Using this jurisdictional claim, the UBC eventually organized an amazing diversity of crafts, including millwrights, pile drivers, boat builders, caulkers, cabinet makers, house movers, loggers, lumber and sawmill workers, furniture workers, and casket and coffin makers.

Other new unions adopted a different form of organizing workers: *industrial unionism*. Instead of defining a jurisdiction in terms of crafts or occupations, an industrial union attempts to organize all production workers in one or more industries, whatever the job title or skill level. The first union to adopt the industrial form appears to have been the American Miners Association (founded in 1861), which attempted to organize all workers "in and around the mines." The Knights of St. Crispin (1867–78), which tried to organize all workers in the shoe industry, became the first really large American union with membership estimated at half a million.

In some important cases, industrial unions replaced sets of craft unions. For instance, iron and steel were once made by a series of skilled craftsmen who worked on separate steps of the production process: heating, puddling, rolling, catching, hooking, straightening, and so on. Individual crafts or groups of related crafts originally organized separate unions. For instance, the Iron City

Forge of the Sons of Vulcan, founded as a secret society of puddlers, became a national union of puddlers, the Grand Forge of the United States, United Sons of Vulcan; workers in the furnaces and finishing departments formed the Brotherhood of Iron and Steel Heaters, Rollers, and Roughers. The National Union of Rollers, Roughers, Catchers, and Hookers organized an even broader set of trades. The Panic of 1873, a series of failed strikes, and rapid change in technology and the organization of work led these two unions to combine to form the Amalgamated Association of Iron and Steel Workers to organize the many crafts involved in this industry.

The history of American unions evidences great diversity of forms. We have noted the standard distinction of form between craft and industrial organizing. Within these two forms, there has been further broad variation in the breadth of types of workers (crafts and occupations, and skill levels) and types of industries that unions tried to organize.

THE DENSITY OF NATIONAL LABOR UNIONS

The term *union density* is used in studies of labor history to refer to the fraction of the (civilian, nonfarm) labor force in unions. Although this measure is useful for many purposes, it does not aid the understanding of the organizational processes that have shaped the union movement, because it does not take account of the number of unions in existence (and the distribution of members among unions). As the introduction to this section points out, organizational ecologists emphasize *organizational density,* defined as the number of organizations in the population.

Figure 6-1 shows how the number of national labor unions in the United States varied by year from 1836 to 1991. There were hardly any unions until the Civil War era. Then the number rose modestly until about 1881, and then it grew explosively until about 1905. From that point on, growth in numbers was slower and more erratic until the number of unions reached its peak level of 211 in 1954. The last portion of the history shows consistent contraction in the number of unions; this decline accelerated in the most recent years as the result of a wave of mergers.

The pattern of growth and decline in numbers over 150 years has a surprising feature, which is the difference between 1880–1910 and the period after 1910. The number of unions grew explosively in a brief period at the turn of the nineteenth century. The number of unions grew sixfold between 1880 and 1910: in 1881, there were 31 unions, and in 1910, there were 183. By contrast, the number of unions fluctuated much less after 1910. Indeed, between 1910 and 1978, the number of unions remained within the range 165–211. The greater stability during most of the twentieth century is astonishing given the changes that took place in the environment of unions after 1910. The stance of the federal government toward unions changed from oppositional to favorable (during the New Deal) to more oppositional. The economy grew and changed greatly. Union membership surged. In other words, the environment of this population

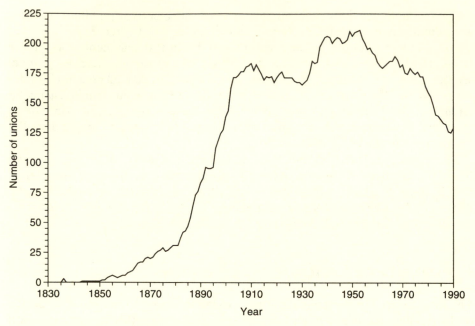

Figure 6–1 Density of American national labor unions. (*Source:* Adapted from Hannan and Freeman 1988. Copyright © 1988 by University of Chicago Press. Used by permission.)

changed much more after 1910 than it did between 1880 and 1910. The pattern in Figure 6-1 suggests, surprisingly, that fluctuation in density in this population had as much or more to do with processes *within* the population of unions as with changes in social, economic, and political environments (which have received enormously more scholarly attention).

The relationship between density and aggregate membership in all unions is especially important. A common way of thinking about the rise of organizations is that they are collective actors appearing in response to existing demand for their services. In the case of unions, they arose when and where workers were ready to use the services of this organizational form. How does this common-sense view fare here? Not very well. Figure 6-2 shows that growth in the number of unions (solid line) *leads* growth in membership (dashed line) by many years for much of the relevant history.[1] (Union membership is expressed in units of 100,000 in Figure 6-2.) Although precedence does not imply causation, this figure does suggest that growth in the number of unions may have played a central role in the growth of union membership. Unions came first and growth in membership came later. This fact has been ignored in the historical and sociological literatures.

Figure 6-2 is informative in another way. It shows that the number of unions peaked long before the growth in membership did. The figure does not support the view that the stabilization and eventual decline in the number of unions reflected an exhaustion of the pool of unorganized workers. Another process

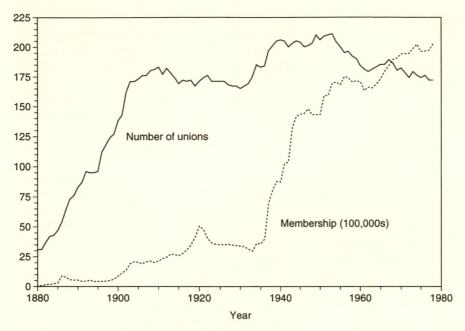

Figure 6–2 Growth in unions and union membership. (*Source:* Adapted from Hannan and Freeman 1988. Copyright © 1988 by University of Chicago Press. Used by permission.)

must have been involved. This chapter holds that the key processes were organizational, that the growth and stabilization in the number of unions reflected processes of legitimation and competition within the population of unions.

LEGITIMATION AND COMPETITION

As the introduction to this section explains, organizational ecology has a theory that explains the growth and decline of organizational populations as a consequence of opposing processes of legitimation and competition (among other causal factors). This theory explains variations in legitimation and competition partly in terms of the density of organizations. Study of the histories of individual unions and of the broader union movement may help to make clear what these abstract ideas mean in a concrete case.

Legitimation refers to the status of an organizational form as a taken-for-granted feature of the society. Absence of legitimation was a major obstacle in the creation and expansion of unions, especially during the early years of the American labor movement. The organizational form was not a taken-for-granted feature of the social structure. Those who tried to begin unions had to expend valuable time and energy just explaining the organizational form and arguing its potential value. They did so in a social climate in which several alternate organizational forms were competing to represent the interests of workers. There were diverse worker political movements, secret societies, utopian movements that sought to create closed communities, and anarchist and terrorist factions (such as the Molly McGuires who waged a kind of guerilla warfare in the Pennsylvania coal country). Absence of a taken-for-granted organizational form to direct the collective action of workers thus made it difficult to succeed in starting unions and in keeping them going.

Unions faced a second kind of legitimation problem. Because unions represented the interests of disadvantaged groups, attempts at unionization usually sparked intense opposition and repression by employers. Because unions were not taken for granted in the society and lacked formal legal rights, such opposition was difficult to overcome.

These problems can be viewed as stemming from a weakness of small numbers (low density). Organizational ecologists have pointed out that a rare organizational form can hardly be taken for granted as a part of the social landscape. Growth in numbers conveys social standing to the organizational form. Low density also hampered attempts to coordinate political actions to protect and defend claims of unions. When unions are rare, their collective voice is weak (unless the unions happen to be very large, which was not so). Increases in density can alleviate these legitimation problems. Growth in numbers of organizations makes them seem natural (or even inevitable) actors, gives force to claims of institutional standing, and provides economies of scale in political and legal action.

According to the theory, continued growth in density eventually sparks *competition*. Many sociologists think it strange that organizational ecologists focused on competition among unions, rather than on competition between unions and employers (or the state). However, there is good reason for thinking that competition among unions has been a potent force, as Robert Michels argued in his classic work on organization theory, *Political Parties* (1949 [1915]). This book examines the paradox of social movement organization: the very creation of an enduring organization alters the character of relations between members and deflects action away from the goals of the members in the direction of preserving the organization (and thus the perquisites of its leaders). In analyzing labor unions, he traced the implications of these tendencies for competition among unions:

> . . . from a means, organization becomes an end. . . . The sole preoccupation is to avoid anything that may clog the machinery. Thus the hatred of the party is directed, not in the first place against the opponents of its own view of the world order, but against the dreaded rivals in the political field, against those who are competing for the same end—power. . . . Evidently among the trade unions of diverse political coloring, whose primary aim is to gain the greatest possible number of new members, the note of competition will be emphasized more. (pp. 338–40)

The case of direct competition for members (often called rival unionism) has been discussed widely in the literature on labor history. It was common for two or more unions to attempt to organize the same set of workers. Such instances of high niche overlap with respect to target membership were sometimes due to expansion of unions that had begun in different regions, typically Eastern versus Midwestern or Western unions. For example, the Western Federation of Miners competed with the (mainly Eastern) United Mine Workers. Sometimes the rivalry reflected disagreements over politics or tactics, as was the case of the politically conservative Journeymen Tailors Union and the mainly socialist Tailors National Progressive Union. At other times a national federation created an affiliated union to compete with an independent union. For example, the American Federation of Labor (AFL) created the American Federation of Musicians to compete with the National League of Musicians after the NLM repeatedly refused to affiliate with the AFL.

Another kind of head-to-head competition pitted craft unions against industrial unions and unions that organized multiple crafts, as noted above. For example, the UBC fought jurisdictional battles with and raided the membership of unions such as the International Union of Timber Workers, the Furniture Makers Union, the Laborers International Union, the Association of Sheet Metal Workers, the Alliance of Theatrical Stage Employees and Moving Machine Operators, the Woodcarvers Association, and the International Woodworkers.

Much rival unionism resulted from strategic competition between national federations that promoted different forms of unionization. The most important example was the competition of the Congress of Industrial Organizations (CIO), a federation of industrial unions, with the American Federation of Labor (AFL), a federation of (mainly) craft unions. After the founding of the CIO within the AFL in 1936 and its expulsion in 1938, the CIO was instrumental in founding industrial unions to compete with AFL unions. For example, the CIO created the United Paperworkers International Union to compete with the AFL-affiliated Brotherhood of Paper Makers and the Retail, Wholesale, and Department Store Union to compete with the Retail Clerks International Association. Sometimes struggles and raids on memberships resulted in mergers. However, commonly one or both of the competitors were destroyed.

When there are few unions (density is low), even unions with broad jurisdictions can avoid direct competition with other unions for members. (This statement, of course, assumes that the small number of unions has not exhausted all of the organizing resources.) As the number of potential competitors grows, avoidance becomes more difficult. For instance, it becomes harder to find target memberships (or jurisdictions) that have not been already claimed. Thus, as density grows, any new union is more likely to claim a jurisdiction that at least partly overlaps that of other unions, thereby creating conditions for rivalry.

Unions have competed for limited resources beside members. Other key, limited resources include the services of skilled organizers and dedicated staff, political support and influence, and attention from the news media. Sometimes such competition involved direct rivalry, as when two or more unions seeking to organize the same workers competed for political and financial support from and membership in a national federation such as the AFL and CIO.

It would be misleading to consider only head-to-head competition or rivalry. More often the competition was *diffuse*, meaning that competition was characterized more by congestion than rivalry. As the number of unions grew large, more of the resources used to build and sustain unions were claimed by other unions that could defend themselves against raids. Such diffuse competition apparently lowered the odds of starting new unions and diminished the life chance of existing unions.

FOUNDING RATES

We begin with the founding rate: the rate at which new unions are formed. Organizational ecologists emphasize organizational foundings as sources of diversity in organizational form. To understand the relation between organizational forms and environments, they try to learn how founding rates vary over time and place. Their approach to this issue points to influences of social, political, and economic environments and to processes that operate within the organizational population. This chapter emphasizes the latter.

The introduction to the Section discusses the theory of density-dependent organizational evolution. This theory posits that organizational founding rates (1) increase with the legitimation of the organizational form, and (2) decrease with the intensity of competition within the population. It holds further that growth in numbers (density) gives legitimation in the sense of taken for grantedness, but that there is a ceiling on this effect. In other words, at some level of density, further increases have a negligible effect on the legitimation of the organizational form. In the case of competition, the theory assumes that competition grows with density at an increasing rate (the higher the density, the greater the increase in competition due to the arrival of another organization).

The combination of these assumptions leads to a testable hypothesis about the relationship of density and the founding rate: the relationship should have the form of an inverted U. That is, growth of density from zero should increase the founding rate, but eventually further growth in density should lower the founding rate. This is because at low density, growth in density increases the founding rate through a legitimation effect; but at some point, further growth in density has a mainly competitive effect that depresses the founding rate. A series of studies of the foundings of American labor unions supported this hypothesis (Hannan and Freeman 1987, 1989; Hannan and Carroll 1992). Here we briefly describe the main findings.

This research analyzed the number of foundings per year and related them to density at the beginning of each year (and to other conditions that held during that year). The data on foundings by year are shown in Figure 6-3. It shows that the number of foundings per year was low for almost fifty years after the first national unions began in 1836. Then a surge in foundings began in 1883 and continued until 1906. This was the most important period of building national unions. The peak years were 1897 and 1903 with nineteen foundings. A second brief peak occurred right after the First World War, and a broader period of high activity occurred during the 1930s. In broad terms, we want to learn whether these fluctuations in foundings were related to density as our theory predicts.

Comparing Figures 6-1 and 6-3 reveals that the number of foundings was highest during 1881–1905, when density was considerably below its maximum. The number of foundings was quite low during the period of peak density (1940–60). In other words, the figures are consistent with the hypothesis that the founding rate rises with early growth in density but then declines when density gets larger. Thus, the raw data are consistent with the theoretical story.

The raw data must be supplemented with some statistical analysis, however, because many things changed over the course of the history of interest. Perhaps the theoretically derived pattern holds in the raw data but this is due purely to changes in the environment over time. Therefore, we have conducted analyses that control for environmental conditions and effects of major events in the legal and legislative environment of unions.[2] These analyses show that the conclusion based on the raw data is not misleading. Even when the relevant environmental conditions are controlled statistically, the inverted-U relationship between density and the founding rate remains.

The main result is illustrated in Figure 6-4, which shows the estimated relationship between density and the founding rate.[3] Note that the predicted founding rate is low at low density but rises substantially as density increases. When density equals 35, the founding rate is roughly six times higher than when density was zero. At this level of density, the relationship changes sign from positive to negative. Further growth in density, to the historical maximum of 211,

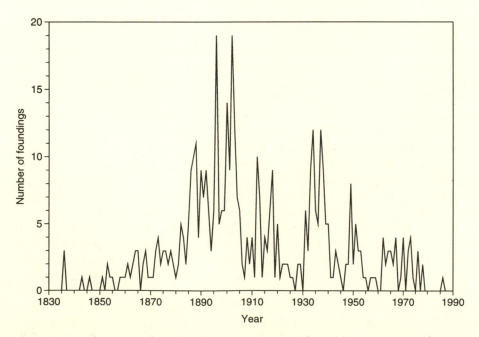

Figure 6–3 Labor union foundings by year. (*Source:* Adapted from Hannan and Freeman 1988. Copyright © 1988 by University of Chicago Press. Used by permission.)

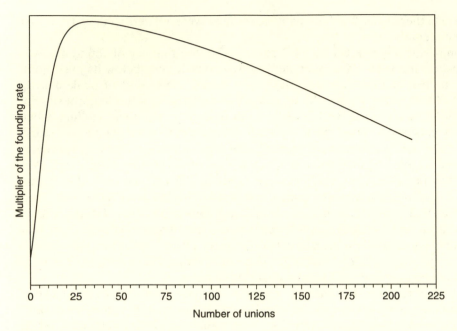

Figure 6–4 Relationship between union density and founding rate. (*Source:* Adapted from Hannan and Carroll 1992.)

cut the founding rate by half. Thus the relationship has the predicted shape, and the effects of density-dependent legitimation and competition have been powerful.

MORTALITY RATES

Although labor historians have paid scant attention to patterns in union foundings, this is not so for union mortality. Most historical studies concentrate on one (or sometimes a few) union and emphasize the particular events that appear to have speeded its end. In these accounts, union disbandings are commonly attributed to some kind of catastrophe, some particular event in the union's operations or in its environment at the time of failure (Hannan and Freeman 1989). Some frequently cited reasons for failures of unions include:

1. *Government intervention.* Government agencies have frequently taken actions to break strikes and these actions have sometimes destroyed the unions. For instance, the Professional Air Traffic Controllers Organization disbanded in 1982 after striking controllers were fired and replaced at the order of President Reagan.

2. *Employer offensives.* Associations of employers sometimes have acted to disrupt union organizing, especially in periods when unions were weak, e.g., unions such as the Oil and Gas Well Workers and the Timber Workers fell victim to such offensives of 1903–8 and 1919–29.

3. *Legislative or judicial rulings*. Some actions have strong effects on particular unions, e.g., the Foremen's Association of America, founded in 1941, had organized 28,000 supervisory employees, mainly in the auto industry, by 1947. The passage of the Taft-Hartley bill that year, which held that existing labor laws no longer applied to supervisory employees, caused many firms to void their contracts with the Foremen's Association, and the union disbanded shortly after that.

4. *Economic contraction*. During financial panics, such as those of 1837, 1853, and 1873, many businesses failed, unemployment surged, and many unions went out of existence, e.g., the three unions formed in 1836 failed during the Panic of 1837.

5. *Waves of immigration*. Labor leaders and scholars have claimed that waves of immigration disrupted the union movement. Although the pool of immigrant labor provided many labor leaders and large numbers of class-conscious workers, immigration lowered the power of unions by providing a source of cheap (and nonunionized) labor and by supplying a ready pool of strikebreakers.

6. *Inability to adapt to technical change*. As employers adopted new technologies, the distinctions among jobs changed quickly and crafts became obsolete. The titles of some disbanded unions from the nineteenth and early twentieth centuries illustrate the problem: the Horse Collar Makers National Union, the Window Glass Snappers Union, the Association Brotherhood of Iron and Steel Heaters, Rollers, and Roughers, and the Union of Shipwrights, Joiners, and Caulkers.

7. *Direct competition* (or interunion rivalry), as discussed above.

8. *Organizational failure*. Some unions never developed reliable structures and routines, e.g., at least three unions disbanded in rancorous internal conflict after officers embezzled their treasuries: the American Longshoremen's Union, the Journeymen Tailors National Trades Union, and the Switchmen's Mutual Aid Association.

Historians have often argued that such catastrophes destroyed unions that were already vulnerable for other reasons such as youth, declining membership, and inability to adjust to technical change. Historical accounts of disbandings are useful for identifying factors that appear to affect union mortality. Hannan and Freeman (1989) argue they are not appropriate for assessing competing arguments about causes of disbandings. Meaningful causal analysis requires study of unions that faced comparable catastrophes and did not disband. That is, restricting analysis to unions that disbanded distorts causal inferences about the causes of disbanding. This is a clear instance of sample selection bias (discussed in Chapter 1). Organizational ecologists have departed from the labor-history tradition by analyzing the entire population of national unions over the full, 150-year-long, historical period. This strategy avoids problems of selectivity bias and permits consideration of the joint operation of the various hypothesized causes of disbanding.

This chapter's focus on organizational density is not meant to suggest that density was the only—or even the most important—determinant of the mortality of unions. Union mortality has surely been affected by changes in the economic, legal, and political environments. In fact, changes in these key environments have altered both the competitive advantages of national unions over local unions and the capacity of the social system to sustain diverse collections of national unions. So, to obtain meaningful estimates of the effects of density on mortality, empirical research on the ecology of unions has considered the effects of a variety of other factors that have been cited as causes of union mortality.

We now briefly consider the results of studies of the effect of density on the mortality of unions. We focus on one ending event: *disbanding of the organization*. By this we mean that a union ceases to operate as an organization and does not merge with another union. Roughly one third of the unions studied disbanded. This is not the only kind of ending event for unions. About one quarter of American national unions were absorbed by other unions, and another 20 percent merged with unions of roughly equal status to form new unions. The remaining 129 unions were still functioning at the end of 1991, the date of the last systematic data.

The theory treats the disbanding rate as the mirror image of the founding rate: anything that increases one, decreases the other. Thus the theory holds that legitimation decreases the risk of disbanding and that competition increases the risk. Continuing to assume that legitimation and competition depend on density in the ways discussed in this chapter, these assumptions imply a U-shaped relationship between density and the mortality rate.

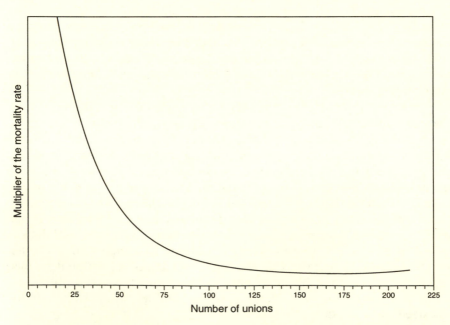

Figure 6–5 Relationship between union density and mortality rate. (*Source:* Adapted from Hannan and Carroll 1992.)

The results of many different analyses reveal that the relationship of contemporaneous density and mortality rates does have the predicated U shape. This is the case even when strong effects of aging, periods, environmental conditions, and founding conditions are considered. Figure 6-5 plots the estimated effect of density on the disbanding rate.[4] The most obvious effect is the strong negative effect of density over much of its range. The predicted disbanding rate drops by 98 percent as density rises from zero to 168. At this point, the relationship changes sign and becomes positive (although this is hard to see in the figure). As density rises further to its historical maximum (211), the disbanding rate rises modestly.[5]

Finally, organizational ecologists have also argued that density has a *delayed* effect on mortality rates, that organizations founded during periods of high density have permanently elevated mortality rates. This turns out to be the case for unions. Density at time of founding has a strong, positive effect on mortality rates. For instance, unions founded when density was at its peak had mortality rates nineteen times higher than unions founded at minimum density, once other relevant conditions have been considered.[6]

NOTES

This chapter draws on Hannan and Freeman (1987, 1988, 1989) and Hannan and Carroll (1992). Its preparation was supported by National Science Foundation Grant SES-9247842.

1. Usable data on aggregate membership are available only beginning in 1880 and are only rough approximations for 1880–89. And, after 1978, the Bureau of Labor Statistics changed its way of calculating membership (by combining employee associations with unions) so that data after this year are not directly comparable with data for earlier years. Thus the figure presents data on aggregate membership for the period 1880–1978.

2. This analysis divides the 150-year history as follows. The first period begins in 1836, the start of national unionization, and ends in 1886, the year in which the AFL was founded. The second period begins in 1887 and ends in 1931. The third period begins in 1932 with the New Deal and the Norris–LaGuardia Act of 1932, which limited the power of employers to gain injunctions against striking unions, and the National Industrial Recovery Act in 1932–33. The subsequent Wagner Act, passed in 1935, gave substantial legal protection to unions and union-organizing campaigns. This third period ends in 1947, when the Taft-Hartley Act rolled back some of the gains that unions won under the Wagner Act. The fifth period begins in 1955, the year of the merger of the AFL and CIO, and runs to 1985. It is characterized by continuous decline in the fraction of the labor force in unions.

3. This figure is based on the estimates reported by Hannan and Carroll (1992, p. 88).

4. The figure is based on results reported by Hannan and Carroll (1992, p. 126).

5. The statistical analyses involved show that the density-dependent competitive effect is indeed statistically significant.

6. This result comes from Hannan and Carroll (1992, p. 140).

BIBLIOGRAPHY

Brody, David. 1980. *Workers in Industrial America*. New York: Oxford University Press.

Commons, J. R. 1918. *History of Labor in the United States*. New York: Macmillan.

Edwards, P. K. 1981. *Strikes in the United States, 1881–1974*. New York: St. Martin's Press.

Fink, Gary, ed. 1977. *National Labor Unions*. Greenwood, AL: Greenwood Press.

Foner, Philip S. 1955. *History of the Labor Movement in the United States*, 4 vols. New York: International Publishers.

Hannan, Michael T., and Glenn R. Carroll. 1992. *Dynamics of Organizational Populations: Density, Legitimation, and Competition*. New York: Oxford University Press.

Hannan, Michael T., and John Freeman. 1987. "The Ecology of Organizational Founding: American Labor Unions, 1836–1985." *American Journal of Sociology* 92: 910–43.

Hannan, Michael T., and John Freeman. 1988. "The Ecology of Organizational Mortality: American Labor Unions, 1836–1985." *American Journal of Sociology* 94: 25–52.

Hannan, Michael T., and John Freeman. 1989. *Organizational Ecology*. Cambridge, MA: Harvard University Press.

Michels, Robert. 1949 [1915]. *Political Parties*. Translated by Edward Cedar Paul. Glencoe, IL: Free Press.

Olzak, Susan. 1989. "Labor Unrest, Immigration, and Ethnic Conflict in the United States, 1880–1914." *American Journal of Sociology* 94:1303–33.

Perlman, S. A. 1932. *A History of Trade Unionism in the United States, 1896–1932*, vol. 4. New York: Macmillan.

Tomlins, Christopher. 1985. *The State and the Unions: Labor Relations, Law and the Organized Labor Movement in America, 1880–1960*. Cambridge, MA: Cambridge University Press.

Troy, Leo. 1965. *Trade Union Membership, 1887–1962*. New York: National Bureau of Economic Research.

Ulman, Lloyd. 1955. *The Rise of the National Trade Union*. Cambridge, MA: Harvard University Press.

7

Credit Unions

DAVID BARRON

The first credit union in the United States was founded in Manchester, New Hampshire, in 1909, the same year that Massachusetts became the first state to enact a general credit union law. From this beginning, credit unions have spread to all fifty states. In 1990, there was a total of 14,533 unions in the nation, with over 61 million members and assets of more than $212 billion. Impressive though these numbers might seem, they actually represent a very small proportion of the wider financial industry. Commercial banks in the United States, for example, had total assets of well over $3 trillion in 1990. Given their relatively small size, why should we single out credit unions for study?

First, the very fact that credit unions and commercial banks differ so profoundly raises interesting questions. We often think of financial institutions as powerful bastions of capitalist economies, huge organizations transacting many millions of dollars each day and making enormous profits. Credit unions are a completely different story. They were founded on the principle of self-help, and continue to be nonprofit organizations, many still relying on the voluntary efforts of their members. How do we explain the simultaneous existence of such disparate organizational forms in the same industry? And how have credit unions, comparative minnows of the financial sector, managed to thrive for so long?

Second, these organizations were pioneers in the field of consumer lending. At the turn of the century, there were strong cultural and legal proscriptions against this form of credit. Consumer lending was left largely to "loan sharks," who normally operated illegally and charged outrageously high rates of interest. Consumer loans have since become one of the most powerful engines of modern economies. Credit unions played a significant role in this development.

Third, particularly in the early years of their history, credit unions had much in common with social movements. Even today, people involved with credit unions refer to the "credit union movement." So credit unions have some attributes of both businesses and social movement organizations. How is this reflected in the development of the credit union movement? In addition, these organizations provide a useful reference point for discussing the broad changes that have taken place in the structure of the financial industry since the 1970s. How have the structures and strategies of credit unions been affected by deregulation and the upheavals in the financial industry?

In this chapter I describe the development of the credit union movement in the United States as a whole, but often refer specifically to the condition of the New York State movement. This is because credit unions in New York have been studied more extensively than those of other states, and hence we know a lot more about them (Barron 1992; Hannan, West, and Barron 1994).

WHAT IS A CREDIT UNION?

Credit unions have a governance and ownership structure that is quite unusual in the United States: they are cooperatives. All U.S. credit unions are constituted as democratic organizations, controlled by their members based on the principle of one member, one vote. That is, voting power does not depend on the size of one's financial investment in the organization. This is, of course, very different from the typical public corporation where number of votes is directly linked to the size of shareholding. An elected committee and officers oversee the day-to-day operation of a credit union. Originally, all operations were carried out by elected members who received no remuneration for the task. Increasingly, however, credit unions have come to rely on professional managers and full-time staffs for their operation.

To become a member of a credit union one must purchase at least one share. In the early days of the credit union movement, shares were usually worth $1, but could be, and often were, purchased in installments. These shares, on which dividends were paid at the end of the year, provided the credit union with capital that it could invest in loans to members or in other ways. The types of investment allowed by law vary somewhat from state to state, but typically include government bonds, deposits in interest-bearing accounts of commercial banks, and sometimes stocks in "blue chip" corporations. However, credit unions have always used the bulk of their capital to provide loans to members.

The pioneers of the credit union movement saw themselves as providing two crucial services: helping people to practice thrift, and providing a source of credit at reasonable rates of interest for people faced with a financial emergency. However, it was the lending practices of credit unions that were to have the most impact. Credit unions helped establish two major innovations in the practice of consumer credit. First, they allowed loans to be repaid in installments. The standard practice at that time was for loans to be repaid in a single lump sum. Second, they did not require security for their loans. To minimize the risks involved in this practice, credit unions are constituted so as to maximize the *social capital* of their members. Membership is restricted to people sharing a common bond. Most credit unions in the United States have a common bond based on employment, but many credit unions take a labor union, fraternal association, church, or other type of organization as their membership base. The common bond can also be residence in a neighborhood, a form known as *open membership,* in contrast to the more common *closed membership* organizations.

Beyond the common bond requirement, credit union members were required to be "mutually acquainted." That is, there had to be some sort of social tie between the members in addition to their connection through the credit union.[1] The common bond and mutual acquaintanceship requirements were imposed on credit unions for two reasons. First, they made it easier for credit unions to assess a potential borrower's credit worthiness. Making loans to an unknown member of the public would have required a credit union to check a person's financial and personal situation—a very costly undertaking. However, if the person requesting a loan was already personally known to the committee members charged with disbursing credit, the assessment of risk was greatly facilitated. Second, a person receiving credit would experience social pressure to meet his or her obligations to the credit union. Failure to repay a debt would become known to co-workers, fraternity members, neighbors, or whichever group formed the basis of the union. These two requirements, then, were intended to keep down the costs involved in making loans and to minimize the nonpayment of debts.

Prior to 1934, all credit unions had to be chartered by a state. After the first state credit union law, that of Massachusetts in 1909, thirty-seven other states enacted legislation permitting the formation of credit unions. However, the provisions of these state laws varied quite widely, as did their success in organizing new unions. In 1934, the Federal Credit Union Act was passed, allowing credit unions to be formed on the basis of a federal charter in all states, including those without their own credit union law.

For a charter, federal or state, to be granted, credit union organizers had to show first that there were sufficient potential members sharing their common bond to make the organization viable, and that enough of these potential members were interested in joining the credit union. However, the minimum initial membership laid down in the Federal Credit Union Act, and in most state laws, was originally only seven people. Organizers also had to show that the new credit union would not overlap with the membership of existing organizations, effectively minimizing direct competition between credit unions.

Although U.S. credit unions have several attributes not found in cooperative financial institutions elsewhere in the world, they did have foreign antecedents. Similar organizations existed earlier in several European countries, including Germany and Italy, and in Quebec, Canada. Furthermore, informal organizations (that is, organizations with no formal legal status) sharing many characteristics of credit unions existed in some parts of the United States before the emergence of credit unions themselves.

PRECURSORS OF THE U.S.
CREDIT UNION MOVEMENT

European Origins

Credit unions have roots in European cooperative banks as well as in the wider cooperative movement.[2] The first people generally associated with the cooperative bank movement in Europe were the Germans Victor Aime Huber, Herman Schulze-Delitzsch, and Friedrich Wilhelm Raiffeisen. Huber was something of a Utopian. He believed that the problems of the world could be traced directly to degradations of poverty, which produced "defects of character" in the poor. In what was to become a common theme among credit union advocates, Huber thought that cooperative, self-help organizations would combat poverty more effectively than purely philanthropic activities because they promoted self-support and self-respect in addition to providing practical assistance.

Huber's interest in cooperative organizations proved to be more theoretical than practical: he was involved in the foundation of just two organizations. However, he influenced another German idealist, Schulze-Delitzsch, who formed his first cooperative credit society in 1850. These organizations had some of the characteristics of modern credit unions. Only members could borrow money from them, membership was obtained by the purchase of shares, and the organizations were under the democratic control of their members on the principle of one member, one vote. These organizations did not provide consumer credit, however, limiting their activities to the provision of credit for productive purposes.

Schulze-Delitzsch's people's banks spread rapidly. Just nine years after the founding of the first association there were 183 organizations in operation with a total of 18,000 members. By 1912, this number had risen to over 1,000 organizations with 641,000 members. These banks were located primarily in urban areas, with members being mainly shopkeepers and craft workers.

In 1846, the first "Raiffeisen Bank" was founded. This was the precursor of a second type of German credit union, based in rural areas, and intended primarily to help farmers. To become a member of a Raiffeisen credit union, one had to have tangible assets and be judged to be of "good character, industrious, and friendly" (Moody and Fite 1984) by one's peers. In contrast to the Schulze-Delitzsch organizations, Raiffeisen banks limited their membership to a single parish, and initially had no share capital. They raised money to finance their lending by borrowing from other financial institutions.[3] Although these organizations spread very slowly at first, by 1913 there were 17,000 of them, in contrast to the 1,000 Schulze-Delitzsch banks.

From Germany, cooperative credit spread to Italy. Luigi Luzzatti, a professor of political economy at the University of Padua, was influenced by Schulze-Delitzsch. He opened his first cooperative bank in Milan in 1866. Although closely modeled on their German precursors, Luzzatti's banks differed in one important respect. While both German pioneers insisted that the members of their credit unions should share unlimited liability for their banks' debts—as a way of boosting their commitment to the stability and success of the organization—Luzzatti argued that this was asking too much of people already under severe financial pressure. His organizations, therefore, were the first cooperative credit associations to adopt the principle of limited liability. These organizations also emphasized the value of a person's character as "security" for a loan—the "capitalization of honesty," as Luzzatti put it (Moody and Fite 1984). However, as these banks grew, they departed from strict cooperative principles in that they began to provide services to the public, member and nonmember alike.

Early Cooperative Credit Organizations in Canada

From these early origins, cooperative credit organizations spread to many other European countries. Not surprisingly, given that German immigration was very high from the end of the Civil War until the 1920s, similar organizations also sprang up in the United States. A few German people's banks, similar to Schulze-Delitzsch banks, were established in New York. The *New York Times* in 1869 suggested that these cooperative banks provided a means of defusing the increasingly violent confrontations between labor and capital, a theme that was to be repeated many times over the next few years by credit union advocates.

These organizations never really established themselves in the United States, however, and soon disappeared from the scene. More successful were the efforts of Alphonse Desjardins in Quebec. He founded the first *caisse populaire* in Lévis, a city in eastern Quebec, in 1901.[4] Desjardins studied the cooperative banks of Germany and Italy carefully, corresponding with several European pioneers, including Luzzatti. He felt that the *Caisse Populaire de Lévis* synthesized those elements of the European organizations that best suited Quebec society at that time (Roby 1975). The *caisses populaires* are particularly interesting for our purposes. As the direct precursors of credit unions in the United States, they share many characteristics. On the other hand, there are also several important differences between these two organizational forms that will prove illuminating.

Several elements of Desjardins' program deserve note. First, following the example of Luzzatti, members of a *caisse populaire* had only limited liability for an organization's debts. Second, he intended the *caisses* to serve the needs of both rural and urban communities, going against the European norm of having specialist organizational forms serving these two types of environment. Third, as Rudin (1990) points out, the *caisses* were closely associated with French-Canadian nationalism and with the Catholic Church. Indeed, Desjardins took great pains to enlist the support of the Catholic clergy, and all the early *caisses* took a church parish as their geographical area of operation.

The *caisse populaire* movement in Quebec was slow to spread at first, and there were many failures among the pioneer organizations. However, by 1920 there were 140 *caisses populaires* operating in Quebec, with combined assets of $6.3 million. The great majority of these organizations were based in rural communities. Managers of *caisses populaires* in cities, and particularly in Montreal, the largest city in the province, believed that the instability of the population within their catchment areas impeded the development of the strong community ties that facilitated the formation and growth of cooperative organizations.

As we discuss the development of credit unions in the United States, we see many similarities between the American organizations and their foreign precursors. However, we also see that U.S. credit unions have evolved their own unique structures and strategies.

Precursors in the United States
Apart from the few Schulze-Delitzsch-style banks that were founded by German immigrants in New York toward the end of the nineteenth century, there were several other organizational forms that can legitimately be seen as forerunners of credit unions. Informal organizational forms appear to have been quite widespread, often within immigrant communities. For example, organizations called *axias* are known to have predated credit unions, and continued to exist even after credit unions became well established. Because of their informal nature, details of these organizations are difficult to obtain. Robinson (1931) mentions them in a comparison of the different interest rates charged by various institutions.[5] They are also mentioned in the 1931 report of the New York Credit Union League, which was concerned that *axias* were trying to pass themselves off as legally constituted credit unions.

Several other types of organization providing credit to working people also existed in the early twentieth century, though these lacked any of the elements of cooperative organizations. Employers, for example, sometimes took it upon themselves to organize savings and loan facilities for their employees. The annual report of the commissioner of banks in Massachusetts for 1908 mentions eight such cases of workplace banking (Moody and Fite 1984). These arrangements were intended to provide similar services to credit unions, though their emphasis tended to be on encouraging saving rather than the provision of credit and they were certainly not cooperatives.

Finally, in several states, including New York, mutual savings banks and savings and loan associations (or building and loan associations as they were sometimes called) existed prior to credit unions (Ranger-Moore, Banaszak-Holl, and Hannan 1991). Although not cooperatives, these organizations shared something of the character of credit unions in that they were not-for-profit concerns intended to provide services to people not served by traditional financial institutions. Mutual savings banks became extremely powerful institutions, attracting huge sums, mostly in the form of small savings accounts. However, they generally did not provide loans to their customers. Savings and loan associations specialized in the provision of real estate mortgages, but did not provide credit for more general purposes. So credit unions, with their emphasis on the provision of small loans, entered a niche that had not previously been exploited by legally constituted financial institutions.

Interestingly, however, credit unions were not the only new type of organization to enter this niche during the early years of the twentieth century. Organizations known as "Morris Plan Banks" were also spreading across the

United States just as the credit union movement was establishing itself. So two very different organizational forms were being created at the same time, both having as their primary aim the provision of consumer credit to working people. What can we learn about the development of new organizational forms by comparing and contrasting these two sets of organizations? To answer this question, we first need to know something about how the Morris Plan Banks operated.

MORRIS PLAN BANKS

The Morris Plan was devised by Arthur Morris, a lawyer from Virginia. He hit upon a way of meeting the demand for small loans, making a profit, and appearing to keep to the legal maximum interest rate, which at that time was 6 percent per annum in most states. Note that Morris Plan Banks were run as businesses. Although we shall see that they portrayed themselves as meeting an urgent social need, they were set up to make a profit for their investors, who included such noted industrialists as Andrew Carnegie. Indeed, they were very successful in this endeavor, and consequently had no trouble attracting capital investment.

The operation of the Morris Plan Banks in various U.S. cities was coordinated by the Industrial Finance Corporation. No city had more than one Morris Plan Bank, though the banks often had several offices in a city. Other organizations also copied the essential elements of the Morris Plan after the courts ruled that Mr. Morris did not have exclusive rights to the idea. These organizations were often known as *industrial banks,* although their primary market was in small loans. When commercial banks started to enter the personal loan field in significant numbers in the 1930s, they also adopted many features of the Morris Plan.[6]

Banks operating under the Morris Plan made small loans to ordinary working people. The minimum loan was $50, quite large by the standards of the day. A borrower had to be in regular employment and had to get two cosigners who agreed to be responsible for the debt if the borrower defaulted. This cosigner arrangement served much the same purpose as the "mutual acquaintanceship" requirement of credit unions; it imposed social pressure on a borrower to repay his or her loan. In practice, the Morris Plan Banks had to be cautious in their enforcement of the responsibility of cosigners. They did not want to frighten people away from assuming this role. In fact, the default rate for Morris Plan Bank loans—like that of credit unions—was remarkably low.

The Morris Plan was devised to enable small loans to be made at the legal 6 percent interest rate. This is how it worked. Say someone borrowed $100 for a year at 6 percent. First, the interest would be discounted at the start of the year, so the borrower actually only received $94. A fee of $2 was also deducted, leaving $92. Then the money was repaid in 50 weekly installments of $2. Consequently, the effective rate of interest was much higher than 6 percent: it was actually around 18 percent. The practice of claiming to charge an interest rate of 6 percent when the true rate is much higher would clearly be illegal today.

It was probably not legal in 1914. However, the practice was never challenged in the courts because, as Robinson and Nugent (1934, p. 92) point out, the Morris Plan Banks ". . . had the moral support of the community." How did the Morris Plan Banks and the credit union movement go about winning this support? Is there evidence of any competition between these organizations? To understand these processes we need to know something about the social and economic conditions that prevailed at the time these new organizational forms were emerging.

THE EMERGENCE OF CREDIT UNIONS
IN THE UNITED STATES

Social and Economic Conditions

What were the important features of the social environment around the time when the first credit unions were being formed? The social and economic situation of the United States at the turn of the century was characterized by rapid industrialization and urbanization. Immigration, particularly from southern and eastern Europe, was also very high during this period. Consequently major cities contained large numbers of people who were dislocated from traditional family and community sources of support. Such people were often in a very precarious financial position, as there was no widely available unemployment or medical insurance. A family could easily be thrown into a financial crisis as a result of sickness or job loss. For want of alternative sources of support in such circumstances, people had to borrow money to pay their debts. However, credit for ordinary working people was not readily available. Consumer borrowing and lending were looked upon as unsavory practices, shunned by respectable people and financial institutions. As Clark (1930, p. 4) put it,

> The workingman who asked for a loan was looked upon as slightly immoral—he must be wasting his substance in riotous living—and those who made him loans had an unsavory reputation as men engaged in a risky and nefarious trade, with whom one would not associate in a business way.

Clark estimates that 90 percent of the U.S. population had no access to credit "on a business basis." Therefore even in 1930 "unlicensed lenders" were the most important source of small loans. They lent some $750 million, an estimated 28.9 percent of the loans made in the United States in that year (Clark 1930, Table 3). People faced with an urgent need for cash usually had no alternative but to go to an unlicensed money lender—universally known as a loan shark—who would typically charge well above the legal maximum interest rate.

At this point in history, then, there is evidently a demand for credit, but a cultural antipathy toward those who borrow or lend money. It is important to note that at this time the demand for credit was almost entirely to meet unexpected expenses such as medical bills. The practice of borrowing money to purchase luxury items—consumer credit as we know it today—was virtually unknown at the turn of the century, at least for the working class. It was in this climate that both credit unions and Morris Plan Banks emerged.

Gaining Legitimacy

What steps did these new organizations take to overcome the widespread aversion toward their activities? As financial institutions, credit unions and Morris Plan Banks faced a particularly difficult task to establish their legitimacy, because the financial sector was so tightly regulated. Support from politicians and officials was crucial if these new organizational forms were to succeed. Each Morris Plan Bank had to obtain a charter from a state banking commissioner. Credit unions faced an even more difficult task: new legislation was required in each state in addition to the chartering of individual unions once such legislation was enacted. We might expect this task to have been fraught with difficulty. First, the spread of these organizations, particularly credit unions, was often opposed by powerful interests representing commercial banks and savings and loan associations, who feared a loss of savings deposits to a new competitor. Second, their principal market—consumer credit—was one that was still viewed by many people as morally questionable and likely to encourage "riotous living" among the working classes.

Both organizational forms had the advantage of being backed by powerful individuals. The Morris Plan Bank, for example, included such people as Andrew Carnegie among its investors. Arthur Morris also created an organization—the Industrial Finance Corporation—designed to promote Morris Plan Banks across the nation. Furthermore, these organizations operated under normal banking laws, and there was less opportunity for opponents to fight them. All they had to do was persuade a state banking commissioner to grant them a charter. Credit unions also had a powerful backer: Edward Filene, the wealthy Boston store owner. He had many contacts with powerful politicians, including Franklin Roosevelt. In addition, Filene financed the Credit Union National Extension Bureau, an organization dedicated to promoting credit unions throughout the United States. In its early years, CUNEB, and in particular its organizer, Roy Bergengren, devoted much of its time to lobbying for the passage of credit union laws in various states and ultimately at the federal level.

McCarthy and Zald (1973) argued that "social movement entrepreneurs" play an important role in modern social movements. Similarly, DiMaggio (1988) argued that "institutional entrepreneurs" are sometimes important in boosting the legitimacy of new organizational forms via their involvement in institutionalizing projects. There can be little doubt that Arthur Morris, Edward Filene, and Roy Bergengren were "institutional entrepreneurs," and that they adopted a clear strategy intended to boost the legitimacy of their organizations with the public and hence with politicians. This institutionalizing project involved linking their organizations with the fight against loan sharks, an issue that was provoking widespread concern (Barron 1992).

A document published by the Industrial Finance Corporation in 1914, for example, went to great pains to point out that the Morris Plan Banks were providing an alternative to the "Loan Shark Evil" (Industrial Finance Corporation 1914). Working people who could get credit from a Morris Plan Bank would no longer need to turn to usurers. Demand for credit from illegal sources would therefore disappear, and loan sharks would be eradicated.

Evidence that the Morris Plan Bank succeeded in getting this message across can be found in several articles published in the *New York Times*. On November 21, 1914, for example, the *Times* carried a story about the Morris Plan Company organizing to make small loans with the express purpose of fighting loan sharks. June 5, 1914, saw the publication of an article explaining how the Morris Plan worked and pointing out that it aimed its business at "workingmen, formerly the prey of loan sharks." And on February 17 the headline was "Get Ready to Rout Loan Sharks Here." This story carried lengthy quotes from Arthur Morris, the author of the Morris Plan.

Like the Morris Plan Banks, credit unions tried to make use of anti–loan shark feeling. CUNEB published a newspaper—*The Bridge*—that contained many statements of the objectives of credit unions and their anti–loan shark, pro-thrift stance. The credit union movement stressed the role of credit unions in the war on usury. It also pointed out that credit unions promoted thrift (they also accepted savings as well as providing loans), and that they were self-help organizations. Hence, the credit union movement, like Morris Plan Banks, stressed that someone availing himself or herself of a credit union loan need feel no loss of self-respect. Credit unions required no collateral or cosigners, stressing instead that, "Character and earning power are collateral." Furthermore, a credit union member should feel proud at being a member of a "people's bank."

The credit unions' campaign, however, was less successful than the Morris Plan Banks' at generating publicity in the *New York Times*. Far fewer reports deal with credit unions than with the Morris Plan Bank. This might well reflect the fact that although there were numerous credit unions, the single Morris Plan Bank in New York was much larger than even the biggest credit union. However, the few articles that did appear certainly reflected the tone of the credit union movement's campaign. On October 16, 1914, for example, the *New York Times* carried a report in which credit unions were described as a means by which "[w]orkers can obtain money without falling into the hands of usurers."

So both the Morris Plan bank and the credit union movement, although very different organizational forms, adopted very similar tactics in their institutionalizing projects. Both these projects appear to have been somewhat successful in the sense that contemporary newspaper accounts accurately reflect the image that the Morris Plan Banks and credit unions were attempting to project.

Credit Unions and Free-Riders

The activities of CUNEB and the Industrial Finance Corporation suggest that credit unions and the Morris Plan Banks were behaving much like social movements conducting a public campaign. In the case of credit unions, the similarity to a social movements is clear. Credit union activists have always seen themselves as part of a "movement." Bergengren, the first head of the Credit Union National Extension Bureau, described his work to spread credit unions as a "crusade." In the case of the Morris Plan Bank the ideological motivation is less obvious, though we have seen that these organizations employed the rhetoric of an anti–loan shark social movement in the years immediately following their establishment.

Social movements are usually concerned with the production of what are known as "public goods." That is, if a social movement is successful in meeting its goals, the benefits of its achievements are often enjoyed by a much larger group than the movement activists. Furthermore, it is often the case that the participation of any one individual has an insignificant effect on the probability that a movement will accomplish its mission. In these circumstances, organizations face the "free-rider problem." People might well reason that there is no point in becoming involved in a social movement. There is little incentive to participate when people believe that their contribution will be of little or no value, and when they can share in the fruits of success whether they get involved or not.

Both credit union activists and the leaders of the Morris Plan Banks argued that they were trying to produce public goods. Their organizations, they claimed, would contribute to reducing poverty and eradicating usury. Yet neither suffered from free-riding. What protected credit unions and Morris Plan Banks from this problem?

This question is least problematic when we consider businesses. When a firm is founded by a single entrepreneur, or when an individual invests capital in a business, it is clear that they have an individual interest in making a profit. More generally, as Adam Smith pointed out, in a market economy collective action can occur as a result of individuals acting to further their own private interests. Hence, there is no difficulty understanding the interests underlying the formation of Morris Plan Banks.

Cooperatives can be seen as a nonmarket means of producing collective action based on individuals acting in their own interests. At least some of the benefits produced by cooperatives accrue *only to members*. To become a member of a credit union, one has to purchase one or more shares. Some benefit is obtained from this alone, in that dividends are paid on the shares. In addition, membership allows one to deposit savings and to obtain credit. If these services either cannot be obtained elsewhere, or if they can be obtained on better terms from a credit union than from other institutions, then this is clearly in the interests of the individual member. Thus a credit union can attract members who have no interest (objective or subjective) in the goals of the credit union movement as set out by the leadership of the movement. Furthermore, they might not share any commitment to the "ideals" of cooperation, such as democracy and self-help. So a cooperative is effective at producing public goods such as reducing poverty when it also produces benefits available only to members.

It is important to remember that the personal interest of an individual in becoming a credit union member is not sufficient to explain the emergence of this organizational form. Presumably this interest existed before credit unions emerged, and presumably it is shared by at least some of the many millions of people who do not become credit union members. Furthermore, cooperative organizations were not the only means of meeting these interests: the simultaneous emergence of the Morris Plan Banks shows that more traditional businesses could operate in a very similar market. But understanding the relationship between the production of public and private goods does help to illuminate the nature of cooperative organizations, and in particular the connection between the ideologically motivated movement leadership and the ordinary member pursuing his or her own interests.[7]

New Organizations Build on Existing Structures

New organizational forms such as credit unions are not created in a vacuum. I have, for example, pointed to the importance of the social and economic conditions that prevailed in the early twentieth century for understanding the process by which these organizations emerged. Another way in which new organizations are influenced by their environment is that they tend to build on existing social structures. For example, Barron (1992) has argued that one of the keys to the formation of new credit unions in the early stages of the population's history was the social network ties of credit union members.

Once the first organization of a particular type has been founded, its members, clients, customers, and staff become potential sources for the further diffusion of information about the organizational form. In the case of credit unions, for example, the first members were likely to have had a more favorable attitude than the general public toward consumer borrowing in general and credit unions in particular. Therefore, it is reasonable to suppose that they acted as sources for the diffusion of such attitudes. Their activities could have had the effect of increasing recruitment to existing organizations. However, someone wanting to avail themselves of the services of a credit union would not be able to do so if they did not share a common bond with an existing organization. But such a person might well be more likely to be involved in the formation of a new credit union than she or he was before being exposed to information about credit unions. Although it is difficult to observe this sort of process directly, evidence has been found that network diffusion did play a role in the founding of a new credit unions, at least in the early years of the population.

Credit unions built on existing social structures in other ways. An innovative practice introduced by credit unions was that they often did not require security for their loans. They treated "character as collateral," to quote one of the movement's early slogans. That is, credit union organizers reasoned that they could safely lend people money on the strength of their future earning potential and their good character. This left the problem of how to assess the character of a potential borrower. Credit unions resolved this problem by insisting that their members be "personally acquainted" with each other and that they all share a "common bond." Not only did this facilitate character assessments, it also provided an incentive for borrowers to repay their debts, because knowledge of their failure to do so would certainly spread through their circle of friends or co-workers. It is not difficult to see that this requirement meant that it was much easier to form a credit union whose common bond was membership of another, preexisting organization. In the United States, the most frequent common bond is based on employment. Most credit unions' members are people who have the same employer. As well as providing a ready-made group of mutually acquainted people, this arrangement had several other significant advantages for a credit union. First, employers would often grant time off for employees to administer the credit union and would provide free office space, effectively subsidizing the operation of the credit union.

Second, credit unions situated within the workplace were very convenient for workers to use, particularly as many of them operated next to the factory cash office from which employees drew their pay. This was a major advantage before the arrival of the automated teller machine. Finally, employees could deposit savings with and repay loans to their credit union by means of direct payroll deduction long before such services were available electronically to bank customers.

It is instructive to compare the experience of credit unions in New York with the *caisses populaires* in Quebec. While the former were mostly found in cities—primarily in New York City itself—and were mostly based in workplaces, in Quebec most *caisses populaires* were founded in rural areas. The few *caisses populaires* that were established in urban areas such as Montreal did not flourish. The *caisse populaire* movement was closely associated with the Catholic Church, and all *caisses populaires* were based on church parishes. That is, they were open to all members of a church, which meant almost all the residents in a parish. Thus, *caisses populaires* too were based on preexisting organizations, in this case churches. This arrangement worked well in rural areas where the population was relatively stable. On the other hand, the population of urban parishes in Montreal was very unstable. Rudin (1990) reports that the managers of the *Caisse Populaire de l'Immaculée-Conception* complained to Desjardins of the struggle they were having to keep the organization viable in the face of a high turnover of people in their parish.

Most of the first credit unions in New York, which followed the Quebec model, were based on geographical units—neighborhoods—rather than on workplaces. However, these "open membership" organizations, as they were called, experienced the same problems as the urban *caisses populaires*. These organizations failed at a much higher rate than "closed membership" unions, whose common bond is membership of another organization. Therefore, open membership credit unions were largely replaced by closed membership organizations, the process being hastened by government policies that discouraged the founding of new open membership organizations.

DEVELOPMENT OF THE CREDIT UNION MOVEMENT

In most states, credit union growth was rather slow. As an example, Figure 7-1 shows a plot of the growth of credit unions in New York State from 1914 to 1990. At the time of the passage of New York's Credit Union Law in 1914 (the second such law in the United States), the prospects for credit union growth seemed bright. The movement enjoyed some powerful friends, including then New York Senator Roosevelt. Furthermore, the Russell Sage Foundation, con-

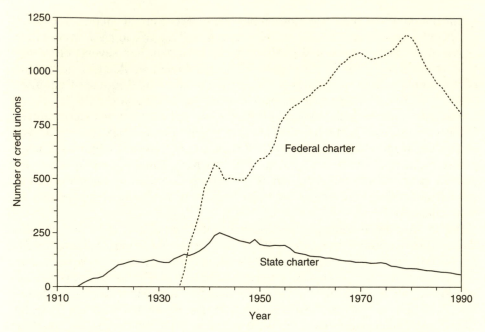

Figure 7–1 Density of credit unions in New York State. (*Source:* Adapted from Barron et al. 1994. Copyright © 1994 by University of Chicago Press. Used by permission.)

vinced that credit unions were an effective means of reducing urban poverty, was also actively involved in the movement. In fact, however, the number of credit unions grew only slowly in the first twenty years of the population's history, as can be seen in Figure 7-1.

Moody and Fite (1984) attribute this slow growth to lack of commitment by the Russell Sage Foundation, which was active in the promotion of credit unions in New York. The Credit Union National Exchange Bureau (CUNEB), a national organization devoted to the promotion of the credit union movement, was not initially involved in New York because of the presence of the Russell Sage Foundation. According to Moody and Fite, however, Bergengren, the leader of CUNEB, quickly became dissatisfied with the progress of the movement in New York, which he attributed to lack of zeal on the part of the Russell Sage Foundation.

On the other hand, the experience of slow initial growth of a novel organizational form is not unusual. We have already mentioned that cooperative banks in Germany spread slowly, and that the *caisses populaires* in Quebec experienced a similar growth trajectory. Furthermore, slow initial growth is a feature common to a wide range of organizational populations. Hannan and Carroll (1992), for example, describe the historical evolution of seven populations—labor unions, breweries, and life insurance companies in the United States; newspapers in Argentina, Ireland, and the San Francisco Bay Area; and banks in Manhattan. Of these seven populations, only one—San Francisco newspapers—did not have a period of markedly slow growth during the first few years of its development.

Perhaps, then, it is possible to understand the slow growth of credit unions in New York in terms of more general processes that affect many, if not all, organizational populations, rather than, or in addition to, unique historical circumstances surrounding the leaders of the credit union movement. Possible candidates for such processes are density-dependent legitimation and competition, described in the introduction to this section. We have already discussed the potential difficulties faced by credit unions in overcoming the antipathy toward the provision of consumer credit. It is also easy to imagine that credit unions would at first have a hard time persuading people to deposit savings with them until they had achieved a reputation for stability. This is particularly true when one recalls that deposit insurance was unheard of at the time credit unions were establishing themselves, and so the risk of loosing one's savings in the event of a credit union's failure was very real. Thinking this way makes it easy to believe that founding and failure rates are linked to social legitimacy. As people begin to believe that credit unions are reliable organizations that are not going to fail, they are more likely to support the founding of a new credit union. People are also more likely to deposit their money in existing credit unions, thereby increasing the capital of these organizations and reducing their risk of failure. Similar arguments can be made regarding the increasing social acceptability of consumer borrowing.

I have already described two mechanisms by which the legitimacy of credit unions and Morris Plan banks was enhanced: an institutionalizing project and diffusion via social networks. The legitimation argument advanced by Hannan and other organizational ecologists suggests that the legitimacy of an organizational form is linked to the number of organizations in existence. Rare organizations, they reason, are less likely to be "taken-for-granted" and trusted. As the number of organizations of a particular type increases, people become more familiar with them; they gradually become an accepted part of the social landscape. Barron (1992) and Hannan, West and Barron (1994) have indeed found evidence that credit union founding and failure rates are affected by processes of density—dependent legitimation. Thus two explanations of the slow initial growth of the credit union population have been advanced. The first stresses a particular historical circumstance—poor movement leadership—while the second invokes a general social process of legitimation. While the former process might well have been important, there is also evidence that more general processes—an institutionalizing project, diffusion, and density-dependent legitimation—were also operating. If we accept that increasing legitimacy increases the rate at which new organizations are founded and decreases the risk of failure of existing organizations, then it is easy to see how these processes would produce a pattern of accelerating population growth.

In 1934, the number of credit unions rose sharply. This precipitate rise is explained by the passage of the Federal Credit Union Act. Before 1934, all credit unions in the United States had operated under the authority of various state laws, though not all states had such statutes. Figure 7-1 shows the com-

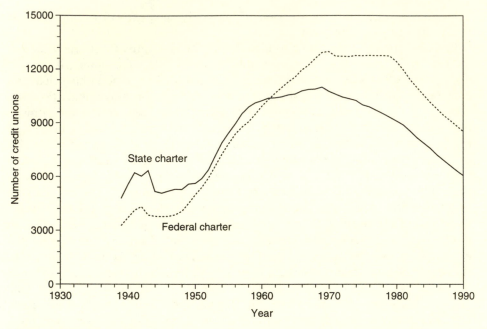

Figure 7–2 Density of credit unions in the United States. (*Source:* Adapted from Barron et al. 1994. Copyright © 1994 by University of Chicago Press. Used by permission.)

plete history of the credit union population in New York State, from the time of the first union's founding in 1914 through 1990. Complete population data are not readily available for other states. However, the Credit Union National Association (CUNA) has compiled data on each state from 1939 onward. Figure 7-2 shows a plot of the number of federally chartered and state chartered unions in the country over this period.

CREDIT UNION GROWTH

Table 7-1 gives some idea of the extent of credit union growth in New York City over the past seventy years or so. Similar trends occurred nationally. Growth has been particularly spectacular since the 1960s. For example, during 1961–76, credit union assets grew by 12.8 percent per year, compared with commercial bank annual growth of only 8.6 percent (Pearce 1984). As the number of credit unions declined during the same period, many of those organizations that survived saw even more spectacular growth than these aggregate figures suggest.

However, this growth was not distributed equally across all credit unions. Perhaps the most striking feature of this table is the increasing asset share held by the largest credit unions. In 1920, the largest 5 percent of the credit union population in New York City controlled 22.6 percent of the assets held by all credit unions in the city. By 1990, the largest 5 percent held 85.1 percent of the

Table 7–1 Descriptive statistics showing how the distribution of real total assets of state-charter credit unions in New York City varied from 1920 to 1990

Year	Number of credit unions	Mean total assets (in thousands)	Median total assets (in thousands)	Percentage of total assets held by largest 5% of CUs
1920	47	1.412	.841	22.61
1930	108	6.838	3.533	31.07
1940	102	7.872	2.308	56.56
1950	89	9.000	1.958	65.18
1960	59	22.80	3.028	76.88
1970	46	59.56	5.740	74.98
1980	32	176.0	18.37	70.64
1990	20	165.7	6.961	85.07

assets. At the national level, in 1976 the sixty largest credit unions (one quarter of 1 percent of the total population of 22,533) held 14.5 percent of all credit union assets (Pearce 1984).[8] At the other end of the spectrum, 80 percent of all credit unions had less than $2 million in assets, accounting for just 18.5 percent of all credit union assets.

Organizational researchers have long been interested in explaining organizational size distributions. Much of this research has involved tests of variations on "Gibrat's law," which holds that an organization's proportional growth rate is independent of its current size. If this law were true, organizations of all sizes would grow at the same rate. For example, if the growth rate is 10 percent per year, an organization that starts the year with assets of $1,000 will amass assets of $1,100 by the end of the year. Similarly, a $100,000 organization will reach a size of $110,000 over a twelve-month period. Simon and collaborators studied the implications of Gibrat's model, proposing variations that produce stable size distributions over time (Ijiri and Simon 1977). Tests of these models have received mixed support. Barron (1992) and Hannan, West, and Barron (1994) have tested Gibrat's law on credit unions in New York, and found that it was not supported. In fact, their findings suggest that large organizations grow at a proportionately *slower rate* than their smaller counterparts. How do we square this finding with the observation, as in Table 7-1, that large organizations have been controlling a larger and larger share of credit union assets? Although this question has yet to be directly addressed by researchers, the answer is likely to be found in the fact that the risk of failure declines sharply as organizational size increases. Thus, though they might be growing at a comparatively slow proportionate rate, large organizations survive longer on average, and thus have the opportunity to become larger and larger over time. Furthermore, as the credit union population has declined in number in recent years, large organizations make up a growing share of the total population.

Cooperative organizations face certain distinctive problems as they get larger. Earlier we pointed out that individuals have an interest in becoming a credit union member, because only members can benefit from the credit union's services. However, consider the position of unpaid volunteers running a union. While a professional manager of a business has a clear interest in the growth of the organization he or she is running, it is not clear that a volunteer has the same interest. The following quotation is taken from a booklet published by CUNA for credit unions themselves (Francis 1968, p. 58):

> Growth has its penalties for the volunteer manager. What he took on cheerfully as a two-hour-a-week adventure becomes a ten- or twenty-hour drain on his time and energies. Credit union income builds too slowly, is committed to too many other things to be used to sweeten the job for the people who carry the load in those early months. Unless the momentum of the enthusiastic charter signers can carry over, the little credit union might never get past the stage of pants-pocket management.

Even slightly larger credit unions that have a paid, part-time manager can face similar problems. Such a manager might not have an interest in the credit union growing to the point where full-time management is required. These factors can result in credit union growth becoming stalled, because the move to employing a full-time manager can be a difficult one for a nonprofessional, elected committee to take.

On the other hand, full-time professional managers of credit unions clearly have the same interest in expanding their organization that managers of businesses have. Thus, while the officers of most credit unions have no pecuniary interest in their organizations' growth, the "cadre of professionals in the credit union trade associations and managers of large credit unions have a clear interest in industry growth" (Pearce 1984).

Besides this potential source of conflict within the credit union movement, it is not completely obvious how one should measure a credit union's growth. The objectives of individual credit unions are not clear. They are not trying to maximize profits; they are nonprofit organizations. If they decide to maximize the dividends paid on shares, this will result in higher interest rates on loans. On the other hand, if they charge as little as possible to lenders, depositors will loose out. Some members join a credit union primarily as savers, and others join primarily to obtain credit. Thus there is a potential conflict of interest among members. Indeed, Rudin (1990) reports that disputes over this question did occur in several of Quebec's *caisses populaires*. However, most credit unions place more importance on the provision of consumer loans, and the bulk of their assets are in this form. Thus most research has used total assets as the best measure of credit union size, and growth in assets as an indicator of growth and decline.

CREDIT UNIONS AND DEREGULATION

In recent years the financial industry has seen wide-ranging deregulation. Simultaneously, the traditional lines of demarcation between the financial institutions have been breaking down. Table 7-2 shows some of the major regulatory changes affecting credit unions between 1977 and 1983.

Table 7–2 Credit union regulatory changes, 1977–1983

1977 Amendments to Federal Credit Union Act
  Increased loan maturities on nonresidential loans to twelve years.
  Allowed thirty-year residential mortgage loans and fifteen-year mobile home and home-improvement loans.
  Permitted self-replenishing lines of credit.
  Permitted participation in loans with other financial institutions.
  Allowed different types of share accounts, including share certificates.

1978 Financial Institutions Regulatory and Interest Rate Control Act
  Restructured NCUA into three-member board.
  Permitted sale of mortgages on secondary market.
  Permitted market rates on large share certificates.
  Permitted six-month, $10,000 certificates paying 0.25 percent above six-month Treasury bill rate.

1980 Depository Institutions Deregulation and Monetary Control Act
  Classified credit unions as depository institutions.
  Gave permanent authority for share draft account.
  Set required reserves for share drafts.
  Raised loan rate ceiling to 15 percent.
  NCUA regulations raised loan ceiling to 21 percent for nine-month period.

1981 NCUA Regulations
  Extended 21-percent ceiling.
  Allowed credit unions to make variable interest rate consumer and mortgage loans.

1982 Garn–St. Germain Depository Institutions Act
  Freed credit unions to set par value of shares and to determine internal organization.
  Eliminated limits on size and maturity of mortgage loans, allowed refinancing of first mortgages, and extended maturity limit on second mortgages.
  Permitted credit unions greater flexibility in the kinds of services they can offer and the joint sharing of activities with other credit unions.

1983 NCUA regulations expanded definition of "family member" in common bond requirement.

Source: Pearce (1984).

These regulations have had several important consequences for the services credit unions can offer. First, the amendments to the Federal Credit Union Act passed in 1977 allowed credit unions to enter the residential mortgage market to a significant degree. Previously, secured credit union loans could not have a maturity of longer than ten years, effectively excluding them from the mass mortgage market. The 1978 act allowing credit unions to sell mortgages on the secondary market enabled even relatively small credit unions to offer this service to their members. Second, the DIDMC (Depository Institutions Deregulation and Monetary Control) Act of 1980 ratified the use of credit union share draft accounts, which are effectively interest-bearing checking accounts. Third, allowing credit unions to offer self-replenishing lines of credit and variable-rate loans effectively opened the door to their entry into the credit card market.

However, deregulation has also allowed other financial institutions more scope to enter the traditional markets of credit unions. Savings and loan associations and mutual savings banks were allowed to make consumer loans. Restrictions on deposit interest rates have also been phased out, putting pressure on one of the traditional advantages of credit unions: the ability to offer higher interest rates on deposits than other depository institutions.

Thus there has been an increasing degree of overlap in the retail banking services offered by the various financial institutions. This raises two important questions: What precipitated the processes of industry homogenization? What effect has this process had on the credit union movement and the other types of financial institutions?

Financial Industry Homogenization

One approach to the question, "What precipitated the deregulation of the financial industry?" would be to look at changes in the ideology of government over the period. The conservative administrations of the 1970s and 1980s espoused an ideological commitment to deregulation across a wide range of industries. Presidents Reagan and Bush argued that deregulation was a means of increasing competition within an industry, and that increasing competitive pressure results in increasing efficiency. Organizations must either adapt to their new, more competitive environment by increasing their efficiency—that is, by cutting unit costs—or they will be forced out of business by those organizations that do change.

However, there is considerable evidence that process of increasing overlap in the services provided by different financial organizations began well before deregulation started. Dugger, Miller, and Wolken (1981, p. 8) write that, "It has been widely and, the authors of this paper believe, accurately observed that DIDMCA did not initiate financial change; it ratified change that had already been underway and in some respects achieved." These authors identify likely causes of the breakdown in the traditional barriers between financial institutions as "advances in data processing technology, the changing structure of the American population, [and . . .] secular increases in inflation and interest rates."

Technological changes have brought powerful computer hardware and software within the reach of even smaller organizations, including credit unions. The ability to process large amounts of data rapidly is particularly important for the operation of share draft accounts, credit cards, automatic teller machines, and so on. So, credit unions' ability to offer a wider range of services has been greatly enhanced by their increased ability to acquire powerful data processing technology.

Another important factor has been the growth of trade associations in the credit union industry. Smaller credit unions, in particular, have been able to provide a wider range of services by becoming part of a trade association. Furthermore, integrating such services as data processing has enabled credit unions to realize economies of scale that would not otherwise have been possible. Pearce (1984) argues that the growth in the significance of trade associations—of which the Credit Union National Association (CUNA) is by far the most important—has resulted in most credit unions being integrated into what is essentially a single financial network. The cooperative nature of credit unions and the existence of the common bond facilitates this industry structure.

Effects of Financial Industry Deregulation

Most researchers agree that the financial industry has become much more competitive since the 1970s as a result of increasing overlap of services (Dugger, Miller, and Wolken 1981; Pearce 1984; Bundt and Keating 1988). Although several scholars have suggested that credit unions are well placed to cope with this increased competition (Pearce 1984), they nevertheless expect there to be a continuing decline in the number of credit unions. Indeed, the National Credit Union Administration—the federal agency charged with regulating federal-chartered credit unions—has a policy of encouraging mergers, believing large credit unions to be better able to survive in this new environment. This opinion is borne out by a recent study (Bundt and Keating 1988), which concluded that there was no evidence that, "Large credit unions, which must compete with other depository institutions, have experienced either increasing costs or declining revenues as a result of the combined effects of enhanced competition and deposit interest rate deregulation."

One of the most important—and controversial—changes in credit union strategy in recent years has been the gradual relaxation of the common bond requirement. Regulators and legislators have acted out of a desire to facilitate credit union growth and to protect credit unions that are associated with a single firm from failing when the host organization fails. Credit unions today can have as members people sharing multiple common bonds: some of the largest have over one hundred common bonds making up their field of membership. Undoubtedly this has helped the growth of credit unions. As one recent report pointed out, new groups that want access to credit union services no longer seek to found a new credit union, but rather to become part of the field of membership of an existing organization. Therefore, the growth of existing credit unions has been associated with a precipitate decline in the number of new credit unions being founded.

While the growth of credit unions must surely have been beneficial in reducing the number of organizational failures, it has not occurred without a price. For many within the credit union movement, the coming of multiple common bonds has seriously undermined a fundamental principle on which the credit union ideal is based. There is a possibility that member cohesion will be undermined, that competition among credit unions for members will grow, and that as a result credit unions will start to act more like profit-maximizing organizations. This, in turn, will further undermine member commitment, and so on. Already, the trend to more open membership has substantially increased the pressure on government from other financial institutions to abolish credit unions' tax-exempt status.

There is also evidence that the credit union population is becoming split into two classes—large credit unions, offering an ever-increasing range of services; and small credit unions that continue to offer limited services and to rely heavily on voluntary help. Table 7-3 shows a list of the twenty largest credit unions

Table 7-3 The twenty largest federally insured credit unions in the United States as of December 31, 1990

Name	City and state	Year chartered	Total assets ($\times 10^3$)	Charter
1. Navy	Merrifield, VA	1947	$4,574,575	Federal
2. State Employees	Raleigh, NC	1937	$2,348,541	State
3. Pentagon	Alexandria, VA	1935	$1,325,059	Federal
4. Boeing Employees	Seattle, WA	1935	$1,310,242	State
5. Hughes Aircraft Employees	Manhattan Beach, CA	1940	$1,034,685	Federal
6. American Airlines Employees	DFW Airport, TX	1982	$993,786	Federal
7. Alaska USA	Anchorage, AK	1948	$924,075	Federal
8. The Golden 1	Sacramento, CA	1933	$820,001	State
9. LMSC	Sunnyvale, CA	1956	$808,153	Federal
10. Eastern Financial	Miami, FL	1937	$758,309	Federal
11. IBM Hudson Valley Employees	Poughkeepsie, NY	1963	$739,010	Federal
12. Orange County Teachers	Santa Ana, CA	1985	$732,703	Federal
13. Telephone Employees	Pasadena, CA	1934	$695,537	State
14. Construction Equipment	Peoria, IL	1984	$664,804	Federal
15. Lockheed	Burbank, CA	1937	$643,810	Federal
16. Pennsylvania State Employees	Harrisburg, PA	1933	$626,484	State
17. America First	Riverdale, UT	1939	$616,189	State
18. Delta Employees	Atlanta, GA	1940	$611,666	State
19. Suncoast Schools	Tampa, FL	1978	$594,997	Federal
20. Tinker	Tinker AFB, OK	1946	$586,797	State

in the United States at the end of 1990. The largest credit union in the country is the Navy Federal Credit Union, based in Merrifield, Virginia. At the end of 1990, this credit union had assets in excess of $4.5 billion. At the same time, there were no less than 2,295 credit unions in the United States with assets totaling less than $500,000.

Discrepancies in size are reflected in large differences in organizational structure and strategy, many of which have been greatly magnified since 1980. For example, all credit unions continue to offer secured and unsecured personal loans, their traditional role, and most also provide automobile loans. During the 1980s, increasing numbers of credit unions began to furnish their members with real estate mortgages as well. In 1980, only 5 percent of credit union assets were held in this form, a figure that had more than quadrupled by 1990. However, only 18 percent of credit unions with assets under $5 million offered this service, compared to 85 percent of the largest credit unions (those with assets over $50 million).

Similarly, the 1980s saw a large increase in credit unions offering share draft accounts (which work like checking accounts). Only 16 percent of credit unions provided this service in 1980, but this figure had risen to 42 percent by 1990, again masking a greater difference among credit unions of different sizes. Even in 1990, only 18 percent of the smallest class of credit unions had share draft accounts, while almost all (96 percent) of the largest organizations could offer members this facility. The discrepancy is even more marked when we look at the provision of credit cards. This service was rare in 1980, but in 1990 fully 90 percent of the largest credit unions could provide their members with a credit card, compared to just 5 percent of small credit unions.

In general, then, credit unions have seen extensive changes in the range of services that they can provide to their customers. In the field of personal finance, the largest organizations now provide services to rival those of the commercial banks. These changes have been accompanied by changes in the structure of the organizations. All large credit unions have full-time employees. Most now have their own marketing directors and in-house training staff. By contrast, only around one fifth of the smallest credit unions have even one full-time employee. So we can see that there has been a radical shift away from the traditional image of the credit union as a small, self-help organization with the emergence of increasing numbers of large, professionally managed organizations offering a full range of financial services.

CONCLUSION

We are now in a position to answer some of the questions that I have raised in the course of this survey of the evolution of credit unions. Credit unions exist as a distinct organizational form because of institutional boundaries that partition the financial industry in the United States. The consumer loan market was ignored by commercial banks, partly out of distaste for the practice, and partly because it was assumed to be unprofitable to provide this type of credit within the law. Of course, these two aspects are connected, as the law restricting interest rates was intended to protect people from usurers. Credit unions helped make the provision of consumer credit respectable, aided by the fact that, as nonprofit organizations, they could not be accused of exploiting people for private gain.

Credit unions were very different organizational forms from existing commercial banks. Furthermore, they were chartered under the auspices of distinct laws, and were subject to different sets of regulations fixing interest rates and the range of services they were allowed to offer. Thus the segmentation of the financial industry was reinforced and institutionalized by legislation. No doubt there has always been some overlap in the niches of the different types of financial institution—the segmentation of the market is not absolute. There is evidence, for example, of early competition between credit unions and Morris Plan Banks. However, even when large commercial banks moved into the consumer loan field, market segmentation provided credit unions with a distinct niche, enabling them to survive despite their relatively small size.

In contrast, Morris Plan Banks were a less distinctive type of organization. They were businesses, and were chartered under preexisting, general banking laws. Their innovation was to introduce a new strategy for making consumer loans that enabled them to stay within the law. However, this innovation was one that other organizations, such as commercial banks, could easily copy. Gradually, the distinction between Morris Plan Banks and commercial banks broke down. Morris Plan Banks ceased to exist as a distinct organizational form, although many of the organizations continue to exist today.

What are the likely ramifications of the recent changes in the regulation of the financial industry for credit unions? There is little doubt that we will see a continuation of the trend toward larger credit unions with multiple common bonds offering a wide range of financial services. The erosion of the distinction between credit unions and other forms of financial institutions is likely to increase. The question for the credit union movement is: If credit unions continue to become more like banks, will there be a distinct niche for credit unions in the future?

NOTES

Elizabeth West made very helpful comments on earlier drafts of this chapter. I would like to acknowledge the support of Fonds pour la Formation de Chercheurs et l'Aide à la Recherche, the Faculty of Graduate Studies and Research, McGill University, and U.S. National Science Foundation Grants SES-9100623 and SES–9196228.

1. While the common bond requirement remains in force today, albeit in a very different form, the mutual acquaintanceship requirement has now virtually disappeared.

2. Much of the information in this section is drawn from Moody and Fite (1984), easily the most comprehensive history of the U.S. credit union movement published to date.

3. This practice is widespread among commercial financial institutions, but is rare among credit unions. It is not allowed by law in the United States.

4. The name *caisse populaire* is difficult to translate exactly into English. "Popular Bank" or "People's Bank" are rough equivalents. Although *banque populaire* would

have been a more obvious choice of name, Moody and Fite (1984) suggest that *caisse populaire* was chosen because it was less controversial.

5. *Axias* were apparently charging interest of around 28 percent compared to credit union interest rates of between 6 percent and 18 percent (Robinson 1931, p. 234).

6. There was a gradual convergence of Morris Plan Banks and commercial banks over time. Eventually, most Morris Plan Banks became commercial banks.

7. As we discuss in this chapter, the situation becomes more complex when individual credit unions hire professional managers and other paid employees.

8. The largest credit union is the Navy Federal Credit Union, which had assets of $568 million in 1976. The sixtieth largest organization had about $56 million in assets.

BIBLIOGRAPHY

Barron, David N. 1992. "An Ecological Analysis of the Dynamics of Financial Institutions in New York State, 1914–1934." Unpublished Ph.D. dissertation, Cornell University.

Barron, David N, Elizabeth West, and Michael T. Hannan. 1994. "A Time to Grow and a Time to Die: Growth and Mortality of Credit Unions in New York, 1914–1990." *American Journal of Sociology* 100: in press.

Bundt, Thomas, and Barry Keating. 1988. "Depository Institution Competition in the Deregulated Environment: The Case of the Large Credit Union." *Applied Economics* 20:1333–42.

Clark, Evans. 1930. *Financing the Consumer*. New York: Harper and Brothers.

DiMaggio, Paul J. 1988. "Interest and Agency in Institutional Theory." In Lynne G. Zucker (ed.), *Institutional Patterns and Organizations: Culture and Environment*. Cambridge, MA: Ballinger, pp. 3–21.

Dugger, Robert H., Randall J. Miller, and John D. Wolken. 1981. "DIDMCA, Depository Institution Failure Probability and the Demand for Supervisory Resources." *Bank Structure and Competition* 17:7–29.

Francis, Kent W. 1968. *Credit Union Dynamics: How to Make Your Credit Union "Go."* Madison WI: CUNA International.

Hannan, Michael T., and Glenn R. Carroll. 1992. *Dynamics of Organizational Populations: Density, Legitimation, and Competition*. New York: Oxford University Press.

Hannan, Michael T., and John Freeman. 1986. "Where Do Organizational Forms Come From?" *Sociological Forum* 1:50–72.

Hannan, Michael T., and John Freeman. 1989. *Organizational Ecology*. Cambridge, MA: Harvard University Press.

Hannan, Michael T., Elizabeth West, and David N. Barron. 1994. *Dynamics of Credit Unions in New York*. Madison WI: Filene Center and Center for Credit Union Research.

Ijiri, Yuji, and Herbert A. Simon. 1977. *Size Distributions and the Sizes of Business Firms*. Amsterdam: North-Holland.

Industrial Finance Corporation. 1914. *The Morris Plan of Industrial Loans and Investments*. New York: Industrial Finance Corporation.

McCarthy, John D., and Meyer N. Zald. 1973. *The Trend of Social Movements in America: Professionalization and Resource Mobilization*. Morristown, NJ: General Learning Corporation.

Meyer, John W., and Brian Rowan. 1977. "Institutionalized Organizations: Formal Structure as Myth and Ceremony." *American Journal of Sociology* 83:340–63.

Moody, J. Carroll, and Gilbert C. Fite. 1984. *The Credit Union Movement: Origins and Development 1890–1980,* 2nd ed. Dubuque IA: Kendal/Hunt Publishing Co.

Morris, Aldon D. *The Origins of the Civil Rights Movement.* New York: Free Press.

Olson, Mancur. 1965. *The Logic of Collective Action.* Cambridge, MA: Harvard University Press.

Pearce, Douglas K. 1984. "Recent Developments in the Credit Union Industry." *Economic Review, Federal Reserve Bank of Kansas City* 69:3–19.

Ranger-Moore, James, Jane Banaszak-Holl, and Michael T. Hannan. 1991. "Density Dependence in Regulated Industries: Founding Rates of Banks and Life Insurance Companies." *Administrative Science Quarterly* 36:36–65.

Robinson, Louis N. 1931. "The Morris Plan." *American Economic Review* 21:222–35.

Robinson, Louis N., and Rolf Nugent. 1934. *Regulation of the Small Loan Business.* New York: Russell Sage Foundation.

Roby, Yves. 1975. *Alphonse Desjardins, 1900–1920: Les Caisses Populaires.* Québec: Federation de Québec des caisses populaires Desjardins.

Rudin, Ronald. 1990. *In Whose Interest?: Quebec's Caisse Populaires, 1900–1945.* Montreal: McGill-Queen's University Press.

8

Health Maintenance Organizations

DAVID STRANG

By Harold Luft's (1978, p. 1336) definition, a health maintenance organization (HMO) "assumes a contractual responsibility to provide or assure the delivery of health services to a voluntarily enrolled population that pays a fixed premium that is the HMO's major sources of revenue." HMOs are best contrasted with the fee-for-service, third-party payment arrangements that dominate American medicine, where an insurer reimburses an independent provider (or indemnifies the insured customer) for services rendered. A short organizational understanding of an HMO is that it combines the health insurance and health delivery functions generally kept separate in American medicine.

Health maintenance organizations thus make up a population of firms set off organizationally, though not technologically, from the larger health industry or medical care system. HMOs are of particular interest from an organizational perspective. They involve an effort to integrate, and thus potentially to manage, the provision of health care. This runs counter to the conventional structure of health-care delivery, where increasingly sophisticated work is characteristically handled not through complexity in organizational design and strategy, but through the complexity of the physician as an autonomous professional. In effect, health maintenance organizations embody a fundamental organizational innovation in health care.

Health maintenance organizations are not only of interest to organizational researchers, however. Health consumers, doctors, purchasers, and policymakers have all seen the HMO as having great promise as a vehicle for consumer control, for expanded collegiality among doctors, and for reducing health costs. At the same time, HMOs have been highly controversial, due to the challenge they pose to the professional autonomy of the physician. With government support in the 1970s and 1980s, the prepaid group movement matured into the HMO industry. HMOs form an increasingly substantial part of the American health-care system, and one with the potential to reorganize standard ways in which medicine is financed and delivered.

TWO HMO PORTRAITS

The leading HMO throughout the post–World War II period has been Kaiser-Permanente. Formed during World War II, Kaiser enrollments topped one million in 1963. In the early 1970s, the Kaiser plans enrolled about half of all HMO members (over two million) in the country. While that figure is now about 15 percent, Kaiser remains by far the largest single HMO (or HMO chain). Further, Kaiser-Permanente has long been regarded not only as one of the biggest HMOs, but one of the best organized. Kaiser-Permanente plans compare favorably to both fee-for-service medicine and other HMOs on a variety of dimensions: controlling costs, maintaining quality of care, providing access, and generating patient and provider satisfaction (for a review, see Somers 1971).

The Kaiser plans began not with Henry Kaiser but with Dr. Sidney Garfield, a physician who in 1933 set up a hospital to care for construction workers in the California desert.[1] Unable to maintain a fee-for-service practice in such a remote location, Garfield started a prepaid health plan. Henry J. Kaiser, a prominent industrialist who had managed some of the California construction sites, then recruited Garfield to set up a similar plan in a remote construction site in Washington. In both places, prepayment proved the best way to organize health care to concentrated groups in areas lacking an existing medical infrastructure.

During World War II, Kaiser and Garfield entered into a closer relationship to provide health care for Kaiser shipbuilding employees in Oakland, California. It was with this practice that Kaiser-sponsored prepaid practice first became a permanent organization. After World War II, Kaiser took formal control of the plan's hospitals and other services, while Garfield's practice became the Permanente Medical Group. The plan began to provide health care not only to Kaiser employees, but to other large corporations as well.

Kaiser-Permanente faced strong opposition from the local medical society, which accused Garfield of advertising and soliciting patients, preventing patients from having a free choice of physicians, rendering inadequate services, and channeling profits into his health plan. But unlike most HMOs, strong financial backing received from the Kaiser industries enabled the Kaiser plans to set up a wholly autonomous medical system. Kaiser-Permanente built its own hospitals and staffed them with a dedicated medical group (i.e., Kaiser hospitals were staffed only by Permanente physicians, and Permanente physicians worked only in Kaiser hospitals). Kaiser set up an in-house research division, and even considered establishing its own medical school. The autonomy of the Kaiser system made it relatively invulnerable to the occupational pressures that overcame many prepaid health plans between the 1940s and the 1960s.

As in many prepaid plans, expansion in size led to tension between Kaiser and the physicians staffing the organization. Physicians resented Henry Kaiser's control over plan expansion, while Kaiser opposed physician initiatives and the threat that Permanente physicians might contract with competing plans. In 1955, Kaiser-Permanente was reorganized to more clearly distinguish areas of authority between the hospital and marketing arms of the plan (run by Kaiser executives) on the one hand, and the health delivery arm (run by Permanente medical groups) on the other. This dual management structure proved highly effective in promoting a strong organizational culture of cooperation between administrators and physicians. It also facilitated the later expansion of Kaiser-Permanente, which was able to organize separate plans on the same model in Hawaii, Colorado, Cleveland, and Washington, D.C.

While Kaiser-Permanente is the outstanding example, a similar story of internal integration, organizational innovation, and steady growth could be told for a number of HMO prototypes: Group Health Association in Washington, D.C., Health Insurance Plan of New York, Group Health Cooperative of Puget Sound. Each of these plans combined some form of entrepreneurial or consumer management with a strong physician staff; faced tensions over plan threats to the professional autonomy of physicians; and provided economical health care to large employee groups in major urban centers.

A more interesting contrast is to United Healthcare (see Moore 1979; Moore, Martin, and Richardson 1983; Martin, Ehreth, and Geving 1985). In the early 1970s, SAFECO Insurance Company began to consider developing a prepaid health plan as part of its insurance offerings. Its interest in doing so was spurred by the shift toward federal support for HMOs (to be discussed). SAFECO sought to make use of its existing network of marketing representatives to promote its medical insurance plan, while contracting with individual physicians and group practices to provide health care.

Between 1974 and 1979, SAFECO sponsored several plans that were eventually combined to form United Healthcare (UHC). United Healthcare contracted mainly with individual primary-care physicians. It was widely noted for making early use of a "gatekeeper" structure, where primary-care physicians controlled referrals to specialists (that is, patients could not self-refer). The plan reimbursed gatekeepers on the basis of their standard fee-for-service charges. Ten percent of physician charges was withheld, to be returned to the physician if his or her total costs per patient were below a target figure.

This structure facilitated rapid growth, with both physicians and members rather easily signed up. By 1978, UHC had expanded into Woodland, California; Seattle, Spokane, and Bellingham, Washington; and Salt Lake City, Utah. The plan grew at a rate of well over 100 percent per year throughout the 1970s, peaking at about 38,000 subscribers in 1980. In 1979, optimistic discussions of United Healthcare and the advantages of a gatekeeper-based system were reported in the *New England Journal of Medicine* and the *Wall Street Journal*.

But United Healthcare costs per enrollee mounted along with the expansion of the plan. United Healthcare had failed to select cost-conscious providers, instead attempting to contract with most physicians in covered areas so prospective enrollees would not have to change doctors. Reimbursement of physicians on a fee-for-service basis with a small withheld amount proved insufficient to induce economizing behavior among physicians.[2] UHC had no controls over specialists, no system for monitoring the physician's utilization of services or certifying hospital stay, and no program for educating physicians about cost-conscious styles of practice.

In 1981, United Healthcare sought to restructure its relation to physicians. Panels of specialists were contracted to bring referral costs under control, high-cost doctors were dropped from the plan, and the size of withheld provider fees was doubled. While costs began to decrease with these organizational reforms, SAFECO sought a buyer for United Healthcare. When several possible purchases fell through, SAFECO terminated United Healthcare in 1982.

The contrast between Kaiser-Permanente and United Healthcare suggests the importance of several features of health maintenance organizations. First, HMOs involve complex relations between groups of physicians and external sponsors (even in those cases where physicians themselves initially sponsor the HMO, a distinction develops over time between the physicians and the plan). Second, the internal structure of the plan is crucial for HMO survival and profitability: of particular importance are modes of reimbursement, relations between physicians, and managerial monitoring and education. Third, the environmental conditions under which HMOs develop have changed dramatically over time, with substantial consequences for organizational strategies and success.

HISTORICAL BEGINNINGS

While the term *health maintenance organization* only gained currency in the 1970s, prepaid practice is a fairly common mode of organizing medicine. Abel-Smith (1988) notes that it was common practice in many European countries before World War II for occupational or social groups to hire physicians to provide medical care for a prepaid fee. Similarly, in the first decades of the twentieth century, company doctors reimbursed on a salaried or prepaid basis were widespread in the railroad, mining, and lumber industries (Starr 1982, p. 202). But these forms of "contract medicine" have largely vanished, due to fierce opposition from increasingly united medical professions (and in Europe, from the implementation of national health insurance).

The roots of the contemporary HMO industry can be located in health co-operatives formed in the 1920s and 1930s. Of particular importance was Dr. Michael Shadid's medical cooperative at Elk City, Oklahoma. Dr. Shadid sought to provide comprehensive and up-to-date medical care in a small rural community by setting up a cooperatively organized prepaid health plan. While colleagues rejected Shadid's idea and sought to deprive him of his medical license, the Oklahoma Farmers Union supported the plan. Fierce opposition from the local medical community eventually led to the dissolution of the Elk City Cooperative. But Shadid lectured widely about the promise of health co-operatives and succeeded in inspiring a number of companion efforts.

Many of the early HMOs (or prepaid group practices, as they were then called) flowed from the aim to increase consumer control and medical cooperation. Labor unions provided an important early impetus through their efforts to make medical care available to workers in isolated company towns. Cooperative designs were realized successfully by Group Health Association, a consumer cooperative begun in 1938 by a group of federal employees, and Group Health Cooperative of Puget Sound, a physician collective founded in 1947.

HMO "prototypes" were also founded by corporate rationalizers aiming for more efficient and accessible health care. The most important corporate rationalizer was Henry J. Kaiser, as detailed previously. Similarly, Fiorello La Guardia set up Health Insurance Plan of New York in 1947 to serve much of the city's public work force. While early prepaid plans responded to various perceptions of the inadequacies of conventional arrangements, they shared much pressure from the medical community. As Paul Starr (1982) details, doctors have vigorously opposed the emergence of organized clients (including the development of health insurance), the imposition of organizational limits on professional autonomy, and the outbreak of price competition among providers. In 1934, for example, the American Medical Association (AMA) described all medical institutions as "but expansions of the equipment of the physician" and insisted that "no third party must be permitted to come between the patient and his physician." The AMA also required that the immediate cost of medical care be borne by the patient, and that health plans should include all physicians who wished to participate in them (Starr 1982, pp. 299–300).

Prepaid plans directly violated these prescriptions, challenging the physician's workplace autonomy and financial control. They could underprice and outcompete solo practitioners, were often sponsored and managed by laypeople, and inserted an organizational structure between physician and patient. In response, the medical profession brought considerable political and organizational pressure to bear on nascent HMOs.

Physicians joining HMOs were barred from memberships in county medical societies and admitting privileges in hospitals, threatened with the loss of their medical licenses, and confronted with general social and professional ostracism. Under pressure from organized medicine, many states passed Blue Cross/Blue Shield laws requiring prepaid plans to be sponsored by physicians or gain county medical society approval, to allow all local physicians to participate, and to guarantee physician control of HMO-governing bodies (Starr 1982, pp. 303–6).

Resistance to HMOs also took the form of organization building. In 1956, solo practitioners in the Sacramento area formed the San Joaquin Foundation for Medical Care to resist the threat posed by an expanding Kaiser-Permanente. The San Joaquin Foundation also delivered medical care to prepaid enrollees, but it was run by and for physicians who maintained their existing private practices. While formed as an oppositional device, these medical-care foundations (or independent practice associations, as they later came to be known) had enough in common with the prepaid group plans that subsequent federal and state HMO policy treated the two as alternative forms of HMOs.

The HMO population grew slowly from the 1930s through the 1960. Kaiser-Permanente and some other plans emerged as major providers, primarily on the West Coast and in some large eastern and midwestern cities. But in general HMOs failed to diffuse widely. While some HMOs grew throughout the post-war period, there were on the order of twenty HMOs in the country in 1960, and less than forty in 1969. The 1960s saw the development of few plans of the stature of the early health cooperatives and industry-organized plan.

On the political side, conditions improved somewhat for HMOs over the de-cades. The courts sometimes blocked the efforts of the medical profession to restrict prepaid plan access to health facilities. Most notably, Group Health Association (GHA) won a suit against the Washington, D.C., medical society, which had attempted to bar GHA physicians from admitting patients to hospi-tals. And some accommodation between prepaid plans and organized medicine was reached in 1960, when the AMA recognized free choice of health plan as a substitute for free choice of physician. But HMOs remained a marginal and delegitimated population within the American health-care system.

Further, the conditions of the early growth of health maintenance organiza-tions—lack of accessible health care for labor unions and businesses on the one hand, and the vigor of the cooperative movement on the other—seemed to be disappearing. When HMOs succeeded in the 1970s and 1980s, it was on the basis of a new sort of appeal: their promise as vehicles of cost containment in an era of health inflation.

INSTITUTIONAL LEGITIMATION

The term *health maintenance organization* itself is tied to this shift. It was coined in the late 1960s by Dr. Paul Ellwood, executive director of the Ameri-can Rehabilitation Federation, a health policy analysis group. Ellwood (and others, notably Alain Enthoven, Jon Christianson, and Clark Havighurst) ad-vocated prepaid group practice as a cure for the rampant cost inflation that had accompanied the infusion of federal funds for Medicare and Medicaid. Mount-ing health costs were traced to misaligned incentives within the health-care system. Fee-for-service, third-party payment arrangements gave the physician a free hand to engage in expensive forms of care. On the other hand, the insurer who footed the bill possessed an incentive to economize on care, but no op-portunity to translate this incentive into policy.

Ellwood argued that an organization that not only insured individuals but provided their health care would realign incentives and capacities in an appro-priate way. Such an organization would have the ability to manage the delivery of health care in an economizing fashion. Ellwood christened prepaid plans as "health maintenance organizations" to summarize his boldest (and least broadly supported) claim, that prepaid groups would achieve these goals by replacing medicine's usual focus on crisis management with attention to pre-ventive care.

Ellwood succeeded in stimulating health bureaucrats at HEW (Department of Health, Education, and Welfare) into putting the newly named health main-tenance organizations on the federal agenda. HMOs proved politically attrac-tive, allowing the Nixon administration to offer a market-based alternative to national health insurance. And the economic arguments of HMO advocates, who emphasized the immediacy of financial incentives and minimized the labor of organizational creation and maintenance, proved highly compelling to health services experts and public policymakers alike. In 1971, Nixon made HMOs the centerpiece of his program for health-care reform. Two years later, legislation was passed by Congress and signed into law.

The HMO Act of 1973 overrode restrictive state legislation, instituted a program of grants and loans, and required employers to offer HMOs as an option within their health-care programs. All these provisions applied to "federally qualified HMOs," however, and leading plans like Kaiser viewed the qualification requirements as burdensome. Rather than seeking qualification, major HMOs campaigned to eliminate the broad benefit packages, unrestricted enrollment, and community rating mandated by federal law. Most of these requirements were lifted or weakened in amendments to the act passed in 1976 and 1978 (for excellent legislative histories, see Falkson 1980; Brown 1983).

The states were quick to follow the lead of the federal government. Within two years of the federal HMO law, twenty-six states had passed enabling acts to certify and regulate HMOs. These laws superseded earlier statutes impeding organizational formation, and put HMO regulation on a more positive and less uncertain basis. Like federal legislation, state laws were not a response to an increasingly active HMO lobby: in fact, seventeen states without HMOs passed HMO-enabling legislation. Instead, HMO laws were passed to counter the rising costs of medicine, with legislation occurring most rapidly and most favorably to HMOs where costs were highest (Strang and Bradburn 1993).

It should be noted that the policy appeal of HMOs remains strong. HMOs continue to figure heavily in plans for the restructuring of medicine, most prominently in the Clinton administration's aim of grouping providers into large HMOs competing for the health dollars of large-scale consumer organizations. This effect draws on the analysis developed by Alain Enthoven and Paul Ellwood in the 1970s, where HMOs are seen as capable of integrating and thus properly aligning financial incentives within the context of a market for medical care.

POPULATION BOOM AND STABILIZATION

Shifts in the legal and policy environment helped trigger a boom in health maintenance organizations. Figure 8-1 plots HMO organizational density (numbers of operating HMOs) over the 1970s and 1980s, and total HMO enrollment. Statistics are not readily obtained for industry size prior to the 1970s, since the various forms of HMOs were not treated as subcategories of a meaningful larger category until that time. For more extensive reviews of HMO demographics, see Gruber, Shadle, and Polich (1988) and Christianson et al. (1991).

HMO growth was steady but unimpressive in the decade following the federal HMO Act. While falling far short of ambitious federal projections that 1,700 HMOs would be in operation by 1975, the number of HMOs increased fivefold from 1971 to 1982 (from 46 to 262 HMOs). Enrollment also increased

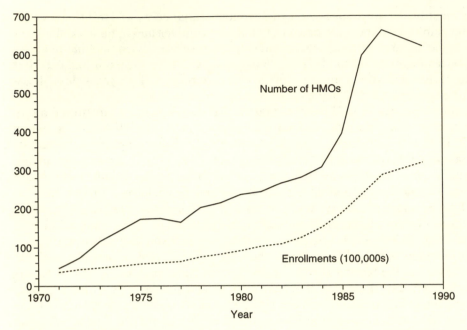

Figure 8–1 Density and enrollment of health maintenance organizations. (*Source:* InterStudy, various years.)

substantially, though not in proportion to growth in organizations (rising from 3.6 million to 10.7 million enrollees).

Industry growth accelerated rapidly in the mid-1980s, sparked by the increasing availability of state Medicare contracts and the development of a highly favorable capital market for HMO start-ups. The number of operating HMOs tripled, reaching some 643 HMOs in 1988. Nearly every major metropolitan market was entered by at least one HMO. HMO enrollment also tripled, increasing from 10 million to over 30 million enrollees.

Rapid industry growth in the 1980s was accompanied by a number of changes in industry composition. In the early 1970s, HMOs were highly concentrated in a few metropolitan areas. In 1975, sixty-eight HMOs with a combined enrollment of 3 million were located in California (making up 40 percent of all plans and 55 percent of all HMO subscribers). Thirty-five of these plans operated in Los Angeles alone. Other centers of HMO development were Minnesota and Wisconsin, while major cities like New York, Chicago, and Boston had few HMOs. And in contrast to the Pacific region, in 1973 the South could boast only five HMOs with a total enrollment of 17,000 subscribers.

By 1988, all states except Alaska were home to at least one HMO. California continued to have more HMOs (51) and HMO enrollment (7 million) than any other state. But now Florida, Illinois, New York, Ohio, Texas, and Wisconsin all had 30 or more operating HMOs. Regional differences were all but invisible, as HMOs were formed wherever population density provided substantial markets. Southern states, perhaps the most inhospitable to prepaid practice in the pre-Ellwood era, had one quarter of all operating plans (167 HMOs).

The 1970s and 1980s also saw important shifts in distributions of organizational size and scope. Before the late 1970s, only Kaiser-Permanente had control over a variety of distinct plans located in several states. But attractive financial markets in the 1980s led to a large-scale flowering of national HMO chains. Through acquisitions and new starts, national HMOs came to control 300 HMOs by 1987, or about half of the entire HMO population. Organizationally, HMOs remained highly local operations, since health care is a highly local activity. But financially, and to some extent strategically, HMO development became a national rather than a local phenomenon.

The nationalization of fiscal control occurred without much change in the average size of operating units. Enrollment per HMO dropped in the 1970s, and then held steady in the 1980s at about 40,000 members per HMO. (Organizational size is better captured by enrollment than by numbers of HMO employees, since different HMOs contract for different percentages of the physician's time). But most HMOs at any one time have fewer than 15,000 enrollees, while the less than 10 percent of HMOs with more than 100,000 members have about two thirds of total HMO enrollment.

The HMO population suffered a shakeout in the late 1980s, with more than 100 organizational failures in the last three years of the decade and a reduction in population size of about 15 percent. (Prior years had witnessed failure rates on the order of 10–20 percent of operating plans per year, but these failures occurred in the context of an overall expansion in the organization's population.) The favorable capital markets that had fueled rapid growth petered out as HMOs not only filled their niche but overflowed it.

In large part this shakeout resulted directly from the rapid expansion of the previous several years. Many of the plans that started during the boom were the product of easy opportunities for external investors (Moran and Savela 1986), who could profit even if HMOs never got off the ground. The national chain–sponsored IPAs founded during the period of the boom were especially likely to fail (Christianson et al. 1991). This pattern is reminiscent of Hannan and Carroll's (1992) arguments about "density delay," where the presence of many similar firms is argued to squeeze newly formed organizations. But for HMOs, it seems even more apparent that periods when many weakly established organizations are carelessly thrown together constitute booms in organizational founding. It is unsurprising that such organizations are failure prone.

HMO DYNAMICS AND LOCAL MARKET CONDITIONS

While most ecological analyses have studied population dynamics in a single site (e.g., Hannan and Freeman 1987) or have analyzed a number of sites independently (Carroll and Hannan 1989), the fundamentally local operation of most HMOs until the mid-1980s encourages simultaneous multimarket analyses. These analyses permit close investigation into the local conditions that facilitate HMO growth and maintenance that is easily achieved in single time series studies. A number of studies by health services researchers have examined conditions associated with HMO presence and size (Goldberg and Greenberg 1981; Morrisey and Ashby 1982; Welch 1984; McLaughlin 1987). More recently, a number of studies have sought to test ecological arguments about patterns of organizational founding (Strang and Uden-Holman 1990; Wholey, Sanchez and Christianson 1993) and failure (Wholey, Christianson, and Sanchez 1992).

This research develops a consistent portrait of the conditions that lead to HMO founding and maintenance. HMOs are found in the larger metropolitan areas, and in areas where their typical enrollees form big segments of the population (areas with large businesses and much in-migration, families with children, individuals with high income or education). They are more likely to be formed where physicians are easily recruited (where there are many physicians per capita, and where many young physicians are struggling to set up practices). HMO growth is also encouraged by high medical costs, since HMOs are seen as vehicles for cost containment. And finally, HMOs are formed more easily where state legislation is favorable (though Wholey, Sanchez, and Christianson [1993] note that by permitting more weak plans to get off the ground, favorable state regulation may also raise failure rates).

Ecologically oriented studies have focused on the influence of organizational density on founding, and organizational size on mortality. Wholey, Sanchez, and Christianson's (1993) study of founding in the 1980s finds the nonmonotonic patterns of density that Hannan and Freeman (1987) argue should result from opposing effects of population legitimacy and competition. (That is, at low densities additional HMOs primarily add to perceptions of the appropriateness of HMOs and the inscription of these perceptions in law; at high densities additional HMOs primarily tighten organizational competition for patients and providers.) Strang and Uden-Holman (1990) show that in the 1970s the HMOs that were strongly opposed by the medical community (the prepaid group practices described later in the chapter) exhibit only positive effects of existing HMO presence in a community. Presumably institutional and attitudinal conditions were sufficiently antagonistic that competitive pressures between HMOs were outweighed by the extent to which later HMOs benefitted from the regulatory and occupational struggles waged by the first HMOs to enter the community.

Wholey, Christianson, and Sanchez (1992) show that HMO mortality rates vary with organizational size, though in different ways for different subpopulations. They interpret low rates of failure for plans organized around a multispecialty group practice or hospital staff as the product of high commitment by cohesive groups of doctors. By contrast, they argue that plans whose physicians do not form integrated groups are likely to experience high rates of failure when small.

THE ORGANIZATIONAL STRUCTURE OF HMOS

While organizational structures and strategies vary widely within the HMO population (typical variations are discussed in the next section), they share a number of basic organizational features. Almost all HMOs employ a dual structure, with separate administrative and provider arms. An executive director heads the administrative side of the organization, which generally includes marketing, financial, personnel, and legal departments or functions (depending on organizational size). A medical director heads the provider side of the organization, typically supported by a variety of physician committees on quality assurance, utilization review, staffing, and the like.

All HMOs face difficulties in organizing and managing the work of the "sovereign" physician (Freidson 1970; Starr 1982). HMO managerial styles emphasize physician education and mutual cooperation rather than discipline, and relations between the plan and the physician involve mutual negotiation rather than control. Nevertheless, HMOs are in the business of containing costs and promoting innovation in physician practice patterns.

Formal management efforts include financial incentives, requirements that the plan authorize some medical decisions (typically hospital admissions and out-of-plan referrals), the collection and dissemination of physician utilization records, and the development of standard practice protocols. Informal efforts include intraphysician socialization to plan norms and advocacy by the medical director and other leading physicians of particular practice patterns. While these efforts can add up to very little (Freidson 1975), most research finds that elaborated and integrated managerial systems can successfully mold physician practice patterns (Eisenberg 1986; Fox and Heinen 1987; Hillman, Pauly, and Kerstein 1989; Strang and Currivan 1992).

The bulk of the health services literature on HMOs is devoted to exploring differences between HMOs and fee-for-service arrangements, particularly with reference to health costs. The most comprehensive analysis of HMO cost-containment performance remains Harold Luft's (1981) integration of a large number of prior studies. Luft found that HMO savings result primarily from the substitution of ambulatory care for expensive hospital care. More recent debate has focused on whether HMO savings are due to changes in provider patterns or to selective enrollment or disenrollment (where HMOs mainly serve the healthy). Important support for the former was found in a massive RAND experiment that randomly assigned individuals to a major HMO or fee-for-service medicine (see Manning et al. 1984).

TYPES OF HEALTH MAINTENANCE ORGANIZATIONS

The conventional HMO typology describes four HMO forms: the staff, group, network, and independent practice association (IPA) models. For many purposes these are usually collapsed into two, contrasting the IPA with the other three plan types, often described jointly as prepaid group practices, or PGPs.

It is important to note that these classifications are generated by industry participants, rather than by academic analysts. This detracts from their analytic clarity, but helps ensure their relevance for immediate organizational concerns.

Plan types are differentiated on the basis of the physician's legal and organizational setting. Staff HMOs are plans where most physicians are directly employed by the HMO. Group HMOs are plans where most physicians are members of a single multispecialty group practice contracting with the HMO, and network HMOs are plans where most physicians are members of two or more such group practices. IPAs are plans where most physicians are solo practitioners contracting with the HMO, either directly or through a physician association.

Distinctions between plan types are important for their historical and structural relation to plan-enrollee relations, and even more to relationships internal to the organization. Along almost all relevant dimensions, IPAs are found at one extreme and staff models at the other, with group and network HMOs closer to staff than IPA plans. To simplify, I mainly compare the three sorts of prepaid group practices to IPAs, with the understanding that staff models best exemplify what is distinctive about PGPs.

First, physicians in the different kinds of PGPs tend to see only or mostly HMO enrollees. By contrast, physicians in IPAs typically maintain a large non-HMO practice, with on the order of 10 percent of their patients enrolled in the HMO. This contrast is grounded in the founding rationales of the different kinds of plans. As noted above, IPAs were generally formed by solo practitioners to oppose the inroads of large PGPs. The aim behind the IPA was thus to preserve the private practices of its physicians, not eliminate them.

Second, PGPs are unlikely to reimburse physicians on a fee-for-service basis, whereas IPAs are. In staff models, physicians are generally salaried; in group and network models, they are capitated. (*Capitation* refers to the payment of fee per enrollee to a medical provider; this approach generally involves some financial risk on the provider's part.) Contrasts in modes of reimbursement arise in part for historical reasons: since IPAs were formed to defend the fee-for-service sector, they were unlikely to pay physicians on any other basis. They also derive from an organizational logic. It is dangerous to capitate individual physicians, since this makes the incentive to underprovide care very stark. It is awkward to pool the risks of solo practitioners who do not work together or even know each other. And it is impractical to salary physicians who work for the HMO on an occasional and individually variable basis.

PGP physicians thus depend rather heavily on the HMO, which generates a large proportion of the patients they see. PGP physicians also interact on a continuous basis with other HMO physicians, who are their colleagues within the group practice or hospital staff. Financial rewards in PGPs are directly tied to HMO outcomes and policy through the setting of salary and capitation levels. (For capitated physicians, income is also directly tied to the practice behavior of other physicians, since groups of doctors generally form a risk pool.) And PGPs are able to influence physicians in a variety of other ways, including informal norm setting within the medical group, advocacy of practice patterns by the medical director, and formal attempts to develop coordinated practice patterns.

IPAs diverge from PGPs along all these dimensions. Their physicians have a weak financial and professional stake in the HMO, interact little with each other,[3] receive modest financial incentives to connect their outcomes with those of the organization as a whole, and are relatively difficult to influence in informal or continuous ways. Management in these plans is frequently contracted out to an HMO management firm, rather than provided by organizational sponsors. Overall, IPAs can be so structurally disarticulated that they resemble a network of contracts more than an authoritatively coordinated organization.

A main result of these structural differences is that PGPs have historically succeeded in lowering health costs, while costs in IPAs are comparable to costs in the fee-for-service sector (Luft 1981). IPAs make frequent use of formal contraints on physician decision making like hospital admission requirements, but do not employ the combination of continuous and informal control mechanisms that translates into successful cost containment (Hillman, Pauly, and Kerstein 1989; Strang and Currivan 1992). This situation may be changing, however, as is discussed in this chapter.

POPULATION DYNAMICS AMONG TYPES OF HMOS

It is of great interest that the IPA blossomed in the 1970s and 1980s. In the early 1970s, a handful of small IPAs was dwarfed by a larger number of well-established, high-enrollment prepaid group practices. But rates of IPA formation exceeded those of PGP formation in the 1970s and 1980s, with virtually all of the mid-1980s boom occurring through new IPA starts. IPA density rose to over 400 organizations in 1987, or two thirds of total HMO density. And IPA enrollment grew to virtually match PGP enrollment. HMO population counts by plan type are given in Figure 8-2.

One source of this shift in relative density is a challenge-response process. As already noted, the initial spur to IPA development was the threat posed by growing PGPs to the fee-for-service sector. This threat grew much more real with federal support for HMOs in the 1970s. IPA founding was thus particularly rapid in these metropolitan areas where PGPs had already appeared (Strang and Uden-Holman 1990). But this competitively induced effect declined in the 1980s (Wholey, Christianson, and Sanchez 1993) as HMOs became a regular and less threatening part of the medical scene. Although a challenge-response process can explain the initial takeoff in IPAs, it cannot account for their increasing predominance within the HMO population.

A second main source of the growth of the IPA subpopulation is its ease of founding and operation. IPAs rely heavily on the existing "building blocks" provided by the health system; most importantly, the ability of physicians to practice individually and through referrals in the absence of a central coordinating mechanism. IPAs are trivial to set up because they involve no necessary

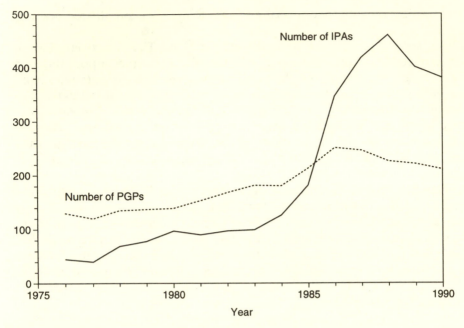

Figure 8–2 Density of health maintenance organizations by type. (*Source:* InterStudy, various years.)

change in physician routines, occasion no strong dependence on the plan for revenues (since physicians maintain their existing practices), and require little managerial expertise or structure. Of course, these are the attributes that led health policy analysts and reformers to disparage IPAs. But they are also attributes that fueled rapid construction once public health policy and market conditions began to favor HMOs.

On the other hand, prepaid group practices are difficult and costly to found. They involve substantial start-up costs, large commitments by physicians and others that can only be met as the plan grows, and specialized forms of managerial expertise not found in the health sector at large. PGPs are difficult to found and to maintain because they differ so importantly from conventional medical arrangements. Brown (1983) is forceful in arguing that the absence of rapid industry expansion in the 1970s was not due to faults in federal legislation, but to the very real costs and difficulties of constructing alternative kinds of health-care organizations.

By this argument, IPAs are what ecologists have dubbed R-strategists: organizations that are able to reproduce rapidly in newly accessible environments. (Their ease of (re)production is contingent on the prior existence of an operating fee-for-service system, of course.) PGPs are K-strategists: organizations with high fitness in stable or crowded environments, but with less capacity to rapidly exploit new opportunities. Some evidence for such an analysis is suggested by fact that IPA formation took off when capital markets made large influxes of money available to plans that could be founded in a hurry.

However, a third account suggests that IPAs have expanded rapidly due to improved operating procedures—that the modern IPA has simply built a better mousetrap. Welch (1987) argues persuasively that in the 1980s IPAs learned from well-publicized failures like that of SAFECO's United Healthcare. Many began to provide a substantial fraction of the patients seen by their physicians, developed risk-sharing reimbursement practices, and instituted more thorough organizational controls.

Welch contends that contemporary IPAs are able to outcompete PGPs because they have come to combine the traditional strengths of the PGP with their structural advantage in flexibility and ease of start-up and expansion. While IPAs grew aggressively at the expense of established staff and group HMOs in some metropolitan markets, however, it is not clear how Welch's arguments can be squared with the fact that IPA failure rates exceeded PGP failure rates throughout the 1980s.

A second set of interform dynamics involves transitions between staff, group, network, and IPA models. As one might expect from the previous discussion, there is little movement between the IPA form and the other three forms, but some movement between different PGP types. In particular, staff and group HMOs fairly often turn into network HMOs. This shift is largely a function of organizational expansion. For example, the growth of a group HMO leads to the development of contracts with additional group practices as much or more than through expansion in the size of the original group.

These last points serve as a useful caution about the permanence of organizational typologies. As Welch argues, aggressive IPAs have taken on many of the attributes traditionally connected to PGPs; in turn, the now less embattled PGPs may likely take on traits of IPAs (see next section in chapter for the example of Group Health Plan in the Twin Cities). As a result, knowledge of plan type conveys less about core internal processes within an HMO now than it once did. Standard industry classifications tend to become institutionalized. In the case of HMOs, the present four-type classification is grounded in federal policy and in Interstudy's (1973–92) HMO census categories.

Welch, Hillman, and Pauly (1990) have argued that new HMO typologies should be developed that better reflect contemporary variations in organizational structure. They propose that the crucial dimensions of HMO structure include how physicians are reimbursed, whether physicians retain a practice outside the HMO, whether physicians contract with the HMO as a group or as individuals, and the type, size, and structure of risk-sharing arrangements between the plan and providers. This reconceptualization may be seen as an effort to more directly characterize the organizational structures of different types of HMOs, and in particular to distinguish between "new" and "old" IPAs.

HMO DYNAMICS IN ONE METROPOLITAN MARKET

HMOs are involved in complex local systems of competition, imitation, and learning. The initial entry of an HMO into a community looks much like a random event, though it is conditioned by the community's existing health system and its demographic structure. Once an HMO enters the community, it tends to foster a variety of reactions. These include expanding competitiveness within the medical sector, imitative formation of similar HMOs, and defensive IPA building. As these new organizations develop, their interaction continues to spur new organizational strategies.

A case history provides the best illustration of some of the possible relationships involved. I focus here on Minneapolis–St. Paul, a city whose relatively longstanding experience with HMOs yields a rich picture of local population dynamics. (The discussion here is based on accounts of Twin Cities HMOs in Anderson et al. 1985; Christianson and McClure 1979; Kralewski et al. 1987; Feldman, Kralewski, and Dowd 1989).

The first prepaid plan in the Minneapolis–St. Paul area was Group Health Plan, founded in 1957. Group Health was organized as a staff HMO employing full-time physicians on a salaried basis to provide health care to union groups and public employees. In the face of considerable opposition from the local fee-for-service community, Group Health grew slowly but steadily. By 1972, it served some 48,000 enrollees.

The HMO population in the Twin Cities expanded rapidly with nationwide shifts in the regulatory climate in the 1970s. In 1972–73, four group practice–based plans were offered. These included MedCenter Health Plan (sponsored by the St. Louis Park Medical Center), Ramsey Health Plan (sponsored by the Ramsey Hospital), SHARE (sponsored initially by a railroad employees association), and the Nicollet-Eitel Health Plan (a joint venture of the Nicollet Clinic and Eitel Hospital). While the largest of these prepaid practices was about a third the size of the older Group Health Plan, they mark the emergence of an accepted HMO presence in the Twin Cities medical market.

Solo practitioners were not long in responding to the growing HMO share in the community. In 1975, the county medical society organized an independent practice association named Physicians Health Plan (PHP). Some 1,200 physicians, about 75 percent of all solo practitioners working in the Twin Cities, contracted with PHP. In 1976, Blue Cross/Blue Shield sponsored a second IPA, HMO Minnesota (HMOM). While the staff and group practice–based plans tended to contract with a single or narrow range of hospitals, the two IPAs provided coverage throughout the Minneapolis–St. Paul metropolitan area.

The Twin Cities thus saw intense competition between HMOs and the fee-for-service sector, and between different kinds of HMOs as well. Some of the group and IPA-based plans had great difficulty limiting hospitalization and expanding enrollment. The Ramsey Health Plan failed to grow due to high inpatient costs, and failed during the 1970s. Physicians Health Plan lost nearly a million dollars in its first two years of operation. But both PHP and HMOM replaced their initially loose controls over physicians with programs for certifying hospital admission and length of hospital stay. While maintaining higher hospital utilization rates than the local group and staff-based HMOs, these IPAs had considerably lower costs than did the fee-for-service sector.

The 1970s and 1980s were a period of expansion in HMO enrollments as well as organizations. Most large corporations in the Twin Cities offered a selection of HMOs as well as indemnity plans to their employees, and HMOs gained much of this market. Total HMO enrollment in 1973 stood at about 65,000 persons, almost three quarters of whom were covered by Group Health. HMO enrollment in the Twin Cities rose to 275,000 in 1979, and stood at some one million subscribers in 1987. At that time, Group Health enrolled 228,000 persons, or about a quarter of all HMO enrollees. The largest plans were now MedCenters (now linked to the PARTNERS national network), with 292,000 enrollees, and Physicians Health Plan, with 324,000 enrollees.

Active competition among HMOs produced a number of important shifts in the internal operations and market offerings of the Twin Cities plans. First, competitive pressure on health costs lowered physician incomes, leading to a "physicians' rebellion" (Kralewski et al. 1987). When PHP failed to return any funds from its physicians' withholding account in 1987, its doctors mounted a campaign to oust the plan's board of directors that succeeded in gaining partial control of the organization. Competitively induced decreases in MedCenter's premiums led to an arbitration fight over physician incomes. HMO Minnesota failed in the late 1980s as a result of rising competition.

While IPAs faced mounting internal tensions in an increasingly tight market, the older, highly integrated plans faced pressure as well. As noted in the figures on enrollment, Group Health Plan was increasingly superseded by the more flexible group and IPA plans. Aggressive IPAs like PHP offered similar premiums and much greater choice of physician and hospital than even a large-staff HMO could make available. As a result, in 1987 Group Health began to offer preferred provider options, where enrollees could see physicians outside the plan (but pay higher rates for such visits).

Finally, Minnesota's Blue Cross responded to HMO growth by adopting many of the practices of HMOs. In the late 1980s, Blue Cross began to aggressively contract with hospitals rather than paying standard fees, and to withhold 10 percent of physicians' income against plan losses. As a result, Minneapolis–St. Paul's conventional fee-for-service sector has moved to a form of "managed care" that is hard to distinguish from the structure of many IPAs.

This brief account of HMOs in the Twin Cities illustrates several population dynamics of broad import. Entry of HMOs into the metropolitan market was slow and contested until the 1970s, when new federal policies and trends in the medical market suggested that more organized forms of health delivery were imminent. A variety of group practice–based, and then solo practitioner–based, HMOs were formed. Most have prospered, but mounting competition leaves decreasing slack for all types of health organizations. The conclusion of some seasoned observers of health care in Minneapolis–St. Paul is that tight competition homogenizes the internal structure and market products of health-care organizations (Feldman, Kralewski, and Dowd 1986).

CONCLUSION

Scott (1987) notes that organizations may face complex technical environments and complex institutional environments, and illustrates the point with the example of health care. Due to their efforts to coordinate and organize aspects of health care usually left to the market or informal relations between physicians, HMOs face more extreme environmental pressures than other medical organizations. Health maintenance organizations must manage a complex and uncertain work process, enroll members in an increasingly tight medical market, and locate their operations within a highly politicized, wealthy industry viewed widely as in crisis.

While the care delivered by HMOs is strongly conditioned by the changing technology of medicine, technological change appears to have played almost no role in the population dynamics of HMOs. Nationwide, it is true that the increasing specialization and complexity of health care has led to the expansion of group practices and the demise of the independent solo practitioner. But this has not had a discernible impact on the HMO industry. As discussed, the largest increase in health maintenance organizations has been through the organization of contractual arrangements among the solo practitioners forming IPAs.

Instead, the historical dynamics of HMOs are most importantly a function of institutional conditions. Prior to 1970, HMO growth was stunted by the political power of the medical profession. Since 1970, health maintenance organizations have received strong support from government policy, not in proportion to their political strength but in proportion to their attractiveness as vehicles for cost containment. Public policy support generated unexpected outcomes, as types of HMOs regarded as little able to contain costs proved the best capable of seizing new opportunities. Given the volatile character of national health policy, institutionally generated change seems likely to continue to dominate the population dynamics of health maintenance organizations.

NOTES

1. A detailed historical portrait of Kaiser, from which this discussion is drawn, is provided by Smillie (1991).

2. Incentives were particularly weak because most United Healthcare doctors had "panels" of less than twenty UHC patients. Whether physicians received money back was primarily dictated by whether they happened to see one or two really ill patients. Further, it was difficult to spread physician risks because UHC physicians were primarily solo practitioners who were unable to exert informal controls over each other, increasing the likelihood that physicians would free-ride on any collective risk pool.

3. In fact, a 1980 survey showed that physicians in IPA talk less frequently with each other than they do with physicians outside the HMO.

BIBLIOGRAPHY

Abel-Smith, Brian. 1988. "The Rise and Decline of the Early HMOs: Some International Experiences." *The Milbank Quarterly* 66:694–719.
Anderson, Odin W. Terry E. Herold, Bruce W. Butler, Claire H. Kohrman, and Ellen M. Morrison. 1985. *HMO Development: Patterns and Prospects*. Chicago: Pluribus Press.

Brown, Lawrence D. 1983. *Politics and Health Care Organization*. Washington, DC: Brookings.

Carroll, Glenn R., and Michael T. Hannan. 1989. "Density Dependence and the Evolution of Populations of Newspaper Organizations." *American Sociological Review* 54:524–41.

Christianson, Jon B., and Walter McClure. 1979. "Competition in the Delivery of Medical Care." *New England Journal of Medicine* 301:812–8.

Christianson, Jon B., Susan M. Sanchez, Douglas R. Wholey, and Maureen Shadle. 1991. "The HMO Industry: Evolution in Population Demographics and Market Structures." *Medical Care Review* 48:3–46.

Eisenberg, John M. 1986. *Doctors' Decisions and the Cost of Medical Care*. Ann Arbor, MI: Health Administration Press.

Falkson, Joseph L. 1980. *HMOs and the Politics of Health System Reform*. Chicago: AHA.

Feldman, Roger, John Kralewski, and Bryan Dowd. 1986. "HMOs: The Beginning or the End?" *Health Services Research* 24:191–211.

Fox, Peter D., and LuAnn Heinen. 1987. *Determinants of HMO Success*. Ann Arbor, MI: Health Administration Press.

Freidson, Eliot. 1970. *Professional Dominance*. New York: Atherton Press.

Freidson, Eliot. 1975. *Doctoring Together*. New York: Elsevier.

Goldberg, Lawrence G., and Warren Greenberg. 1981. "The Determinants of HMO Enrollment and Growth." *Health Services Research* 16:421–38.

Gruber, Lynn R., Maureen Shadle, and Cynthia L. Polich. 1988. "From Movement to Industry: The Growth of HMOs." *Health Affairs* 7:197–208.

Hannan, Michael T., and Glenn R. Carroll. 1992. *Dynamics of Organizational Populations: Density, Legitimacy, and Competition*. Oxford, MA: Oxford University Press.

Hannan, Michael T., and John Freeman. 1987. "The Ecology of Organizational Founding: American Labor Unions, 1836–1985." *American Journal of Sociology* 92:910–43.

Hillman, Alan L., Mark V. Pauly, and Joseph J. Kerstein. 1989. "How Do Financial Incentives Affect Physicians' Clinical Decisions and the Financial Performance of Health Maintenance Organizations?" *New England Journal of Medicine* 321:86–92.

InterStudy. 1973–92. *National HMO Census*. Minneapolis: InterStudy.

Kralewski, John E., Brian Dowd, Roger Feldman, and Janet Shapiro. 1987. "The Physician Rebellion." *New England Journal of Medicine* 316:339–42.

Luft, Harold S., 1978. "How Do Health-Maintenance Organizations Achieve Their 'Savings'?" *New England Journal of Medicine* 298:1336–42.

Luft, Harold. 1981. *Health Maintenance Organizations: Dimensions of Performance*. New York: Wiley.

Manning, Willard G., Arleen Leibowitz, George A. Goldberg, William H. Rogers, and Joseph P. Newhouse. 1984. "A Controlled Trial of the Effects of a Prepaid Group Practice on Use of Services." *New England Journal of Medicine* 310(23):1505–10.

Martin, Diane P., Jenifer L. Ehreth, and Anita R. Geving. 1985. *A Case Study of United Healthcare*. Menlo Park, CA: Henry J. Kaiser Family Foundation.

McLaughlin, Catherine G. 1987. "HMO Growth and Hospital Expenses and Use: A Simultaneous-Equaltion Approach." *Health Services Research* 22:183–205.

Moore, Stephen. 1979. "Cost Containment Through Risk-Sharing by Primary-Care Physicians." *New England Journal of Medicine* 300:1359–62.

Moore, Stephen, Diane P. Martin, and William C. Richardson. 1983. "Does the Primary-Care Gatekeeper Control the Costs of Health Care: Lessons from the SAFECO Experience." *New England Journal of Medicine* 309:1400–4.

Moran, D., and T. Savela. 1986. "HMOs, Finance and the Hereafter." *Health Affairs* 5:51–65.

Morrisey, Michael A., and Cynthia S. Ashby. 1982. "An Empirical Analysis of HMO Market Share." *Inquiry* 19:136–49.

Scott, W. Richard. 1987. "The Adolescence of Institutional Theory." *Administrative Science Quarterly* 32:493–511.

Smillie, John G. 1991. *Can Physicians Manage the Quality and Costs of Health Care?* New York: McGraw-Hill.

Somers, Anne R., ed. 1971. *The Kaiser-Permanente Medical Care Program.* New York: Commonwealth Fund.

Starr, Paul. 1982. *The Social Transformation of American Medicine.* New York: Basic Books.

Strang, David, and Ellen M. Bradburn. 1993. "Theorizing Legitimacy or Legitimating Theory? Competing Institutional Accounts of HMO Policy, 1970–89." Presented at the annual meetings of the American Sociological Association, Miami, FL.

Strang, David, and Douglas Currivan. 1992. "Incentives, Controls, and Communication: The Impact of Managerial Strategies on Hospital Occupancy in Health Maintenance Organizations." Presented at the annual meetings of the American Sociological Association, Pittsburgh, PA.

Strang, David, and Tanya Uden-Holman. 1990. "The Emergence of Health Maintenance Organizations." Paper presented at the annual meetings of the American Sociological Association, Washington, DC.

Welch, W. P. 1984. "HMO Enrollment: A Study of Market Forces and Regulations." *Journal of Health Politics, Policy and Law* 8:743–58.

Welch, W. P. 1987. "The New Structure of Independent Practice Associations." *Journal of Health Politics, Policy and Law* 12:723–39.

Welch, W. Pete, Alan L. Hillman, and Mark V. Pauly. 1990. "Toward New Typologies for HMOs." *Milbank Quarterly* 68:221–43.

Wholey, Douglas R., Jon B. Christianson, and Susan M. Sanchez. 1992. "Organizational Size and Failure Among Health Maintenance Organizations." *American Sociological Review* 57:829–42.

Wholey, Douglas R., Susan M. Sanchez, and Jon B. Christianson. 1993. "The Effect of Physician and Corporate Interests on the Formation of Health Maintenance Organizations." *American Journal of Sociology,* 99:164–200.

9

Newspaper Publishers

GLENN R. CARROLL

Newspapers have been part of American life for over three hundred years. The beginning of the industry is usually placed at 1690, which marked the appearance of the first known American paper, *Publick Occurrences Both Foreign and Domestick*. Since then, thousands of newspapers have been started in the United States, penetrating virtually every locale. The industry's period of greatest organizational growth was the nineteenth century, when the number of papers went from 150 to over 20,000. Most counts suggest that the number of newspapers in the country peaked at about 23,000 immediately prior to World War I. Throughout the rest of the twentieth century, numbers of American papers have generally declined.

The last decade or so has witnessed a major development in the newspaper industry—the emergence of a national press in the United States. Although the *Christian Science Monitor* and the *Wall Street Journal* had long operated on a national basis, they were considered specialized anomalies. The launching of Gannett's *USA Today* in 1982 and the subsequent expansion of the *New York Times* into many far-flung metropolitan areas represented a shift in size and scale of potential newspaper markets. According to many observers, this shift was made possible by modern advancements in information technology.

Prior to the national press's emergence, newspapers in the United States typically focused on a single metropolitan area. This is still true of most American newspapers. However, the persisting local character of the press does not mean that the organizational structure of the industry has remained stable. Indeed, the transformations of the industry across the many and varied places of the country are remarkably similar and dramatic. They also foreshadow the national press, making it appear as the natural outgrowth of a long-term trend.

This chapter reviews organizational transformations that occurred in the American local newspaper industry in the years prior to the development of the national press (up to about 1975). It describes several long-term trends in the industry as well as ecological research on the processes behind them. It looks at the industry from the perspective of the nation as well as from that of several specific metropolitan areas. I also mention some related research on the newspaper industries of Argentina and Ireland.

Newspapers are especially interesting organizations for ecological study because they are of both commercial and political importance. As commercial entities, newspapers face the same sort of market pressures and economic forces as any profit-oriented business. Yet the political potential of a newspaper has led many to enter the industry with little regard for financial implications. It should be no surprise, then, to discover that both economic and political processes have played roles in shaping the organizational populations of newspapers.

CONCENTRATION IN THE NEWSPAPER INDUSTRY

Few Americans have failed to hear the occasional outbursts of critics bemoaning the impending demise of the press. Usually prompted by highly visible newspaper failures, such as the *Chicago Daily News* in 1978 or the *Washington Star* in 1981, these observers think that the American newspaper industry has become politically unhealthy because of ownership concentration.

Just how concentrated is the U.S. newspaper industry? Table 9-1 presents some relevant data for the period 1920 to 1976. It shows that the American press has experienced dramatic economic changes. For instance, the number of general circulation dailies declined severely: 2,200 dailies operated in 1920; only 1,756 dailies operated in 1976. By 1975, most of the country's urban areas did not have local dailies, and of those cities with dailies, only 2.5 percent had more than one.

Newspaper chains—firms owning and operating papers in more than one locale, e.g., Gannett or Hearst—also gained more of the market in this period. In 1920, only 13 chains operated in the United States; by 1976, the number had risen to 167. The incidence of chain-owned dailies also increased from 2.8 percent to 59.4 percent in this period. By 1976, a typical chain-owned daily had greater circulation than that of an independent daily (Bagdikian 1980). Moreover, more than 70 percent of the nation's total daily circulation was in the hands of the chains.

Table 9-2 shows the largest newspaper chains in 1972, ranked by total circulation. Obviously, the chains differed in structure, with some holding a few large papers and others maintaining a portfolio of smaller papers. Moreover, the market was highly fluid in this period. For instance, in 1976 the new leader was the combined Knight-Ridder chain, with thirty-four dailies and a total circulation of 3,725,000. Newhouse had moved up to second place by adding seven dailies. But the most acquisitive company among the leaders was Gannett, which increased its holdings to seventy-three daily newspapers (Bagdikian 1977).

Table 9–1 Concentration in the American newspaper industry

	1920	1940	1960–61	1970–71	1976
Number of English-language general-circulation dailies	2,200	1,878	1,763	1,748	1,756
Total daily circulation (millions)	22.4	41.1	58.9	62.1	60.6
Cities with dailies	1,207	1,426	1,461	1,511	1,550
One-daily cities	509	1,092	1,222	1,312	1,369
Percentage of daily cities with competition	57.1	12.7	4.2	2.4	2.5
Number of chains	13	60	109	157	167
Percentage of dailies with chain ownership	2.8	17.0	31.8	50.3	59.4
Percentage of daily circulation by chains	n.a.	n.a.	46.1	63.0	71.0

n.a. = not available
Sources: Emery and Emery (1978), Dertouzos (1978), Sterling and Haight (1978), Ayer (various years).

Analysts often debate what effects concentration in the press has had. But there is far less disagreement on the causes of concentration in the daily newspaper market. Most analysts (e.g., Rosse 1978, 1980) recognize that newspaper production costs and advertising rate structures possess strong economies of scale. An economy of scale exists when one large firm can supply a product at lower cost than can a combination of small firms. Scale economies occur in newspaper production because the overwhelming proportion of production costs accrues in the first copy of each press run; the marginal cost declines sharply for the second copy, and even further for additional copies. Advertising costs display a parallel logic: to reach an audience of a given size, it is generally less expensive to advertise in one larger paper than in several smaller ones. Both factors allow large newspapers to offer readers and advertisers a better

Table 9–2 Largest chains of daily newspapers, 1972

	Total circulation	No. of dailies owned
Chicago Tribune	3,600,000	8
Newhouse	3,300,000	23
Scripps	2,400,000	49
Gannett	2,300,000	50
Knight	1,950,000	10
Hearst	1,750,000	8
Times-Mirror	1,700,000	5
Dow Jones	1,500,000	15
Ridder	1,300,000	17
Cox	1,000,000	12

Source: Baer et al. (1974).

product at a lower price than smaller competitors. And the industry concentrates because, in the long run, the disadvantaged position of the smaller papers forces them out of business.

DENSITY DEPENDENCE AMONG NEWSPAPERS

Taking a longer view of American newspapers suggests that the declines in dailies reflects, at least in part, the operation of density-dependent processes of legitimation and competition. For example, Figures 9-1 and 9-2 show the density of newspapers operating in various metropolitan markets across time. In each instance, the trajectory of density is consistent with that predicted by the theoretical model. Institutional history also coincides with the model's depiction of organizational evolution driven initially by legitimation and then later by competition.

Legitimation
The first papers in the United States found it difficult to continue publishing without the endorsement of authorities. *Publick Occurrences Both Foreign and Domestick* lasted only one issue—its publisher was jailed for printing "the truth as he saw it" (Emery and Emery 1978). America's second paper, John Campbell's *Newsletter,* had its copy approved by the governor. Subsequent papers

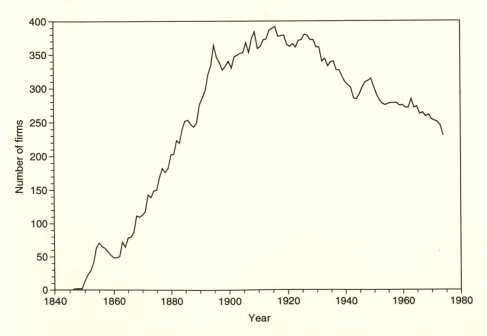

Figure 9–1 Density of newspapers in San Francisco Metropolitan Bay Area. (*Source:* Adapted from Carroll and Hannan 1989. Copyright © 1989 by American Sociological Association. Used by permission.)

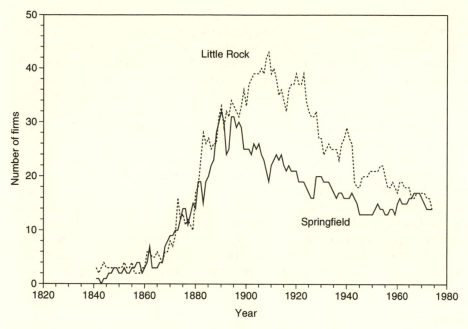

Figure 9–2 Density of newspapers in two metropolitan areas. (*Source:* Adapted from Carroll and Hannan 1989. Copyright © 1989 by American Sociological Association. Used by permission.)

were typically published by postmasters who noted that they were circulated "by authority." In 1721, James Franklin challenged the authorities with his *New England Courant*. Although he wound up in jail, the paper operated for five years and gave strong impetus to the development of an independent press. By 1785, all thirteen of America's colonies had at one time or another been home to a newspaper. Most of these were private enterprises.

Early newspapers had very high failure rates. More than half of the 2,100 papers founded before 1820 are thought not to have survived for two years (Emery and Emery 1978). Financial difficulties accounted for many of these failures. However, early papers also encountered legal, political, and civil difficulties. One of the more interesting obstacles involved libel, a charge that could result in jail sentences or bankruptcy. Early courts recognized the principle, "the greater the truth, the greater the libel" (Emery and Emery 1978), and did not allow a defendant to introduce evidence as to the truth of an alleged libel until at least 1805 (Mott 1962).

American newspapers prior to 1830 were basically of two types: mercantile papers (which printed commercial information) and partisan papers (which reported political news and printed opinions, usually on behalf of the political parties supporting them).[1] Both kinds of enterprises were typically small, often one-person operations. In the 1830s, the so-called "Penny Press" (named after its retail price) emerged, marking the first independent, mass-based newspapers (Schudson 1978). These papers gained independence from political parties because their broad-based readership generated ample revenues from sales and advertising. In terms of content, the penny papers opted for objectivity: accounts of trials and the like were often published verbatim from official proceedings. The established press of the day labeled such contents sensational, but social historian Schudson (1978) credits the Penny Press with inventing the modern concept of "news." By the turn of the century, the job of newspaper reporter had been transformed into a profession. Many cities formed press clubs. And, the journalism profession began to increasingly stress fairness, objectivity, and dispassion (Schudson 1978).

These and other developments led to the social acceptance of the newspaper, its taken-for-granted right of existence, and its commonly regarded value as a source of information. Yet the process by which this occurred was uneven in both time and space. For instance, publishers still found themselves on occasion dueling with the angry subjects of editorials until at least the mid-nineteenth century (Mott 1962). Battles in the newly settled areas of the South and the West showed that while national events set the stage for legitimation, new papers on the expanding frontier often needed to establish their own claims.

Competition

Journalism history of the nineteenth century contains many accounts of bitter local newspaper rivalries. Yet from the perspective of organizational mortality, competition intensified in the twentieth century. The best data on competition and consolidation in the newspaper industry pertain to general-circulation dailies (Rosse, Owen, and Dertouzos, 1975; Emery and Emery, 1978). The first daily newspaper appeared in 1783; it was the *Pennsylvania Evening Post*. Dailies remained relatively uncommon until the middle of the nineteenth century. By 1880, the number of daily newspapers had grown to 850. The peak number of 2,200 was reached immediately prior to World War I; numbers of dailies then declined to about 1,750 between World Wars I and II. The density of dailies remained roughly stable until 1980, with periodic small fluctuations.

As suggested by Table 9-1, this national trend masks an underlying process of severe local competition. Within cities, there has been a steady downward trend toward a single daily. Among all cities with dailies, the percent with two or more competing dailies has fallen from 61 percent in 1880 to 57 percent in 1910, to 20 percent in 1930, and to 1.9 percent in 1981.

Empirical research on density dependence among newspapers provides more direct support for the model. Studies by Carroll and Hannan (1989) show that in large newspaper markets, the nonmonotonic relationships between density and foundings and failures are strong. Density at founding also shows the expected position effects on mortality (Hannan and Carroll 1992).

POLITICAL ENVIRONMENTS

Because the press can be used to influence opinions, interpret events, recruit followers, and increase solidarity among those already holding a particular view, its potential as a political tool is great. Systematic empirical research on newspapers in Argentina, Ireland, and San Francisco has uncovered important ways that the press's political sensitivity shapes organizational populations (Carroll 1987). In all three locales, newspaper founding rates increased sharply in years characterized by political turmoil, and newspapers founded in these years had shorter lifetimes.

How might these associations be explained? Three arguments seem plausible. The first recognizes that political turmoil is news. All other things equal, political turmoil means there is more news to report; it is also a situation likely to motivate potential readers to buy newspapers to find out what is going on. If we regard news as an environmental resource, then, as with any environmental resource, an increase in its supply will likely lead to a larger organizational carrying capacity (see the introduction to Section II). And, because turmoil is episodic, a greater number of newspapers can be sustained for only a short period.

A second explanation realizes that those behind political turmoil might be publishing their own newspapers. If so, then the new papers that appear in these periods are likely to be explicitly political, serving the purposes of recruitment, organization, solidarity, or propaganda. Such political papers would not be reacting to the turmoil so much as they would be instigators of it; they would likely lose their purpose after the turmoil subsides.

A third interpretation relies on the research of sociologist Charles Tilly and colleagues, who have demonstrated that collective violence is essentially political in nature, involving interest-oriented groups created by broad social and economic transformations, exhibiting high levels of solidarity, and articulating specific complaints (Tilly 1978; Tilly, Tilly, and Tilly 1975). If collective violence does reflect an impending or ongoing restructuring of the social and economic order, then the newspapers appearing in these periods may be designed to appeal generally to recently mobilized groups. Although such groups may be real contenders for power, their motivations are not solely political. Instead, they tend to be organized around specific local problems that are not being addressed properly by the ruling groups. The differences between this explanation and the previous one are subtle but important. Whereas in the previous explanation groups are fighting for power and using *political* newspapers as a tactical tool, in this explanation the contending groups publish *general* newspapers that appeal to their members.

Research on newspapers in Argentina, Ireland, and San Francisco suggests strongly that the third interpretation is most plausible. Years of turmoil are associated with higher founding rates of general, not political, newspapers. These papers have shorter lifetimes on average. Analysis of circulation patterns also supports their interpretation.

A closer look at a year of political turmoil provides some insight into the underlying processes. In 1907, San Francisco witnessed a violent year related to a tumultuous local history of labor struggle (McGloin 1978). The 1906 earthquake and fire had disabled many of the city's businesses, but the major operator of the local streetcar lines, United Railroads, was quick to recover. Owned by an investment company in New Jersey, United Railroads decided to resist wage demands and pressure for an eight-hour day from Local 205 of the Carmen's Union. Led by union officials and publicly supported by Father Peter C. Yorke—a prominent citizen and editor of the local newspaper, *The Leader*—about 2,000 streetcar workers went on strike in early May after negotiations with the company broke down. Prepared with 400 armed strikebreakers, United Railroads gave the strikers a two-day warning and then resumed operation on May 7. An enraged mob of strikers and sympathizers attacked the operating streetcars with rocks and bricks on that day, nicknamed "Bloody Thursday."

Company personnel and strikebreakers retaliated with gunfire. At least one striking worker was killed and nineteen others were wounded. Violence and sabotage persisted through the middle of the month, when the San Francisco Labor Council endorsed a boycott of the streetcars, reducing the daily passenger load by 75 percent. The strike went on successfully for three months, but labor leaders then became preoccupied with local elections. In March 1908, the strike was officially ended, although its effectiveness had already been diminished months earlier by attrition. Total estimated casualties from the strike range from 39 dead and 700 injured (Wood and Bush 1962) to six dead and 250 injured (McGloin 1978). The Union Labor party was defeated in the November elections, handing the labor movement a general political setback.

As depicted by Tilly's model, the violence of 1907 in San Francisco was not connected with "homogeneous masses of angry or desperate people, but to a large extent with specific groups" (Tilly, Tilly, and Tilly 1975, p. 225), namely, the local labor unions. The election-oriented Union Labor party exemplified the political nature of the local unions of this time. As Tilly and colleagues have argued, collective violence is "closely connected with nonviolent struggles for power" (Tilly, Tilly, and Tilly 1975, p. 242). Such struggles for power arise when newly mobilized groups appear and articulate special-interest concerns.

Further insight into the process comes from examining the forty-six specific papers founded in the years 1907 (nineteen newspapers) and 1908 (twenty-seven newspapers). A few of these were explicitly political in purpose, such as the *San Francisco Observer* (a weekly founded by convicted former mayor Eugene Schmitz in an effort to clear his name and attack his local political enemies) and the *World* (a weekly Oakland labor paper published by the Socialist party "to organize the slaves of capital to vote their emancipation"). But the vast majority of these papers were not political. Instead, they signified the commercial, occupational, ethnic, religious, and territorial differentiation rampant in the area at the time, and by Tilly's model, connected to the sources of political turmoil. Consider, for instance, these papers expressing commercial differentiation:

Construction News (1907–10), a six-page daily reporting on the building trades industry

Coast Banker (1907–75), a 64-page monthly devoted to the financial community

Hotel News (1907–18), an eight-page weekly devoted to the local hotel industry

Inter City Express (1908–   ), a four-page, local, legal, and commercial index published weekly in Berkeley

And these papers connected to occupational differentiation:

Franklin Printer (1908–10), a 42-page monthly published for typographers by the Franklin Association of San Francisco; and

Pacific Pharmacist (1907–22), a 76-page monthly directed to the pharmaceutical community.

The following papers are related to ethnic differentiation:

Resurrection (1908–11), a Spanish-language 32-page semimonthly of general interest

Jadran (1908–22), an eight-page independent weekly published in Croatian

Sokoshi Mbun (1908–12), a Japanese-language newspaper

New Korea (1908–37), a Korean newspaper

L'Echo del L'Ouest (1908–28), apparently a French paper

California (1907–50), a general-interest Greek weekly

Or the following papers stemming from territorial differentiation:

Mill Valley Independent (1907–11), a four-page independent weekly with a circulation of 700–900

Centerville Register (1908–11), a four-page Republican weekly with a circulation of 500

Fairfield Enterprise (1908–42), a four-page nonpartisan weekly with a circulation of 500

Berkeley Independent (1908–13), a six-page independent daily with a circulation of 2,000–2,750

Alameda Times (1908–   ), an eight-page daily of general interest

What about the contents of these papers? Many of them are difficult to find today. However, the few that can be found contain, as would be expected, specialized information of interest to the target audience. But many of these papers also contained general information written in interpretive fashion for the target audience. Consider, for example, the editorial philosophy proclaimed in the first issue of Berkeley's *The Church Messenger,* an eight-page interdenominational weekly:

We want to state for those that do not know, what *The Church Messenger* is, and is going to be. First of all, it is a newspaper. It is to be conducted along the lines of a modern newspaper, and as long as it is to be published, it will endeavor to be up-to-date and newsy. And it is to be devoted exclusively to the interests of the Berkeley Churches, and Berkeley Righteousness . . . Not righteousness in church matters, but in all matters—religious and secular, municipal as well as clerical,

Table 9–3 Nondaily newspapers

	1920	1940	1960–61	1970–71	1976
Number of weekly newspapers	16,227	10,796	8,953	8,888	8,506
Number of semiweeklies and triweeklies	672	412	372	469	621
Total circulation of weeklies (millions)	n.a.	n.a.	21.0	29.4	38.0

n.a. = not available

Sources: Emery and Emery (1978), Sterling and Haight (1978), Ayer (various years).

political as well as spiritual. . . . [The paper] is to be the means of expressing to the public through its editorials, the sentiment of the united church of Berkeley, in all matters that it may be interested. . . . This paper will pave the way for . . . concerted action, it will give the churches a bond of unity and a chance to become better acquainted with each other through its columns. (Vol. 1, No. 1, p. 1, 1908)

SPECIALIST NEWSPAPERS

Although most Americans know about the one or two specialized newspapers that are relevant to their specific world, few understand the size and diversity of the whole specialist segment of the newspaper industry. Specialist newspapers are often invisible to those outside their target audiences. Data on specialist papers are also hard to come by.

Table 9-3 presents some imperfect data on the specialist newspaper population of the United States from 1920 to 1976. The data concern nondaily newspapers rather than specialists. However, because few specialists publish on a daily basis, there is likely to be a positive correlation between specialist and nondaily newspapers. So the table provides some suggestion as to the size of the specialist press—it is substantial. Moreover, the number of papers in this segment remained fairly stable in the post–World War II era. And, because total circulation has grown, so too has the average size of these papers.

It may seem paradoxical that at the same time the daily press was becoming more concentrated, the specialist nondaily press was apparently expanding. The two trends are likely linked, and in Section IV we describe a model that can explain the relationship. The model is known as a resource-partitioning model and it predicts that as the market for generalist organizations becomes more concentrated, specialists will experience enhanced life chances. The data presented here are consistent with this prediction. So too are journalistic reports about the specialist press.

CONCLUSION

Long before the national press emerged, organizational transformations were well under way in the American newspaper industry. Most major cities and metropolitan areas witnessed a precipitous drop in the number of daily newspapers operating in their market. This decline was driven by intense competition in what was by the twentieth century a mature industry. That organizational evolution in this period was driven primarily by competition is consistent with the density model of organizational ecology.

Earlier history of the industry also agrees with the expectations of the density model in that the press encountered many obstacles to legitimation. The sensitivity of the press to political turbulence and other political processes underscores the precarious early evolution of the newspaper organizational form.

Finally, in the more recent era, the specialist press has secured a stable and substantial market segment. The forces producing concentration in the daily press have not undermined this trend—in fact, they have likely enhanced it.

NOTES

Sections of this chapter are adapted from G. R. Caroll, 1985, "Concentration and Specialization: Dynamics of Niche Width in Populations of Organizations," *American Journal of Sociology* 90:1262–83; G. R. Carroll and Y. P. Huo, 1986, "Organizational Task and Institutional Environments in Ecological Perspective: Findings from the Local Newspaper Industry," *American Journal of Sociology* 91:838–73; and G. R. Carroll and M. T. Hannan, 1989, "Density Dependence in the Evolution of Newspaper Populations," *American Sociological Review* 54:524–41.

1. For instance, commenting on the 360 papers in print in 1810, I. Thomas (1970, p. 17) wrote: "A large proportion of the public papers . . . were established, and supported, by the two great contending political parties, into which the people of these states are usually divided and whose numbers produce an equipollence; consequently, a great augmentation of vehicles for carrying on the political warfare have been found necessary."

BIBLIOGRAPHY

Ayer, N. W. Various Years. *American Newspaper Directory Annual*. Philadelphia: Ayer Press.

Baer, Walter S., et al. 1974. *Concentration of Mass Media Ownership*. Santa Monica: Rand Corporation.

Bagdikian, Ben. 1977. "Newspaper Mergers—The Final Phase." *Columbia Journalism Review* 15:17–22.

Bagdikian, B. 1980. "Conglomeration, Concentration and the Media." *Journal of Communication* 30:59–64.

Carroll, G. R. 1985. "Concentration and Specialization: Dynamics of Niche Width in Populations of Organizations." *American Journal of Sociology* 90:1262–83.

Carroll, G. R. 1987. *Publish and Perish: The Organizational Ecology of Newspaper Industries*. Greenwich, CT: JAI.

Carroll, G. R., and M. T. Hannan. 1989. "Density Dependence in the Evolution of Newspaper Populations." *American Sociological Review* 54:524–41.

Carroll, G. R., and Y. P. Huo. 1986. "Organizational Task and Institutional Environ-

ments in Ecological Perspective: Findings from the Local Newspaper Industry."
American Journal of Sociology 91:838–73.

Dertouzos, J. N. 1978. *Media Conglomerates: Chains, Groups, and Crossownership.*
Technical Report No. 96. Studies in Industry Economics, Stanford University.

Emery, E., and M. Emery. 1978. *The Press and America,* 4th ed. Englewood Cliffs, NJ:
Prentice-Hall.

Hannan, M. T., and G. R. Carroll. 1992. *Dynamics of Organizational Populations.* New
York: Oxford.

McGloin, J. B. 1978. *San Francisco: The Story of a City.* San Rafael, CA: Presidio.

Mott, F. L. 1962. *American Journalism,* 3rd ed. New York: Macmillan.

Rosse, J. N. 1978. *The Evolution of One-Newspaper Cities.* Technical Report. Studies
in Industry Economics, Stanford University.

Rosse, J. N. 1980. "The Decline of Direct Newspaper Competition." *Journal of Communication* 30:65–71.

Rosse, J. N., B. Owen, and J. Dertouzos. 1975. "Trends in the Daily Newspaper Industry." Technical Report. Studies in Industry Economics, Stanford University.

Schudson, M. 1978. *Discovering the News.* New York: Basic.

Sterling, C., and T. Haight. 1978. *The Mass Media: Aspen Institute Guide to Communications Trends.* New York: Praeger.

Thomas, I. 1970 (1810 original). *The History of Printing in America.* New York: Weath-
ervane.

Tilly, C. 1978. *From Mobilization to Revolution.* Reading, MA: Addison-Wesley.

Tilly, C., L. Tilly, and R. Tilly. 1975. *The Rebellious Century 1830–1930.* Cambridge,
MA: Harvard University Press.

Wood, R. D., and L. Bush. 1962. *California History and Government.* San Francisco:
Fearum.

10

Automobile Manufacturers

GLENN R. CARROLL AND MICHAEL T. HANNAN

Some organizational theorists regard organizational ecology as useful primarily for understanding a limited range of industries. These are industries in the periphery of the economy and those populated by small and mid-sized organizations. Supposedly, firms in the core of economy can manipulate their environments and immunize themselves from competition and selection pressure. Those in peripheral industries presumably cannot, thus making selection analysis relevant. Moreover, large organizations have low failure rates. Thus only populations that contain mainly small organizations are subject to selection processes, according to this interpretation (Scott 1992).

Sociologist Charles Perrow (1986), a critic of organizational ecology, has pointed to the American automobile industry as a prototypical context in which ecological theory does not apply. This industry clearly stands in the center of the economy, and it has been dominated by a few giant firms. Moreover, Perrow contends that these firms can manipulate their economic and political environments to serve their own ends, thereby avoiding competitive and selective pressures.

How credible are these claims? Can ecological theory illuminate historical and contemporary developments in the automobile industry? We have begun to address these questions as part of a new long-term research project. We do so by examining the number and diversity of firms in the automobile manufacturing industry. Our investigation looks both at the modern industry and its history. We rely primarily on archival data about the industry and its firms in historical sources. The data span the period from 1885 to 1986. In surveying the organizational history of the industry, we pay special attention to issues concerning the theory of density-dependent legitimation and competition.

Most industries pale in comparison with the American automobile industry in terms of scale of production, employment, and revenues. In 1986, the end of our study period, over 750,000 persons were employed in the domestic manufacture of motor vehicles in the United States. Another 3.1 million earned their living through automotive sales and servicing. Domestic firms produced over 7.8 million passenger cars. Another 500,000 automobiles were produced in the United States by Japanese firms. Total motor vehicle output was valued at over $120 billion, almost 3 percent of the gross national product. Overall, no industry has had a better claim to occupying the center of the economies of the rich countries of the world. What role did ecological processes play in shaping this industry? We begin to answer this question by considering the origins of the industry in Europe.

DEVELOPMENT OF THE EUROPEAN INDUSTRY

Although American firms dominated the world market for much of the twentieth century (from roughly 1920 to the late 1970s), the industry did not emerge initially in the United States. A recognizable automobile industry started and first flourished in Europe. Moreover, since the mid-1980s, American firms have lost their clear dominance of the worldwide industry (although they retain the largest share of production). For these reasons, much can be learned from placing the population of American manufacturers in a worldwide context.

It is not a simple matter to date the start of the worldwide industry. Experimentation with the application of mechanical energy (steam initially) to propel vehicles began during the late eighteenth century. In some sense, the motor vehicle, as a technical product, has existed for two hundred years. However, this early experimentation did not produce an industry. It was not until the closing years of the nineteenth century that a recognizable industry emerged, with firms declaring intentions to manufacture automobiles for the market. Most historians of the industry place its start between 1885 and 1895. We use the earlier date in our research. Our reading of the histories of the firms involved suggests that firms devoted to producing automobiles for the general market began in 1885 in France and Germany.

Although the French and German populations began nearly simultaneously, France quickly became the center of the industry. The population of automobile manufacturers in France grew more rapidly and to a higher density (Figure 10-1). Almost a decade passed before auto firms appeared in two other major European automobile-producing countries: Britain (1894) and Italy (1895). The trajectories of density for the four countries (Figures 10-1 and 10-2) show strong similarities. Density grew slowly initially, and then soared for a time. The most striking growth occurred during the closing years of the nineteenth century and the first few years of the twentieth century. For instance, French density grew from 20 firms in 1895 to 121 in 1900, and British density grew from 32 in 1898 to 120 in 1903. Densities remained high (though variable) until the onset of the First World War. In each country, the number of producers dropped by at least a third from 1913 to 1918. However, numbers rebounded quickly after the war. By 1922–23, densities had returned to prewar levels (and for Germany surpassed the prewar level). The onset of the worldwide Great Depression in 1929 began a continuous decline in densities, accelerated by World War II. Over the

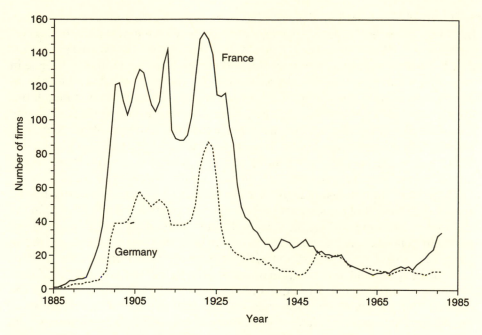

Figure 10–1 Density of French and German automobile producers. (*Source:* Adapted from Hannan et al. 1995. Copyright © 1993 by Michael T. Hannan and Glenn R. Carroll. Used by permission.)

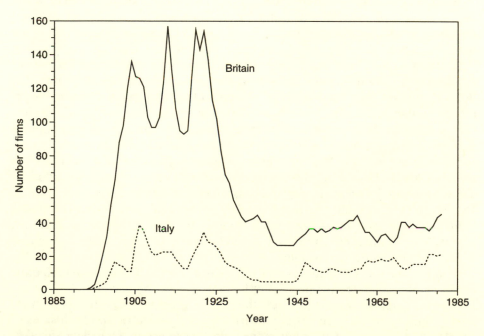

Figure 10–2 Density of British and Italian automobile producers. (*Source:* Adapted from Hannan et al. 1995. Copyright © 1993 by Michael T. Hannan and Glenn R. Carroll. Used by permission.)

post–World War II period, densities have remained stable and sometimes have begun to grow, as a variety of specialist producers have entered the industry.

The early takeoff in France seems surprising. Economic historians report that British and German manufacturing industries surpassed those in France in technology during this period. In particular, Britain dominated the bicycle industry, which was a very important source of entrepreneurs and skilled labor for the new automobile industry. The key innovations in propulsion, involving the internal combustion engine, were perfected in Germany. Why, then, did France take the lead and hold it in Europe until the onset of World War II? This question strikes us as a fruitful one, because it draws attention to the importance of social movement activities in the formation of an industry.

The French automobile industry's early lead can be explained partly by the spatial distribution of the supporting industries, especially metalworking, in the main manufacturing nations. In France, the machine industry was centered in Paris. In contrast, the machine and metalworking industries were dispersed in Germany, and they were concentrated—but away from London—in Britain. Several early manufacturers set up operations in Paris. The presence of a large pool of potential suppliers of components and of a large labor force with the requisite mechanical skills supported the nascent industry. Concentration of the support industries and labor force allowed geographic concentration of the industry in both Britain, in the Midland cities of Coventry and Wolverhampton, and France. But the British automobile industry still lagged behind the French. Why?

What seems to have mattered most is that the French industry began at the nation's political and cultural center.[1] Location in Paris, the center of commerce, journalism, fashion, and wealth, eased the development of the social movement activities that solidify an emerging industry. Concentration of the industry in such a center eased the flow of information about the product, technological innovations, and business activities in the industry. Such information flows encouraged the establishment of a collective identity as a distinctive industry (rather than some extension of metalworking, carriage making, etc.) Easy access to the country's centralized journalism industry allowed cultural images of the automobile and of the organizational automobile manufacturer form to spread widely. The community of early enthusiasts, led by the Automobile Club de France, used two strategies to call attention to their industry. They sponsored races on public roads between major cities, e.g., Paris-Bordeaux-Paris, which generated much international journalistic attention. And they produced specialized publications: first the monthly magazine *La Locomotion automobile* appeared in 1894 and then the daily newspaper *L'Auto* began publication in 1900.

In short, the fortuitous location of the early French automobile manufacturers in Paris accelerated the process of industry formation and gave France the lead in automobile production. Yet, the rise to prominence of the French industry quickly encouraged entrepreneurial action in countries on both sides of the Atlantic. The industry rapidly gained worldwide scope. One clear signal of the impact elsewhere of developments in France can be seen in language. The French term for the product, automobile, diffused throughout the world, replacing the many alternative names in use.[2] We discuss research that investigates the possibility that growth in density of the French industry had legitimation effects that spilled over the borders of France.

It is important to recognize that the automobile industry has had a strong international dimension from the start. Even the early developments in France reflected international flows of information, as Laux (1976, p. 9) points out:

> The entry into the automobile industry of the pioneer firms in France, Panhard et Levassor, Peugeot, and Roger, was marked in each case by some initiative coming from Germany, showing in this way the international character of the industry from the very beginning.

In turn, France exported many automobiles to Britain, Germany, and even the United States during the closing years of the nineteenth century. For instance, it was only after 1908 that Britain produced more autos than it imported from France.

American automobile enthusiasts and entrepreneurs apparently paid close attention to developments in France and elsewhere in Europe. Several European manufacturers licensed their designs to American firms during the 1890s. For instance, the New York piano manufacturer William Steinway obtained the right to produce Daimler engines and automobiles from the German firm in 1888, and he established the Daimler Motor Co. in Connecticut in 1891. This firm produced Daimler engines but never actually produced automobiles. Several American firms were formed to import French automobiles during the late 1890s. It is striking to us how much attention American automobile publications of the period gave to technical and commercial developments in Europe.

The American industry lagged initially. Historians estimate it was ten years behind the French in 1895. However, it made up the gap in design and production very quickly.[3] By 1905, American firms produced as many cars as the French; by 1908, they produced as many as all of Europe. In 1913, the Ford subsidiary in England was the largest producer in Europe. The low-cost, high-quality vehicles eventually overwhelmed the European industry. By the outbreak of World War II, American manufacturers had 85 percent of the world's automobile sales.

DEVELOPMENT OF THE AMERICAN INDUSTRY

Let us consider the American developments in some detail. Figure 10-3 and Table 10-1 show trends in the industry's annual production. Of course, production figures have grown steadily over most of the history of the industry. Although early production was slight compared with contemporary levels, this does not mean that the industry was unimportant to the economy. As early as 1912, total American production passed the one-million mark; the 50-million mark was passed in 1935. The period of greatest production growth followed World War II, peaking in the 1970s.

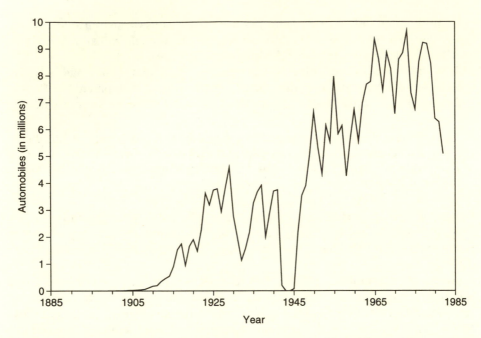

Figure 10–3 Domestic production of passenger cars in the United States. (*Source: Automotive News* 1993.)

General Motors Corp., Ford Motor Co., and the Chrysler Corp. (the so-called Big Three) have dominated the American industry for most of its history. Given the eventual success of these firms, their origins were surprisingly inauspicious. Henry Ford failed in his first two attempts to build automobile manufacturing firms, first with the Detroit Automobile Co. and then with the Henry Ford Co. He then founded the Ford Motor Co. in 1903. Its initial capitalization was a modest $100,000, with only $28,000 paid in; the assembly plant employed about a dozen workers, and operated within about 10,000 square feet.

General Motors was founded in 1908 by William C. Durant, who already controlled the Buick Motor Car. Durant was an ambitious and skillful corporate entrepreneur. In the next couple of years, he acquired thirteen automobile manufacturers and placed them under the GM holding company. Of these, only Buick and the Cadillac Co. were profitable enterprises; several, such as Cartercar, faltered badly and were quickly closed down. Durant lost control of the company in 1910 to a banking syndicate. He regained control in 1915 from a different organizational base, Chevrolet Motor Car Co., in collaboration with the DuPont family. However, the company foundered in the 1920–21 depression, and Durant was again forced out. Pierre DuPont assumed the helm this time, and he appointed Alfred P. Sloan as executive vice-president. Sloan reorganized the company, using the innovative divisionalized organizational structure.

The Chrysler Corp. came into existence in 1927, when Walter Chrysler reorganized the ailing Maxwell Motor Co. Chrysler had earlier come out of retirement to aid the Willys Corporation, which failed in 1921. The newly formed

Table 10–1 Car sales in the United States (in thousands of automobiles)

	1922	1925	1928	1930	1931	1940	1950	1960	1970	1980	1990
Ford	753	1,257	488	1,059	532	644	1,519	1,749	2,216	1,544	1,944
GM	289	601	1,289	905	825	1,625	2,871	2,870	3,333	4,116	3,309
Chrysler	—	105	365	225	228	809	1,114	921	1,350	789	861
Imports	17	8	8	43	21	5	19	499	1,231	2,375	3,045
Total	1,569	2,968	3,169	2,627	1,908	3,416	6,327	6,577	8,388	8,975	9,296

Sales data are usually based on new car registration information. Prior to 1960, import figures may include some small domestic products.
Source: Automotive News (1993).

Chrysler Corp. subsequently purchased Dodge Brothers Manufacturing Co., which gave the company a valuable established network of dealers.

Figure 10-3 shows historical production data for Ford, GM, and Chrysler. The rapid early growth of Ford reflected its success in producing what Henry Ford called "a car for the great multitude." With the Model N in 1906 and the Model T in 1908, Ford offered light, tough cars priced within the means of the growing middle class. Early sales of the Model T were so encouraging—28,000 cars in its first two years—that Ford dropped all other models and concentrated his firm's energies on efficient production of this car.

After experimenting for several years with various production techniques at its new Highland Park plant, the Ford Motor Co. came up with the stunning innovation of the moving assembly line in 1913. This new production process allowed for increased output and continuing declines in the price of the Model T. By 1927, Ford had produced over 15 million units of the car. It was by far the most successful firm in the worldwide industry at this time. If dominance of a core market allows a firm to manage its environment and escape competitive pressure, Ford was so far ahead that it would never have lost its position at the top.

Nonetheless, rivals, especially GM and Chrysler, gained considerable ground on Ford in the 1920s. Many historical accounts of this era blame Ford's losses in market share on the eccentricities of the colorful Henry Ford, who steadfastly refused to abandon the Model T and expand the company's product line. Such a singular focus made sense in the face of phenomenal demand for the Model T. However, it also meant that the company failed to develop any experience or expertise at transforming its production system.

Although Ford might have stayed too long with the Model T, his greater blunder was to overlook the organizational difficulties of changing over to a new model.[4] When the Model T was finally abandoned in 1927, Ford planned a quick introduction of a new model, just as revolutionary as the Model T. The new Model A did eventually succeed in the market. However, its introduction was greatly delayed by the havoc its development and initial production wrought throughout the company. Unanticipated design problems occurred, the layout of the plant had to be revamped, and most production machinery had to be replaced. Along the way, many managers and production workers were fired for being thought too closely associated with the Model T. These various organizational problems caused the Ford assembly line to be shut down for six months. Industry historian David Hounshell (1984) estimates the total cost of the changeover to be $250 million; he comments that, "Ford had driven the strategy of mass production to its ultimate form and thereby into a cul-de-sac" (p. 267). These delays provided an opportunity for rivals to close the gap with Ford.

The contrast with GM is striking. Much of GM's success has been attributed to its multidivisional organizational structure. This design was put in place in the 1920s, during the reign of DuPont and Sloan. The design separates operational business units from the corporation's long-term planning and administration. One of GM's divisions, Chevrolet, managed to offer a highly successful challenge to the Model T in the mid-1920s. This success relied partly on use of

Ford-like production techniques. However, the Chevrolet division's success was due largely to an innovation in business strategy: regular introduction of styling changes. This strategy resonated well with the increasingly affluent citizenry.

The division's capacity to make frequent model changes depended on innovations in organizational structure and physical infrastructure. Most notable among these were the use of general-purpose machine tools (rather than the single-purpose tools used at Ford) and the adoption of a highly decentralized organizational structure that placed primary responsibility for major systems (engine, body, etc.) in separate plants (Hounshell 1984). Both factors eased "the development of changeover know-how and procedure" within GM and enabled it to become the innovator of the annual model change.

Ford and Chrysler eventually got better at model changeover as the industry moved toward flexible mass production in the 1950s. Ford moved toward the divisional organizational structure with the establishment of its ill-fated Edsel division. Chrysler retained its functional (nondivisional) organizational structure until the 1970s. GM's lead in administration and organization allowed it to remain the largest auto manufacturer, however. Each large automobile company generated above-average profits from 1945 to 1970, but GM's were especially high. So too was its share of the market. Why? After thorough study, economist Lawrence White (1971, p. 265) concluded: "General Motors' superior profitability must be attributed to its superior management: a superior ability to utilize differently the resources at hand and to make decisions under conditions of uncertainty." In short, GM was an "excellent" organization. From the perspective of 1971, it was inconceivable that GM would bleed multi-billion-dollar yearly losses only twenty years later.

The years since the Second World War have seen continued high levels of industry concentration. Of course, this does not imply that the large firms found the going easy. From its position of seeming invincibility in the late 1960s and early 1970s, GM lost much of its market share. Chrysler almost went under in 1979, only to be saved by government loan guarantees. A major precipitating event for the American losses was the OPEC (Organization of Petroleum Exporting Countries) oil embargo of 1979, when fuel prices rose sharply. This changed the competitive conditions in the industry. The small-car share of the U.S. market went from 27 percent in 1978 to 54 percent in 1979 to 61 percent in 1981. Unfortunately, the U.S. industry had focused its efforts on larger, standard-sized cars that had higher prices and profits. The small-car market was better served by the foreign manufacturers, who increased their market share from 17.8 percent in 1978 to 28.8 percent three years later.

The oil crisis of 1979 did not by itself cause the slide of the dominant domestic producers; it only speeded the downturn. Foreign automakers had been steadily making inroads to the American market since the early 1950s. The earliest successful arrival was Volkswagen, whose Beetle found a market for those wanting a reliable and inexpensive automobile. Other European manufacturers followed; again, usually with "specialty" products such as the British MG and Triumph roadsters. Nothing transformed the market and threatened the American industry like the large-scale entry of Japanese automakers, however. Although companies such as Nissan and Toyota entered the American market in the late 1950s and early 1960s, their presence was not felt strongly until the 1970s. In the 1980s, Japanese market share continued to increase from 22.8 percent at the beginning of the decade to 25.3 percent at the end. Moreover, the higher quality and lower cost of Japanese automobiles became so widely accepted by the American public that commentators far and wide began to speculate about the demise of the American industry.

Why were foreign companies suddenly at the forefront of an industry that some of America's best companies had long dominated? Scores of books and articles have examined this complex question. For purposes here, the important conclusion of this research is that much of the change can be accounted for by organizational factors. Differences between the structures of the major American manufacturers and both European and Japanese manufacturers are key to understanding these changes.

Large American firms initiated mass production. They excelled at manufacturing large quantities of standardized products by long-established methods. Their heavily bureaucratized organizational structures were tuned to this emphasis. So too were their generalist business strategies, which targeted the center of the market.

European firms typically specialized. They offered differentiated products to diverse market segments, often using advanced technologies. Japanese firms, especially Toyota Motors with its "lean production techniques," virtually reinvented the mass production system. They introduced new processes such as total quality management and just-in-time inventory. They also used employment relations very different from those in Detroit. These systems allowed Japanese firms to produce cars with less labor and fewer defects. By most analyses, automation of production per se played at best a small part, much smaller than did differences in organizational structures (Dertouzos et al. 1989).

ORGANIZATIONAL ABUNDANCE AND DIVERSITY

The large producers of the modern era emerged as the result of a long and severe selection process. Evidently, many Americans saw the potential future of the automobile market in its formative years. Literally thousands of them attempted to enter the market. According to the historian John B. Rae (1984, p. 17), entry into the early industry was easy:

> All that was required was some mechanical skill and a building where the vehicle could be assembled from parts made elsewhere. The cars were sold for cash . . . and the parts bought on credit, so that if production could be achieved and if buyers could be found, the operation could finance itself.

Figure 10-4 suggests that these conditions were abundant. It shows the number of individuals and groups who annually either entered production or began preproduction activities, meaning usually that an intent to produce was announced (a price quoted or a catalogue published) and a prototype was made.[5]

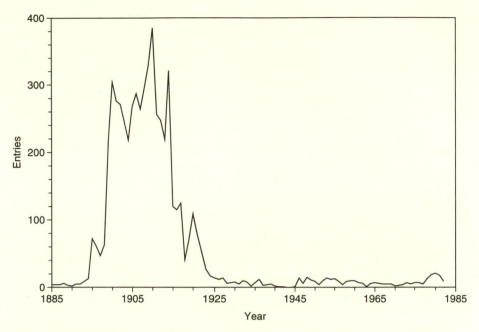

Figure 10–4 Entries of automobile producers and would-be producers in the United States. (*Source:* Authors' analysis. Copyright © Glenn R. Carroll and Michael T. Hannan. Used by permission.)

For at least a quarter of a century—from 1900 to 1925—entrepreneurial activity was rampant in this industry. A total of over 3,300 formal attempts at automobile production were launched.

Much selection occurred in the earliest stages of organization. Many individuals and groups who entered a preproduction phase of activity never made it into production. In other words, these enterprises failed before they could be said to have entered the market. Remarkably, entrepreneurs continued to attempt to enter the industry well after the obvious failures of many prior efforts.

Figure 10-5 shows the annual number of actual producers in the American industry. The abundance of producers, especially from 1900 to 1925, is startling, given the common image of the industry as made up of a few large companies. Most of these found it rough-going, no doubt; the median longevity of automobile producers was one year. Over 68 percent left the market within two years.

Many early automobile manufacturers came from other industries in which they were established manufacturers. Many of these made bicycles, which seemed an ideal background from which to begin automobile manufacture. Both bicycles and automobiles involved the assembly of self-propelled private transport vehicles with wheels. Moreover, early cars were much closer in design to bicycles than to modern cars. The cyclecar, essentially a motorized adaptation of the bicycle (often with three wheels), was a common product. So too was the "buggy with engine," a horse carriage with the engine mounted

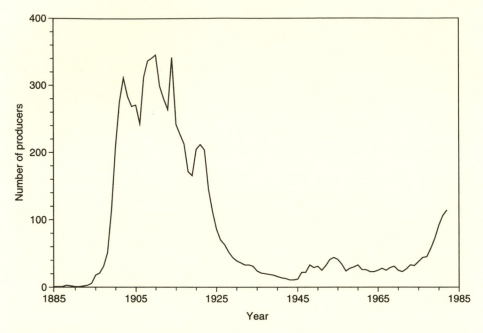

Figure 10–5 Density of automobile producers in the United States. (*Source:* Authors' Analysis. Copyright © Glenn R. Carroll and Michael T. Hannan. Used by permission.)

below the seat. Not surprisingly, many early makers of such models came from the carriage industry.

Bicycle and carriage manufacturers did not fare well in the automobile industry. As in many other emerging industries, established entrants from related industries failed to reap the benefits of what seemed to be an advantaged position. For instance, one of the first American firms to produce automobiles was the Pope Manufacturing Co. of Hartford, Connecticut. Pope was the largest bicycle manufacturer in the country (it had integrated backward into production of steel tubes and tires as well). There were virtually no other large companies in the automobile industry at the time. Between 1897 and 1899, Pope made between 500 and 600 cars, most with electric power. Despite the pleading of the chief engineer of the Motor Carriage Department, the general manager of the company would not support development of cars powered by internal combustion. He did not believe that the public would accept the "exploding" gasoline-powered engine. In 1899, the department was acquired by the trust-minded Electric Vehicle Co., and it went into receivership eight years later.

What about other producers? What kinds of cars did they make? The variety of early designs boggles the mind. Consider, for example, the following early cars and their makers:

• Riker, an electric car produced from 1896 to 1902, initially by Riker Electric Motor Co. in Brooklyn, New York. The Riker line included two-seaters, four-seaters, and heavy trucks.

- Roberts Electric, a two-seat electric car produced in 1897 by C. E. Roberts of Chicago. The car was powered by two 60-volt motors, one for each rear wheel.
- Waltham, a steam-powered auto that was steered with a tiller. This car was manufactured by the Waltham Automobile Co. of Waltham, Massachusetts, which operated from 1898 to 1900.
- Kent's Pacemaker, a steam car with three rear wheels and a single wheel in front for steering. The Colonial Automobile Co. of Boston manufactured this car from 1899 to 1901.
- Luxor, a gasoline-powered vehicle that resembles a Roman chariot. The car's designer, C.R. Harris of Williamsport, Pennsylvania, never managed to get his automobile into production, despite attention in the trade in 1900.
- Cotta Steam, a steam automobile with four-wheel-drive and steering. This car was produced in very limited numbers by the Cotta Automobile Co. of Rockford, Illinois, in 1903.
- Pullman, a six-wheel vehicle initially in 1903, this car survived until 1917 after it switched to a more convenient four-wheel design. The Pullman was made by the Hardinge Co. of York, Pennsylvania. There was no connection with the railway car manufacturer of the same name.
- Rotary, a gasoline-powered car with a single-cylinder engine and two crankshafts. The Rotary was made in Boston from 1904 to 1905 by the Rotary Motor Vehicle Co.
- Sears, a tiller-steered automobile sold by the mail-order company from 1906 to 1911 and made by the Sears Motor Car Works of Chicago.
- Pratt, a car with four rear wheels and two front ones. It boasted a 75-horsepower engine and was built in 1907 by Pratt Chuck Works of Frankfurt, New York.
- Ruler, an automobile using instead of a chassis "a three-point arrangement with the rear wheels acting as two points and stretching to a ball-and-socket joint in the center of the front cross member as the third point" (Kimes and Clark 1988, p. 1269). It was made by the Ruler Motor Car Co. of Aurora, Illinois, in 1917.
- Templar, a modern touring roadster manufactured by the Templar Motors Corp. of Cleveland from 1917 to 1924.
- Scarab, a V-8 powered car whose seats could be moved so that a card table could be put in place. It was built by Stout Engineering of Detroit from 1934 to 1939.
- Menkenns, a three-wheeled car powered by a front-mounted airplane propeller. It was made in 1937 by Willie Menkenns of Hillsboro, Oregon.

As bizarre as some of these product ideas now seem, it was far from obvious to contemporaries what basic features the successful car would have. A major choice involved type of engine or propulsion: steam, electric, and gasoline engines were all available to early car makers. At the turn of the century, roughly

130 automobile manufacturers used engines powered by technologies and fuels other than gasoline. Many early analysts thought that steam was the inherently superior technology. The eventual dominance by gasoline power might show they were wrong. However, historians and social scientists have recently offered two other possible explanations for the rise of the gasoline engine. First, because more early manufacturers used the gasoline engine, refinement of this technology went more quickly. Second, several highly publicized races in the United States and Europe in the late nineteenth century were won by gasoline-powered automobiles, giving the impression of superiority.

Some technology analysts claim that the automobile locked into a dominant design of all-steel-enclosed body with gasoline engines around 1920.[6] This view probably understates the importance of earlier convergence on a few simple principles, such as having all passengers face in the same direction and having all of the operations of the car done by one person (many early designs required one person to steer and another to operate the brakes). This view also slights the many important subsequent technological innovations that appeared, including the V-8 engine (introduced by Cadillac in 1924), automatic transmission (Olds in 1940), automated stamping and welding of body parts (a process innovation introduced by Ford in 1950), front-wheel-drive with torsion bar suspension (Olds in 1966), use of robots in production (GM in 1967), and four-wheel power disc brakes (Chrysler in 1974). These and many other innovations were more than incremental changes in the design of the automobile; they were marked departures from prior designs and production processes.

The diversity in designs and organizations supporting them continued into the modern era. For example, in the late 1970s and early 1980s, there were roughly a hundred domestic producers of automobiles.[7] Almost half were small manufacturers producing "replicars" and "exoticars." An example would be Berlina Motor Car Sales of Knoxville, Tennessee. This company offered several versions of its Berlina coupe, which were assembled in a 13,000-square-foot plant. Twenty-four companies produced "kitcars," cars manufactured by mounting a customized body on an available chassis and engine. The 1979 *Complete Guide to Kit Cars, Auto Parts and Accessories* claims that, "The kit car phenomenon . . . began more than a decade ago as an alternative to mass automotive conformity" (Kutner 1979, p. 3). An example of a kitcar manufacturer is Elite Enterprises of Cokata, Minnesota. This company was established in 1968 and sold two models of kitcars in the early 1980s: the Elite Laser J2X (a roadster) and the Elite Laser 917 (a modern-looking coupe). Both kits sold for around $5,000 and were to be mounted on another (major) manufacturer's chassis and engine.

Five of these manufacturers produced custom sports cars. For example, American Custom Industries, Inc., of Sylvania, Ohio, sold an extensively modified Corvette in the early 1980s by two names, American Turbo and Duntor Turbo Convertible. The company had forty employees and its cars sold for over $30,000.

Nine American automakers manufactured electric cars in this period. These included B and Z Electric Car Co. of Long Beach, California. This firm began making cars in the early 1960s and advertised them as "The King of Electric Cars." They could run up to 30 miles per hour.

Of course, most—if not all—of these specialist producers seem insignificant in comparison with the major manufacturers. And, most types of organization theory would pay no attention to them. But a breakthrough in the technology of batteries, for instance, could change the situation. How likely is such a development? By most accounts, this is not very likely in the near future. Alternative fuel propulsion systems lag severely behind gasoline engines in terms of power, range, and efficiency. Still, the emissions problems created by gasoline have prompted governments to pressure for faster development of alternative technologies. In California, for instance, the Air Resources Board has dictated that by 1998 at least 2 percent of every manufacturer's auto sales must be zero-emission vehicles. The percentage jumps to 10 percent five years later.

Specialist automobile producers have also occasionally outcompeted the major producers in particular market niches. In Great Britain, for instance, TVR has been successful in the British sports car market against GM's Lotus subsidiary. TVR sells a sports car named the Griffith, which was developed in eighteen months with a small budget. The Griffith is essentially handcrafted from advanced composite materials. The costs of manufacturing are low, and the quality of the car is exceptionally high. Griffith's success and the profitability of TVR in this market forced Lotus to withdraw its Elan model (*The Economist* 1992b). In 1993, GM sold Lotus to Bugatti.

PATTERNS OF DENSITY DEPENDENCE

Even this brief sketch of the automobile industry in Europe and the United States reveals that many complex processes shaped its evolution. These include technological innovations, organizational innovations (e.g., Ford's assembly line, GM's divisional structure, Toyota's lean production system), and relations of automobile manufacturing firms with national governments. Given this complexity, we questioned whether density dependence characterizes this industry as it does the others discussed in earlier chapters.

In research conducted to this point, we have analyzed entry rates for the United States and the countries that became major European producers: Belgium, Britain, France, Germany, and Italy. We have explored two issues. First, have entry rates into the industry in these five countries been related to the country's density of automobile producers in the way predicted by the theory discussed in previous chapters? Our analyses suggest that they were. There is a strong relationship between density and the entry rate of automobile manufacturing firms in each of these countries.[8] The general pattern of results suggests that the pattern of density dependence shown in previous research holds for the automobile industry and that the model is general enough to apply to diverse national contexts.

Our second question concerns the links between industries in the different countries within Europe (later we will investigate connections with the American population). In discussing the early evolution of the European industry, we emphasized that events in one country quickly brought responses in others. One obvious question is whether we can represent these effects with a modification of the theory of density dependence. We think we can by using a simple theoretical idea, namely, cultural images of organizational forms diffuse through social systems with less friction than the material resources used to build and sustain organizations. Put differently, competitive environments tend to be more local than institutional environments.

Organizational forms in one area might gain legitimation from the growing density of such organizations in other areas long before competitive influences exert themselves. This is because the resources (whose limits cause competition) tend to be localized. Organizations compete for members and employees in local populations and local labor markets. They tend also to compete locally for capital and material inputs. Moreover, competitors and others can more successfully block the inflow of labor, capital, and material inputs than those of ideas and cultural understandings. For these varied reasons, we think that legitimation processes typically operate at broader scales than competition processes.

National political boundaries should be especially important in differentiating these processes. Nation-states try to create and enforce all sorts of rules and regulations to protect their industries and labor markets from outside competition. However, even totalitarian states find it difficult to control the cultural images that shape their inhabitants' tastes. Witness the widespread appeal of Western music, literature, clothing, and cigarette brands under the old regime of the Soviet Union.

So we investigated the hypothesis that density-dependent legitimation operates on a broader scale than does density-dependent competition (still concentrating on entry rates). We used models in which the entry rate in each country depends, first, on the country's density and, second, on the density in the rest of Europe. When we introduced effects of European density, we found a sharp difference in results for Britain and the four continental countries. In every variation we have tried, British entry rates have no relation with other European density. As far as these results are to be believed, the British auto industry was indeed insular, as some historical accounts suggest.

European density does, however, have a sizable positive effect on the entry rate of each continental country. That is, adding European density to the model makes a big difference in the effects of national density. For each continental country, the effect of the country's own density becomes negative. We interpret these results as saying that European density had a legitimating effect in each continental country but that national density had mainly competitive effects.

Given these results, we think that the automobile manufacturing organizational form was legitimated broadly within Europe. Competition, however, tended to take place on a national scale, as it affected entry rates. In other words, the start of a firm in Germany increased the legitimation of the organizational form within Germany but also increased the level of competition within the German population of auto manufacturing firms. But the start of a firm in France enhanced the legitimacy of the form with Germany without increasing the level of competition there.

It is important to note that our tests have so far involved only one set of empirical implications of the theory—those concerning organizational founding rates. What of organizational mortality? Should we expect the same pattern of legitimation driven by European density and competition driven by national density? It would be simple if that turned out to be the case. From a substantive viewpoint, one might expect that the effects of legitimation and competition on founding rates interact differently with national political boundaries than do mortality rates. In particular, effects of legitimation on founding rates might pertain primarily to entrepreneurs. Entrepreneurs and their backers often scan other markets in search of ideas. Their broader awareness might make founding rates sensitive to density in other areas. By contrast, legitimation in mortality might pertain more to potential employees and customers. If these groups are more parochial, then density dependence in organizational mortality rates has mainly a local character.

What about the American industry? We have yet to conduct systematic studies of the effects of developments in Europe for the population of American producers. However, anecdotal historical evidence suggests that American awareness of European developments speeded legitimation. Historian Flink (1970, p. 21) reports that even though most Americans had not seen a car by 1895,

> The Paris-Bordeaux-Paris race demonstrated to many Americans the feasibility of using motor vehicles for long-distance high-speed transportation, and an aura of optimism about the automobile prevailed among technical experts in the United States throughout 1895.

He further notes that after initial development of the American population, "Little popular prejudice toward the motor vehicle was evident either in absolute terms or compared with earlier responses to innovation in transportation, particularly the bicycle and the self-propelled trolley car" (1970, p. 34). This situation still did not mean automobiles and their producers gained immediate social taken-for-grantedness. As producer density increased, the reliability of the automobile was displayed and the necessary material social infrastructures developed. Widely publicized races, demonstration drives, and exhibitions helped the process. So too did the formation of many automobile clubs and several industry associations.

CONCLUSION

We conclude this historical sketch of the automobile industry by reexamining the question we began the chapter with, namely, how applicable is ecological theory to an organizational population dominated at certain times by very large and powerful organizations? Even the brief review we have undertaken here shows that when placed in historical relief, this question loses much of its force. The early American industry witnessed an abundance of diverse organizational forms and an early period of intense selection. The same was true in Europe. Obviously, it makes little sense to deny the value of ecological models of selection in such contexts.

Our research efforts to date on this industry have gone some way toward amplifying this point. Tests of the theory of density-dependent legitimation and competition have not only been generally supportive, they have suggested a refinement in the theory. Specifically, legitimation processes might operate at a broader scale than competition processes and, in doing so, transcend political boundaries.

NOTES

Financial support for the research reported in this chapter has been provided by the Institute of Industrial Relations, University of California at Berkeley, and National Science Foundation Grants SES-9123708 and SES-9247842. We appreciate the research assistance of Lyda Bigelow, Elizabeth Dundon, Marc-David Seidel, Albert Teo, John Torres, and Lucia Tsai.

1. Other factors also clearly operated. For instance, Great Britain had passed laws restricting the speed of motorized vehicles on public roads to only 2 miles per hour in towns. During some of this period, the law also required that such vehicles be preceded by a person on foot carrying a red flag (hence the laws are called the Red Flag Laws). These restrictions clearly discouraged the development of an automobile industry in Britain before motorcars were accepted in 1896. France's road system was the best in the world at this time.

2. The editor of the American weekly *The Horseless Carriage* attempted to block the term. The lead editorial, entitled "Terminology," in the issue of June 7, 1899, argued that sensible Americans would keep with the name "motor vehicle." "As for the word 'automobile,' it is French, and may be said in its present currency to represent the faddish and speculative phases of the motor vehicle movement." The futility of this argument is clear in the announcement (with great fanfare) in the same issue of the formation of the American Automobile Club.

3. One possible explanation for the fast catch-up of the American industry was the superior American machine tool industry. Some historians of the industry claim that this superiority allowed American firms to lead in taking advantage of machine tool innovations.

4. Despite the image of the Model T as "never changing," Ford Motor Co. actually made several major changes in the model and in its production technology during its heyday. Most of these changes were initiated by the company's engineering department and concerned ways to lower costs. (Similar goals steered Ford's early and extensive backward vertical integration.)

5. Our primary sources for data on producers and would-be producers in the American industry are the three volumes by Krause Publication, entitled *Standard Catalog of American Cars*. The first volume by Kimes and Clark (1988) spans the period of 1805–1942. The second volume by Gunnell (1987) covers 1946–76. And the third volume by Flammang (1989) is for 1976–86. These volumes represent massive undertakings that involve numerous historians, archivists, collectors, and museums. They build on pre-

vious compilations of automobile producers and attempt to be comprehensive and accurate. The volumes have won numerous prizes from associations of historians and
journalists. Because the volumes report information on automobile makes rather than
firms, we had to aggregate by firm to obtain the data reported here. We have spent over
two years coding and checking these data.

6. Others claim that the dominant design emerged much earlier: seats facing forward
and controlled by one person (many early models required one person to steer and
another to brake).

7. Because they were small and specialized, data on these producers collected from
industry sources seem less reliable.

8. This relationship changes sign—from positive to negative, as predicted—at a density below the maximum level for all five countries. Thus in these four cases the predicted relationship between entry rates and density has an inverted U shape within the
range of density actually observed.

BIBLIOGRAPHY

Altshuler, Alan, et al. 1984. *The Future of the Automobile: The Report of MIT's International Automobile Program*. Cambridge, MA: MIT Press.

Automotive News. 1993. *100 Years of the Automobile in America*. September 27, 1993,
edition. Flint, MI: Automotive News.

Baldwin, Nick, G. N. Georgano, Michael Sedgwick, and Brian Laban. 1987. *The World
Guide to Automobile Manufacturers*. New York: Facts on File Publications.

Bardou, Jean-Pierre, Jean-Jacques Chanaron, Patrick Fridenson, and James M. Laux.
1982. *The Automobile Revolution*. Chapel Hill: University of North Carolina
Press.

Cusumano, Michael A. 1985. *The Japanese Automobile Industry*. Cambridge, MA: Harvard University Press.

Dertouzos, Michael L., et al. 1989. *Made in America*. New York: Harper-Collins.

Flammang, James M. 1989. *The Standard Catalog of American Cars 1976–1986*, 2nd
ed. Iola, WI: Krause.

Flink, James L. 1970. *American Adopts the Automobile, 1895–1910*. Cambridge, MA:
MIT Press.

Flink, James J. 1975. *The Car Culture*. Cambridge, MA: MIT Press.

Flink, James J. 1988. *The Automobile Age*. Cambridge, MA: MIT Press.

Georgano, G. N. (ed.) 1982. *The New Encyclopedia of Motorcars: 1885 to the Present*,
3rd ed. New York: E. P. Dutton.

Gunnell, John A. 1987. *The Standard Catalog of American Cars 1946–1975*, 2nd ed.
Iola, WI: Krause.

Hannan, M. T., G. R. Carroll, E. A. Dundon, and J. C. Torres. 1995. "Organizational
Evolution in Multinational Context: Automobile Manufacturers in Belgium, Britain, France, Germany, and Italy." *American Sociological Review*, in press.

Hounshell, David A. 1984. *From the American System to Mass Production*. Baltimore:
Johns Hopkins University Press.

Kimes, Beverly Rae, and Henry Austin Clark. 1988. *The Standard Catalog of American
Cars 1805–1942*, 2nd ed. Iola, WI: Krause.

Kutner, Richard M. 1979. *Complete Guide to Kit Cars*. Wilmington, DE: Auto Logic
Publications.

Laux, James M. 1976. *In First Gear: The French Automobile Industry to 1914*. Montreal: McGill-Queen's University Press.

Laux, James M. 1992. *The European Automobile Industry*. New York: Twayne.

Lawrence, Paul, and Davis Dyer. 1983. *Renewing American Industry*. New York: Free Press.

MVMA (Motor Vehicle Manufacturers Association). 1989. *Facts and Figures of the Automobile Industry*. Detroit: Motor Vehicle Manufacturers Association.

Perrow, Charles. 1986. *Complex Organizations: A Critical Essay,* 3rd ed. Glenview, IL: Scott, Foresman.

Rae, John B. 1959. *The American Automobile Manufacturers: The First Forty Years*. Philadelphia: Chilton.

Rae, John B. 1984. *The American Automobile Industry*. Boston: Twayne.

Scott, W. Richard. 1992. *Organizations: Rational, Natural and Open Systems,* 3rd ed. Englewood Cliffs NJ: Prentice-Hall.

The Economist. 1992a. "The Endless Road: A Survey of the Car Industry." *The Economist,* October 17 (special insert).

The Economist, 1992b. "Lotus-eater." *The Economist,* June 20, pp. 66–67.

White, Lawrence J. 1971. *The Automobile Industry Since 1941*. Cambridge, MA: Harvard University Press.

IV

RESOURCE PARTITIONING

Another distinctive model of organizational ecology concerns resource partitioning. Originally developed by Glenn Carroll (1985) in a study of newspaper markets, this model addresses questions about the distribution of generalist and specialist organizations in a population. It asks, in particular, under what conditions will the specialist form be viable and why.

Generalist and specialist forms of organization are defined by niche width. A population's niche width is the variance of its resource utilization. So, for example, a set of construction firms that bids only on contracts for renovations of residential housing has a low variance of utilization of the resource base in terms of size of contract. This population has a narrow niche and its constituent organizations are considered specialists. A population of firms that bids on those projects as well as on many other types has a broad niche; it is composed of generalist organizations.

As with all ecological theory, the resource partitioning model assumes that organizations cannot freely change form. That is, adaptation constraints prevail in moving from generalism to specialism or vice versa. The model also assumes that consumers in the market are heterogeneous; that is, tastes of buyers differ.

The resource partitioning model applies especially to contexts in which production or marketing activities exhibit economies of scale and price competition among producers is weak or nonexistent. An economy of scale exists when the per-unit cost of providing a product or service declines with the number of units produced. A firm enjoying an economic scale advantage over its competitors usually passes along some savings to its customers as a lower price. However, when price competition is weak, the portion of the advantage passed on to consumers manifests itself as a superior product. Either scenario implies that rational consumers will prefer products of the larger firms. As such a market unfolds over time, smaller producers are no longer able to compete effectively, and the population of producers tends toward oligopoly or even monopoly.

Although economies of scale might let us predict how a market will look after time passes, making predictions about the fates of specific firms can be quite another matter. Of course, if one firm holds a significant size advantage over its rivals, then it is easy to predict its continued dominance. But what about the market with roughly equal-sized competitors? If strong economies of scale exist, then eventually one or several firms will come to dominate. However, identifying the exact firms that will prevail typically proves elusive. In accounting for the evolution of one-newspaper cities, for instance, the economist James Rosse (1978, 1980) claims only that newspapers compete on roughly equal terms until by luck, chance, skills, or whatever, one paper gains a substantial size advantage. In other words, the causes of early size differentials are idiosyncratic or random.

Once in place, a firm's size advantage provides strong economies of scale in both production and advertising; this advantage makes competition an uphill battle for other firms and they eventually fail. So, as with many self-reinforcing processes, economies of scale yield an equilibrium prediction but are indeterminate about the exact composition of this equilibrium. The appeal of this type of explanation is that it can account for many anomalies of success, such as in the newspaper industry the dominance of the lowbrow *San Francisco Chronicle* in a highly educated and culturally sophisticated area and the success of the highly regarded *Louisville Courier-Journal* in an area not acclaimed for its enlightened citizenry.

Rosse's scenario describes well the behavior and fates of generalist firms in a market with scale economies. Indeed, scale economies favor generalist organizational forms: generalist organizations are likely to be larger than specialists. When there is little or no price competition, the generalist form is reinforced further by product enhancements that frequently take the form of inclusiveness appeals to a broad range of consumers. So the best competitive posture for a large firm is generalism and firms are unlikely to become large unless they adopt that posture.

The more interesting question about this kind of market context concerns what goes on with specialist organizational forms. The resource partitioning model relates the life chances of specialist organizations to the level of concentration among generalists. Early in these markets, when the arena is crowded, most firms vie for the largest possible resource base. Competition forces each to specialize to some extent to differentiate itself, although the overall strategy adopted by most firms is generalist in nature.

As scale economies come to dominate, only a few generalists survive and they move toward the center of the market. This lessened crowding of generalists and their move to the center opens small pockets of resources on the periphery of the market, and it is here that specialist forms usually appear and thrive. In fact, the market at this point has been partitioned into generalist and specialist resources.

The key predictive variable in the model is the overall level of *market concentration*. When the market is not highly concentrated, specialist organizational forms will not do as well as they do when it is highly concentrated. The reason is that specialists and generalists compete directly for the same resources under these conditions. So, increasing market concentration enhances the life chances of specialist organizations.

Figures IV-1, IV-2, and IV-3 illustrate resource partitioning in terms of consumer tastes. The three graphs show the process at three points in time, t_1, t_2, and t_3, which represent successively increasing concentrated markets. In each graph, the horizontal axis indicates the values of some dimension X of the industry's products of interest to consumers (a single dimension is shown for ease of illustration; the model is generalizable to multiple dimensions). The vertical axis measures the proportion or relative frequency f of consumers who prefer any particular value of X. The curved plots of functions show the distributions of consumer preferences about X. The area under any given segment of the curve tells how many resources are potentially available to a firm operating in that part of the market.

Figure IV-1 shows a relatively concentrated market. Here two generalist firms, A and B, jockey for the attractive center of the market. The resource bases of A and B overlap to some extent, but there is also differentiation. At time t_2, represented by Figure IV-2, Firm B has failed because A's economies of scale have given it an unsurmountable advantage. Firm A moves, of course, to absorb the resources freed up by B's departure and mainly succeeds in this effort. Only the

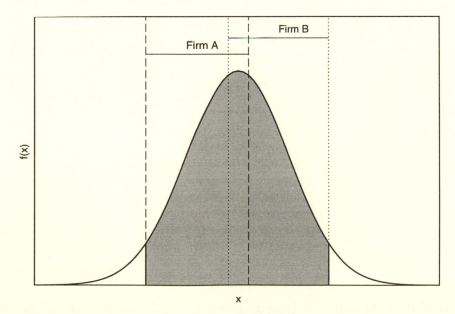

Figure IV–1 Market resources accruing to two generalist firms. (*Source:* Authors' analysis. Copyright © Glenn R. Carroll and Michael T. Hannan. Used by permission.)

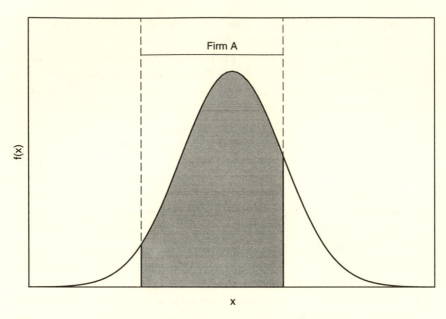

Figure IV–2 Market resources accruing to firm A after firm B departs. (*Source:* Authors' analysis. Copyright © Glenn R. Carroll and Michael T. Hannan. Used by permission.)

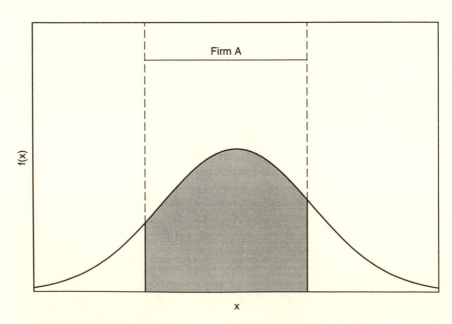

Figure IV–3 Market resources accruing to firm A after distributional shifts. (*Source:* Authors' analysis. Copyright © Glenn R. Carroll and Michael T. Hannan. Used by permission.)

most distant of B's resource base remains outside its reach. Note that firm A grows considerably in the process, making the general level of market concentration higher at t_2 than t_1. Note also that the total area under the curve, which falls outside the domain of the generalists A and B (the unshaded areas), is larger at t_2 than t_1. This space represents the resource base available to specialists, and the transition from t_1 and t_2 depicts how the life chances of specialists improve as the market becomes more concentrated.

The curves in Figures IV-1 and IV-2 are identical, showing that consumer preferences do not change between t_1 and t_2. This assumption is reasonable in the short term and might also be so in the long term if tastes are exogenous. H owever, consumer tastes often change in response to market developments. Figure IV-3 shows how tastes typically change in markets of the kind under consideration. Specialist appeals to the peripheries of the market unlock new tastes and tap new consumers. And some consumers develop reactions to the ever-broadening mass production generalists. This reaction is reinforced by specialists who make nostalgic and emotional appeals to individuals about self-expression. Consequently, tastes often shift, yielding a flatter distribution of preferences, and thereby providing even more of a resource base for specialists (compare the unshaded areas under the curve).

A fair amount of systematic empirical evidence supports the resource partitioning model. The initial study of newspaper markets by Carroll (1985) showed that the death rates of specialist papers were lower in highly concentrated markets than in less concentrated ones. Generalist papers' death rates increased with market concentration. In a study of the early American telephone industry, Barnett and Carroll (1987) found a different type of supporting finding. Estimating models of the rate of firm start-up, they discovered a positive relationship between the average size of currently operating companies (a variable akin to market concentration) and the emergence of new, primarily small and geographically specialized telephone companies.

Freeman and Lomi (1994) found a similar relationship among banking cooperatives in Italy: the founding rates of rural cooperative banks increased with the size and market share of the larger national banks. In a study of the brewing and wine industries in post–Prohibition America, Swaminathan (1993) found a comparable set of patterns. Swaminathan (1993) concludes that resource partitioning can account for the microbrewery movement in brewing (see also Carroll and Swaminathan 1992) and the rise of boutique wineries in wine making. Finally, in a study of the microprocessor production market of the United States, Wade (1993) reported consistent findings. His study showed that market concentration is positively related to the entry of firms sponsoring new architectural innovations in microprocessors.

Anecdotal evidence suggesting the operation of resource partitioning has also appeared in the organizations literature. Carroll (1987) sketched developments in the music recording industry in a way compatible with the model. And Walter

Powell (1985) has suggested that resource partitioning can explain well the recent history of the American book publishing industry.

Despite the considerable evidence for the resource partitioning model, some observers still regard the main finding that concentration raises rates of start-up as paradoxical (see Acs and Audretsch 1989). We can only speculate about the source of this view but our guess is that it comes from the prevalence of economic thinking about the problem. As Freeman and Lomi (1993) note, the conventional view in economics considers high levels of concentration to be a barrier to the entry of new firms. In this respect, the resource partitioning model appears to make a very different prediction than conventional economic theory. However, as Swaminathan (1993) illustrates, the differences can be resolved by viewing concentration as an entry barrier to only the generalist market. The advantage of this reconceptualization is that it yields additional predictor variables for resource partitioning theory, namely, those factors associated directly with generalist entry barriers. Swaminathan shows that the additional variables perform well in empirical research; see also Lomi (1994).

Resource partitioning has implications for the study and analysis of strategic groups of firms. As originally outlined by Caves and Porter (1977), strategic groups are clusters of relatively homogeneous sets of firms within an industry. Mobility barriers block the movement of firms from one group to another. Many economic and organizational processes might produce an industry with a stable set of strategic groups but resource partitioning seems to be a fairly general process.

This section opens with Swaminathan and Carroll's account of organizational evolution in the American brewing industry (Chapter 11). Their account of the recent proliferation of brewpubs and microbreweries, discussed briefly in Chapter 1, provides a clear illustration of the operation of resource partitioning processes. Will Mitchell's treatment of the medical diagnostic imaging industry (Chapter 12) provides another.

BIBLIOGRAPHY

Acs, Z., and D. B. Audretsch. 1989. "Births and Firm Size." *Southern Economic Journal* 56:467–75.

Barnett, W. P., and G. R. Carroll. 1987. "Competition and Mutualism Among Early Telephone Companies." *Administrative Science Quarterly* 30:400–21.

Carroll, G. R. 1985. "Concentration and Specialization: Dynamics of Niche Width." *American Journal of Sociology* 90:1262–83.

Carroll, G. R. 1987. *Publish and Perish: The Organizational Ecology of Newspaper Industries.* Greenwich, CT: JAI.

Carroll, G. R., and A. Swaminathan. 1992. "The Organizational Ecology of Strategic Groups in the American Brewing Industry from 1975 to 1990." *Industrial and Corporate Change* 1:65–97.

Caves, R. E., and M. E. Porter. 1977. "From Entry Barriers to Mobility Barriers." *Quarterly Journal of Economics* 91:421–62.

Freeman, J., and A. Lomi. 1994. "Resource Partitioning and Foundings of Banking Cooperatives in Italy." In J. A. C. Baum and J. V. Singh (eds)., *Evolutionary Dynamics of Organizations*. New York: Oxford University Press, pp. 269–93.

Lomi, A. 1994. "The Population and Community Ecology of Organizational Founding: Italian Cooperative Banks, 1936–1989." *European Sociological Review,* in press.

Powell, W. W. 1985. *Getting Into Print*. Chicago: University of Chicago Press.

Rosse, J. N. 1978. *The Evolution of One Newspaper Cities*. Technical Report. Studies in Industry Economics, Stanford University.

Rosse, J. N. 1980. "The Decline of Direct Newspaper Competition." *Journal of Communication* 30:65–71.

Swaminathan, A. 1993. "The Evolution of Specialist Organizational Forms in Mature Industries: Beer Brewing and Wine Making in Post-Prohibition America." Unpublished doctoral thesis, University of California at Berkeley.

Wade, J. B. 1993. "Dynamics of Organizational Communities and Technological Change: An Empirical Investigation of Technological Variation, Innovation, and Performance in the Microprocessor Market." Unpublished doctoral thesis, University of California at Berkeley.

11

Beer Brewers

ANAND SWAMINATHAN AND GLENN R. CARROLL

Over the last hundred years or so, the most striking organizational trend in the American brewing industry has been the severe and steady decline in the number of brewing firms or density. This pattern was evident before national Prohibition in 1933: The 2,473 breweries operating in 1880 had dropped to 766 by 1919. And, the pattern continued after repeal in 1933 (following a few years of growth driven primarily by firms reentering the industry).

THE POST-PROHIBITION ERA

Figure 11-1 shows the number of American breweries operating over the period 1933–92. Most of the breweries founded immediately after Prohibition operated before Prohibition: 709 out of the 934 breweries founded in 1933–34 were "restarts," meaning that the firms involved had produced beer prior to the Prohibition. The number of breweries declined from a maximum of 926 in 1934 to a minimum of 43 in 1981 and 1983. The decline in numbers was even more severe in certain cities. For example, Chicago had 32 breweries in 1937, 18 in 1950, 10 in 1960, and 2 in 1969 (McNulty 1986). Peter Hand, the last Chicago-based brewer, exited the industry in 1979.[1]

Since the repeal of Prohibition, and particularly in the post–World War II period, the American brewing industry has undergone rapid concentration. The industry four-firm concentration ratio rose from 11 percent in 1935 to 78 percent in 1982 (U.S. Bureau of the Census 1982). By 1991, this figure was 88.9 percent (*Modern Brewery Age Bluebook* 1992, p. 222). Several researchers believe that increasing economies of scale are responsible for this industry trend (Scherer 1980; Elzinga 1986). If so, the decline in the number of firms does not represent unfavorable general conditions for the industry. Indeed, total sales of beer in-

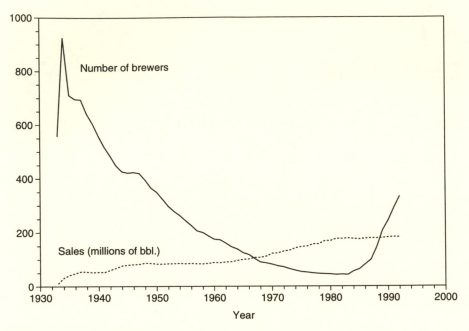

Figure 11–1 Density and sale of beer brewers. (*Source:* Authors' analysis.)

creased over this period. Figure 11-1 also plots total industry sales (tax-paid withdrawals) in millions of barrels over 1933–92.[2] While the number of firms fell from 710 in 1935 to 43 in 1981, the total sales of the industry increased from 42 million to 176 million barrels over the same period. Thus, surviving firms typically grew considerably larger over time. For instance, the largest firm, Anheuser-Busch, held 30.4 percent of market share in 1981 and increased its market share substantially to 46.4 percent by 1991 (*Modern Brewery Age Bluebook* 1992, p. 222).

Structural changes occurring in the American brewing industry during 1933–92 can be seen clearly through the number of foundings and deaths by year in the brewing industry, shown in Figure 11-2. In all, 1,447 breweries were founded during this period. Not surprisingly, the highest number of foundings occur immediately after the repeal of Prohibition—557 in 1933 and 377 in 1934. The other significant aspect is the recent increase in the number of foundings from about 1983 onward. As many as 363 firms were founded in 1983–92. Between 1933 and 1992, a total of 1,131 firms exited the industry. Of these, 196 firms had to cease operations because they were unable to obtain an operating license. The number of deaths reached a maximum of 247 in 1934. Most of the deaths in the immediate post-Prohibition period occurred as a result of firms not acquiring legal permits. In comparison to the period 1971 to 1992, the number of deaths was higher from 1933 to 1970 as the industry underwent consolidation. As mentioned earlier, growing economies of scale are widely held responsible for this spate of brewery failures (Keithahn 1978; Lynk 1984).

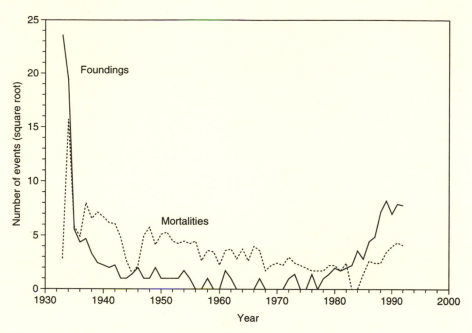

Figure 11–2 Foundings and deaths of brewers by year. (*Source:* Authors' analysis.)

Why have economies of scale in brewing increased during the post-Prohibition period? A number of technical developments played major roles. First, significant improvements occurred in the packaging process. Tremblay (1987) points out that a modern canning line can fill 2,000 twelve-ounce cans per minute, whereas one in 1952 could only fill 300 cans per minute. Tremblay (1987) estimates that to keep a modern canning line operating efficiently, a brewer would have had to increase production capacity from 0.3 million to 2.2 million barrels between 1952 and 1986. Similarly, it has been estimated that a minimum-cost bottling line requires an annual rate of production of 600,000–800,000 barrels and a minimum cost kegging line requires 1 million to 2.2 million barrels of production per year (Tremblay 1987). Second, the introduction of automated brewhouses reduced the amount of labor required to operate a production shift (Keithahn 1978, p. 37). These technological changes implied that the production process had become more capital intensive. The number of production workers in the brewing industry has declined from a high of 61,537 in 1953 to 23,500 in 1990, while production during the same period rose from 90.4 million to 201.7 million barrels (U.S. Brewers Association 1992).[3]

Multiplant scale economies that developed in the late 1940s and 1950s also increased the optimal firm size in the brewing industry. Prior to World War II, most brewers operated in small local areas, though some operated regionally. Even those selling nationally, such as Anheuser-Busch and Schlitz, operated out of a single brewery. By the mid-1950s, most of the major brewers operated multiple plants.[4] Scherer and colleagues (1975) found that multiplant operations

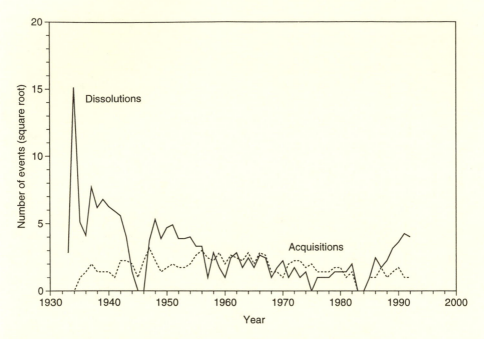

Figure 11–3 Deaths of brewers by type. (*Source:* Authors' analysis.)

reduced distribution costs marginally, but the biggest gains were in the area of advertising and product promotion. Scherer et al. (1975) estimated optimal firm size at three to four plants. Keithahn (1978) argues that at least four plants are required to exploit multiplant economies of scale. Keithahn's study provides the largest estimates of minimum efficient firm size. According to his study, an efficient-size firm should have had national capacities of 4 million, 8 million, and 18 million barrels in 1960, 1970, and 1978, respectively.

The decline in the number of firms reflects not only brewery failures, but also a greater incidence of mergers and acquisitions (Tremblay and Tremblay 1988). Of the 1,131 firms that exited the industry, 870 were dissolved, 55 suspended operations, and 206 were acquired by other firms. Figure 11-3 shows the number of deaths by type from 1933 to 1992. The early years are characterized by a large number of dissolutions and suspensions. The large number of dissolutions may reflect the operation of economies of scale in the industry. But from 1970 onward, it appears that the number of acquisitions is equal to, if not greater than, the number of dissolutions. Some mass producers such as the G. Heileman Brewing Company grew largely by acquiring smaller breweries—since the 1960s, it has acquired, among others, such brands as Sterling,[5] Weidemann, Pfeiffer, Jacob Schmidt, Drewry's, Cook, Kingsbsurg, Grain Belt, Hauenstein's, Rainier, Falls City, Carling's, Atles, Colt .45, National, Tivoli, Stag, Dutch Treat, Van Lauter, Red, White and Blue, Lone Star, Champale, Blatz, and Blitz-Weinhard (Foley 1990).

However, Elzinga (1973) finds that mergers and acquisitions accounted for only 2.7 percent of the 2.3-percentage-point increase in the four-firm concentration ratio between 1959 and 1972, and therefore concludes that the increase in concentration in the brewing industry is largely the result of internal expansion. Strict enforcement of antitrust laws by the Justice Department may have contributed both to the low impact of mergers and acquisitions on concentration and an unanticipated focus of large breweries on internal expansion (Ornstein 1981). Industry concentration may have been accelerated by the fact that internal expansion by national brewers usually involved larger, more efficient, new plants. Further, the inability of smaller brewers to merge among themselves because of antitrust regulations may have weakened their position. Most acquisitions that did occur involved a plant or a brand that was in decline with the acquiring firm making the purchase: (1) to gain barrelage to bring one plant to full capacity; (2) to gain access to stronger distribution networks or a new sales territory; (3) to fill gaps in a product line; or rarely (4) to acquire needed plant capacity (Elzinga 1973, pp. 104–5).

As mentioned earlier, most of the firms founded in 1933 and 1934 are restarts. New firm foundings are also high in these two years (56 in 1933 and 169 in 1934). Both restarts and new firm foundings decline to an insignificant number after 1950. The declining trend in the number of breweries has reversed itself because of the emergence of two new specialist organizational forms in the late 1970s—the microbrewery and the brewpub (Erickson 1987; Institute for [Fermentation and] Brewing Studies, various years; see also Carroll and Swaminathan 1992).[6] New firm foundings increased dramatically starting in 1977. All 377 firms founded during 1977–92 were new firms. This recent burst of foundings has been driven by the emergence of these two specialist organizational forms.

MICROBREWERIES AND BREWPUBS

Both microbreweries and brewpubs produce ale and beer by traditional "handcrafted" processes. According to the Institute for Brewing Studies (1993, p. 19), a microbrewery is "a brewery that produces less than 15,000 barrels of beer per year. Microbreweries sell to the public by one or more of the following methods: the traditional three-tier system (brewer to wholesaler to retailer to consumer); the two-tier system (brewer acting as wholesaler to retailer to consumer); and in some cases, directly to the consumer through carryouts or on-premise tap-room sales." The second form, commonly referred to as the brewpub, involves the sale of malt beverages directly to the consumer at the site of production. A brewpub, as defined by the Institute for Brewing Studies (1993, p. 19) is "in simple terms, a restaurant-brewery that sells at least 50 percent of its beer on premise. The beer is brewed for sale and consumption in the adjacent restaurant and/or bar. The beer is often dispensed directly from the brewery's storage tanks. In states where it is allowed, some pubs package their beer for carryout and off-site sales." Brewpub products usually resemble those of microbreweries except that they are fresher and are typically never bottled.

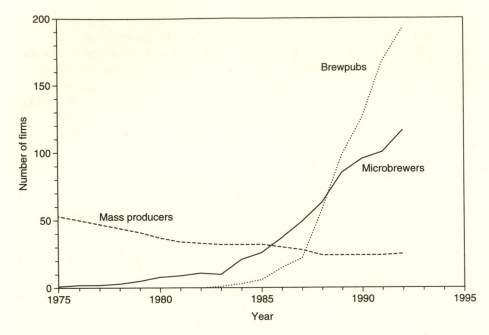

Figure 11–4 Density of brewers by organizational form. (*Source:* Authors' analysis.)

Figure 11-4 shows the number of brewing firms by organizational form. It shows separately the number of mass producers, microbreweries, and brewpubs from 1933 to 1992. While the number of mass producers continues to dwindle over this period, the two specialist organizational forms exhibit considerable growth in numbers.

Like other small firms, microbreweries and brewpubs face a higher risk of failure in the first few years after their founding (Mayer and Goldstein 1961). Almost two fifths of the forty-one microbreweries that had failed by the end of 1992 did so within three years after being established. The initial risk of failure is even higher in the case of brewpubs—as many as three fifths of the forty defunct brewpubs discontinued operations within two years of founding.

MICROBREWERY OVERVIEW

The New Albion Brewing Company of Sonoma, California, is widely recognized to be the first microbrewery (Kureczka 1988). In an effort to produce a "real beer," Jack McAuliffe, a former Navy electrician, raised $10,000 from friends, hand-built his initial equipment, and began brewing English- and Scottish-style ales in 1977. At its peak production, New Albion made sixty cases of beer each week for sale to local stores and restaurants. Finally, New Albion failed in 1982 after not raising another $750,000 in capital, which would have allowed it to reach a more cost-efficient scale of 10,000 to 15,000 barrels of production per year.

Although not officially classified as a microbrewery, Anchor Brewing Company of San Francisco serves as the inspiration for microbrewers nationwide.[7] Anchor's primary product is Anchor Steam Beer. The origins of the name are unknown. The most likely explanation is that it was a nickname for beers that were brewed quickly without ice (Hartman 1983). Lager beers are fermented at 45°F and aged at near-freezing temperatures, a process that required large amounts of ice, a rare commodity in California in the mid-1800s. Brewed and stored at a high temperature, the beer was highly volatile, and when a bartender tapped a keg, it would make a loud hissing sound—like steam. The brewery, founded in 1896, was restarted after Prohibition and was operated by Joe Allen from 1933 to 1958. It temporarily suspended operations for a three-year period when Allen retired in 1958.

Lawrence Steese bought the brewery in 1961 and revived Anchor Steam Beer. But by 1965, the brewery was once again sliding toward bankruptcy. Maytag paid about $5,000 for the controlling interest and the debt of the brewery in 1965. At the time, it was producing about 600 barrels a year for about ten to twelve customers (Hartman 1983). In 1969, Maytag assumed complete ownership. By 1975, the brewery was making a profit. By 1977, the brewery was running at full capacity, producing 12,500 barrels of beer for sale in ten western states, Minnesota, and New Jersey. In 1979, the company shifted production to a larger brewhouse with a capacity of 25,000 barrels per year. Plant capacity has since been extended to 83,000 barrels (*Brewers Digest* 1993).

Anchor brews its beer to exacting and expensive standards. It uses only the more costly two-row barley chosen by European brewers, rather than the common, blander six-row variety favored by mass-production breweries. And Anchor does not use barley substitutes, such as corn or rice, which typically replace 40 percent of the barley in mass-produced beer. Rather than pellets or extracts, Anchor uses whole hops, one pound per barrel, three or four times the industry average (Hartman 1983). Most important, Anchor's products do not contain any of the almost 100 additives that brewers are allowed to use: enzymes, foaming agents, heading agents, spark enhancers, colorings, and a wide variety of other chemicals (Persinos 1988). Anchor Steam Beer, the brewery's flagship product, accounts for about 80 percent of total sales. Anchor Porter, introduced in 1976, and Anchor Liberty Ale, introduced in 1983, account for another 10 percent of total sales. The remainder of Anchor's sales volume is made up by its Old Foghorn barley wine-style ale, its Christmas Ale, and its Wheat Beer (Blair 1985).

The microbrewery segment of the brewing industry is characterized by small craft-like producers such as the Abita Brewing Company of Abita Springs, Louisiana (which brewed 10,900 barrels of beer in 1992), the Millstream Brewing Company of Amana, Iowa (which brewed 1,875 barrels in 1992), and the Bar Harbor Brewing Company of Bar Harbor, Maine (which brewed only 130 barrels in 1992). Virtually all microbreweries adhere strictly to the Reinheitsgebot, or Bavarian Purity Laws, of 1516, specifying that only barley malt, yeast, water, and high-grade hops should be used in the brewing of beer. In doing so, they cater to the current trend toward the consumption of products containing fresh and all-natural ingredients.

In comparison, mass-production breweries use chemical preservatives, antioxidants, foam stabilizers, and artificial coloring among a host of other additives (Moon 1987). Anchor Brewing Company's large size has often been used as an argument for excluding it from the microbrewery category—total annual production amounted to 82,600 barrels in 1992.[8] However, a definition of a microbrewery in terms of product characteristics and marketing strategy would suggest that Anchor Brewing Company is the first microbrewery in the post-Prohibition period. Anchor is also considered by brewers to be the flagship of the microbrewery movement.

BREWPUB OVERVIEW

The brewpub is an adaptation of microbrewing that combines manufacturing and retailing. Prohibition-era laws in most American states mandated separate ownership for brewers and retailers. States have increasingly amended these laws to allow brewpubs, although in some cases opposition by distributors or temperance groups has been effective. By the end of 1992, forty-three states and the District of Columbia had legalized brewpubs in one form or another. Laws allowing brewpubs typically place an upper limit on brewpub production and often require them to sell food as well. Some state laws prohibit the sale of packaged beer by brewpubs, but such restrictions are being gradually dismantled.

Since Washington (in 1982), California (in 1983), and Oregon (in 1983) were the first states to legalize brewpubs, it is not surprising that the largest number of brewpubs are found here.[9] The proliferation of brewpubs in western states has been facilitated by the greater availability of space and the services of consultants who can provide a "turn-key" operation in a few months (Prial 1989). However, the trend has rapidly spread to other states such as Florida, where the number of brewpubs increased from one to thirteen between 1988 and 1992 (see also Brooks 1990). Colorado is another high-growth area with fourteen brewpubs at the end of 1992, barely four years after legalizing the organizational form (see Morris 1990 for an entertaining account of a brewery tour across the United States).

Brewpubs are now legal in one form or another in all but eight states. Moreover, they now outnumber mass production breweries and microbreweries. At the end of 1992, 183 brewpubs were known to be in operation (Institute for Brewing Studies 1992, 1993). Moreover, the brewpub could potentially become the most prevalent organizational form in the brewing industry—in comparison to the 183 brewpubs, there were 108 microbreweries and only 25 mass producers in existence at the end of 1992. Bill Owens, the owner-operator of Buffalo Bill's Brewpub in Hayward, California, and the publisher of *American Brewer* magazine, predicts that there will be 1,500 brewpubs in the state of California alone by 1998 (Hartman 1988). Some observers of the industry project as many as 15,000 brewpubs nationwide in coming years (Charlier 1990).

The identity of the first brewpub in the United States is open to dispute. According to our data, the Switzer Opera House in downtown Yakima, Washington, is the home of America's first brewpub founded in 1982, the Yakima Brewing and Malting Company (see also Erickson 1987). Herbert Grant, the founder and brewmaster, has worked in the brewing industry for over forty years, beginning as a 16-year-old apprentice at a Toronto brewery and progressing to his present position of technical director at S. S. Steiner, a Yakima hopgrower. All ales brewed by Grant use locally grown hops from the Yakima Valley, one of the world's largest hop-growing regions. Yakima ales include Grant's Scottish Ale, India Pale Ale, Celtic Ale, and Imperial Stout. Grant's brewpub serves English-style "pub-grub" such as sausages, sausage rolls, and "ploughman's lunch."

According to another source, the distinction of being the first brewpub belongs to the Mendocino Brewing Company of Hopland, California, founded in 1983 (Institute for Fermentation and Brewing Studies 1987). The brewpub, also known as the Hopland Brewery, is certainly the first one in California since Prohibition. Michael Laybourne, president and general manager of the Mendocino Brewing Company, and his two partners purchased their brewing equipment from the New Albion Brewing Company when it ceased operations in 1983. Housed in a 100-year-old brick building that was once called the Hop Vine Saloon, the Mendocino Brewing Company emphasizes its local character in its interior decor, a tactic that is followed by most brewpubs (see also Lubenow 1987; Fussell 1989). Through a glass partition, Donald J. Barkey and Michael Lovett, who had earlier worked at New Albion, can be seen brewing traditional ales and lagers.

Brewpubs typically showcase their copper brewing kettles to promote an image of freshness and to display their direct kettle-to-glass delivery system (Fisher 1986). Like most brewpub operators, Laybourne and his partners are veteran home brewers and their beers tend to reflect their idiosyncratic tastes. Brewpub products are remarkably fresh, and even the inconsistency has been turned into a selling point (Moon 1987). John Martin, who, together with his brother Reid, founded the Triple Rock Brewing Company in Berkeley, California, says: "I try to look at that [inconsistency] as an interest point in beer. People say, 'That last pint was especially good.' But we're constantly fooling around with it, making adjustments to make it perfect" (Fisher 1986).

Most brewpubs produce top-fermenting beers such as ales, bitters, stouts, and related products. Top fermentation is so called because the strains of yeast rise to the top during fermentation. Fermentation occurs rapidly in about two weeks or so, a turnaround time that is ideal for a small brewpub. In contrast, lager and pilsner-type beers are produced through bottom fermentation, a colder and slower process that may take up to several months (Fisher 1986; Evangelista 1988).

The larger and more successful brewpubs brew between 1,500 and 3,000 barrels of beer per year. Among the firms that fall into this category (with their

1992 production in parentheses) are: "Sudwerk Privatbrauerei Hübsch, Davis, California (2,900 barrels); Gordon Biersch Brewing Company, San Francisco (2,700 barrels); Tied House Cafe and Brewery Mountain View, California (2,600 barrels); Rock Bottom Brewery, Denver (2,500 barrels); Wynkoop Brewing Company, Denver (2,450 barrels); and Boston Beer Works, Boston (2,300 barrels). Brewpubs of this size usually have substantial production facilities. Smaller brewpubs—and they range in size down to the minuscule operator— often use "turn-key" brewing equipment that can be operated with ease by a single person (Mares 1991, p. 137). These turn-key operations are built from kits sold by brewery manufacturers such as JV Northwest of Wilsonville, Oregon. Since 1985, JV Northwest has designed and installed over forty-five microbrewery and brewpub systems ranging in size from 700 to 6,000 barrels per year (Institute for Brewing Studies 1991, p. 90). Other firms that provide similar services including Brewing Systems, Inc., of St. Petersburg, Florida; J. E. Siebel Sons Co., Inc., of Chicago, and The Pub Brewing Co. of Santa Rosa, California.

In keeping with their localized specialist strategies, the microbreweries and brewpubs are small in size. For 1938–92, the average annual production capacity of firms ranged from 1,405 barrels for brewpubs to 7,450 barrels for microbreweries to 857,129 barrels for mass producers.[10] This difference in size is reflected in the total production of each organizational form, which is plotted in Figure 11-5. Mass-production totals (in millions of barrels) are scaled on the left axis. Microbrewery and brewpub production totals (in thousands of barrels)

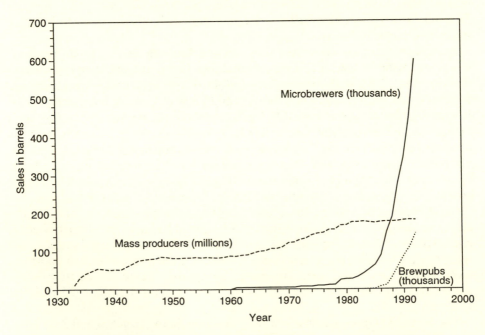

Figure 11–5 Sales of brewers by organizational form. (*Source:* Authors' analysis.)

are scaled on the right axis. Despite the proliferation in numbers, the total production of the two specialist organizational forms taken together constitutes less than 1 percent of total industry production (see also *Modern Brewery Age,* 1990).[11]

This enormous difference in operational scale raises the question as to whether microbreweries and brewpubs are in the same industry as the mass-production breweries. Such an argument confuses the boundaries of organizational forms with the boundaries of industries. As we argue below, the three organizational forms face different competitive opportunities and constraints. However, it should be noted that all three organizational forms manufacture a product—beer—that serves the same functional purpose, the basis of which defines the industry. Most importantly, brewers themselves socially construct the boundaries of their industry to include all three organizational forms (Institute for Brewing Studies 1992; U.S. Brewers Association 1992).

STRATEGY AND ORGANIZATION

Carroll and Swaminathan (1992) argue that mass producers, microbreweries, and brewpubs constitute distinct organizational forms to the extent that they encounter very different environments and respond differently to the distinct environments. The mass-producer segment of the industry is characterized by strong economies of scale in production and advertising and extensive distribution networks. The microbrewers, by contrast, cater to customers looking for a beer with a more unique taste and who are willing to pay premium prices to get it. English and German imports were the first choice for these adventurous, image-conscious, upscale beer drinkers seeking an alternative to generic, mass-produced American beers, the aptly named "wet-air" or "Velveeta" beers (Moon 1987). One result of this quest for distinctive beers has been an increased exposure to classic European brewing styles among the general population. Current societal norms of moderation in alcohol consumption help as well, as customers prefer fewer but heartier beers.

Sierra Nevada Brewing Company's approach to marketing is representative of the efforts of microbrewers to target their products at upscale niches. Sierra Nevada does not advertise, apart from merchandising some T-shirts carrying the company logo and other point-of-purchase materials. Instead of advertising, which brewery executives say they cannot afford, Sierra Nevada relies on beer-tasting events, newspaper articles, and word of mouth (Kaplan 1986; Allman 1988). Since most microbrewers survive on niche marketing, considerable effort goes into packaging that is intended to stimulate consumer interest. Brand names and labels are carefully designed to be eye-catching and distinctive. This is particularly important, because microbrewery products need to stand out among imports and mass-produced beers on crowded store shelves.

One of the thorniest problems facing microbrewers is gaining access to their target customers. Due to their low sales volumes, distributors are hard to find.

For instance, it took an entire year of preselling before the now-defunct Thousand Oaks Brewing Company of Berkeley, California, could generate sufficient sales to interest a distributor in carrying its line. Some microbreweries opt for self-distribution. Others use the services of distributors of imported beers or wines (Mares 1991). Microbreweries with access to distribution channels face yet another problem—an inability to exercise control over these channels. Sometimes this lack of control can result in grievous damage. In 1985, for example, Boulder Brewing Company of Boulder, Colorado, had to destroy more than 2,000 cases of beer (25% of annual sales) after they were mistakenly stored in a hot warehouse. Since most microbreweries do not pasteurize their beer, it is essential that distributors use refrigerated trucks and warehouses.

Microbrewers almost always operate initially in geographically localized markets (Prial 1988). Some of these small brewers face an inherent paradox. They would like to grow and extend distribution of their products beyond local markets. But growth also implies that they lose the uniquely local flavor that made them special in the first place (Loomis 1986; Fenn 1987). According to Fritz Maytag, the owner of Anchor Brewing company, microbreweries that grow rapidly find it difficult to maintain product quality (Berger 1990). As described earlier, Anchor Brewing Company provides an exceptional case of managed growth. Other microbreweries have not been as fortunate as they have attempted to grow. Consider, once again, the case of Boulder Brewing Company. The company, founded in 1979, produced 4,708 barrels in 1986, a tenfold increase from 1985, making it one of the fastest-growing breweries in the country that year. In 1986, the company embarked on an ambitious growth plan. It extended distribution to eight western states and New England. Also that year, the company spent $1.3 million on a new 1.5-acre site and brewery (Bilby 1988). Sales remained stagnant and then declined precipitously in 1989 and 1990. After being on the verge of closure in 1990, the company radically shifted its strategy. It reversed gears and decided to focus once again on the local draft market for Boulder Beer. Its ratio of bottled-to-draft sales changed from 90/10 to 40/60 from 1990 to 1991. Boulder Brewing's sales for 1991 increased by 80 percent over 1990, for a total of 6,100 barrels (Edgar 1992).

Brewpubs face a different kind of challenge—a decision as to what extent they define themselves as restaurants. Perceptions vary even among brewpub operators and this is reflected in the relative emphasis on beer versus food (see Aidells and Kelly, 1992) for an inventory of brewpub food). Some brewpubs such as Buffalo Bill's Brewpub in Hayward, California, emphasize the beer. Bill Owens, the original owner-operator at Buffalo Bill's Brewpub argues: "This should be a brewing business with food on its coattails, not a restaurant with a brewery as a gimmick to lure customers. With 49 percent food costs versus the cost of manufacturing beer at 3 percent, common sense says emphasize the beers" (Hartman 1988, p. 93).

The risk involved in offering an ambitious menu in addition to the distinctive beers is illustrated by the case of brewpubs such as Sieben's River North Brewery in Chicago, which was irreparably damaged by scathing restaurant reviews in major local newspapers (Hartman 1988; Brokaw 1989). Sieben's went out of business in 1990, three years after it opened. The Los Angeles Brewing Company/Eureka Brewpub, which boasted the services of Wolfgang Puck, the celebrated chef, also suffered a similar fate, failing within a year of its opening in 1990. Puck and his partners invested $8.5 million in the 26,000-square-foot brewpub that could seat 214 customers. The marketing plan was ambitious—it called for a sales target of 12,000 barrels in the first year of operation with a long-term goal of 50,000 barrels, most of it through the wholesale and retail trade (Martin 1990). Although the restaurant was profitable, the brewing operations lost money because the wholesale demand did not materialize, possibly due to insufficient funds for marketing its Eureka California Lager brand (Martin 1992).

While the flavor of fresh "real ale" might be sufficient to keep the brewpub operating for six months, maybe even a year, some operators stress that it takes quality food to ensure long-term success for the brewpub. For example, Loggerhead Brewing Company of Greensboro, North Carolina, had to overhaul its menu four times in a sixteen-month span since its opening in 1989. Loggerhead has abandoned its original Bavarian food theme for more traditional fare such as sandwiches and steaks, a change that has resulted in increased sales (Hayes 1991). The Los Angeles area's first brewpub, City of Angels, located in Santa Monica, is widely thought to have failed because of losses sustained in its restaurant operations (Johnson 1989).

In general, brewpubs require a smaller initial investment than microbreweries because there is no need for bottling and warehousing facilities. A small brewpub may have only $100,000 to $200,000 invested in equipment, compared to the capital costs of $500,000 to $1,000,000 that are typical of a mid-sized brewery (Anderson 1986). Rather than struggle for scarce space on distributors' trucks and store shelves, a brewpub need only attract customers into the establishment. Quality control is firmly in the hands of the manufacturer. The absence of kegging or bottling lines implies lower line costs, while the brewer captures the retailer's, the wholesaler's, and the manufacturer's profit. At an average price of $2.15 a pint, gross manufacturing margins can exceed 97 percent (Hartman 1988). Other estimates suggest typical gross profits of $350 per barrel of brewpub sales versus a maximum of $150 per barrel for a traditional microbrewery that wholesales bottled beer (Kureczka 1988).

A specialist strategy is not the only factor differentiating microbreweries and brewpubs from mass producers. Unlike mass producers, they lack access to capital markets. So they tap the sources of capital that support small businesses: family, friends, and personal assets. For example, Paul Camusi and Ken Grossman, partners in Sierra Nevada Brewing Company, initially raised $110,000 from their families to set up the microbrewery on the outskirts of Chico, California, a college and farming town near Sacramento (Lindley 1983). Similarly, Randall Sprecher launched Sprecher Brewing Company in 1985 in Milwaukee, Wisconsin, with $50,000 from his personal savings. He raised another $100,000 from fourteen shareholders, all of whom contribute skills besides their capital to the company. The shareholders include a lawyer, a plumber, and a welder (Connole 1987).

Microbreweries and brewpubs also differ from mass producers in terms of their internal organizational structures. In accordance with their smaller size, microbreweries and brewpubs have fewer employees. More importantly, however, the owner or managing partner typically doubles as the technical expert or brewmaster. Even a large microbrewery such as Anchor Brewing Company has only fourteen full-time employees and seven part-time employees on its payroll. According to Fritz Maytag, owner of Anchor, smaller work groups tend to be more quality oriented and more creative (Gumpert 1986). Maytag's management style is nearly as unusual as his products. He runs Anchor like a family, with shared responsibility, although without profit sharing or bonuses. There are no supervisors or foremen or job titles for that matter, with the sole exception of "brewmaster," which belongs to him. Full-time workers are salaried and earn slightly above union wages for brewery workers in California (Hartman 1983). Task rotation is an established practice. While some specialization has inevitably occurred, everyone has been sent to both brewing and packaging courses. The workers are remarkably similar in terms of age. Turnover is minimal and the working atmosphere is casual.

Like Anchor, most microbreweries and brewpubs have simple organizational structures with a minimum of administrative personnel. According to Jim Schlueter, the founder of River City Brewing Company, a now-defunct microbrewery, microbrewers need to possess a wide variety of mechanical skills in addition to their knowledge of the brewing process. Skills in areas such as electrical work, plumbing, welding, tile work, carpentry, and refrigeration are necessary in order to maintain and repair equipment (Mares 1991, p. 139). Mass producers may be family-run enterprises, but they usually hire technical staff for daily operations. Also, mass producers are characterized by highly differentiated administrative hierarchies. The proportion of administrative (nonproduction) employees in the industry is significant at about 27.9 percent of total industry employment in 1990 (U.S. Brewers Association 1992, p. 27). It can be safely assumed that virtually all of these nonproduction employees are employed by mass producers.

The normative order among microbreweries and brewpubs is also considerably different. Cooperation rather than competition seems to be the norm in mutual interaction. For example, it is common for microbreweries and brewpubs in the same area to negotiate shared bulk purchasing agreements with suppliers of raw materials. It is also common for various firms in a region to sponsor together festivals, tours, clubs, newsletters, and tasting events. The cooperative approach also extends to distribution: several Northern California microbreweries combined to put together a Microbrew Discover Pack (cost: $20) that includes six different beers and a video tour of twenty microbreweries and brewpubs in the area (*Newsweek* 1989). Many microbrewery and brewpub operators approach their business with an almost missionary zeal. In that respect, the proliferation of these two specialist organizational forms bears an uncanny resemblance to the growth of social movements. Indeed, industry publications frequently refer to this segment of the industry as "the microbrewery movement."

INTERPRETATION

Recall that the resource-partitioning model holds that as the market becomes increasingly concentrated, the life chances of specialist organizations will be enhanced. Generalists move toward the middle of the market, opening up pockets of resources for specialists. In brewing, the conditions that might initiate this process have certainly occurred: concentration has increased steadily due to economies of scale in production and advertising. In addition, consumer taste tests demonstrate that even regular brand-loyal drinkers of beer cannot identify or discriminate between the generalists' products in blind taste tests (Allison and Uhl 1964; Jacoby, Olson, and Haddock 1971).

The recent and increasing number of microbreweries and brewpubs suggests that at least some entrepreneurs believe new opportunities have been created as a result of market concentration. When asked about the market, these entrepreneurs usually offer resource-partitioning types of scenarios. As one individual associated with the microbrewery movement told us in an interview, "There is very little difference left in the big brewers—it's all generic. . . . People are looking for something different and unique."[12]

Obviously, the emergence of the micro and brewpub segments are consistent with the resource-partitioning model. So too is the small and specialized organizational nature of microbreweries and brewpubs. Systematic empirical research (Carroll and Swaminathan 1992) also shows that mortality rates of microbreweries and brewpubs respond to concentration levels in the manner predicted by the resource-partitioning model. As overall market concentration rises, the mortality rate drops. So although the brewing industry has become considerably more concentrated, the abundance and longevity of these specialist producers have been enhanced. So too have those of the smaller mass-producer breweries; selection of this organizational form appears to have been greatest for mid-sized firms, a finding consistent with the resource-partitioning model.

NOTES

1. The Sieben Brewing Company and the Tap and Growler, both brewpubs, were founded in 1987, the first brewing operations in the Chicago area since the exit of Peter Hand. By the end of 1992, the Chicago area featured a total of six brewpubs and three microbreweries.

2. Throughout this chapter we define total sales both for the industry and for each organizational form in terms of tax-paid withdrawals of beer. This is an estimate of the actual volume of beer entering the domestic market and can be interpreted as sales volume.

3. Total industry sales (tax-paid withdrawals) for 1953 and 1990 were 84.6 million barrels and 181.5 million barrels, respectively. In addition to tax-paid withdrawals, the total production figures include tax-free withdrawals and production losses.

4. By 1956, Anheuser-Busch, Associated, Carling, Drewry's, Falstaff, Hamm, Lucky, National, Pabst, Rheingold, Schafer, Schlitz, and C. Schmidt all operated more than one brewery. Heileman purchased its second plant in 1961, as did Miller in 1962 (Tremblay 1987).

5. Sterling was eventually spun off and formed the basis for the new Evansville Brewing Co.

6. Microbreweries and brewpubs are not historically new organizational forms. They are new in the context of the mature post-Prohibition brewing industry.

7. Maytag referred to this definitional issue in his opening address to the 1988 Microbrewers Conference at Chicago: "Over the years, we've watched the definition of microbrewery grow and grow—to our great amusement. I read the other day that a microbrewer produces something around 20,000 barrels. As last we have discovered what a microbrewer is, and I can offer you a definition: A microbrewery is a brewery that brews as much as the brewer that is just under Anchor thinks they might brew next year" (Evangelista 1988).

8. Other large microbreweries that exceed the size criterion include the Sierra Nevada Brewing Company of Chico, California (which brewed 68,000 barrels in 1992), the Redhook Ale Brewery of Seattle, Washington (which brewed 49,000 barrels in 1992), the Full Sail Brewing Company of Hood River, Oregon (which brewed 28,500 barrels in 1992), and the Widmer Brewing Company of Portland, Oregon (which brewed 27,500 barrels in 1992).

9. Of the 183 brewpubs in existence at the end of 1992, California, Oregon, and Washington were home to fifty-one, fifteen, and five brewpubs, respectively.

10. These estimates are based on available firm-level capacity data. These data are available for 626 of the 687 brewpub firm-year spells, for 621 of the 657 microbrewery firm-year spells, and for 10,142 of the 10,536 mass-producer firm-year spells.

11. In some states such as Oregon, craft-brewed beers account for as much as 3.1 percent of the total market. Craft-brewed beers have outsold imported beers in Oregon since 1991.

12. We are grateful to Dennis Wheaton for conducting this and numerous other interviews with microbrewery and brewpub operators.

BIBLIOGRAPHY

Aidells, Bruce, and Denis Kelly. 1992. *Real Beer and Good Eats: The Rebirth of America's Beer and Food Traditions*. New York: Alfred A. Knopf, Inc.

Allison, Ralph I., and Kenneth P. Uhl. 1964. "Influence of Beer Brand Identification on Taste Perception." *Journal of Marketing Research* 1:36–39.

Allman, Kevin. 1988. "Beer Tastings at Pub Create Big Brew-Haha: Americans Seem to Be Acquiring a Thirst for Knowledge on Relatively New Topic." *Los Angeles Times*, Sunday, Valley Edition, December 11, 1988. Section: Calendar, p. 107.

Anderson, A. Donald. 1986. "What's New in Specialty Beers." *New York Times*, April 10, 1986.

Berger, Dan. 1990. "Anchor Steam: The Giant of the Micro-Breweries." *Los Angeles Times*, Thursday, Home Edition, August 30, 1990. Section: Food, part H, p. 42, column 1.

Bilby, Wynne. 1988. "Boulder Beer: From Goat Shed to Brewery to, Perhaps, Profitability." *Denver Business*, May 1988, vol. 10, no. 9, section 1, p. 10.

Blair, Ian C. 1985. "Is There Strength in Diversity?: Although Their Ranks Have Dwindled Over the Years, America's Small Regional Brewers May Be on the Brink of a Renaissance." *Beverage World,* 104(October):26–34, 135–9.

Brewers Digest Buyers Guide and Brewery Directory. 1993. Chicago, IL: Siebel Publishing Co.

Brokaw, Leslie. 1989. "Anatomy of a Start-Up Revised: The Beer's Great, But." *Inc.,* May 1989, p. 59.

Brooks, Christopher. 1990. "Fare of the Country: From Florida, Bar-Made Brews." *New York Times,* Sunday, Late Edition—Final, April 29, 1990, section 5, p. 6, column 1.

Carroll, Glenn R., and Anand Swaminathan. 1992. "The Organizational Ecology of Strategic Groups in the American Brewing Industry from 1975 to 1990." *Industrial and Corporate Change* 1:65–97.

Charlier, Marj. 1990. "Brew Pubs Pour into Restaurant Market Creating Their Own Beers and Ambiance." *Wall Street Journal,* February 22, 1990, pp. B1, B5.

Connole, Peter. 1987. "Sprecher Built His Microbrewery with Sweat Equity." *Business Journal-Milwaukee,* March 23, 1987, vol. 4, no. 23, section 1, p. 17.

Edgar, David. 1992. "1992 Industry Review." *New Brewer* 9(3):10–30.

Edgar, David. 1993. "1993 Industry Review." *New Brewer* 10(3):10–28.

Elzinga, Kenneth G. 1973. "The Restructuring of the U.S. Brewing Industry." *Industrial Organization Review* 1:105–9.

Elzinga, Kenneth G. 1986. "The Beer Industry." In Walter Adams (ed.), *The Structure of American Industry,* 7th ed. New York: Macmillan.

Erickson, Jack. 1987. *Star Spangled Banner: A Guide to America's New Microbreweries and Brewpubs.* Reston, VA: Red Brick Press.

Evangelista, Joe. 1988. "Did You Wash Your Hands First?" *Beverage World* 107 (October):208–11.

Fenn, Donna. 1987. "The Rediscovery of Local Pizzazz: Small Businesses That Market Regional Products." *Working Woman,* July 1987, vol. 12, p. 66.

Fisher, Lawrence M. 1986. "Small Breweries Enjoying a Revival." *New York Times,* Late City Final Edition, October 29, 1986, section C, p. 14, column 3.

Foley, A. M. 1990. "Cambridge Beer Holds Head High: British Biochemist Sets Up Brewery in Maryland." *Washington Post,* Thursday, February 8, Final edition, section: Maryland Weekly (Montgomery), p. M1.

Fussell, Betsy. 1989. "Fare of the Country: Bay Area Brewpubs—Beer at the Source." *New York Times,* Sunday, Late City Final Edition, May 7, 1989, section 5, p. 6, column 1.

Gumpert, David E. 1986. "Growing Concerns: The Joys of Keeping the Company Small. An Interview with Fritz Maytag." *Harvard Business Review,* July–August, pp. 6–14.

Hartman, Curtis. 1983. "The Alchemist of Anchor Steam." *Inc.* 5(1):31–39.

Hartman, Curtis. 1988. "New Brew: Microbrewery and Restaurant Become One." *Inc.* 10(4):86–88, 92–93.

Hayes, Jack. 1991. "Bible Belt Brew-Pubs Sprout Up as Old Laws Crumble in Many States." *Nation's Restaurant News,* September 2, p. 1.

Institute for (Fermentation and) Brewing Studies. 1986. *Microbrewers Resource Handbook and Directory.* Boulder, CO: Institute for Fermentation and Brewing Studies.

Institute for (Fermentation and) Brewing Studies. 1987. *Microbrewers Resource Handbook and Directory.* Boulder, CO: Institute for Fermentation and Brewing Studies.

Institute for (Fermentation and) Brewing Studies. 1988. *North American Microbrewers Resource Handbook and Directory*. Boulder, CO: Institute for Fermentation and Brewing Studies.

Institute for Brewing Studies. 1989. *North American Microbrewers Resource Directory*. Boulder, CO: Institute for Brewing Studies.

Institute for Brewing Studies. 1990. *North American Brewers Resource Directory*. Boulder, CO: Institute for Brewing Studies.

Institute for Brewing Studies. 1991. *North American Brewers Resource Directory*. Boulder, CO: Institute for Brewing Studies.

Institute for Brewing Studies. 1992. *North American Brewers Resource Directory*. Boulder, CO: Institute for Brewing Studies.

Institute for Brewing Studies. 1993. *North American Brewers Resource Directory*. Boulder, CO: Institute for Brewing Studies.

Jacoby, J., J. C. Olson, and R. A. Haddock. 1971. "Price, Brand Name and Product Compositional Characteristics as Determinants of Perceived Quality. *Journal of Applied Psychology* 55:570–9.

Johnson, Greg. 1989. "Brew Pubs Tapping into Trend of Designer Suds." *Los Angeles Times,* Sunday, San Diego County Edition, December 10, 1989, section: Metro, part B, p. 1, column 4.

Kaplan, Michael. 1986. "Tiny Breweries Work to Build Impact." *Advertising Age* 57(25):S12–14.

Keithahn, Charles F. 1978. *The Brewing Industry*. Washington, DC: Bureau of Economic Research.

Kureczka, Joan. 1988. "From California Here They Come: There's Microbreweries in Them Thar Hills." *Beverage World* 107(October):216–18, 222–24.

Lindley, Daniel. 1983. "Small Beer: But Microbrewers Are a Yeasty Lot." *Barron's* 63(19):16–20, 41.

Loomis, Susan H. 1986. "Fare of the Country: Seattle, Microbrews Are Big in Flavor." *New York Times,* Sunday, Late City Final Edition, May 11, 1986, section 10, p. 12, column 1.

Lubenow, Gerald C. 1987. "A New Thirst for Brewpubs." *Newsweek,* February 9, 1987, section: Business, p. 49.

Lynk, William J. 1984. "Interpreting Rising Concentration: The Case of Beer." *Journal of Business* 57:43–55.

Mares, William. 1991. *Making Beer*. New York: Alfred A. Knopf, Inc.

Martin, Richard. 1990. "Eureka! Puck Unveils Brewery." *Nation's Restaurant News,* June 11, 1990, vol. 24, no. 24, p. 1.

Martin, Richard. 1992. "Reorganization Brewing at Puck's Dormant Eureka." *Nation's Restaurant News,* June 15, 1992, vol. 26, no. 24, p. 3.

Mayer, Kurt B., and Sidney Goldstein. 1961. *The First Two Years: Problems of Small Firm Growth and Survival*. Washington, DC: Small Business Administration.

McNulty, Timothy J. 1986. "Image and Competition Keep Beer Industry Foaming." *Chicago Tribune,* Monday, Sports Final Edition, August 11, 1986, section: News, p. 1, Zone C.

Modern Brewery Age. Various Years. *Modern Brewery Age Bluebook*. Norwalk, CT: Modern Brewery Age.

Modern Brewery Age. 1990. "Microbrewing '90: Industry Forecast and Analysis, 1990 Microbrewery Report." *Modern Brewery Age,* May 14, 1990, vol. 41, no. 20, p. 4.

Moon, William Least Heat. 1987. "A Glass of Handmade." *The Atlantic,* 260(5):75.

Morris, Stephen. 1990. *The Great American Beer Trek,* rev. ed. New York: The Stephen Greene Press/Pelham Books.

Newsweek. 1989. "A Sophisticated Sampler for Joe Six-Pack." January 23, 1989, section: Business, p. 44.

Ornstein, Stanley. 1981. "Antitrust Policy and Market Forces as Determinants of Industry Structure: Case Histories in Beer and Distilled Spirits." *Antitrust Bulletin* 26:281–313.

Persinos, John F. 1988. "Heady Brews: Amber Waves of Grain." *Venture* 10(1):58–61.

Prial, Frank J. 1988. "Summer Drinks: America's New Regional Brews." *New York Times,* Sunday, Late City Final Edition, May 15, 1988, section 6, part 2, p. 44, column 1.

Prial, Frank J. 1989. "Spirits: Western Flair—Home Brew." *New York Times,* Sunday, Late Edition—Final, August 6, 1989, section 6, p. 57, column 1.

Scherer, Frederic M. 1980. *Industrial Market Structure and Economic Performance,* 2nd ed. Chicago, IL: Rand McNally.

Scherer, Frederic M., Alan Beckenstein, Erich Kaufer, and R. D. Murphy. 1975. *The Economics of Multi-Plant Operation: An International Comparisons Study.* Cambridge, MA: Harvard University Press.

Tremblay, Victor J. 1987. "Scale Economics, Technological Change, and Firm-Cost Asymmetries in the U.S. Brewing Industry." *Quarterly Review of Economics and Business* 27(2):71–86.

Tremblay, Victor J., and Carol Horton Tremblay. 1988. "The Development of Acquisition: Evidence from the U.S. Brewing Industry." *Journal of Industrial Economics* 37:21–46.

U.S. Brewers Association. Various Years. *Brewers Almanac.* Washington, DC: U.S. Brewers Association.

U.S. Bureau of the Census. Various Years. *Census of Manufacturers.* Washington, DC: U.S. Government Printing Office.

ADDITIONAL READINGS

Books and Articles

Anderson, Will. 1986. *Beer, USA.* Dobbs Ferry, NY: Morgan and Morgan.

Apps, Jerold W. 1992. *Breweries of Wisconsin.* Madison, WI: The University of Wisconsin Press.

Baron, Stanley. 1962. *Brewed in America.* Boston: Little Brown.

Boeker, Warren. 1991. "Organizational Strategy: An Ecological Perspective." *Academy of Management Journal* 34:613–35.

Carroll, Glenn R., and Anand Swaminathan. 1991. "Density Dependent Organizational Evolution in the American Brewing Industry From 1633 to 1988." *Acta Sociologica* 34:155–76.

Carroll, Glenn R., Peter Preisendoerfer, Anand Swaminathan, and Gabriele Wiedenmayer. 1993. "Brewery and Brauerei: The Organizational Ecology of Brewing." *Organization Studies* 14(2):155–88.

Cockerill, Anthony. 1977. "Economies of Scale, Industrial Structure and Efficiency: The Brewing Industry in Nine Nations." In E. P. Jacquemin and H. W. de Jong (eds.), *Welfare Aspects of Industrial Markets.* Leiden: Martinus Nijhoff Social Sciences Division.

Greer, Douglas F. 1971. "Product Differentiation and Concentration in the Brewing Industry." *Journal of Industrial Economics* 19:201–19.

Greer, Douglas F. 1981. "The Causes of Concentration in the Brewing Industry." *Quarterly Review of Economics and Business* 21:100–17.

Hatten, Kenneth J., and Dan Schendel. 1977. "Heterogeneity Within an Industry: Firm Conduct in the U.S. Brewing Industry, 1952–71." *Journal of Industrial Economics* 26:97–113.

Hatten, Kenneth J., Dan Schendel, and Arnold C. Cooper. 1978. "A Strategic Model of the U.S. Brewing Industry." *Academy of Management Journal* 21:592–610.

Hawkins, Kevin, and Rosemary Radcliffe. 1971. "Competition in the Brewing Industry." *Journal of Industrial Economies* 20:20–41.

Horowitz, Ira, and Ann Horowitz. 1965. "Firms in a Declining Market: The Brewing Case." *Journal of Industrial Economics* 13:129–53.

Peles, Yoram. 1971. "Economies of Scale in Advertising Beer and Cigarettes." *Journal of Business* 44:32–37.

Salem, Frederick W. 1880. *Beer, Its History and Its Economic Value as a Beverage.* Hartford, CT: Salem.

Tremblay, Victor J. 1985. "Strategic Groups and the Demand for Beer." *Journal of Industrial Economics* 34:183–98.

Data Sources

Bull, Donald, Manfred Friedrich, and Robert Gottschalk. 1984. *American Breweries.* Trumbull, CT: Bullworks.

Institute for Fermentation and Brewing Studies. 1986. *Microbrewers Resource Handbook and Directory.* Boulder, CO: Institute for Fermentation and Brewing Studies.

Institute for Fermentation and Brewing Studies. 1987. *Microbrewers Resource Handbook and Directory.* Boulder, CO: Institute for Fermentation and Brewing Studies.

Institute for Fermentation and Brewing Studies. 1988. *North American Microbrewers Resource Handbook and Directory.* Boulder, CO: Institute for Fermentation and Brewing Studies.

Institute for Brewing Studies. 1989. *North American Microbrewers Resource Directory.* Boulder, CO: Institute for Brewing Studies.

Institute for Brewing Studies. 1990. *North American Brewers Resource Directory.* Boulder, CO: Institute for Brewing Studies.

Institute for Brewing Studies. 1991. *North American Brewers Resource Directory.* Boulder, CO: Institute for Brewing Studies.

Institute for Brewing Studies. 1992. *North American Brewers Resource Directory.* Boulder, CO: Institute for Brewing Studies.

Institute for Brewing Studies. 1993. *North American Brewers Resource Directory.* Boulder, CO: Institute for Brewing Studies.

Modern Brewery Age. Various Years. *Modern Brewery Age Bluebook.* Norwalk, CT: Modern Brewery Age.

Siebel Publishing Co. 1993. *Brewers Digest Buyers Guide and Brewery Directory.* Chicago, IL: Siebel Publishing Co.

U.S. Brewers Association. Various Years. *Brewers Almanac.* Washington, DC: U.S. Brewers Association.

U.S. Bureau of the Census. Various Years. *Statistical Abstracts of the U.S.* Washington, DC: U.S. Government Printing Office.

U.S. Department of Commerce. Various Issues. *Survey of Current Business.* Washington, DC: U.S. Government Printing Office.

U.S. Government Printing Office. Various Years. *Economic Report of the President.* Washington, DC: U.S. Government Printing Office.

12

Medical Diagnostic Imaging Manufacturers

WILL MITCHELL

This chapter describes key commercialization patterns in the medical diagnostic imaging device industry in the United States since 1950. Physicians and other health-care workers use diagnostic imaging devices to obtain pictures of structures and systems with the human body. X-ray instruments, which were introduced during the last decade of the nineteenth century, were the first imaging devices to receive broad use in medical practice. Since 1950, imaging devices that are based on nuclear medical, ultrasonic, computed tomographic, and magnetic resonance technology also have entered medical practice. By commercialization, I mean the process of acquiring an idea for a product, augmenting it with complementary knowledge, developing and manufacturing a salable item, and offering to see it to one or more sets of users. The commercialization history of the diagnostic imaging industry, comprising several hundred manufacturers that have participated in the American diagnostic imaging equipment market since the mid-1950s, is an important example of business success and failure during industry evolution.

The imaging devices and the firms that commercialize the instruments encompass several distinct technical subfields of the medical diagnostic imaging industry. An industry is a group of firms that manufacture products having "reasonable interchangability of use or cross-elasticity of demand" (U.S. Supreme Court 1964, p. 76), while a technical subfield of an industry (Mitchell 1989) is a set of products that draw on knowledge bases not required for traditional goods in the same industry. A knowledge base is a combination of "information inputs, knowledge, and capabilities" (Dosi 1988, p. 1126). The emergence of a new technical subfield within an established industry occurs when products that draw on a new knowledge base serve as substitutes and complements for goods used within an existing market.[1] Table 12-1 lists several imaging technical subfields, key differences in their underlying knowledge

Table 12–1 Technical subfields of the medical diagnostic imaging industry

Imaging technical subfield	Knowledge base	Introduction	
		World	U.S.
X-ray	X radiation	1896	1896
Nuclear medical	Gamma radiation	1954	1954
Ultrasonic	Sonic waves	c. 1954	1957
Computed tomographic (CT)	X radiation computer interpretation	1972	1973
Magnetic resonance (MR)	Resonance of nuclei of atoms	1980	1980

bases, and when the first commercial systems were introduced to world and U.S. markets.[2]

I first describe the early commercialization of x-ray imaging devices and the emergence of four new imaging technical subfields in the United States, along with key environmental factors and organizational forms that have emerged since 1950. I next describe commercialization patterns in the four new technical subfields of the industry. I then discuss the patterns in the context of the resource partitioning and inertia arguments of organizational ecology and review several other issues, including the technical contribution of later entrants, the incentives for industry newcomers to enter new subfields, the circumstances in which newcomers are most likely to survive, and whether the patterns will be found outside the United States.

IMAGING INDUSTRY COMMERCIALIZATION HISTORY

Early Evolution

The beginning of the imaging industry is generally traced to November 1895, when German physicist Wilhelm Roentgen discovered that particle-like short electromagnetic rays would produce fluorescence in mineral salts.[3] Working in his laboratory at the University of Wurzburg, Roentgen created the first diagnostic images by passing the rays through his wife's hand and producing shadows of the bones on mineral salts. (Roentgen called his discovery the x-ray after the mathematical symbol signifying the unknown quantity.) Within a year, researchers at universities in Europe and the United States developed intensification screens to improve image sharpness, focusing tubes to reduce imaging times, and emulsion film on which to record the images.

The first commercial producers of x-ray equipment entered the market in 1896. The early instruments consisted of tubes to generate the rays and pieces of cardboard coated with metal salts on which to detect them. During the next sixty years, the commercial equipment improved drastically with the introduction of better tubes, full-wave rectification methods that reduced imaging times, equipment to focus the radiation, better film, cathode-ray tube monitors, and many other innovations. By the 1950s, diagnostic use of x-ray images had become an important part of health care throughout the world.

The earliest firms to offer commercial x-ray equipment included established electrical goods firms and small start-up ventures. Initially, the imaging industry was segregated into distinct national and subnational markets in the United States, Japan, and the larger countries of the European continent, mainly served by domestically based firms. Siemens and General Electric were among the earliest entrants in their respective countries, each offering commercial x-ray instruments in 1896. The German and American firms were soon followed in other countries by other established companies with experience in many industrial sectors. Many smaller companies also entered as the x-ray industry developed, especially in the United States, often offering innovative product changes. Dr. William Coolidge, for instance, established a company that commercialized an x-ray device incorporating a "hot cathode" tube that replaced more temperamental gas tubes and allowed more powerful and reliable pictures to be obtained. Most such new ventures competed for a few years and then disappeared, after either shutting down their business or being acquired by a more established company.

By the early 1950s, the major players in each country were mainly firms with businesses in many electrical equipment industries, such as General Electric and Westinghouse in the United States, Siemens in Germany, GEC in Britain, Philips in the Netherlands, and Toshiba, Shimadzu, and Hitachi in Japan. Some x-ray equipment specialists also prospered and attained strong market positions, particularly in the United States, where firms such as Picker, Stanford, and Profexray served regional markets and were often somewhat quicker than their more broadly based competitors to incorporate product advances. Newcomers, including start-up and diversifying firms, continued to enter and exit the industry and often introduced x-ray product innovations that were then adopted and refined by the industry leaders. The industry and markets continued to be nationally based in the 1950s.

New Technical Subfields

Several new technical subfields of the industry emerged between 1950 and 1980, as Table 12-1 notes, and now comprise important parts of medical technology and industrial activity. The imaging instruments all draw from physical science and applied engineering but use several scientific and technical knowledge bases within those fields. X-ray instruments record the absorption of short waves of radiation after they have passed through the body. Electrodiagnostic devices interpret electrical signals. Nuclear medical imaging instruments measure the gamma-ray emissions of radioactive materials that have been administered to a patient. Ultrasonic imaging instruments produce pictures by interpreting either sonic echoes from organs or frequency shifts induced by moving objects such as fetuses or blood. CT (computerized tomography) scanners record x-radiation and use computers to interpret the absorption patterns. Magnetic resonance imaging devices subject the body to a large magnetic field and then interpret changes in the resonance of atomic nuclei when a smaller radio frequency electromagnetic force disturbs the original field. Because they draw on different knowledge bases, the instruments within each class constitute technical subfields of the imaging industry.

Most early research prototypes in each new diagnostic imaging technical subfield were constructed in academic laboratories, although some corporate researchers also undertook important early involvement with development of imaging systems and key components. Key academic and corporate contributions emerged from many countries, with perhaps the most frequent contributions emerging in the United States, Britain, Germany, and Japan. Transfer of the results of the academic research to corporate development generally occurred informally rather than through formal licenses between the universities and corporations, usually when key researchers set up their own companies or were hired by established corporations.

The first commercial instruments in each new technical subfield were introduced by newcomers to the diagnostic imaging industry, including start-up ventures and established firms diversifying into the diagnostic imaging industry. Prototype nuclear medical imaging instruments were introduced in the early 1950s by several small American firms that drew on academic and industrial research carried out in the United States, Britain, and Germany. Firms manufacturing commercial prototype ultrasonic imaging equipment in Japan, Europe, and the United States during the late 1950s and early 1960s included small firms established by or consulting with university medical researchers and several industrial firms with prior experience with industrial or military ultrasonic equipment. The first CT instrument was introduced in 1972 by a British recording firm, EMI, which drew on its own experience as an electronic components manufacturer and on academic imaging research carried out in the United States. The first commercial magnetic resonance imaging instrument was introduced in 1980 by an American start-up venture, Fonar, drawing on academic research begun at SUNY Brooklyn and other institutions.

The industry newcomers were soon followed by leading incumbent imaging equipment manufacturers. In the nuclear imaging subfield, Picker X-ray began work on an innovative nuclear imaging scanner during the 1950s and was eventually followed by the other leading manufacturers. In the ultrasound subfield, Siemens, Picker, and Toshiba each introduced commercial instruments during the 1960s. In the CT subfield, which represented a direct substitute for many existing nuclear imaging and x-ray procedures, most leading nuclear and x-ray instrument manufacturers had followed EMI into the market by the mid-1970s. In the magnetic resonance imaging subfield, the leading imaging incumbents reacted even more quickly, with all major players offering commercial instruments by 1985. The incumbents drew on their existing technical skills to develop instruments for the new subfields, usually adding to their internal know-how by consulting with academic researchers, licensing or copying ideas introduced by earlier entrants, or acquiring earlier entrants.

Market Environment

Hospital-based radiology departments became the principal market for x-ray equipment during the first half of the twentieth century and remain the primary market for most new imaging equipment. Nuclear medicine, which became established as a medical specialty during the 1950s and 1960s, soon became closely associated with radiology departments in most hospitals. Computed tomographic and magnetic resonance imaging instruments were quickly adopted by radiologists. Ultrasound was the primary exception to the radiology trend, as ultrasonic imaging instruments found much initial use in other departments, including obstetrics, ophthalmology, and urology.

For all subfields except ultrasound, therefore, technical innovation led to relatively little new market segmentation. Even for ultrasound, radiology became a growing market segment during the 1980s. In general, the marketing and service systems required for the radiology products enjoy significant complementarities and economies of scope, which provide cost and quality advantages to firms that offer a broad range of imaging devices used by radiologists. Most firms that have enjoyed long success in the industry have offered a broad product line of goods across all subfields, although some manufacturers have enjoyed temporary success by specializing narrowly within a single subfield.

Prices of different imaging devices range widely, and assigning specific prices to different types of imaging equipment is impossible, owing to differences in sophistication and quality of different systems offered within each subfield and to widely varying discount practices followed by the manufacturers. Nonetheless, several important price trends are clear. During the 1950s and 1960s, x-ray, nuclear, and ultrasonic imaging devices were inexpensive. Prices ranged from a few thousand dollars to perhaps $100,000, depending on the sophistication of the device. The introduction of CT changed the price structure drastically. CT instruments entered the market at about a quarter of a million dollars and CT prices rose to more than $1 million during the 1980s. Prices of sophisticated MRI (magnetic resonance imaging) devices soon reached $2 million or more. Conventional x-ray, nuclear medical, and ultrasonic imaging devices remained relatively inexpensive during the 1970s, but prices rose substantially with the introduction of computer-based technology during the 1980s. Sophisticated digital x-ray and nuclear medical systems now command more than $1 million, while top-end ultrasound systems may cost a quarter of a million dollars.

Organizational Structure of the Market Environment

The structure of the relationship between hospital administrators, physicians, and national health-care payment systems has had important influences on imaging equipment use. In the United States, some key features of this environment began to change during the mid-1980s, which I discuss when I describe imaging equipment sales growth, but the structure described here had the major influences on the commercialization patterns described in this chapter.

Most diagnostic imaging equipment is purchased by hospitals and used under the direction of physicians. Traditionally, in the United States, most physicians are independent agents rather than hospital employees and are free to choose the hospitals in which they practice. A physician's choice of hospitals is often influenced by the availability of advanced medical technology, so that equipment availability has been an important competitive factor for hospital administrators as they seek to attract and retain physicians.[4]

Since the mid-1950s, hospital administrators had relatively little incentive to resist strong demands by physicians for new equipment. Employment-based not-for-profit insurance systems such as Blue Cross and Blue Shield have been responsive to hospitals' requests to set reimbursement schedules at high-enough levels to purchase equipment and attract physicians. The formation of the Medicare public health-care payment program in 1966 accelerated the trend toward a near cost-plus payment environment for medical procedures. Although most capital costs were not covered by the Medicare system, hospital administrators could often negotiate sufficiently high reimbursement rates for medical operating procedures to recover capital expenditures. Although the public program covered only a minority of the population, Medicare influenced overall medical trends because the program is used by the elderly, who tend to require medical care more frequently than the younger population. In addition, other insurers tended to follow the lead of the public agency in setting billing practices.

Radiologists have particularly strong voices within many hospitals. In part, the power stems from the relative ease with which radiologists can move between hospitals and from the high public profile of their services. Therefore, hospital administrators tend to be particularly responsive to radiologists' requests for new imaging instruments. The strong independent role of radiologists within hospitals combined with the weak constraints on hospital capital expenditure has contributed to rapid diffusion of imaging equipment through the American medical system.

Imaging Industry Sales And Manufacturer Density

Figure 12-1 plots annual American imaging market sales and manufacturer density figures between 1950 and 1988. The right vertical axis reports sales, recorded in constant 1982 dollars (deflated by the Producer Price Index), while the left vertical axis reports the number of participants active in the market at each year end.

Between 1950 and 1988, sales of imaging systems in the United States rose from a few million dollars to almost $3 billion, representing about half of world sales of imaging systems. These figures report only purchases of imaging systems, thereby omitting costs of supplies, facilities, and personnel. Such ancillary costs total several multiples of the annual expenditure on imaging systems.

The most striking sales growth occurred during the late 1960s and early 1970s, following the creation of the Medicare public insurance program, and continued until about 1977. A brief sales decline occurred during the late 1970s, following the diffusion of hospital capital expenditure controls to many states. These controls most often took the form of Certificate of Need programs that required hospitals to argue that equipment requiring large capital outlay was not available in nearby institutions (Joskow 1981). In part, the controls were a response to rising health-care costs in the United States, including a public perception that expensive CT equipment was causing part of the expenditure growth. The controls contributed to a brief decline in CT instrument sales. Technological confusion also contributed to the decline, as three different CT systems designs were competing for market acceptance during the late 1970s and many buyers were waiting for a dominant design to emerge before purchasing a system.

Sales began to rebound about 1980. Part of the rebound occurred when the CT system being offered by General Electric became the clear winner in the

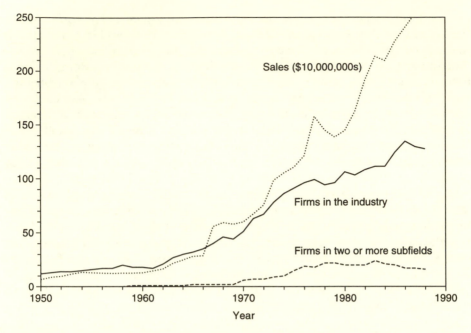

Figure 12–1 Density and sales of medical diagnostic imaging manufacturers. (*Source:* Author's analysis.)

design race and market uncertainty subsided. In addition, many nonhospital imaging facilities were created, often with equity and organizational participation by hospitals and hospital-based radiologists. By 1985, more than 200 facilities' were in operation or under construction in the United States, about 85 percent of which were associated with hospitals. The outpatient facilities could charge insurers for imaging procedures but were not affected by most capital expenditure control programs. Hence, the facilities became important purchasers of CT systems and then of MRI devices. Initially, some firms saw the new facilities as the creation of a new market segment, outside the traditional sphere of the established industry leaders. However, many of the new facilities followed much the same buying practices as hospital radiology departments, stemming in part from the strong role played by hospitals and radiologists. As a result, established imaging industry manufacturers tend to dominate sales to the new institutions.

Imaging equipment sales declined briefly about 1984, but then recovered again. Part of the reason for the decline can be traced to the creation of Medicare's Prospective Payment System, which began to replace the earlier cost-plus payment approach about 1983. Under the new system, hospitals are paid a fixed amount to treat a patient, with the amount varying depending on the diagnosis of the patient's problems. Public agencies expected this system to curb rising health-care costs, including payment for expensive capital equipment (United States Congress 1984; Hillman and Schwartz 1986). Imaging sales quickly rebounded, however, with the strong pressure of MRI innovation and the growing role of nonhospital imaging facilities leading the market growth.

One interpretation of the sales trends between 1977 and 1988 is of an ongoing interplay between public agencies that are trying to stem rising costs and medical equipment purchasers who want new technology. Purchasers took about four years to adapt to the capital expenditure controls on CT equipment during the late 1970s, with a major aspect of the adaptation being the creation of a new demand-side organizational form, the outpatient imaging clinic. The adaptation to the Prospective Payment System in the 1980s then took place much more quickly, because purchasers were able to use the now-widespread outpatient organizations as important purchase sites for new devices.

The number of firms selling imaging systems in the United States rose from about 10 in 1950 to almost 150 in 1988. Figure 12-1 shows that participant density and industry sales followed related trends in cyclical growth and decline. The figure also reports that some firms began to operate in two or more imaging industry subfields during the late 1950s and early 1960s as nuclear medical and ultrasound imaging equipment entered the market, but that most such multiple-subfield activity began during the 1970s when imaging sales grew rapidly. The number of firms selling imaging systems from more than one imaging subfield reached a peak of about 25 companies by the late 1970s. Multiple-subfield participation then declined slightly, with the decline stemming from growing volume economies in design, manufacturing, and marketing.

Industry Globalization

In addition to growing volume economies, industry globalization has contributed to the decline of multiple-subfield incumbents. Most imaging markets remained nationally based, in the sense that distinct sales and service systems are required for each national market, but a few companies now dominate all major national markets, most notably General Electric and Siemens, along with Philips, Toshiba, and Hitachi. All dominant players are now broad-based electronics firms with extensive international operations. Diagnostic imaging equipment specialists and firms that continue to operate primarily in a single country have either exited the industry or, in the case of past leaders such as Picker in the United States and Shimadzu in Japan, become second-tier players. By the late 1980s, foreign-owned firms held almost 50 percent of the market share in the United States. Similar trends are found in national imaging equipment markets in Western Europe, and foreign firms such as General Electric and Siemens now have major presences in the Japanese imaging equipment market.

The globalization of the imaging industry stems in part from the general postwar resurgence of European and Japanese firms. In equal or greater part, two factors concerning the technologies underlying the industry also have led to the extensive globalization of the industry. First, imaging technical advances occur in academic and corporate laboratories throughout the world, so that firms with effective international operations gain technical advantages over firms that operate in a single country. Second, imaging technical advances now draw heavily from many industrial sectors, including aerospace and computers. Firms with broad industrial experience have advantages relative to companies with businesses only in the medical sector. Therefore, firms that operate primarily in a single country or in a single industry can no longer compete as sales leaders in medical diagnostic imaging equipment markets.

TECHNICAL SUBFIELD
COMMERCIALIZATION PATTERNS

The commercialization history in each of the four new subfields has followed similar general patterns. This section first describes several examples of product introduction and business acquisition.

Examples

A product introduction and business acquisition series that begins in the ultrasound subfield provides a useful example of the commercialization process in the new technical subfields. The story begins in 1958, when an engineer at the General Precision Company, which manufactured scientific instruments, and an ophthalmic researcher at the Albert Einstein School in New York initiated commercial development of an experimental ultrasonic eye scanner. General Precision introduced a commercial prototype of the instrument in 1959 and then, in 1961, formed a joint venture with the pharmaceutical manufacturer Smith Kline French to further commercialize the device. After the instrument achieved only limited success, Smith Kline took over the joint venture in 1964. The following year, Smith Kline acquired Branson, a manufacturer of industrial ultrasonic flaw detectors that had begun medical ultrasonic research in 1962, and soon introduced a neurological ultrasonic instrument. The eye and brain devices were only moderately successful, but Smith Kline used its experience with them to help achieve a major breakthrough in cardiac ultrasound during the mid-1960s, after commercializing a device initially developed at Indiana University.

Smith Kline achieved significant commercial and innovative success in the ultrasound subfield through the 1970s, especially in the cardiac sector. By 1980, however, the company was finding it difficult to adapt to the ongoing technical innovation in the subfield and faced pressure from innovative newcomers. In 1981, Smith Kline sold its ultrasound division to Xonics, which was attempting to become an imaging industry generalist. Xonics was a start-up venture that had introduced specialized x-ray equipment in the early 1970s and then acquired several moderate-sized x-ray equipment companies, including the long-established regional companies Profexray and Standard. Xonics had entered the ultrasound subfield in 1978, by acquiring Litton's ultrasound operations (along with Profexray, which Litton had acquired in 1964). Xonics was also working with several universities and venture companies to develop prototype CT, digital x-ray, and MRI instruments. Xonic's attempt to expand ended in bankruptcy, however, and its ultrasound assets were acquired by Picker and several other established imaging industry companies in 1984.

A second development and acquisition series begins in the nuclear imaging subfield in 1967 when Ohio Nuclear, a start-up company in Cleveland, introduced the first whole-body nuclear scanner. The Ohio Nuclear scanner was technically successful, but the company lacked the financial and managerial resources to fully commercialize the device and was acquired by a financial services company, Technicare, in 1971. As Technicare, the imaging business continued to develop nuclear imaging instruments and introduced an early whole-body CT scanner in 1974. Technicare entered the ultrasound subfield in 1975 by acquiring Unirad, a start-up firm that had commercialized an innovative ultrasonic scanner in 1969 (drawing in part on research carried out at the University of Colorado). Technicare also initiated an early MRI development program. However, Technicare soon faced serious financial difficulty after coming under technical and market pressure from General Electric and other imaging industry generalists, especially in the CT subfield. Technicare was acquired by Johnson and Johnson, the pharmaceutical and medical supplies company, in 1978, which was particularly attracted by the company's MRI research skills.

Johnson and Johnson provided the financial resources needed for Technicare's commercialization programs. Within J&J, Technicare continued to make major technical contributions to the new subfields of the imaging industry, particularly in the MRI subfield, where it introduced one of the earliest commercial instruments in 1981. By the mid-1980s, however, J&J had lost several hundred million dollars in the effort to develop the new products and compete with the established players in the industry. In 1986, J&J sold the Technicare business to General Electric.

A third example begins in 1977 when Diasonics, a start-up company founded by people with experience at other imaging firms, introduced an innovative ultrasonic scanner and soon became an important ultrasound participant. Diasonics then worked with researchers at the University of California at San Francisco to develop one of the earliest commercial MRI devices, which the company introduced in 1981. The MRI device was technically successful and achieved substantial market success until the late 1980s, when it incurred increasing competitive pressure from imaging industry generalists, particularly General Electric. Diasonics then sold its MRI business to Toshiba, which had financed part of the company's research program.

Density and Sales Trends
Figures 12-2 through 12-6 depict density and sales trends in the x-ray subfield and in each of the four new subfields. In the x-ray subfield, sales growth began in the late 1950s and then accelerated during the 1960s. The growth was accompanied by a concurrent or slightly lagged increase in manufacturer density, suggesting that some manufacturers entered in response to market growth. In the new subfields, by contrast, density growth often preceded sales growth, suggesting that firms entered the new subfields in anticipation of market growth. Only in the CT subfield, where the extremely quick success of the new instruments took the industry by surprise, did density and sales growth occur concurrently. Sales decreases in all subfields, meanwhile, were usually accompanied by reductions in the number of firms selling the products.

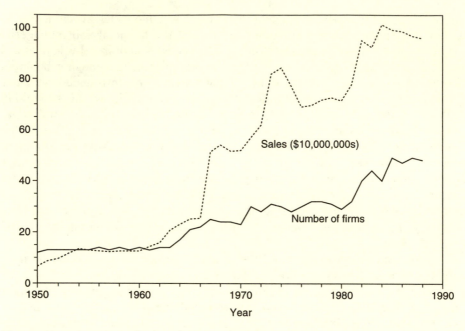

Figure 12–2 Density and sales of x-ray manufacturers. (*Source:* Author's analysis.)

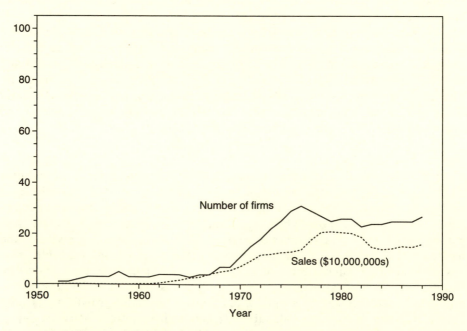

Figure 12–3 Density and sales of nuclear medical imaging manufacturers. (*Source:* Author's analysis.)

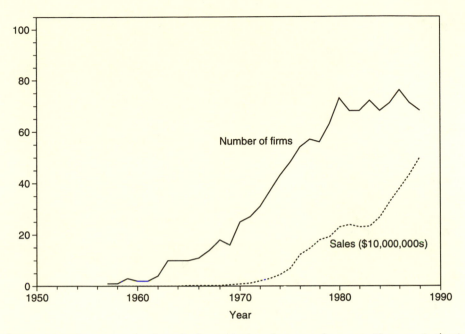

Figure 12–4 Density and sales of ultrasonic imaging manufacturers. (*Source:* Author's analysis.)

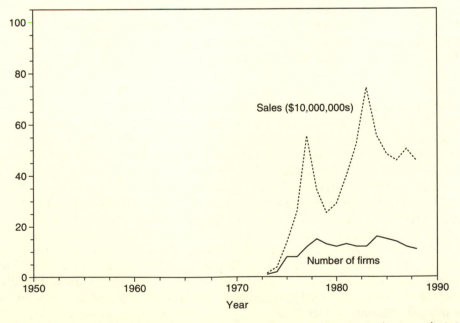

Figure 12–5 Density and sales of CT scanner manufacturers. (*Source:* Author's analysis.)

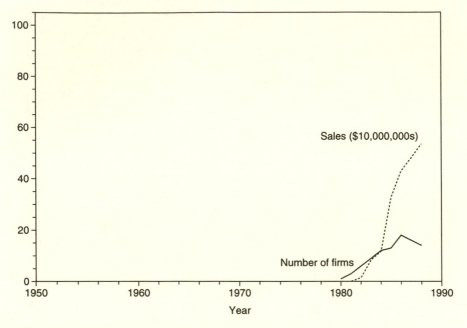

Figure 12–6 Density and sales of MRI manufacturers. (*Source:* Author's analysis.)

Two differences among the subfield trends are notable. First, average sales per firm (sales/density) was relatively low in the nuclear and ultrasound subfields and relatively high in the CT and MRI subfields, owing to much larger volume economies available for the later products. Second, extremely rapid density growth took place in the CT and MRI subfields, compared to the nuclear medical and ultrasound cases, corresponding to the rapid sales growth that occurred for CT and MRI devices.

Newcomer and Incumbent Entry and Exit Frequency
Within the overall record of participant density and sales, industry newcomers and incumbents have followed substantially different entry and exit patterns. Firms that did not sell other medical diagnostic imaging systems before they entered a subfield, which include start-up ventures and firms diversifying from other industries, introduced the first products in each new technical subfield and continued to enter throughout the history of each new subfield. Entry by such industry newcomers was somewhat more common during rising sales periods, but substantial newcomer entry occurred throughout the periods, whether sales were rising, stable, or declining. The newcomer exit rates (proportion of existing firms that exited in a given year) in each subfield tended to decline somewhat over time. Nonetheless, newcomer exit is common throughout the life of each subfield, suggesting that new entrants often replaced or displaced other newcomers.

By contrast with newcomer entry incidence, which was common throughout subfield life, entry by industry incumbents took much more of an inverted U pattern. The peak of entry by incumbents, who already sold devices in at least one imaging industry subfield before entering another imaging subfield industry, tended to occur during a period of high subfield sales growth. Few incumbents entered before subfield sales began to be substantial. Many incumbents then entered in quick response to the first wave of incumbent entry, whereas few incumbents entered once some firms established dominant positions. Although somewhat fewer incumbents than newcomers exited the subfields, nontrivial numbers of incumbents did leave, with the exit waves tending to follow incumbent entry waves. The lagged exits suggest that some incumbents that entered during the peak of incumbent entry displaced weaker incumbents as well as industry newcomers.

Although newcomers continue to enter each new subfield, the density of companies that had prior imaging industry experience before entering eventually surpassed the density of newcomers in three of four cases. Only in the ultrasound subfield did the number of newcomers continue to exceed incumbent density in 1988. The likely reason for the exception is that ultrasonic scanners are sold in several medical market segments other than the hospital radiology departments dominated by the industry incumbents.

Newcomer and Incumbent Market Share

Industry newcomers and incumbents also have achieved very different market success. As the density of incumbents grew, the market share held by newcomers fell. Although substantial numbers of newcomers participated in each subfield in 1988, newcomer share fell to 10 percent or less in all but the ultrasound case. Even in ultrasound, where newcomers held a density majority, newcomer market share was less than 50 percent in 1988.

Despite the overall downward trends in newcomer share, some declines did not occur smoothly. Nuclear imaging and ultrasound, in particular, experienced marked fluctuations in newcomer share. In the nuclear subfield, newcomer share rose from about 1963 to 1968 and again from 1977 to 1980. In the ultrasound subfield, increased newcomer share occurred in at least four periods. The increases were associated with major product innovations introduced to the nuclear and ultrasound imaging subfields by industry newcomers. The newcomers enjoyed temporary success, but industry incumbents subsequently recovered their market positions in all but the most recent upsurge in ultrasound newcomer share. Whether incumbents recover in that case remains to be seen.

As newcomer share declined, and incumbent share rose accordingly, market concentration in each subfield also declined. The highest concentration, measured by the Hirschman Herfindahl Index (HHI), occurred with the earliest entrants and then declined to fairly stable levels as more firms entered.[5] Although concentration sometimes rose again when one firm gained an advantage in a subfield, other manufacturers (usually industry incumbents) variably overcame the temporary edge and the downward trends reappeared. Concentration levels were highest in the two newest subfields (CT and MRI), stemming in part from their younger age and in part from their greater volume economies.

Early Entrant Survival and Market Share
Table 12-2 describes the long-term survival and market share of early entrants to each of the four new subfields. For this table, early entrants are defined as the first three newcomers and the first three industry incumbents to enter each new subfield, plus any firms that entered during the same calendar year as the third entrant. The bottom rows of the table note that only two of fifteen early-entrant newcomers remained in the relevant subfield by 1990 (column 4) and that neither of the two surviving firms was among the top three in subfield market share during 1988 (column 5). Ten of fifteen early-entrant incumbents survived in 1990 (column 4), by contrast, and five of the ten survivors were market share leaders in 1988 (column 5). Moreover, the five incumbents that exited did so after participating more than twice as long as the exiting newcomers, nine years versus four years (column 3). The table shows clearly that the newcomers that introduced new technology to the industry realized little long-term success, but that the earliest incumbents to enter the new subfields often fared very well.

Early-entrant incumbents tended to fare poorly only in the CT and MRI subfields, where incumbent entry occurred almost as rapidly as newcomer entry. In these cases, it appears that some industry incumbents helped create the new subfields and then were displaced by stronger incumbents that entered as the subfields became established. Therefore, incumbents that help create a subfield, rather than wait for industry newcomers to introduce the new products, face some of the same competitive pressures from later entrants that are faced by early-entrant newcomers.

Cumulative Entry Incidence and Type
Start-up ventures and incumbents undertook about the same number of entries until after about twenty-five years of subfield life, when incumbent entry largely ceased but start-up entry continued. More than 20 percent of diversifying firms entered the subfields by acquiring earlier entrants, whereas only about 5 percent of incumbents and almost no start-ups entered by acquisition (management buyouts of incumbents were classified as start-up firms that entered by acquiring earlier entrants).

The low incidence of acquisition entries by incumbents stands in marked contrast to their more frequent use of preentry alliances. Mitchell and Singh (1992) showed that incumbents frequently undertook alliances with earlier entrants prior to entering a new subfield. In 30 percent of eighty-seven cases in which industry incumbents eventually entered new subfields, the incumbents distributed other firms' products or conducted joint research with an earlier entrant before introducing their own products to the subfield. Preentry alliances were most common for incumbents with large industry market shares and for incumbents that were relatively late entrants to new subfields. One might ex-

Table 12–2 Relative success of early newcomers and early incumbents: Survival and market leadership

Subfield	First year	First three entrants and ties (No.)	(1) Average entry year	(2) Exit by 1990 No.	(3) Average life (years)	(4) Survive to 1990 No.	(5) No. in top 3 in 1988
Nuclear	1952	Newcomers (3)	1954	3	6		
		Incumbents (4)	1967	1	19	3	2
Ultrasound	1957	Newcomers (3)	1958	3	4		
		Incumbents (4)	1966			4	1
CT	1973	Newcomers (5)	1974	5	4		
		Incumbents (3)	1975	2	5	1	1
MRI	1980	Newcomers (4)	1983	2	3	2	0
		Incumbents (4)	1982	2	8	2	1
All		Newcomers (15)		13	4	2	0
		Incumbents (15)		5	9	10	5

pect that many incumbents would then acquire their preentry partners as a means of entering the new subfield. However, the figure shows that most incumbents undertook independent entry. Although incumbents have acquired many smaller players in the new subfields, most such acquisitions took place after the incumbents had already entered the new subfields.

Cumulative Exit Incidence, Type, and Timing

Overall, incumbents were much more likely to survive than newcomers, as 84 percent of incumbent entrants and only 39 percent of newcomers (44 percent of diversifying firms; 29 percent of start-ups) remained in the subfields in 1988. The type of exit also differed among the firms. Start-up firms were more likely to exit by shutting down than by being acquired, as about 70 percent of exiting start-ups were dissolved. By contrast, only about 30 percent of firms that existed before entering a subfield, whether diversifying entrants or industry incumbents, shut down their imaging businesses upon exit. Instead, most sold their businesses to another firm.

The likelihood of dissolution and acquisition exits changed as firms gained experience in the subfields. The proportion of firms that exited by shutting down their imaging business rather than by selling to another firm generally declined over time until stabilizing after about eight years. By contrast, the proportion of exits that occurred through acquisition initially increased and then stabilized. Thus, for all types of entrants, dissolution exits tended to occur relatively soon after a firm entered a subfield, whereas acquisition exits were more common as firms gained experience.

Whether a firm leaves a subfield by dissolving its business or by selling it to another company will often be influenced by whether the exiting firm possesses valuable industry-specific organizational routines. Organizational routines, which are patterns of activity embodied in human or capital assets (Nelson and Winter 1982), serve as an organization's memory and contain much of its ability to operate (Hannan and Freeman 1984; Cohen 1991). The continued existence of a routine depends on the continued existence of the organization in which it is embedded, so that a firm that values some of another firm's capabilities often must acquire the company rather than simply purchase some of its assets or hire away a few key employees (Mitchell 1992). The differences in the proportion of dissolution and acquisition exits in the technical subfields of the diagnostic imaging industry likely occurred because established firms that are not suited to independent operation within a subfield often possess organizational routines that have value to other firms. By contrast, unsuccessful start-up ventures frequently possess little organizational value to other companies.

The difference in the timing of dissolution and acquisition exits also likely stems from a routine-based explanation. Firms that leave a subfield soon after entry usually do so because their business has not developed routines required to design, produce, or sell a successful product. This idea is at the core of studies of the liability of newness, which find that the rate of business dissolution declines over time and attribute part of the decline to increasing development of successful organizational routines as firms gain experience (Stinchcombe 1965; Freeman, Carroll, and Hannan 1983). Businesses that do not develop successful routines offer little organizational value to other companies and tend to be broken up (Mitchell 1992). The longer a business operates, the more time it has to build organizational routines that may be valuable to other companies. The longer a firm operates in a subfield before exiting, therefore, the greater the incentive for another firm to acquire its business.

Routines may have more expected value for an acquiring firm that believes it can commercialize the products more effectively than the exiting company. Some such cases arise when an exiting business has designed a potentially valuable good but lacks financial resources or key organizational capabilities required for commercialization (Williamson 1985). In other cases, the routines used by the exiting business may conflict with routines of the parent corporation (Scott 1984; Stinchcombe 1990), leading to divestment to another corporation.

Summary

The commercialization histories of the imaging industry technical subfields conform to a general pattern found for many biomedical innovations, as well as for many other industrial sectors. Basic research underlying major biomedical innovation often occurs in academic institutions, whereas most applied product development is undertaken after the research is transferred to commercial entrants. Industry newcomers, including start-up ventures and diversifying firms, usually introduce the major technical changes that create a new technical subfield of an industry. Industry incumbents tend to enter a new subfield as it becomes established, usually commercialize products that are more advanced than the earlier goods, and often displace the newcomers when market segments remain largely unchanged. The rate of incumbent entry often peaks after a few years of subfield maturation and then declines, while newcomer entry is likely to be more constant throughout subfield history.

Newcomers enjoy their greatest market success when substantial market change occurs in concert with technical innovation. Both newcomers and industry incumbents may acquire earlier entrants in order to enter a subfield. Start-up firms that exit a subfield are more likely to do so by dissolving their businesses than are industry incumbents and other established companies, which are more likely to sell their businesses to other firms. For all entrants, the rate of exit by dissolution tends to peak earlier than the rate of exit by acquisition.

This pattern describes a dynamic process of technical and organizational experimentation, in which industry newcomers and incumbents play complementary roles in introducing and commercializing new goods but compete for eventual market success. Usually, industry incumbents dominate, while newcomers' efforts contribute more to the long-term evolution of the new subfield than to the firms' own successes. Only when substantial new market segments emerged did newcomers fare reasonably well and even in these cases the earliest newcomers did not enjoy long-term success. These general trends suggest several additional questions.

RELATED ISSUES

Resource Partitioning

On first reading, the technical subfield commercialization patterns described in the previous section may appear to conflict with ecological resource-partitioning arguments, which predict that increased market concentration will be associated with greater entry incidence by specialists and lower specialist exit rates. Instead, the imaging technical subfields reveal the opposite patterns if we view industry newcomers and incumbents as specialist and generalist firms respectively. As concentration declined over time in each new technical subfield of the imaging industry, specialist entry remained fairly constant and specialist exit rates tended to decline.

The apparent contradiction is resolved when we recognize that the appropriate level of analysis is the imaging industry, because of the substantial market overlap across the individual technical subfields. Figure 12-7 shows plots of industry market concentration (Herfindahl Index) and the proportion of industry participants that were newcomers when they entered a subfield. The newcomer proportion records the aggregate trend in the relative success of newcomers and incumbents, because the proportion increases when newcomers enter more often and/or exit less often than incumbents.

The overall concentration and newcomer proportion patterns both take U shapes, so that decreased concentration is associated with decreased newcomer participation and increased concentration with greater relative represen-

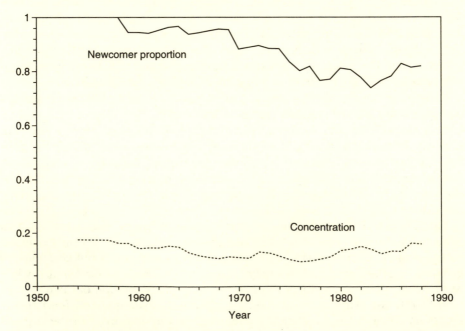

Figure 12–7 Concentration and newcomer proportion of imaging manufacturers. (*Source:* Author's analysis.)

tation by newcomers.[6] Even with the overall U shapes of concentration and newcomer proportion, temporary increases and decreases of concentration tend to be associated with short-term increases and decreases in the newcomer proportion. The aggregate and short-term industry level trends are consistent with the resource-partitioning argument.

Inertia

The tendency for industry incumbents to dominate sales in each new technical subfield may appear to conflict with ecological structural inertia arguments in Chapter 2. Rather than finding it difficult to change, some incumbents appear to have been remarkably able to adapt to changing diagnostic imaging technology. Moreover, Mitchell and Singh (1993) found that incumbents that expanded into a new technical subfield tended to survive longer than those that did not expand, which also seems to conflict with the notion that changing core structures will harm firms' survival chances. But does introducing products in a new technical subfield of an industry represent changing the core structure of an incumbent's organization, even when the products themselves require new technology? In some cases, the answer to this question will be "no."

Instead, the organizational changes required to commercialize products in the new diagnostic imaging technical subfields may be more peripheral adaptation than core transfiguration. Incumbents' marketing, manufacturing, and administrative systems may form as much or more a part of the firms' cores as the specific products they sell. That is, the products that a firm sells may be less important to its success than the commercialization systems within which the products are sold. Think of the Procter and Gamble Company, for instance, which owes its ongoing success much more to its marketing and supplier management systems than it does to any particular product. Thus, the mission, the forms of authority, and the marketing strategy of the organization, which are three of the generic core organizational features that were listed in Chapter 2, may sometimes be more important than the basic technology of the products that it sells, which is the fourth generic feature.

Cases in which product changes represent peripheral adaptation rather than core organizational change will be most pronounced when the market environment within which components are acquired and products are sold does not change drastically when products undergo major technological change. In such cases, a firm's supporting supply and marketing systems will retain much of their value from one type of product to the next. The supporting systems that comprise barriers to successful entry, so that industry newcomers might introduce the first products in a new technical subfield but often will be displaced by incumbents. This appears to have been the case in the diagnostic imaging industry, where market changes have occurred relatively smoothly over time and industry incumbents have been able to adapt to major technical shifts.

Incumbents may be less likely to succeed when markets or supply systems undergo major transformations. Massive changes in consumer electronics markets that followed the introduction of the semiconductor, for instance, contributed to the decline of established vacuum tube manufacturers. Thus the structural inertia arguments may apply most strongly when several aspects of the organizational core are affected by an environmental change.

Associating products with the periphery of a business and supporting systems with its core may run counter to some intuition. However, it is generally recognized that replicating supporting systems is often more costly and difficult than imitating product innovations (e.g., Lippman and Rumelt 1982; Teece 1986). In such cases, it is the supporting systems that provide value and give a business its strength, which is the essential nature of the core features of a business. This argument is consistent with the notion that firms can be viewed as bundles of resources, routines, and competencies, many of which are only indirectly related to the physical products marketed (Penrose 1959). The argument is also consistent with the idea that firms tend to grow through expansion of core activities into new technological and market arenas (e.g., Thompson 1967; Lawrence and Lorsch 1967; Meyer and Scott 1983).

Do Incumbents Free-ride on Innovators' Efforts?

Although the overall pattern of early entrant failure and incumbent success may suggest that incumbents free-ride on innovators' efforts, industry incumbents often play critical roles in technical innovation and product development. The commercial prototypes introduced by early entrants often work badly or do not meet users' needs well, and the early entrants frequently lack the technical capability to refine and redesign the instruments. An incumbent's success in the market stems as much or more from its ability to carry out product technical refinement, which often involves substantial advances, as from the firm's market-related power.

Moreover, industry incumbents introduce many technical advances that draw on knowledge bases currently used within their industry. Digital radiographic instrumentation, for instance, combined radiographic imaging knowledge with computerization skills. The first digital radiographic instruments, introduced commercially during 1981, were developed and marketed by industry leaders with strong positions in the x-ray and computed tomographic subfields of the industry. In addition, incumbents must continually introduce incremental innovations of existing products or they will eventually lose their leadership positions. Often, so-called incremental innovations are anything but minor, requiring major insight as well as substantial outlays of time and money.

An incumbent's contribution also extends to manufacturing the new goods. Just as the instruments introduced by early entrants often have design flaws, many early entrants also lack the production capabilities needed to create high-quality, cost-effective products. By contrast, leaders in the existing industry almost always control strong manufacturing capabilities, either through in-house production facilities or through extensive networks of external suppliers. Their entry brings the production capabilities to the new subfield, which often contributes importantly to the commercial success of the new types of goods. Therefore, an incumbent's technical design and manufacturing skills must match its distribution and service strength.

Why Do Newcomers Enter?

The failure of most newcomers leaves us with a perplexing question. Why would newcomers create a new technical subfield of an industry when the chance that they will survive for many years is so small? One explanation is simply hubris, that managers of early entrants are driven by technical pride in what they hope to accomplish and believe that the market will reward them for technical success. The managers are then fated to discover that the market rewards firms with broader commercialization skills far more than it rewards the design skills of early innovators.

An alternative economically rational explanation to the hubris argument is that early entrants expect to exit as organizations but hope to achieve enough technical success that they will be purchased at a profit by later entrants. This explanation is partly supported by the dissolution and acquisition trends reported earlier. The longer a newcomer survives before exiting, the more likely it is to exit by being acquired rather than shutting down. One explanation for this result is that longer life is a sign that an entrant has created some valuable successful routines, such as basic technical skills required for a new product, that are of value to a firm that believes it has stronger commercialization skills. The rational acquisition goal argument appears stronger for diversifying firms than for start-up ventures, however, because only 30 percent of exiting start-up firms did so by being acquired, compared to almost 70 percent of exiting diversifying firms.

When we examine the fate of the early-entrant newcomers from Table 12-2, which were the firms that created the new subfields, the rational explanation becomes weaker still. Table 12-3 reports that 69 percent (nine of thirteen) of the early entrants that exited did so by shutting down their imaging businesses rather than by selling them to other firms. Start-up firms were particularly likely to exit by dissolution: only one of eight was acquired by a later entrant. Moreover, to the extent that one can identify the financial terms of the four acquisitions, none were especially profitable for the exiting companies. Therefore, we are left with the technical hubris explanation as at least part of the explanation for industry evolution.[7]

Where Do Incumbents Come From?

Although we may conclude that industry incumbents enjoy the greatest success in the new subfields, we should be led to ask how newcomers survive to become incumbents. After all, many current leaders did not begin to participate in the American market until long after 1896. Some firms must survive their

Table 12–3 Fate of early-entrant newcomers

Type of newcomer	No.	Acquired	Shut down
Diversifying firms	5	3	2
Start-ups	8	1	7
All	13	4 (31%)	9 (69%)

initial entry to the industry in order to expand and become entrenched competitors, and some newcomers survived in each subfield in 1988. The newcomers' greatest success was in the ultrasound subfield, in which market segmentation included positions away from the established firms, but some newcomers survived even in the most radiology-dominated subfields.

The answer has at least three parts. First, some surviving newcomers are foreign firms that built strong bases in their home country and then expanded into the United States. By 1988, 35 percent of the firms selling imaging systems in the United States were based outside the country. Overall, foreign firms were far less likely than American companies to exit after entry (Mitchell 1991). Some foreign firms expanded from an initial entry into a single imaging subfield to become broad-based multiple subfield incumbents, as slightly more foreign-owned than American-owned firms participated in two or more subfields of the industry in 1988.

Second, there is an element of firm-specific managerial capability and random chance to newcomer success, as some firms are particularly skillful and fortunate in their design and marketing choices. Third, some paths of expansion from an initial subfield into other parts of the industry offer newcomers a greater chance of becoming successful multiple-subfield incumbents than other paths.

Mitchell and Singh (forthcoming) found that industry newcomers that survived their initial entry and then expanded into other subfields in which goods did not compete directly with the firms' original base were more likely to survive than newcomers that expanded into subfields in which products substituted more directly. Expansion that was undertaken after a firm built a broader base in two subfields often succeeded, even when the later expansion involved substitute goods. Thus newcomers may survive to become the incumbents that expand successfully into new subfields through prior foreign experience, managerial skill and luck, and fortunate choice of expansion paths.

Are These Patterns Peculiar to the United States?

The case in this chapter concerns industry evolution in U.S. markets, although the industry includes many entries by foreign firms. An interesting issue concerns what differences we might expect in other markets, especially in Japan or in Western European countries. Perhaps the major difference is the reduced role played by start-up ventures in many countries other than the United States. Lesser availability of venture capital, different attitudes about job mobility, and other factors often make it much more difficult for new companies to form, especially in Japan but also in many European nations.

Nonetheless, newcomers also play important roles in industry evolution in Europe and Japan. In part, new firms make important contributions, although usually with lower frequency than in the United States. In equal or greater part, diversifying firms often act as industry innovators outside the United States. In Japan, for instance, medical ultrasonic devices were introduced by industrial ultrasound companies. Similarly, several biotechnological innovations were introduced to the Japanese pharmaceutical industry by chemical companies with no prior pharmaceutical industry experience. In addition, American and European firms play the role of diversifying entrants to Japanese markets just as Japanese firms may be newcomers to American markets. Thus the general form of the pattern can be applied internationally, but sometimes with a lesser role for start-up ventures.

CONCLUSION

This chapter describes common commercialization patterns that occur as new technical subfields emerge within an industry. The pattern applies most strongly to cases in which product innovation occurs in the context of an existing market, leading to relatively little new market segmentation. In such cases, industry newcomers tend to introduce the first goods in a new subfield, while industry incumbents tend to refine the goods and ultimately dominate the new subfield. The most likely case in which industry newcomers survive and prosper occurs when new market segments emerge, as in the ultrasound subfield in this study. Overall, this chapter describes industry evolution as a dynamic process of technical and organizational experimentation, in which industry newcomers and incumbents play complementary roles in introducing and commercializing new goods but compete for eventual market success.

NOTES

1. Another example of technical subfields is found in the computer printer industry, where dot-matrix, laser, and ink-jet printers draw from different knowledge bases.

2. The medical diagnostic imaging equipment industry contains other technical subfields. Electrodiagnostic equipment such as electrocardiographs and electroencephalographs, which were introduced during the early decades of the twentieth century, produce two-dimensional depictions of physiological activity. Many diagnostic imaging industry leaders once offered electrodiagnostic devices but exited the subfield by the 1960s owing to relatively low sales. Radiology departments are the most important market segment for most imaging devices, while electrodiagnostic instruments are sold in cardiology and other departments and so fall outside the principle market-related capabilities of the industry leaders. I omit digital radiographic imaging instruments as a distinct technical subfield of the imaging industry, instead treating the devices as a combined extension of the x-ray and CT subfields. I address the differences between commercialization of digital radiographic and other new imaging devices in the discussion.

3. Identifying a specific event as the beginning of any technological sequence is impossible. Many critical discoveries underlay Roentgen's first x-ray image, dating back at least to 1815 when clinical pathologist William Prout obtained a sample of boa constrictor feces. Prout isolated uric acid from the defecation and calculated the atomic weight of urea; in doing so, he measured the weights of other chemical elements and observed a remarkable consistence in atomic proportions. Prout then hypothesized that all atomic weights were multiples of the atomic weight of hydrogen. Prout's hypothesis led William Crookes to construct a vacuum tube to weigh the element thallium during the 1870s, which in turn led Crookes to make a vacuum-encased balance wheel that

rotated in sunlight. Crookes then used the tube to show that light acted as though it were composed of particles, because it possessed enough mass to rotate the wheels. Roentgen used a Crookes tube to carry out his investigation of particle-like rays and mineral salts (Brucer 1978).

4. The hospital market can be segmented by size, level of care provided, and teaching orientation. Large tertiary-care hospitals that are associated with medical schools are the most likely to require expensive, leading-edge imaging devices. Smaller primary- and secondary-care institutions may require less sophisticated instruments. The purchase decisions of the larger institutions have a major impact on the smaller institutions, however, because physicians who receive their education in medical-school hospitals later influence what equipment will be purchased by the smaller hospitals in which they practice. Therefore, most imaging equipment manufacturers serve all types of hospitals.

5. The Hirschman Herfindahl Index is calculated by summing the squared shares of all industry participants ($E_i s_i^2$, where s_i is the market share of firm i). When market shares are stated in decimal form, the HHI has a maximum of one and a minimum that approaches zero.

6. Although concentration in each individual subfield has declined over time, the aggregate U-shaped concentration pattern emerges for two reasons. First, concentration was higher during the 1980s in the two more recent subfields than in the nuclear imaging and ultrasound subfields. Second, incumbent domination of subfield sales accelerated during the 1980s, when subfield sales were increasingly dominated by a few players with strong positions across the industry.

7. Of course, managers of newcomer firms are not the only people who make mistakes owing to hubris. Managers in established firms also often overestimate their chances of succeeding. However, newcomers may be more likely than established firms to face challenges that they cannot overcome when they make mistakes or, at least, face the hurdles sooner, because of their lack of position in the industry.

BIBLIOGRAPHY

Brucer, M. 1978. "Nuclear Medicine Begins with a Boa Constrictor." *Journal of Nuclear Medicine* 19:581–98.

Cohen M. D. 1991. "Individual Learning and Organizational Routine: Emerging Connections." *Organization Science* 2:135–9.

Dosi, G. 1988. "Sources, Procedures and Microeconomic Effects on Innovation." *Journal of Economic Literature* 26:1120–1230.

Freeman, J. H., G. R. Carroll, and M. T. Hannan. 1983. "The Liability of Newness: Age Dependence in Organizational Death Rates." *American Sociology Review* 48:692–710.

Hannan, M. T., and J. H. Freeman. 1984. "Structural Inertia and Organization Change." *American Sociological Review* 49:149–164.

Hillman, A. L., and S. Schwartz. 1986. "The Diffusion of MRI: Patterns of Siting and Ownership in an Era of Changing Incentives." *American Journal of Roentgenology* 146:963–9.

Joskow, P. L. 1981. *Controlling Hospital Costs: The Role of Government Regulation.* Cambridge, MA: MIT Press.

Lawrence, P. R., and J. W. Lorsch. 1967. "Organization and Environment: Managing Differentiation and Integration." Graduate School of Business Administration. Boston: Harvard University.

Lippman, S. A., and R. P. Rumelt. 1982. "Uncertain Imitability: An Analysis of Inter-firm Differences in Efficiency Under Competition." *Bell Journal of Economics* 13:418–38.

Meyer, J., and W. R. Scott. 1983. *Organizational Environments: Ritual and Rationality*. Beverly Hills: Sage.

Mitchell, W. 1989. "Whether and When? Probability and Timing of Incumbents' Entry into Emerging Industrial Subfields." *Administrative Science Quarterly* 34: 208–30.

Mitchell, W. 1991. "Dual Clocks: Entry Order Influences on Industry Incumbent and Newcomer Market Share and Survival When Specialized Assets Retain Their Value." *Strategic Management Journal* 12:85–100.

Mitchell, W. 1992. "Climbing Two Mountains: Risks of Business Unit Dissolution and Acquisition in Medical Sector Product Markets." University of Michigan working paper.

Mitchell, W., and K. Singh. 1992. "Incumbents' Use of Pre-entry Alliances Before Expansion into New Technical Subfields of an Industry." *Journal of Economic Behavior and Organization* 18:347–72.

Mitchell, W., and K. Singh. 1993. "Death of the Lethargic: Effects of Expansion into New Technical Subfields of an Industry on Performance in a Firm's Base Business." *Organization Science* 4:152–80.

Mitchell, W., and K. Singh. Forthcoming. "Spillback Effects of Expansion on a Base Business When Product-types and Firm-types Differ." *Journal of Management*.

Nelson, R. R., and S. G. Winter. 1982. *An Evolutionary Theory of Economic Change*. Cambridge, MA: Harvard University Press.

Penrose, E. 1959. *The Theory of the Growth of the Firm*. New York: Wiley.

Scott, J. T. 1984. "Firm Versus Industry Variability in R&D Intensity." In Zvi Griliches (ed.), *R&D, Patents and Productivity*. Chicago: University of Chicago Press, pp. 233–45.

Stinchcombe, A. L. 1990. *Information and Organizations*. Berkeley: University of California Press.

Stinchcombe, A. L. 1965. "Organizations and Social Structure." In J. G. March (ed.), *Handbook of Organizations*. Chicago: Rand-McNally, pp. 142–93.

Teece, D. J. 1986. "Profiting from Technological Innovation: Implications for Integration, Collaboration, Licensing, and Public Policy." *Research Policy* 15:285–305.

Thompson, J. 1967. *Organizations in Action*. New York: McGraw-Hill.

United States Congress, Office of Technology Assessment. 1984. *Federal Policies and the Medical Devices Industry*. Report OTA-H-230. Washington, DC: Government Printing Office.

United States Supreme Court. 1964. *Brown Shoe Co. v. United States*. 370 U.S., 294.

Williamson, O. E. 1985. *The Economic Institutions of Capitalism: Firms, Markets, Relational Contracting*. New York: Free Press.

DIAGNOSTIC IMAGING INDUSTRY INFORMATION SOURCES

Corporate annual *"Form 10-K" Reports* to the Securities and Exchange Commission.

Articles and Books

Brucer, M. 1966–78. *Vignettes in Nuclear Medicine*. St. Louis, MO: Nuclear Consultants Division of Mallinckrodt Chemical Works.

Comroe, J. H., Jr., and R. D. Dripps. 1977. *The Top Ten Clinical Advances in Cardiovascular-Pulmonary Medicine and Surgery: 1945–1975*. U.S. Department of Health, Education and Welfare, Public Health Service, National Institutes of Health, DHEW No. (NIH) 78-1521. Washington, DC: Government Printing Office.

Donner Laboratory. 1987. "Fifth Years of Progress: 1937–1987." PUB-268, Lawrence Berkeley Laboratory, University of California.

Friar, J. H. 1986. "Technology Strategy: The Case of the Diagnostic Ultrasound Industry." Unpublished doctoral dissertation, Alfred P. Sloan School of Management, MIT.

Gottschalk, Alexander, and E. James Potchen. 1976. *Diagnostic Nuclear Medicine*. Baltimore: Williams & Wilkins Company.

Grossman, C. C., J. H. Holmes, C. Joyner, and E. W. Purnell. 1966. *Diagnostic Ultrasound: Proceedings of the First International Conference, University of Pittsburgh, 1965*. New York: Plenum Press.

Hamilton, B. (ed.) 1982. *Medical Diagnostic Imaging Systems: Technology and Applications*. New York: F&S Press (Distributed by Ballinger, Cambridge, MA).

Hayaishi, Osamu, and Kanji Torizuka. 1986. *Biomedical Imaging*. Tokyo: Academic Press.

Hodges, P. C. 1945. "Development of Diagnostic X-ray Apparatus During the First Fifty Years." *Journal of Roentgenology* 45:438–48.

Hollis, D. P. 1987. *Abusing Cancer Science: The Truth About NMR and Cancer*. Chehalis, WA: Strawberry Fields Press.

King, Donald L. (ed.) 1974. *Diagnostic Ultrasound*. St. Louis: C. V. Mosby Company.

McKay, N. L. 1983. "The Economics of the Medical Diagnostic Imaging Equipment Industry." Unpublished dissertation, Department of Economics, MIT, Cambridge, MA.

Peterson, R. D., and C. R. MacPhee. 1973. *Economic Organization in Medical Equipment and Supply*. Lexington, MA: D. C. Heath.

Russell, L. B. 1977. "The Diffusion of Hospital Technologies: Some Econometric Evidence." *Journal of Human Resources* 12:482–502.

Strauss, W. William, Bertram Pitt, and A. E. James, Jr. 1974. *Cardiovascular Nuclear Medicine*. St. Louis: C. V. Mosby Company.

Business and Clinical Press

Biomedical Business International.
Diagnostic Imaging.
Electronics: Buyer's Guide.
Hospitals, Journal of the American Hospital Association.
Medical Device Register.
Medical Electronics & Data: Equipment Buyer's Guide.
Modern Healthcare.
Year Book of Nuclear Medicine.

Market Studies

Creative Strategies International. 1981. *Diagnostic Imaging: 1981 Ultrasound Update*. San Jose, CA.

Dun's Marketing Services. *Dun's Guide to Healthcare Companies*. Parsippany, NJ.

Frost & Sullivan, Inc. 1974. *The Computer-Assisted Electrocardiography*. New York.

Frost & Sullivan, Inc. 1974. *Medical Diagnostic Equipment Market*. New York.

Frost & Sullivan, Inc. 1975. *Ultrasonic Medical Market*. New York.

Frost & Sullivan, Inc. 1975. *Advanced Medical Imaging Market*. Report No. 252. New York.

Frost & Sullivan, Inc. 1976. *The U.S. Market for Computerized Axial Tomography Equipment*. New York.

Frost & Sullivan, Inc. 1976. *European Markets for Medical Ultrasonic Equipment*. New York.

Frost & Sullivan, Inc. 1977. *Neuroelectric Diagnostic and Therapeutic Devices Market*. New York.

Frost & Sullivan, Inc. 1978. *Government Sponsored Medical Instrumentation, Device, and Diagnostics Research and Development*. New York.

Frost & Sullivan, Inc. 1979. *Nuclear Medical Market*. New York.

Frost & Sullivan, Inc. 1980. *Cardiac Diagnostic Equipment, Supplies, and Services Market*. New York.

Frost & Sullivan, Inc. 1980. *Medical Ultrasound Imaging Equipment Markets in the U.S.* New York.

Frost & Sullivan, Inc. 1981. *Cardiac Diagnostic and Therapeutic Equipment Markets in EEC*. Number E431. New York.

Frost & Sullivan, Inc. 1982. *Nuclear Medical Imaging Markets in the U.S.: Equipment and Radiopharmaceuticals*. New York.

Hale, A. B., and A. B. Hale. 1975–90. *Medical and Healthcare Marketplace Guide*. Miami, FL: International Bio-Medical Information Service, Inc.

National Science Foundation. 1974. "Nuclear Scintillation Camera." Report prepared by Arthur D. Little, Inc. Washington, DC: National Science Foundation.

Office of Microelectronics and Instrumentation Sciences and Electronics. 1988. *Competitive Assessment of the United States Diagnostic Imaging Industry*. Washington, DC: International Trade Administration. U.S. Department of Commerce.

Office of Technology Assessment. U.S. Congress. 1978. *Policy Implications of the Computed Tomography (CT) Scanner*. Washington, DC: Government Printing Office.

Office of Technology Assessment. U.S. Congress. 1978. *Health Care Study 27: Nuclear Magnetic Resonance Imaging Technology: A Clinical, Industrial, and Policy Analysis*. OTA-HCS-27. Washington, DC: Government Printing Office.

Office of Technology Assessment. U.S. Congress. 1981. *Policy Implications of the Computed Tomography (CT) Scanner: An Update*. Background paper. Washington, DC: Government Printing Office.

Office of Technology Assessment. U.S. Congress. 1984. *Medical Technology and Costs of the Medicare Program*. OTA-H-227. Washington, DC: Government Printing Office.

Office of Technology Assessment. U.S. Congress. 1984. *Federal Policies and the Medical Devices Industry*. Washington, DC: Government Printing Office.

Stason, W. B., and E. Fortess. 1982. *The Implications of Cost-Effectiveness Analysis of Medical Technology—Background Paper #2: Case Studies of Medical Technologies. Case Study #13: Cardiac Radionuclide Imaging and Cost Effectiveness*. Washington, DC: U.S. Congress, Office of Technology Assessment.

Stewart, H. F., and M. E. Stratmeyer. 1982. *An Overview of Ultrasound. Theory, Measurement, Medical Applications and Biological Effects*. HHS Publications FDA

82-819. Washington, DC: U.S. Department of Health and Human Services, Public Health Service, Food and Drug Administration.

U.S. Department of Commerce. 1969–87. *U.S. Industrial Outlook*. Washington, DC.

U.S. Department of Commerce. Bureau of the Census. 1955–85. *Census of Manufacturers: Industry Series, 1954, 1958, 1963, 1967, 1972, 1977, 1982*. Washington, DC: Government Printing Office.

V

SEGREGATING PROCESSES AND COMMUNITY DYNAMICS

Each ecological process discussed to this point—environmental selection, density-dependent selection, and resource partitioning—operates within a set of pre-specified *boundaries*. We have assumed that conventional definitions of industries provide the relevant boundaries. As we have progressed from treatments of environmental selection and density dependence to discussion of resource partitioning, our notion of boundaries has become more dynamic. That is, theories of density dependence and especially resource partitioning are more responsive to the actions of organizations and organizational populations than is environmental selection theory. In this section, we continue this theoretical trend and pay explicit attention to the dynamics of boundaries within the organizational world.

In considering boundaries between organizational populations, we consider processes of segregation. When segregating processes are strong, we observe real and consequential discontinuities between industries and between organizational forms. For instance, many observers believe that the modern telecommunications industry is separating into a segment associated with basic telephone service and a segment providing wireless communications. Such observations prompt the question, Why do populations segregate? Hannan and Freeman (1989) point to a variety of generic segregating mechanisms. For example, closure of social networks within which firms recruit members can create and maintain boundaries, giving rise to distinct organizational forms. Idiosyncratic language and culture develop and diffuse through the closed population, sharpening the differences between insiders and outsiders. Idiosyncratic language and culture tend to become markers of competence, causing inbreeding to feed on itself.

Successful collective action by organizations in a population also creates boundaries. For example, the creation of industry associations can produce a sense of collective identity and a sense of distinctiveness. Moreover, lobbying by such associations often stimulates laws and other rules that reinforce boundaries.

In the brewing industry, microbrewers and brewpub operators have used this strategy. After the repeal of Prohibition, states instituted laws requiring in most instances that the production and sale of beer be undertaken by independent firms. Brewpub operators lobbied to have the laws changed to allow vertically integrated breweries—but only below a certain scale of production, usually small. Small-scale brewers have also managed to get lower tax rates. Thus brewpubs operate in ways and under conditions that are not available to the mass-production breweries. The legal system has strengthened the boundary between organizational forms.

Hannan and Freeman (1989) argue that the most important segregating mechanisms arise from institutional processes. In the introduction to Section III, we discussed legitimation as taken-for-grantedness. Organizational theorists also use another form of institutionalization: an organizational form is institutionalized to the extent that other powerful actors in the system endorse its claims in disputes (Stinchcombe 1968). Becoming part of the institutional landscape provides powerful advantages. It allows an organization to call upon other powerful actors for aid in resisting raids on their resources; in other words, institutionalization lowers mortality rates. Unless this tendency is offset by a founding process that blurs boundaries between organizational populations, such a process generates sharp boundaries. That is, selection in favor of institutionalized forms strengthens the boundaries around the forms that emerge from the selection process.

The varied segregation processes can transform arbitrary differences into differences with real social consequences. In this sense, classifications that are initially largely arbitrary become real. They become real when they serve as bases for successful collective action, when powerful actors use them in defining rights and access to resources, and when members of the general population use them in thinking about organizations. Thus the realism of distinction among forms depends on the degree to which the distinctions become institutionalized.

Blending processes are the counter to segregation. They work to erode boundaries among populations. The design of each new organization provides an occasion at which forms and routines can be consciously and intendedly changed from orthodoxy. Much entrepreneurship involves conscious attempts to revise forms and routines to take advantage of changing opportunities and constraints or to avoid defects in orthodox designs. Another blending process involves recombination of existing routines and structures into new packages. Managers often deliberately seek to adapt to changing technical and institutional environments by copying routines and structures, what DiMaggio and Powell (1983) call mimetic isomorphism. Cultural norms about the way an organization should be designed also create (less conscious) pressures for isomorphism. Unconstrained copying—whether intentional or not—can erode boundaries among forms if not opposed by strong segregating processes.

Because inertial forces are strong and the liabilities of initiating new routines and forms are high, organizations often change structures by merging with other organizations or by acquiring them. Joint ventures provide another opportunity to recombining existing structures in ways that blur boundaries between forms.

Finally, legal or other rules maintaining boundaries between populations with similar structures are sometimes relaxed. For example, the boundary between banks and other financial institutions such as so-called thrift institutions (savings and loan association, mutual savings banks, and credit unions) and stock brokerages was eliminated by federal legislation in 1981. As Barron's analysis of credit unions (Chapter 7) pointed out, the boundaries among financial institutions have become increasingly blurred as regulations have been relaxed.

Hannan and Freeman (1989) refer to the joint operation of segregating and blending processes as an editing process operating on a continuous supply of new diversity. At any moment, new organizational forms are being created. However, much potential diversity is edited out. Organizations attempt to filter out mistakes in copying procedures. Key actors in the environment often resist attempts at building novel kinds of organizations. However, when a new form establishes a foothold, the situation often changes quickly. If a new form conveys real advantages in mobilizing resources or generating favorable outcomes, institutional arrangements can change quickly to adapt to it. That is, long-term evolution in organizational populations tends to be *punctuational*. Long periods of relatively minor change are punctuated with brief periods of very rapid alteration in forms and boundaries.

The chapters in this section illustrate a rich variety of segregating mechanisms. William Barnett's analysis of the telephone industry (Chapter 13) emphasizes the interactions of organizational population dynamics and legal constraints on organizing. Joel Podolny (Chapter 14) shows that the seemingly homogeneous population of investment banks is organized into a distinct and stable status structure and that position in this structure has a strong impact on performance. In this case, status ranking segregates firms. Huseyin Leblebici (Chapter 15) details the historical shift in the population of radio stations from independent to network-based and back. Finally, Alan Ryan, John Freeman, and Ralph Hybels (Chapter 16) show that the biotechnology industry is segregated into an array of different types of organizations based on their product offerings and interorganizational network position.

BIBLIOGRAPHY

DiMaggio, P. J., and W. W. Powell. 1983. "The Iron Cage Revisited: Institutional Isomorphism and Collective Rationality in Organizational Fields." *American Sociological Review* 48:147–60.

Hannan, M. T., and J. Freeman. 1989. *Organizational Ecology*. Cambridge, MA: Harvard University Press.

Stinchcombe, A. L. 1968. *Constructing Social Theories*. New York: Harcourt, Brace and World.

13

Telephone Companies

WILLIAM P. BARNETT

Since the breakup of the Bell System and the deregulation of telecommunications in the U.S., we have seen thousands of companies entering the industry. The actions of the U.S. Department of Justice and Judge Harold Green triggered an explosion of strategic activity, with telephone equipment manufacturers, long-distance service providers, so-called "interconnect" firms that connect subscribers to the telephone system, and cellular companies all parceling out the industry's sectors as the traditional operating companies see their domain changing substantially. But this surge of new organizing is only half of the story. Table 13-1 describes the development of the interconnect (or CPES—customer premises equipment and service) sector from 1981 through 1986, and shows that market exit rates have been high across the sector's strategic groups even as this part of the industry has expanded.

Many are surprised to learn that such volatility is not new to the U.S. telephone industry. From the first commercial application of the telephone in 1877 until FCC regulation began in 1933, over 30,000 companies populated this industry in the United States. Some were large, viable rivals to Bell, and even the many small companies were formidable when taken collectively—controlling over half the U.S. telephone market in their heyday. However, even as the "independent" telephone movement seemed to be succeeding, thousands of these companies failed. For instance, Figure 13-1 shows foundings and failures among all telephone companies that operated in the state of Pennsylvania over the early competitive period—a volatile pattern seen throughout the nation at the time. Thus instability is not new to the U.S. telephone industry. Rather, today's upheavals are in some ways a return to the patterns of the industry's first half-century.

Why has the organization of this industry been so volatile? We try to answer this question by looking historically at the evolution of the industry. This approach differs from the methods typically used when teaching organizational strategy. For example, the CEOs of these organizations cannot be interviewed

Table 13–1 The development of the CPES market in the United States, 1981–86

	1981	1982	1983	1984	1985	1986	1981–86
All firms							
Total number nationally	490	635	777	870	858	856	1117
No. of state-level operations	641	836	977	1091	1259	1245	1577
Exits from state markets	10	53	35	52	112	119	381
% Exiting from state markets	.016	.063	.036	.048	.089	.096	.242
Single-state CPES firms							
Total number nationally	444	585	723	809	788	783	1037
No. of state-level operations	444	585	723	809	788	783	1037
Exits from state markets	10	38	28	47	74	69	266
% Exiting from state markets	.023	.065	.039	.059	.094	.088	.257
Multistate CPES firms							
Total number nationally	31	33	36	40	41	41	45
No. of state-level operations	77	88	92	113	205	200	235
Exits from state markets	0	8	2	5	11	14	40
% Exiting from state markets	0	.091	.022	.044	.054	.070	.170
Integrated manufacturers							
Total number nationally	11	13	14	16	18	21	24
No. of state-level operations	75	107	105	109	165	160	200
Exits from state markets	0	6	5	0	26	31	68
% Exiting from state markets	0	.056	.048	0	.158	.194	.340
Utility affiliates							
Total number nationally	4	4	4	5	11	11	11
No. of state-level operations	45	56	57	60	101	102	105
Exits from state markets	0	1	0	0	1	5	7
% Exiting from state markets	0	.018	0	0	.010	.049	.067

because they are dead. And, obviously, students cannot contemplate working in long-gone organizations. We can, however, use the benefit of hindsight to understand the actual, possibly unanticipated results of strategies that seemed like rational moves at the time. In short, we can learn.

As we look back on the evolution of the telephone industry, I report facts and regularities that come from a study conducted by me and several of my colleagues. This study drew on four data sources, each of which shed light on specific aspects of the industry's evolution:

1. Qualitative institutional information was found in archival documents—especially those in the AT&T archives—describing the strategies and motives of many individual companies, government regulators, and other social actors.
2. A nationwide data set was collected covering the more than 30,000 independent telephone companies that operated in the contiguous United States from 1902 until 1942. These data allowed both cross-sectional and temporal statistical comparisons to see the effects of different regulatory policies on the telephone company population.
3. A more detailed sample was collected including the life histories of the 298 telephone companies that operated in southeast Iowa at any

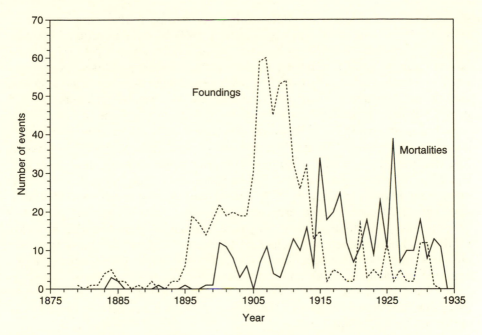

Figure 13–1 Foundings and deaths of telephone companies in Pennsylvania. (*Source:* Adapted from Barnett and Amburgey 1991. Copyright © by Sage Publications. Used by permission.)

    time from the turn of the century until 1933. These data allowed the investigation of industry evolution in rural areas.

4. Another detailed sample included the life histories of the 707 companies that operated at any time in Pennsylvania from the invention of the telephone until 1933. The Pennsylvania sample permitted inquiry into the industry's evolution in more urban areas, as well as a look at the interactions between large and small companies.

    Here I describe only the results of the study, without elaborate theorizing or technical details. Those interested in more in-depth reports should read the works listed in the Bibliography. To keep the chapter straightforward, I review the dynamics of the industry's evolution by time period. This kind of approach often is misused, implying a "life-cycle" or some other stage-wise inevitability in industrial evolution. No such implication is intended here. In fact, many of the regularities reported for one or another time period likely occurred at other times as well.

1861–94: FROM INVENTION TO LITIGATION

The late nineteenth century was a time when curious tinkerers and scientists alike experimented with what electricity could do. Some investigated the transmission of sound, leading to innovations such as the telegraph, the phonograph, and the telephone. The earliest reference I have found to an electronic telephone was the invention of Phillip Reis in Germany in 1861, but interest in telephony was widespread among electricity buffs all over Europe and America. The high-tech dreamers of those times no doubt saw a vision of isolated farmers able to call for supplies, or even of business deals closed from miles away. Yet none of the dozens of early telephone designs were commercially viable. Not until the development of the liquid transmitter was the telephone's sound quality sufficient to sustain organizations specializing in telephone service.

So it was that when Elisha Gray and Alexander Bell each separately invented liquid transmitters in 1875, Bell's earlier arrival at the patent office was pivotal. The Bell patents acted as a *segregating mechanism*—a barrier that protected Bell from thousands of other potential entrepreneurs as he began the first commercial telephone company in 1877. Widespread interest in telephone technology continued to grow, however, so that during the period of the Bell patents— 1876 to 1894—hundreds of new telephone companies were founded anyway. While the Bell company was reluctant to expand beyond the most lucrative business markets, the independent companies wasted no time—attempting to organize in small and large communities across the nation. When it came to taking legal action, however, the Bell company was fast to act; Bell brought more than 600 patent suits over the period, in most cases driving these rivals out of business (Phillips 1985).

Judged in terms of its effects on market power, Bell's litigation strategy was successful. Only about 100 independent companies were in operation by the time the most important Bell patents expired in 1893–94, and the monopoly power enjoyed over that period made Bell very profitable. Judged in terms of its effects on legitimacy, however, the strategy backfired. "The monopoly," as it became known, had built a reputation as a ruthless, arrogant trust. To those with populist sentiments, Bell was an archetype of how large-scale organization runs afoul of the national interest. In this light, those who would build competing telephone organizations were seen as "telephone pioneers," a name that reflected the legitimacy conferred on anyone with the salt to take on Bell.

Meanwhile, by the 1890s the social requirements for building telephone organizations were well developed in the United States. Knowledge of telephone technology was relatively widespread (although equipment was often in short supply). More important, the quarter-million telephone instruments in place in the United States by the 1890s showed a broad acceptance of the technology— if not the company that had monopolized it. What was once a novelty gadget had become a tool for doing business or being sociable (Fischer 1992).

In general, this sort of increasing legitimacy stimulates an increase in the numbers of organizations in an industry. In telephony, however, Bell's patents and its litigation strategy limited this proliferation, so that increasing legitimacy only ripened the industry's potential. When the Bell patents expired, then, the way was clear for the independent telephone movement to grow.

1894–1913: ORGANIZATIONAL PROLIFERATION

From the hundred or so companies that operated when the Bell patents expired in 1894, the industry exploded to number more than 9,000 organizations by

1902. The numbers of companies grew more slowly after that, peaking at well more than 10,000 in operation by 1912. Seen through the lens of economics, this clearly was an aberration. After all, the telephone industry is a "natural" monopoly due to demand-side economies of scale, where the value of a technology increases with the number of users. Small companies thus provided less value to customers. Furthermore, they were poorly organized and technically primitive—far less likely to offer long-distance service than were the larger, firmly established survivors of the Bell patent era. Most did not and often could not issue stock to raise capital. In fact, only a small minority were explicitly organized for the purpose of making profits. Each of these factors made the small, independent companies very likely to fail.

Viewed in terms of the organizational population, however, a different picture appears. Through this lens *population dynamics*—the comings and goings of organizations—catches our attention. As quickly as these organizations failed, new ones were founded to take their places. Just as small and primitive, these successors also were likely to fail when considered individually. But through this process of replenishment the independents were a robust organizational population, despite being individually insignificant and fragile. Consequently, this organizational population expanded collectively to control over half the U.S. telephone market by 1903, and clearly dominated the industry in some states.

Nonetheless, it is hard to believe that this was an efficient way to organize the telephone system. Why didn't competitive selection processes consolidate the independent movement into one or a few large companies? This question directs us to look for segregating mechanisms that would have retarded competition. In this case, political boundaries maintained a large population of smaller organizations, each specialized to one or a few local political areas such as towns or counties. This situation occurred because local governmental units were the first political actors to regulate telephony. They issued permits and franchise rights to telephone companies, and otherwise settled jurisdictional disputes among rival firms.

Furthermore, telephone entrepreneurs typically defined their own service territories by the taken-for-granted boundaries implied by county borders—a "normative" segregating mechanism. All in all, political boundaries retarded competition, so that the industry was organized by many more companies than efficiency alone might dictate. For instance, the Pittsburgh & Allegheny Telephone Company was the largest independent company in the Pittsburgh, Pennsylvania, area in 1910—but it shared the region's independent markets with 11 other companies, each specializing to some of the 120 distinct political units in the vicinity. This pattern occurred throughout the United States, so that a good predictor of the number of telephone companies in a state was its number of incorporated places as illustrated in Figure 13-2.

Finding so many different organizations leads naturally to another question: What were the organizational forms that developed in the industry? The idea here is that while all organizations are idiosyncratic in many ways, it is helpful to categorize organizations into groupings according to general similarities that make them operate alike in similar parts of the environment. In this case, two general organizational forms appeared among the thousands of early indepen-

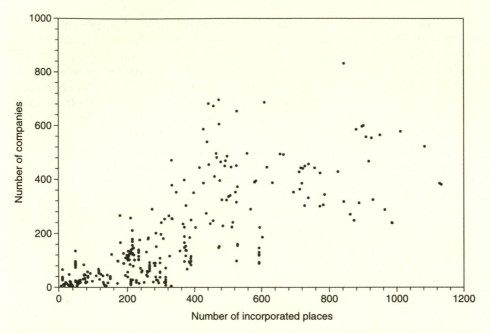

Figure 13–2 Political differentiation and telephone companies. (*Source:* Author's analysis.)

dent companies: cooperatively run *mutual companies,* including a large number of lines run by farmers, and for-profit *commercial firms.*

The mutual companies usually operated in rural areas, benefitting from the loyalty and volunteerism of locals who were often suspicious of large companies, especially Bell (Atwood 1984). For example, in 1900 residents in and around Marengo and Ladora, two towns in rural southeastern Iowa, could solicit telephone service from several commercial telephone companies in Iowa county. However, over 100 residents instead purchased shares in a new cooperative venture, the Iowa County Mutual Telephone Company. Staying in rural areas where distrust of commercial ventures was strong, the company supported only about five telephones per pole mile. Yet by relying largely on voluntary labor and the capital of members it grew modestly and continued to operate in the area for years to come.

By comparison, commercial telephone firms usually located in more densely populated areas and were professionally managed. The Marengo Telephone Company was founded in 1901, one year after Iowa County Mutual and in the same general area. Although it began with only ninety subscribers, the Marengo company grew rapidly by serving townsfolk, with a system supporting double the number of instruments per pole mile than Iowa County Mutual. In this way, the mutual and commercial forms operated in distinct *niches* for which each was particularly well suited.

Once one attends to differences between organizational forms, other patterns become easier to see, since different organizational forms tend to pursue different *strategies*. In this case, mutual companies were not well suited to growth, since they lacked professional management and the more sophisticated technical know-how that growth would require. But they were quick to establish. Thus this form expanded its service area by proliferating in numbers—an appropriate strategy given the scattered, disparate nature of the rural communities that comprised the mutuals' niche. Meanwhile, the commercial firms tended to grow in size individually—again a fit strategy considering the more populated areas they inhabited.

All this talk of niches would be fine for many other kinds of organizations, one might say, but how could telephone companies provide service when they were limited to particular communities? After all, a telephone system that does not reach out of town would not be of much use. The answer, it turns out, was that the independents often connected their lines to one another, forming loosely organized networks of interconnected systems. Typically, several mutual companies would connect to a commercial firm, which in turn would be connected to other commercials and possibly to a long-distance network—or maybe to Bell (Atwood 1984).

For any individual telephone company, connecting to neighboring companies was done on a case-by-case basis rather than as part of some grand strategy. Consequently these networks were poorly coordinated, leaving islands of isolated subscribers disconnected from the wider world—a situation often made worse when feuding companies reneged on connection arrangements. Yet in the aggregate, the thousands of effective connections among companies turned out to be of great strategic importance. Because of these connections, the fates of companies within common networks became linked in a positive way, so that an organization's viability was increased as its partners expanded and prospered. This kind of relationship, known as *mutualism*, can be thought of as the opposite of competition.

Viewed from the organization level, mutualism usually is seen as something that benefits individual companies: "linked" organizations are better off than "unlinked" organizations. Ecologists take mutualism a step further, however, noting that it gives rise to *organizational communities*—collectives of organizations that share a common fate because they work together. Organizational communities are important strategically because they shift the level where natural selection occurs. Individual companies within such communities become less vulnerable to exogenous factors, since mutualism helps them survive hard times.

Instead, selection shifts more to the community level, so that success or failure occurs not so much for isolated organizations as for entire networks. Consequently, whether an individual company succeeded or failed increasingly depended on whether it was part of a larger network of companies that, in turn, succeeded or failed in competition with other such networks. In this light, it is no coincidence that the Marengo Telephone Company and the Iowa County Mutual Telephone Company, along with several dozen other companies, all were founded at about the same time and place and continued to survive alongside one another: they were separate companies, but as an organizational community they shared a common fate.

It is important to keep in mind that these organizational communities were not understood to be formal alliances among large numbers of companies. Indeed, archival records suggest that those who managed these companies typically were aware only of the few firms to which they connected directly, not the hundreds of other companies that may also have been within their wider networks. Neither, then, would they have been aware of community-level regularities in performance. Rather, patterns of success and failure probably appeared chaotic to those in the trenches, where managers of independent companies usually saw neighboring companies as rivals—working with one another out of necessity while squabbling more often than not (Atwood 1984). It is only with the bird's-eye-view of the analyst that we detect patterns at the community level that likely seemed random to any particular strategist.

Meanwhile, the Bell System did not sit by while its market share plummeted. To the contrary, Bell responded by refusing to sell equipment to the independents at any price. (In rural areas, in fact, it was not unusual to see fence wire used for telephone lines!) As fast as it could, Bell moved into direct price competition with the independents wherever it stood even a remote chance of regaining market share, and practically any tactic was considered fair game if it would beat the independents. This meant acquiring pesky rivals, of course, but even included such tactics as operating "independent" companies that were secretly owned by Bell (Fischer 1992).

Although these tactics slowed the independents' surge, they forced Bell to operate unprofitably in many areas while serving to reinforce Bell's onerous reputation. So it was that when J. P. Morgan led a group of bankers to take over the Bell System in 1907, Theodore Vail—once the mastermind behind the initial Bell expansion—was returned to Bell's helm. Vail immediately changed Bell's strategy to one of systems awareness in which Bell aggressively acquired large independent companies. Meanwhile, Bell also shifted its treatment of small independent companies, connecting with and supporting them in order to place the large independents in a competitive squeeze.

Altogether, the period up to 1913 saw the development of a collectively formidable, although fragmented, independent telephone movement facing an aggressive, predatory Bell System. With this stage set, changes then unfolded very quickly over the next few years—but in some entirely unexpected ways.

1913–21: COLLECTIVE STAGNATION

It is difficult, in hindsight, to see the independents as anything but underdogs in their battle with Bell. As the struggle climaxed, however, several forces were pushing strongly in favor of the independents. Distress over Bell's predatory behavior spread from the populists to the growing "progressive" political movement of the times. More generally, concern was widespread that the U.S. telephone system was becoming impossibly fragmented. Consequently, from 1904 to 1919, thirty-four states passed laws requiring neighboring companies to connect their lines. We found that these laws increased mutualism among the independent companies while reducing the strength of competition from Bell.

Meanwhile, the federal government also reacted to the anti-Bell wave with the Department of Justice preparing to investigate possible antitrust violations by the company. To head off this investigation, Bell agreed in 1913 to what would become known as the *Kingsbury commitment* with the U.S. attorney general. In this, Bell agreed to stop acquiring directly competing independent companies and to allow toll connections to the independents at a reasonable rate. All in all, by 1913 the independent movement was supported by a range of powerful institutional measures.

Around the same time, technologies appeared that also increased the potential for coordination among the independents. The first independent companies used magneto instruments. This name refers to the hand-cranked magneto that supplied ringing current, but the more important characteristic of these instruments was the use of a separate battery in each instrument to power sound transmission. Because of this decentralized power supply, systems using these instruments suffered serious problems of incompatibility and poor maintenance. By 1915, however, independent companies were adopting the common-battery-power technology, which featured an organizationally controlled power source housed in a central office or switchboard. By ensuring proper maintenance and a uniform standard in power supply, the common battery helped greatly in the coordination of the independent movement. Meanwhile, a technology known as line loading also was spreading among the independents. This technology increased the range of a telephone central office from 30 miles to 300 miles, permitting the development of long-distance companies within the independent movement.

These technical developments dramatically increased the potential for mutualism among the independent companies. Smaller, single-exchange systems and the larger, multiexchange systems worked together as complements—at least so long as they all adopted common-battery systems. As a result, these organizations increased one another's growth rates while decreasing one another's failure rates. Thus the new technologies gave the loose affiliations of commercial and mutual companies the potential to compose smoothly functioning, viable networks capable of large-scale operation.

It is important to emphasize the community-level logic here. These technologies did not aid the independents by making individual companies technically superior so that they could break from their fellow independents and compete on their own. In fact, we found that head-on competition among the most technically sophisticated independents did more harm than good to these companies. On the one hand, having the most sophisticated technologies would reduce a company's failure rate by 94 percent, but head-on competition from other sophisticated companies more than offset this advantage, with the net effect actually doubling failure rates on average. Rather, the benefits from these technologies came from allowing organizations to coordinate their systems with one another—a gain not so much for any single company as for entire networks of standardized, complementary organizations.

Despite the institutional supports and technical developments, however, the independent telephone movement stopped growing after about 1913, losing ground in terms of the numbers of companies as well as market share. Why?

The answer, it appears, is found in the very same forces that were expected to bring success to the independents. The evidence suggests that both the institutional and technical developments of the time seriously (albeit unintendedly) harmed the independent movement.

On the institutional side, after celebrating Bell's retreat under the Kingsbury commitment, the independent companies then turned their attention to competing ferociously with one another. Our results show that this increase in competition was strong—powerful enough to turn what was a mutualistic relationship among the independents into a competitive one. This is a specific example of a more general process known as *competitive release,* where organizations relieved of rivalry from one source increase the strength of their competition with others. Given that the independents relied—even if unknowingly—on collective success, this competitive release was extremely damaging to the movement.

If that was not bad enough, the movement also became seriously fragmented technologically during this period, which may seem surprising, given all that was just said about new technical developments that could aid coordination. Many students assume that the various organizations involved would behave rationally and adopt the technologies that would bring them success. Ecologists are more skeptical about making such a jump from a rational prescription to an expectation about what really goes on in organizational life. In the case of the telephone industry, this skepticism seems to have been well-founded for two reasons.

First, although many companies did attempt to change technologies—adopting line loading and common-battery power—this attempt to change often caused them to fail. This result is a specific case of a more general process, where change disrupts reliable organizational functioning. According to *structural inertia* theory, changing organizations must develop new capabilities, new roles for members to fill, new routines to coordinate behavior, new formal and informal structural arrangements, and new ties to different suppliers and other social actors in the environment. In sum, by changing, these telephone companies became as vulnerable to failure as a new firm.

For example, the Blairsville Telephone Company in Pennsylvania was founded in 1896, and it had grown to nearly 1,000 subscribers by 1925. It then made an apparently sensible strategic move, adopting common-battery technology. The adjustment to the new technology proved to be too difficult, however, and within two years the Blairsville telephone company failed.

More broadly, the study found that these companies doubled their failure rates, on average, due to the disruption caused when they adopted more advanced technologies. Figure 13-3 illustrates this result in terms of the multiplicative effect that change had on failure rates. It also illustrates, however, that these organizations recovered from the shock of having changed technologies—if they did not die first—after about sixteen years on average. It took that long to restore these organizations to the level of functioning and institutional support that they knew before the change.

Second, despite these new technologies, large numbers of primitive, magneto companies entered the industry during this period. It would be difficult to

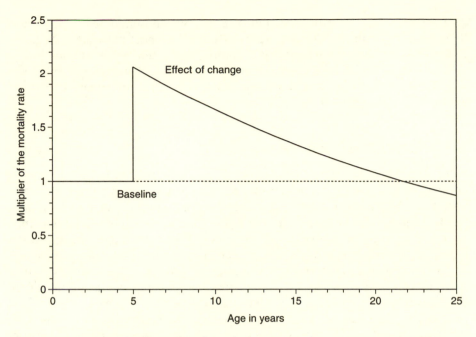

Figure 13–3 Estimated effect of technical change on the organizational failure rate. (*Source:* Author's analysis.)

make sense of this situation if we think of these foundings as the calculated acts of fully rational entrepreneurs. However, if we view the entrepreneur as constrained by existing social and economic conditions, this surge of new magneto firms is less surprising. The new technologies and the know-how to operate them were not commonplace, nor was the needed financial support in many areas. Thus telephone entrepreneurs, no doubt encouraged by Bell's surrender under Kingsbury, mustered whatever primitive resources were available and entered the industry.

With the flood of these magneto companies, the independent movement became increasingly fragmented. Although individually harmless, these small, often incompatible companies collectively crippled the movement, increasing failure and decreasing growth rates for all independent companies. In fact, these effects were so powerful that they more than offset the benefits that had been gained by those parts of the movement that had adopted the new technologies.

While the independent movement was collectively stagnating, Bell was busily expanding into latent markets all over the United States. As Bell grew, it occupied more and more of the potential telephone market, reducing the growth rate of the independent movement. At the same time, Bell took a highly visible role as a patriotic institution during World War I—a move that built public confidence in Bell at the same time the independents were being blamed for ongoing problems with the coordination of the nation's telephone system. Fairly or unfairly, the independents were then roundly blamed when telephone rates skyrocketed at the end of the war as price controls were lifted. (The industry was nominally nationalized in 1918–19, but this amounted to little more than price regulation.) With the winds of public support blowing in its favor, Bell was freed from its Kingsbury commitment by the Willis-Graham Act of 1921, which exempted the telephone industry from antitrust review. What was to have been the heyday of the independent telephone movement ended dismally, with Bell again on the offensive.

1921–33: CONCENTRATION

After 1921, the independent movement continued to lose market share, and the number of companies fell as the independent market became more concentrated. These trends, it turns out, resulted in part from the aging of the independent telephone population. By the 1920s, independent telephone companies were, on average, older than at any time in the past. With age, organizational growth rates tend to fall (other things being equal), since both an organization's internal potential and external opportunities for growth are depleted over time.

Furthermore, increasing ages imply that the existing organizations of the 1920s were survivors—they were the ones that endured even as their fellow companies were failing. Thus the telephone companies of the 1920s were stronger competitors on average. As such, they were more capable of harming one another than had been the case in earlier eras. Consequently, the 1920s saw founding rates fall, failure rates increase, and growth rates flatten—a pattern that seems to result generally when organizational populations mature.

Bell's expansion remained steady and rapid. Although Bell and most other companies declined slightly in size at the onset of the Depression, Bell clearly had risen to its position of dominance in the industry by 1933, when active national regulation began under the Federal Communications Commission (FCC). Through several decades of relative stability, Bell would then be known as the nation's telephone company, even as several thousand independent telephone companies continued to exist as regulated monopolists in various locations throughout the United States.

CONCLUSION

Today, the U.S. telecommunications industry again is an arena where new firms and new strategies are experimenting, succeeding and failing. Although it is still too early to know how the current era will evolve, students may find it valuable to conduct an ecological analysis of the modern telecommunications industry or one of its major sectors using the ideas developed in this and other chapters. (For an example, see Barnett 1993b.) In doing so, it may help to structure your investigation by asking: What are the segregating mechanisms that shape competition in the industry or sector? What organizational forms have appeared? What are their strategies? Where are their niches? Are any organizational forms complementary, so that you would expect to see mutualism between them? Do organizational communities exist? Are any forms sufficiently protected from competition that you expect to see competitive release? What strategic changes are firms attempting? What will happen to these changing organizations? As you ask these questions, make predictions about how the population dynamics of the industry would look if you were right. Seek out data about the industry to see whether your analysis appears to be correct.

BIBLIOGRAPHY

Atwood, Roy. 1984. "Telephony and Its Cultural Meanings in Southeastern Iowa, 1900–1917." Unpublished Ph.D. dissertation, University of Iowa.

Barnett, William P. 1990. "The Organizational Ecology of a Technological System." *Administrative Science Quarterly* 35:31–60.

Barnett, William P. 1993a. "The Liability of Collective Action: Growth and Change Among Early American Telephone Companies." In J. Baum and J. Singh (eds.), *Evolutionary Dynamics of Organizations*. New York: Oxford.

Barnett, William P. 1993b. "Strategic Deterrence Among Multipoint Competitors." *Industrial and Corporate Change* 2:249–78.

Barnett, William P. 1993c. "The Dynamics of Competitive Intensity." Working paper, Graduate School of Business, Stanford University.

Barnett, William P., and Terry L. Amburgey. 1990. "Do Larger Organizations Generate Stronger Competition?" In J. Singh (ed.), *Organizational Evolution: New Directions*. Beverly Hills: Sage.

Barnett, William P., and Glenn R. Carroll. 1987. "Competition and Mutualism Among Early Telephone Companies." *Administrative Science Quarterly* 32:400–21.

Barnett, William P., and Glenn R. Carroll. 1993. "How Institutional Constraints Affected the Organization of Early American Telephony." *Journal of Law, Economics and Organization* 9:98–126.

Brock, Gerald W. 1981. *The Telecommunications Industry*. Cambridge, MA: Harvard University Press.

Brooks, John. 1976. *Telephone: The First Hundred Years*. New York: Harper & Row.

Danielian, Noobar R. 1939. *AT&T: The Story of Industrial Conquest*. New York: Vanguard.

DuMoncel, Theodore A. L. 1879 (1974 trans.). *The Telephone, Microphone and the Phonograph*. New York: Arno Press.

Federal Communications Commission. 1938. *Proposed Report: Telephone Investigation*. Washington, DC: Government Printing Office.

Fischer, Claude S. 1992. *America Calling: A Social History of the Telephone to 1940*. Berkeley: University of California Press.

Fischer, Claude S., and Glenn R. Carroll. 1988. "Telephone and Automobile Diffusion in the United States, 1902–1937." *American Journal of Sociology* 93:1153–78.

Gabel, Richard. 1969. "The Early Competitive Era in Telephone Communications, 1893–1920." *Law and Contemporary Problems* 34:340–59.

MacMeal, Harry B. 1934. *The Story of Independent Telephony*. Chicago: Independent Pioneer Telephone Association.

Phillips, Charles F., Jr. 1985. *The Regulation of Public Utilities: Theory and Practice*. Arlington, VA: Public Utilities Reports, Inc.

Schlesinger, Leonard A., David Dyer, Thomas N. Clough, and Diane Landau. 1987. *Chronicles of Corporate Change: Management Lessons from AT&T and Its Offspring*. Lexington, MA: Lexington Books.

Wasserman, Neil. 1985. *From Invention to Innovation: Long Distance Telephone Transmission at the Turn of the Century*. Baltimore: Johns Hopkins University Press.

14

Investment Banks

JOEL PODOLNY

Stated broadly, the business or function of investment banks in the primary securities markets is to reduce the transaction costs associated with market exchanges, where transaction costs can be defined roughly as the costs of "getting together" issuers and investors.[1] Issuers and investors confront considerable uncertainty in these markets. Since no issuers and few investors are always in the primary capital markets looking for exchange partners, both sets of actors potentially face the difficult problem of locating actors from the other side of the market with whom to trade. Even if issuers and investors can identify potential exchange partners, issuers face uncertainty about the nature of the demand on the investors' side, and investors confront uncertainty regarding the financial soundness of the issuers. Rather than searching for actors from the other side of the capital market and establishing a price themselves, issuers and investors seek and are sought by investment banks that maintain an essentially permanent presence in the market.

The fee that a bank earns for fulfilling this function is the difference between the price that the bank pays the issuer for the securities and the price at which the banks sells the securities to investors. This fee is referred to as the *spread*. A variety of factors—most importantly, the size of the offering or risk associated with the placement—affect whether or not the spread is especially large or small, but underwriting spreads typically range from one tenth of 1 percent of the dollar value of the offering to about 4 percent of the value.

There are two general classes of corporate securities that investment banks underwrite in the primary securities markets: equity and debt. A purchaser of equity gains stock, or an ownership stake, in the corporation and a share of the profits of the firm. A purchaser of debt acquires a bond that specifies terms of repayment for an initial loan to the corporation. There are two types of offerings within each of these two broad classes. Equity is divided into initial public offerings (IPOs) and common stock offerings. An IPO is a company's first sale of stock to the public; a common stock offering is a sale of equity by a publicly traded firm that by definition has previously had its initial public offering. Debt is divided into investment-grade securities, which may be colloquially referred to as "vanilla" debt, and noninvestment-grade securities, which may be labeled high-yield or "junk" debt. What distinguishes investment-grade debt from non-investment-grade debt is the risk that the issuing corporation will default on the loan repayment to the bondholder. This risk is determined by the major bond ratings agencies: Moody's and Standard and Poor's.

Investment banks reduce the uncertainty confronted by actors in these four primary markets through two interrelated activities. First, they develop an extensive network of relations to issuers, investors, and even other investment banks. Second, they cultivate a distinct status vis-à-vis their competitors, which provides a tangible foundation for the rational calculations of potential exchange partners. We shall consider each of these activities in turn.

Strong and varied connections to a relatively large number of issuers and investors, a state sometimes referred to by industry participants as "being in the deal stream," provide the bank with intimate knowledge of supply and demand in the market (Eccles and Crane 1988). The greater this knowledge, the better the investment bank can take on a role approximating that of the mythical Walrasian auctioneer, finding possible exchange partners and setting a market-clearing price for the issue.

In addition to cultivating an extensive network of relations with investors and issuers, investment banks also form extensive ties to one another through participation in syndicates, a collection of banks that jointly underwrite a security offering. Despite intense competition among investment banks for the opportunity to lead a security offering, the selected bank will invariably not underwrite the entire offering itself. Rather, it will form and lead a syndicate. The leader of the syndicate is referred to as the lead manager. Either by itself or with the assistance of one or several banks who receive the title of co-managers, the lead manager determines the composition of the syndicate and the proportion of securities to be allocated to each syndicate member. Occasionally an issuer will request that a manager include a particular bank or set of banks as comanager(s) on an issue because of some connection between the issuer and the chosen comanager, such as common regional affiliation or prior business dealings; however, the choice of comanager is usually at the discretion of the lead manager. In addition to assisting with the allocation of securities among syndicate members, comanagers may also assist the lead manager by helping to "make a market" for the security once the initial distribution is completed and subsequently traded in secondary markets. To "make a market" for a security is to announce a price at which the bank is willing to buy the security and a price at which it is willing to sell the security to ensure the security's liquidity.

Not all banks depend equally on syndicates for the initial distribution of the security in the primary markets and the subsequent trading of the security among investors in the secondary markets. Indeed, a particularly salient dimension along which banks differ in organizational form is the degree to which they depend on ties internal or external to the firm for the distribution and trading of the security. Among the more notable banks during the 1980s, Morgan Stanley was at one extreme in that its connections to investors were mediated externally by large syndicates. As it had done since the turn of the century, Morgan Stanley relied almost exclusively on these syndicates for distribution and trading in secondary markets. At the other extreme during the 1980s were Merrill Lynch, which internalized the ties to the investor side of the market through the development of an extensive in-house sales network, and Salomon Brothers, which internalized connections through the development of a vast trading force. These firms with internalized networks of exchange relations still use syndicates, but their extensive internal resources allow them to rely on smaller syndicates or to underwrite a moderately sized offering alone if the need arises.

It is noteworthy that there is considerable variance among the leading firms in the degree to which they rely on internal versus external ties, and there is considerable variance among the internalized firms in their reliance on a vast trading force or sales force. All of the leading firms in the industry are generalists, competing in each of the primary securities markets for essentially the same clients, and yet competitive pressures do not seem to engender conformity among the leaders in organizational form.

So far, we have observed that a bank reduces its own uncertainty about market conditions through the formation of ties to other actors in the market. As noted, such ties are crucial to the knowledge of supply and demand for particular securities. Yet, also as noted, the performance and survival of a bank is contingent not on the reduction of its own uncertainty about market conditions, but on its ability to reduce the uncertainty or risk that permeates the decisions of other actors in the market. Issuers and investors confront considerable risk in their selection of an investment bank. The issuer depends on the bank for advice regarding the optimum price for the particular security. If the price is too low, the issuer will not receive as much capital for the offering as it otherwise could have. If the price is too high, the issuer will still receive all of the capital from the investment bank or syndicate for the security, but a quick fall in the value of the security will anger investors and make them fearful of investing in, and thus providing money to, the issuer in the future. The issuer is also at risk because the success of the offering depends not only on the bank's pricing ability, but also on its ability to place the security. If the security is not adequately distributed to a sufficiently large number of investors and if the bank does not facilitate the trading of the securities in the secondary markets, the price of the security will decline, and again investors will be much more hesitant to direct financial resources to the company in the future.

Investors are obviously at risk because they are in effect betting on the future performance of the company and the security. They depend on the investment bank's ability first to discriminate between good and bad investments and second to place the offering and support the subsequent trading of the security.

Finally, it should be noted that potential syndicate members also confront uncertainty similar to that faced by the investors. They depend on a lead manager's ability to select offerings for which there is sufficient demand that they can be placed. Thus a lead manager confronts three potential constituencies, each of which faces some uncertainty in its decision to enter into an exchange relationship with the lead manager. A bank seeks to reduce the uncertainty of these constituencies through the formation of a distinct identity or status vis-à-vis the other banks.

STATUS DETERMINATION

Part of the bank's status is determined by the bank's performance in underwriting the securities. Banks that demonstrate superior competence in the underwriting function will be regarded as higher in status than banks that do not demonstrate this superior competence. However, past performance is often difficult to evaluate. Market participants can engage in considerable speculation over such questions as whether a bank might have underwritten an offering at terms more favorable to the issuer or whether problems encountered in an offering were due more to factors within a bank's control than to factors outside of the bank's control. Moreover, industry participants and observers regard the investment banking arena as an extremely dynamic and even volatile environment. As a result, the connection between past performance and present ability is often considered quite tenuous. There is invariably a loose linkage between a bank's status and the qualities or attributes for which that status might be regarded as a signal.

On account of that loose linkage, a bank's status is not only a function of the bank's performance but a function of the relational position that a bank cultivates in the market. Investment bankers are extremely concerned about the identity of actors with whom their bank is associated because such associations affect how the bank is perceived. Probably the clearest evidence of such a concern comes from a consideration of *tombstone advertisements,* announcements of security offerings that appear in the major financial publications such as the *Wall Street Journal, Institutional Investor,* and *Investment Dealer's Digest.* Figure 14-1 presents an example of such an advertisement.

Around the beginning of the twentieth century, such advertisements existed to inform investors of the existence of a new security offering. However, since the emergence of an electronically integrated market, such advertisements no longer serve this function. The major investors are aware of an offering within minutes of its release, and such advertisements typically appear the day after the offering. Therefore, the primary function of these advertisements is no longer to notify investors of a recently issued security. Rather, as several scholars have noted, such advertisements serve to clarify and reinforce the status distinctions among the banks (Hayes 1971, 1979; Eccles and Crane 1988; Chenrow 1990; Podolny 1993).

There are well-defined norms for the allocation of banks to positions on the tombstone. The highest-status position in the tombstone is the one that is the uppermost and furthest to the left. This position is always occupied by the lead manager of the syndicate. Salomon Brothers is the lead manager in Figure 14-1. If there is one comanager for an offering, that comanager is invariably listed to the right of the lead manager. Merrill Lynch is the comanager for the Chrys-

New Issue / February 13, 1985

$100,000,000

CHRYSLER
FINANCIAL CORPORATION

12⅛% Subordinated Notes due February 15, 1990

Price 100% and accrued interest from February 15, 1985

Copies of the Prospectus Supplement and the related Prospectus may be obtained
in any State in which this announcement is circulated only from such of the
undersigned as may legally offer these securities in such State.

Salomon Brothers Inc	**Merrill Lynch Capital Markets**

The First Boston Corporation	**Goldman, Sachs & Co.**

Lehman Brothers Shearson Lehman/American Express Inc.		**Morgan Stanley & Co.** Incorporated
ABD Securities Corporation	**Bear, Stearns & Co.**	**Alex. Brown & Sons** Incorporated
Deutsche Bank Capital Corporation	**Dillon, Read & Co. Inc.**	**Donaldson, Lufkin & Jenrette** Securities Corporation
Drexel Burnham Lambert Incorporated		**EuroPartners Securities Corporation**
E. F. Hutton & Company Inc.	**Kidder, Peabody & Co.** Incorporated	**Lazard Frères & Co.**
PaineWebber Incorporated	**Prudential-Bache** Securities	**L. F. Rothschild, Unterberg, Towbin**
Smith Barney, Harris Upham & Co. Incorporated		**Swiss Bank Corporation International** Securities Inc.
UBS Securities Inc.	**Wertheim & Co., Inc.**	**Dean Witter Reynolds Inc.**

American Securities Corporation	**Daiwa Securities America Inc.**

A. G. Edwards & Sons, Inc.	**Interstate Securities Corporation**	**McDonald & Company** Securities, Inc.
Moseley, Hallgarten, Estabrook & Weeden Inc.		**The Nikko Securities Co.** International, Inc.
Nomura Securities International, Inc.		**Thomson McKinnon Securities Inc.**
Tucker, Anthony & R. L. Day, Inc.		**Yamaichi International (America), Inc.**

Figure 14–1 Example of a tombstone advertisement. (*Source: Investment Dealers Digest* 1985. Copyright © 1985 by Salomon Bros. Inc. Used by permission.)

ler offering. If there is more than one comanager, they will be arranged beneath the lead manager.

Following the comanager(s) are the rest of the banks in the syndicate arranged hierarchically into brackets; the higher the bracket, the more prestigious the position. The number of brackets varies, depending primarily on the number of banks. There may be as few as one or as many as ten.

The highest bracket on many ads is labeled the *bulge bracket* or *special bracket* because its members' names historically have appeared in larger typeface than the names of banks in the lower brackets. The bulge-bracket firms invariably included the five or six highest-status firms in the industry. Over the period of the 1980s, the bulge-bracket firms were Morgan Stanley, First Boston Corporation, Goldman Sachs, Salomon Brothers, and Merrill Lynch.

Banks are listed alphabetically within each bracket. For example, in Figure 14-1, the first bracket begins with The First Boston Corporation and ends with Morgan Stanley. ABD Securities Corporation is the first bank listed in the second bracket, and Dean Witter Reynolds is the last bank in this bracket.[2] Finally, the third bracket begins with American Securities Corporation and ends with Yamaichi International (America), Inc. There are, therefore, no formally designated status distinctions within brackets. However, the fact that banks are listed alphabetically to downplay any possible status distinctions within brackets does not mean that there is a complete absence of such subtle distinctions. For example, at least during the early and mid-1980s, Merrill Lynch was considered a special-bracket firm, but it was typically regarded as being slightly lower in status than other banks in the special bracket, as suggested by an article revealingly entitled "Will the Sun Ever Shine on Merrill's Investment Bankers?" (Kadlec 1986).

If such informal differences become sufficiently acknowledged, then a bank's typical bracket position will change to reflect its change in status. Even out-of-order brackets exist for the one or two banks in a syndicate that occupy an intermediate status between two relatively large brackets of banks. There may be minor fluctuations in a bank's bracket position between underwritings that are not due to changes in status, but to the fact that a bank obtains an unusually large or small share of an offering for some idiosyncratic reasons, such as a regional connection between the bank and the issuer. For example, in Figure 14-1, Lehman Brothers appears with the special-bracket firms in a position that is slightly higher than is typical. As recently as the mid-1970s, such shifts due to volume were extremely infrequent; however,they became much more common throughout the late 1970s and early 1980s. Nevertheless, these fluctuations are invariably limited to one bracket higher or lower than the bank's typical position in the advertisement.

Position in the tombstones is not a trivial matter. There are economic advantages associated with bracket position; the higher a bank's bracket, the greater the share of an offering that is allocated to the bank to underwrite. Nevertheless, concern with position extends beyond the desire to obtain a large share of the offering. A bank's concern with the status associated with a tombstone position is sufficiently great that it will withdraw from an offering if it is given a position in the syndicate and thus a place on the tombstone that the bank managers believe to be incommensurate with the bank's status. For example, in a 1985 offering for which it was lead manager, Goldman Sachs sought to divide the bracket directly beneath the bulge bracket into two distinct brackets. However, nine of the firms that would have ended up in the lower division refused to participate in the offering (Monroe 1986). Similarly, in 1987 five high-status firms refused to participate in a $2.4 billion financing for the Farmers Home Administration when thirteen regional, small minority-owned firms were to receive a larger share of the offering and thus a higher place on the tombstone (*New York Times*, Sept. 21, 1987). In both of these examples, banks preferred to withdraw from the deals rather than accept a tombstone position they felt to be diminutive.

Since a bank's underwriting ability is a function of its presence in the "deal stream" and since participation in syndicates is one of the ways that a bank can more accurately assess the supply and demand for particular securities, such a refusal to appear in a syndicate underscores the tension between activity that is conducive to the better performance of the bank and behavior that enhances or at least preserves the status of the bank. While underwriting ability and status ought be positively correlated, the relational components of status and market knowledge occasionally force a bank to sacrifice an improvement in one for enhancement of the other.

Just like for bracket positions beneath them, manager and comanager positions on an offering are desired not simply for the economic rewards that they bring but for the status entailed by their occupancy. For example, from at least the turn of the century until late in the 1970s, Morgan Stanley was generally regarded as the flagship firm of the investment banking industry. Even the other special-bracket firms were not considered to be close to Morgan Stanley in status. Consistent with such an image, Morgan Stanley not only refused to accept any position on the tombstone less than that of the lead management position but also refused to accede to a given issuer's request to allow any comanagers on the offering.

To preserve its policy, Morgan Stanley would forego what could be quite lucrative business opportunities from such potential corporate clients as Houston Industries and Singer and even from such political entities as the government of Japan (Chenrow 1990). The test of the policy came in 1979 when IBM, one of the world's largest corporations and a client of twenty years, requested that Morgan Stanley accept Salomon Brothers as comanager on a $1 billion debt issue. Morgan Stanley was to receive approximately $1 billion for leading this issue; however, Morgan Stanley refused to accept Salomon Brothers as comanager. IBM responded by not only using Salomon Brothers as the sole manager for that particular issue but also by relying primarily on that firm for its subsequent issues throughout the 1980s. Following the confrontation with IBM, Morgan Stanley gradually revised its policy.

This preoccupation with tombstone position is simply a particular manifestation of a bank's more general concern with the identity of those actors with whom the bank is associated. Journalistic accounts will highlight the prestige that accrues to a rising bank when it occupies a management or comanagement position on an offering that would typically only be managed by one of the special-bracket firms. For example, a 1976 *Forbes* article on the investment banking firm Bache Halsey Stuart (later to become Prudential Bache Securities) noted that, "On May 18, American Telephone & Telegraph announced that Bache Halsey Stuart would comanage its huge 12-million-share offering scheduled for June 16. In cracking AT&T's traditionally exclusive fraternity of investment bankers—Morgan Stanley, Goldman Sachs, Merrill Lynch, and Salomon Brothers—Bache gained new status" (*Forbes* 1976).

Such articles are notable not only because they further underscore the importance that bankers ascribe to status but because they highlight the relational underpinnings of status. Status comes not just from performance or underwriting volume but from association with others of a given status, as suggested by the reference in the *Forbes* article to AT&T's "exclusive fraternity of bankers." For Bache Halsey Stuart, a client as prominent as AT&T reflected positively on the firm. Conversely, for a bank to be in a bracket position lower than its status reflects negatively on that bank.

From the perspective of the bank, status carries with it considerable economic advantages. The first economic advantage is suggested by an observation offered by the head of a middle-sized investment banking firm:

> Typically if you hear that Goldman Sachs or Salomon or whatever is doing an underwriting, they usually have pretty stringent requirements, and it is usually a plus for the company that they are doing work for that Goldman Sachs wants to be their investment banker or underwrite or whatever, [that is], a plus with reference to the market place. Half the time, if Goldman Sachs calls or Salomon calls us and says we are going to be an underwrite for Ford Motor or whatever and asks, "Do you want to be part of the underwriting group?" we almost don't have to do any diligence; you just say yes. On the other hand, if a smaller firm which just doesn't have the credentials calls us, we will probably do more diligence and will probably be less likely to follow suit.[3]

This investment banker points to an inverse relationship between the status of a bank and the transaction costs associated with facilitating the exchange between issuer and investors. The higher the status of the bank, the easier and hence less costly for a bank to put together a syndicate for a given issue.

A higher-status firm not only realizes such advantages in its relations with syndicate members; it accrues them in its relations with investors as well. Just as the syndicate member is more likely to believe that an issue is of high quality because it is distributed by a high-status underwrite, so an investor is more likely to believe that an issue is of superior quality if it is underwritten by a higher-status firm than by a lower-status firm. Given that the primary function of an investment bank is to reduce the transaction costs associated with the placement of a security, such transaction cost advantages are quite significant.

Moreover, it can be argued that transaction advantages are not the only cost advantages of status. A second cost advantage that accrues from higher status is savings on advertisement expenditures. Higher-status banks receive more "free advertising" as a result of published inquiries from the business press. In the previously mentioned article, "Will the Sun Ever Shine on Merrill's Investment Bankers?," investment bankers from Merrill Lynch lamented the fact that though they had a larger market presence than several of the special-bracket firms, their lower status meant that they would frequently be ignored by the business press who sought advice from industry leaders on trends in the primary securities markets (Kadlec 1986).

A third type of lower costs that accrue from status is reduced labor costs. If an individual values the status of the institution for which she works, then she ought to be willing to exchange some monetary compensation for the benefits she derives from the status of the organization (Frank 1985). In other words, she ought to be willing to accept a less favorable compensation arrangement from a high-status firm than from a low-status firm. Note that such a willingness does not imply that high-status firms will pay lower salaries than low-status firms. On the contrary, if high-status firms can only maintain their status by hiring more skilled employees, then they ought to offer higher salaries; however, if the skill of the individual is taken as a given, then the higher-status firm ought to be able to employ the individual with a compensation arrangement that is more favorable to the firm. Merrill Lynch once again serves as an example. In seeking to recruit MBAs from top business schools, Merrill Lynch would have to offer more appealing compensation arrangements to potential recruits than would the other special-bracket firms to attract the same talent (Kadlec 1986).

Such a reduction in costs is nontrivial because the primary securities markets can be quite sensitive to price. Eccles and Crane (1988) comment that the phrase "loyalty" is a basis point" was particularly common among investment bankers in the 1980s. A basis point is .01 percent. Though this phrase was perhaps an exaggeration, the statement was a manifestation of investment bankers' strong belief that price was critical to an issuer's selection of an investment bank. Therefore, even if the status of a bank could reduce its costs by a few hundredths of a percent of the value of the offering, such a reduction could have a significant impact on the bank's ability to successfully bid for the opportunity to manage the offering of the firm.

STATUS AS A SEGREGATING FACTOR

So far, we have considered status as an attribute of individual banks. However, when considering the industry as a whole, it is possible to regard the status ordering as a structure that segregates the competition among the various banks. Because of the cost advantages of status, the higher-status bank is insulated from the competitive pressures of lower-status counterparts. Holding other factors constant, lower-status banks cannot outbid higher-status banks for the opportunity to manage a given offering. Of equal importance, just as the status ordering implies boundaries that cannot be permeated from below, so the relational nature of status implies boundaries that cannot be permeated from above. To the extent that higher-status firms seek to enter into exchange relations with issuers or investors at the lower end of the market, they will cease to be perceived as high status. Higher-status firms thus need to display a certain restraint in pursuing opportunities in the lower end of the market.

The general consequence is that banks come to adopt distinctive niches in the overall status ordering. Lower-status banks are effectively blocked out of the higher-status niches, and higher-status banks must avoid encroaching on the lower-status niches, or they will be perceived as lower status.

Thus, despite the cost and revenue advantages that accrue to the higher-status producers, market share in the underwriting markets over the 1980s was on average quite stable. Table 14-1 and Figure 14-2 depict information on market share and concentration in the markets for both investment-grade and non-

Table 14-1 Interyear Correlations in the Debt Markets, 1982–87

Investment-Grade Debt	Noninvestment-Grade ("Junk") Debt
.91	.87
(p = .0001)	(p = .0001)
N = 191	N = 393

Source: Securities Corporation Database.

investment-grade debt. Specifically, Table 14-1 lists the correlations of market share between years t and $t-1$ in the two debt markets from 1982 to 1987. In the investment-grade market, the correlation is 0.91, and in the noninvestment-grade market, the correlation is 0.87.

Figure 14-2 shows the market-level consequence of this correlation over market share at the firm level by depicting the Herfindahl Indices for these two markets over this period. The Herfindahl Index is a measure of market concentration; it is defined as the sum of squared market shares across producers in the market. The measure approaches zero as the market nears a perfectly competitive situation, with an infinite number of producers each possessing an infinitely small share of the market. At the other extreme, it approaches one as the market becomes a complete monopoly. The index reveals a rise in concentration in 1984 in both markets, but no consistent trend toward increasing monopolization in either market. In effect, the status ordering segments the market by impeding the direct competition of higher- and lower-status compet-

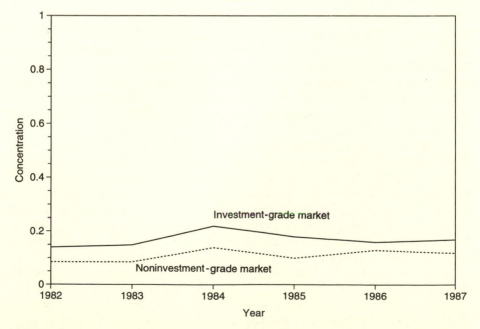

Figure 14-2 Herfindahl Indices for debt markets. (*Source:* Adapted from Podolny 1993. Copyright © by University of Chicago Press. Used by permission.)

itors. Market stability is thereby assured even given the economic advantages that accrue from status.

Though status can be regarded as a symbolic force underlying market competition, it is worth observing the relationship between the status ordering and the flow of resources to banks in the market. On the one hand, since the highest and lowest status banks participate in the same syndicates and thus underwrite the same securities, there is reason to conclude that there is an absence of strong resource partitioning in the investment banking community. On the other hand, if we consider that the higher-status firms find it easier to attract the more qualified individuals, and if we recognize that they gain greater access to investors and thus obtain a better knowledge of demand, it becomes clear that certain resources flow to the higher-status firms and do not flow to the lower-status firms. Status differences thus engender differences in how resources are distributed across firms.

One implication of this relationship between status and the flow of resources is that it reverses the conventional causal connection posited between status differences and quality differences. Typically, we think that quality differences cause status differences. But, if higher status makes it easier and less costly to attract talented bankers and prominent investors, then status differences engender or at least reproduce quality differences. Therefore, what may be falsely perceived as a difference in quality between two banks may actually become a valid distinction through a self-fulfilling prophecy.

UNCERTAINTY AND STATUS

I have argued that banks cultivate distinct status positions to reduce the uncertainty confronted by issuers and investors in the market. These identities provide a tangible foundation on which issuers and investors can make decisions in the primary securities markets. I have further argued that due to the difficulty inherent in observing true quality differences, status positions are relationally constructed, contingent upon a bank's pattern of associations in the markets.

To the extent that these claims are true, we ought to expect that higher-status banks will display greater restraint in an uncertain context than in a certain one. Specifically, the more risk confronted by issuers and investors, the more that status ought to rest on the relational position that banks confront in the market, and the more concerned that higher-status banks ought to be about using their cost advantages to expand into the lower ranges in the market. Some evidence consistent with this expectation comes from a comparison of the investment-grade and noninvestment-grade debt markets.

Using the data from 180 tombstone advertisements for investment-grade offerings and 101 tombstone advertisements for noninvestment-grade offerings that appeared in the *Wall Street Journal* throughout the 1981 calendar year, Podolny (1991, 1993) derived status scores for 170 banks that participated in the market for investment-grade debt and 171 banks that participated in the market for noninvestment-grade debt. Separate status rankings were con-

Table 14–2 Representative status scores from the investment-grade and noninvestment-grade debt markets

Bank	Investment-grade debt		Noninvestment-grade debt	
	Status score	Rank	Status score	Rank
Morgan Stanley	3.30879	1	3.99696	1
First Boston Corporation	3.03206	2	3.69273	2
Goldman Sachs	2.87465	3	2.58810	4
Merrill Lynch	2.84215	4	2.51190	5
Salomon Brothers	2.82667	5	2.42783	6
Lehman Brothers Kuhn Loeb	2.19846	6	2.31416	9
Prudential Bache Securities	2.09874	8	3.03846	3
Dean Witter Reynolds	2.04583	9	2.17970	14
Warburg Paribus Becker	2.02556	10	2.16743	20
Smith Barney Harris	2.01689	11	2.17789	17
Dillon Read	2.01074	12	2.17666	18
Bear Sterns	2.00232	13	2.26895	8
Kidder Peabody	1.99902	14	2.22815	10
Shearson	1.99621	15	2.17894	16
E.F. Hutton	1.99388	16	2.19418	11
Donaldson Lufkin Jenrette	1.98863	17	2.17939	16
Lazard Freres	1.98856	18	2.16955	19
Wertheim Securities	1.98685	19	2.18137	12
L.F. Rothschidh Unterberg	1.98629	20	2.18054	13
Drexel Burnham Lambert	1.98431	21	2.15789	21
Alex. Brown and Sons	1.07966	28	1.21547	25
Burns-Fry and Timmins	0.85649	50	0.80712	46
Nikko Securities	0.62842	80	0.72837	50
Sanford C. Bernstein and Co.	0.44116	100	0.49928	65
Cyrus J. Lawrence	0.34032	110	0.22257	100
Anderson & Strudwick	0.07925	150	0.00177	154
Thomas & Company	0.01166	162	0.01606	150

Source: Podolny (1991). Copyright © 1991 by Joel Podolny. Used by permission.

structed for each market because a bank's status in one primary security market need not be identical to its status in another, though the Spearman correlation for status scores in the two markets is extremely high, .96.

Representative status scores are listed in Table 14-2. It is notable that Drexel Burnham Lambert ranks twenty-first in status in the noninvestment-grade market despite being the innovator and volume leader of the market. This result, along with the high correlation in status scores, suggests that tombstone position for noninvestment-grade issues is influenced by the firm's reputation in the other markets. Such a carryover effect of reputation is not surprising given the newness of the high-yield market at the time. The first originating noninvestment-grade issue was underwritten in 1977, whereas the investment-grade debt market had existed since the turn of the century. Equally important, the low-status ranking of the volume leader alludes to a disjuncture between sheer volume and status.

Figure 14-3 shows how the offerings between 1982 and 1986 are distributed across the banks in both markets. Status percentiles are represented on the horizontal axis; the vertical or response axis denotes the cumulative percentage

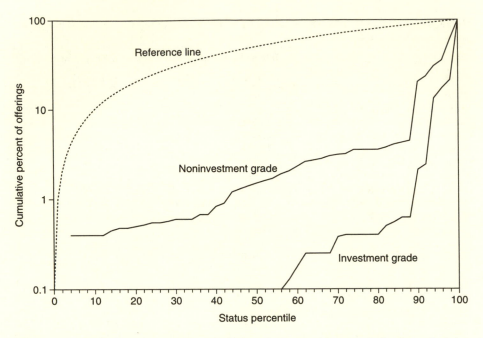

Figure 14–3 Cumulative percentage of offerings by status. (*Source:* Author's analysis.)

of deals (not dollars) lead-managed by the banks in the given percentile rank or lower. This response axis has been plotted on a natural logarithmic scale to better illustrate the distinctions in the lower and middle percentile ranks.[4] Therefore, the lines for both markets begin where the cumulative percentage of offerings is at least 0.1 percent. The dotted reference curve in each figure identifies the cumulative distribution that would occur if the number of deals were equally distributed across all the banks.

In both markets, we observe a significant divergence from this reference line; in neither market are more than 10 percent of the offerings underwritten by those banks below the eightieth percentile. Nevertheless, the figure illustrates that over the vast majority of the percentile distribution, the cumulative percent of offerings underwritten in the junk market at or beneath a given status percentile is at least several times greater than that in the investment-grade market. Hence, from the perspective of a given bank in the middle or lower range of the status order, the relative proportion of deals that seems available to it in the junk market is noticeably greater than in the investment-grade market even if the absolute proportion of deals that it lead-manages in one market is not significantly greater than the proportion that it lead-manages in the other.

Stated another way, the lower-status banks in the noninvestment-grade market occupy much smaller niches than the lower-status banks in the investment-grade market. Conversely, the higher-status banks occupy much larger niches in the investment-grade market than in the noninvestment-grade market. Therefore, while the status ordering is quite stable, the distribution of offerings across that ordering is quite different.

Such a difference is quite consistent with the expectation that higher-status banks ought to display greater restraint in a more uncertain context. Since junk debt is by definition at greater risk of default, there is much greater uncertainty about the future performance of a particular junk bond. Moreover, because the noninvestment-grade debt market had only been in existence since 1977, there is much greater uncertainty about the ultimate demand for securities in this market and thus about a bank's ability to place the security. Given the greater certainty about underlying quality, it seems reasonable to assume that status in the investment-grade market can be based more on observable differences than can status in the noninvestment-grade market. Conversely, status in the noninvestment-grade market must depend more on relational position because true quality differences are much more difficult to infer. Accordingly, the higher-status banks must be much more cautious about extending their presence into the lower end of the junk market since such an extension is a greater threat to identity in the more uncertain context.

CHANGES IN THE STATUS ORDERING

So far we have considered status only as a stabilizing force that segregates the competition in the industry. Yet, despite the stabilizing dynamics that we have considered, change obviously occurs in the investment banking industry. Some changes follow "exogenous shocks" resulting from the introduction of legislation. For example, one noteworthy piece of legislation in the 1980s was the Security and Exchange Commission's (SEC) Rule 415, which was instituted on a permanent basis in November 1983.

Prior to Rule 415, when a firm decided to issue a security, it had to undergo a lengthy registration and approval process with the SEC. However, under Rule 415, an experienced issuer could preregister with the SEC as much as two years prior to actually making an offering, wait for beneficial fluctuations in interest rates, and then call up one or several investment banks and request bids for the securities. Banks are expected to respond to the request for bids within the space of a few hours. Because the solicitation for bids under shelf-registration did not lend itself to an extensive consultation period between bank and issuer, shelf-registration undercut the formation of strong ties between investment banks and issuers, and it increased the degree to which investment banks competed on price.

Moreover, because investment banks needed to be able to place an offering at a competitive price within just a few hours, shelf-registration favored the firms that relied more on internal ties than external ties for the distribution and trading of securities, like Salomon Brothers or Merrill Lynch. Correspondingly, it disadvantaged firms that depended much more on external ties through syndicates to place offerings, like Morgan Stanley. Shelf-registration also disadvantaged the smaller firms in the industry that relied on their participation in syndicates managed by firms like Morgan Stanley for a significant proportion of their business.

In 1981, Morgan Stanley was the largest firm in underwriting volume, as it had been nearly every year since 1935, but as a result of shelf-registration, it quickly fell to the lowest volume of the special-bracket firms (Chenrow, 1990). Salomon Brothers and later Merrill Lynch, the lower-status members of the bulge bracket, would become the most dominant firms in the primary securities market during the rest of the decade.

Nevertheless, while we see evidence that the change in the legislative environment disadvantaged the organizational form based on external ties, it is noteworthy that Morgan Stanley's underwriting volume did not decline to a point where it was surpassed by a fair number of lower-status firms, such as Paine Webber, Dean Witter Reynolds, Prudential-Bache Securities, and E. F. Hutton, that had extensive retail networks that should have made them extremely competitive under the new system. As Chenrow (1990) observes, "[Rule 415] merely led to a reshuffling among the top firms."

Chenrow argues that the mere reshuffling resulted from the fact that only the top firms had the capital to purchase large blocks of shares and resell them to investors quickly. However, Table 14-3 presents the largest fifteen investment banks as ranked by their total capital in 1986. Morgan Stanley is ranked thirteenth behind quite a few of the retail firms. Thus, capital availability does not seem to explain how Morgan Stanley retained its position in the special bracket.

Once again, some insight might be gained by considering the implications of status. I have argued that status lowers the costs associated with underwriting a given deal; as such, status provides a bank like Morgan Stanley with a certain advantage to fend off the competitive pressures that would be brought to bear by some of the competitors from the major bracket ranks. Status serves as a stabilizing force insofar as it dampens selection pressures operating at the organizational level. Yet while the status ordering may undercut selection on organizational form, the fact that status flows through exchange relations means

Table 14–3 Ranking of firms' total capital

1	Salomon Brothers	$2,315,287,716
2	Shearson Lehman Brothers	2,251,000,000
3	Merrill Lynch, Pierce, Fenner & Smith	2,169,521,000
4	Prudential-Bache Securities	1,259,260,000
5	Goldman, Sachs, & Co.	1,201,000,000
6	First Boston Corporation	1,042,200,000
7	Drexel Burnham Lambert	958,250,000
8	Dean Witter Reynolds	884,030,000
9	Bear, Sterns & Co.	800,000,000
10	E.F. Hutton & Co.	755,936,000
11	Paine Webber	532,168,322
12	Donaldson, Lufkin & Jenrette	479,000,000
13	Morgan Stanley & Co.	454,609,000
14	Stephens	376,669,499
15	Kidder, Peabody, & Co.	363,210,000

Source: Institutional Investor.

that selection processes are felt strongly at another level—the level of interorganizational ties.

When new industries first come into existence, they are typically ignored by the special-bracket firms. So, for example, at the turn of the twentieth century, the major investment banks of the time "neglected or overlooked" the financial needs of expanding firms in light industry and retail (Carosso 1970). It is not surprising that firms in less established industries should be overlooked by the higher-status banks. Fombrun and Stanley (1990) have noted several correlates of corporate status, such as profits, total assets, charitable contributions, and market share. All of these characteristics are ones that newer firms are more likely to lack, and thus the reticence of higher-status banks to engage in relations with lower-status issuers creates opportunities for other firms. The failure of high-status banks to serve retail firms, for example, created the initial opportunities for firms like Goldman, Sachs & Co. and Lehman Brothers. Hence, in 1906, when Sears, Roebuck, and Co. needed significant funds, it turned to Goldman, Sachs & Co., which contracted Lehman Brothers as a comanager to help underwrite the issue (Carosso 1970). As the size and status of the issuers in a particular industry rose, the size and status of the underwriters associated with that industry rose as well. Both bank and issuer would find its status reflected in and reinforced by the status of the other.

As another example, in the early twentieth century, Kuhn Loeb became one of the highest-status firms by cultivating extensive ties to the railroad industry. The significance of the railroad industry in the capital markets at the turn of the century was great; between 1900 and 1910, the securities of the railroad companies accounted for the majority of those traded on all of the major exchanges (Carosso 1970). As the railroad industry grew in size and status, Kuhn Loeb grew in size and status as well, to the point where it was clearly one of the special-bracket firms. Yet, in the mid-twentieth century, the railroad industry began to decline. As a consequence of the decline in status of the firms to which it had been tied, Kuhn Loeb's status deteriorated. In 1971, one researcher observed that the general view among the investment banking community was that, "While [Kuhn Loeb] could certainly hold its own as a major-bracket firm, it could no longer lay legitimate claim to special-bracket position" (Hayes 1971). Moreover, as we observe in Table 14-2, the descendant of Kuhn, Loeb via merger, Lehman Kuhn Loeb, is beneath the special-bracket firms in the 1981 tombstones.

One can point to more recent examples of firms whose status seems to rise and fall with an industry. For example, Hambrecht and Quist, a San Francisco–based firm, gained considerable stature as a major underwriter for the initial public offerings of the growing high-technology firms in Silicon Valley. However, when Silicon Valley firms experienced economic difficulty during the mid-1980s, Hambrecht and Quist did as well.

An examination of change in the investment banking industry thus reveals selection processes at the level of the interorganizational network. Instead of isolated firms rising and falling in status, selection processes work at the level of *firm-issuer* networks. Again, it is the relational constraints implicit in the occupancy of a high-status position that at least partially accounts for this dynamic. The fact that a firm's status is dependent on the status of the other firms to which it is tied implies that a firm will experience a change in status to the degree to which the firms to which it is tied undergo changes in their status. In effect, there is a status-based mutualism between a firm and its clients, and it is through this mutualistic dynamic that status contributes not only to stability but to change.

CONCLUSION

Our examination of the investment banking industry has highlighted the significance of status as a segregating factor underlying market competition. The economic advantages of status insulate higher-status banks from lower-status competitors, and the relational nature of status prevents the higher-status banks from using these economic advantages to monopolize the market. One might reasonably ask whether or not these observations on the significance of status are applicable in alternative contexts.

Consider as a concluding example the situation confronted by the publisher of the book that you are now reading. There are many similarities between the situation faced by a high-status publisher and a high-status investment bank. Like the high-status investment bank that receives frequent mention by the business press, so the high-status publisher is more likely to receive free advertising in the form of book reviews. Moreover, if an individual or librarian knows nothing about the underlying quality of a book, he or she is more likely to purchase it if it is published by a high-status press. Thus, like the high-status investment banks, the high-status press faces lower transaction costs than its lower-status competitors. However, also like the high-status investment banks, the high-status presses cannot dominate the market by underbidding their lower-status competitors for the rights to every profitable book, because doing so would necessarily undermine the source of their greater status.

Along these lines, it is perhaps worth noting that at least some of those in the investment banking community regard the concern with relational underpinnings of status not as a distinct facet of their industry but as a general feature of markets. As one investment banker has observed, "If you had a choice of an accountant, or lawyer, or brokerage firm, or doctor, you'd rather be with a doctor that was at Beth Israel or Mass General than at an outlying hospital, you'd like to be with a Coopers & Lybrand rather than a two-man accounting firm, you'd like to be with a big New York firm to do certain types of business, and it is very much so in the investment banking area. In many respects, the reputation of the underwriter is very much a direct reflection on the company that they are doing work for."

In observing that, "the reputation of the underwriter is very much a direct reflection on the company that they are doing work for," this individual highlights the relational underpinnings of status. In drawing comparisons to law firms and hospitals, he alludes to the generalizability of the status processes that we have observed. Further empirical work will hopefully validate such assertations of generality.

NOTES

The author is indebted to Toby Stuart for helpful comments on an earlier version of this chapter.

1. This function is distinct from the brokerage activity that investment banks undertake in the secondary markets, where previously issued securities are traded among investors.

2. Since Dean is a first name, and not a last name, this firm is listed alphabetically by Witter.

3. In forming the syndicate, the lead manager along with the issuer may participate in what could be quite a number of due diligence meetings, where syndicate members "kick the tires" of the corporation to assess its financial soundness. These meetings are part of an investment bank's fiduciary responsibility to its investors.

4. Because of the distribution of this axis, the curves do not cross the origin since the log of zero is undefined.

BIBLIOGRAPHY

Carosso, Vincent P. 1970. *Investment Banking in America: A History*. Cambridge, MA: Harvard University Press.

Chenrow, Ron. 1990. *The House of Morgan: An American Banking Dynasty and the Rise of Modern Finance*. New York: Touchstone.

Eccles, Robert, and Dwight Crane. 1988. *Doing Deals: Investment Banks at Work*. Boston, MA: Harvard Business School Press.

Fombrun, Charles, and Mark Shanley. 1990. "What's in a Name? Reputation Building and Corporate Strategy." *Academy of Management Journal* 33:233–58.

Forbes. 1976. "Tradeoff." *Forbes,* June 15, p. 36.

Frank, Robert H. 1985. *Choosing the Right Pond: Human Behavior and the Quest for Status*. Oxford: Oxford University Press.

Hayes, Samuel L. 1971. "Investment Banking: Power Structure in Flux." *Harvard Business Review* (March–June):136–52.

Hayes, Samuel L. 1979. "The Transformation of Investment Banking." *Harvard Business Press* (Jan.–Feb.) 153–70.

Kadlec, David J. 1986. "Will the Sun Ever Shine on Merrill's Investment Bankers?" *Investment Dealer's Digest,* April 21, p. 21.

Monroe, Ann. 1986. "Just Like Film Stars, Wall Streeters Battle to Get Top Billing." *Wall Street Journal,* January 15, p. 1.

Podolny, Joel. 1991. "Status, Status Processes, and Market Competition." Ph.D. dissertation, Harvard University.

Podolny, Joel. 1993. "A Status-based Model of Market Competition." *American Journal of Sociology* 98:829–72.

15

Radio Broadcasters

HUSEYIN LEBLEBICI

This historical case study describes the evolution of American radio broadcasting from its initial inception in 1920 to its present situation in 1990. It attempts to provide a broad historical overview tracing the evolution of its various participants, and their role in the organization of this unique industry that evolved from a collection of amateur radio activities to a complex set of economic transactions.

Today there are more than 9,000 radio stations in the United States. About half of these stations are located in communities with fewer than 25,000 residents where there is little competition. However, stations located in metropolitan areas may sometimes share the airwaves with thirty or more broadcasters, and they fail or succeed based on their showing in the latest listener surveys. Faced with an audience whose needs and tastes change very rapidly, today's radio stations must be in tune with the latest fads and fashions. They are in a sense at the leading edge of American culture, and thus must be aware of the changes in their own local communities, as well as the cultural movements occurring in other parts of the country.

The majority of U.S. radio stations (about 90%) are owned by corporations and the rest are owned by individuals or partnerships. The general ownership patterns can be divided into five distinct groups. One group represents media conglomerates. These are firms (e.g., Newhouse, CBS, Time, Gannett, Tribune) operating in two or more distinct media such as newspapers, broadcasting, cable, magazines, books, and film. The second group is the manufacturers of broadcasting equipment who are also in broadcasting such as GE, Westinghouse, and RCA. The third major group is called cross-ownership, which combines newspapers and radio. In the 1980s, about 7 percent of all FM and AM stations were owned in this form. The fourth category is the group ownership in which two or more stations are owned by one firm. The overall trend here is the growing concentration of station ownership, with more than half of all stations held in such arrangements. Finally, there is the network ownership that includes the owned and operated (O&O) stations of the major networks such as ABC, CBS, and NBC. These categories are not completely distinct, however, and a given firm, e.g., ABC, can be included in more than one category.

Even though their ownership patterns vary, most radio stations operate similarly and have similar organizational structures. The structure is functionally designed with sales, programming, and engineering. Traditionally, stations are classified as being, small, medium, and metro market outlets. The size of the community that a station serves usually reflects the size of its staff and the extent of division of labor. In a town with 5,000 residents, the station manager may assume the duties of sales manager, and the announcers may handle news. The average size of the staff is about six full-time employees. In medium markets (population size 100,000–500,000) stations may have an average of twelve to twenty employees. In metro markets the size of the staff may range from twenty to sixty full-time employees depending on the nature of the programming format (Keith and Krause 1989).

Ultimately what distinguishes radio stations from each other is their programming format. The basic objective of any station is to air the type of format that can attract a sizable portion of the local audience to satisfy the advertisers. There are approximately 15 major formats, but together with their subformats, or variations, this number is well over 100. The following are the major formats and their national distribution as of Fall 1987 (Radio and Records 1987):

Format	Popularity (%)
Adult Contemporary	20.7
Contemporary Hit (Top 40)	19.4
Country	14.0
Album-Oriented Rock	10.7
Easy Listening	9.7
Urban Contemporary	8.0
News/Talk	6.4
Golden Oldies	5.1
Big Band	2.1
Ethnic (Spanish)	1.8
Religious	1.0
Classical	0.8
Middle-of-the-Road	0.6
New Adult Contemporary	0.6
Jazz	0.1

Some of these formats, such as Adult Contemporary, or Middle-of-the-Road, are highly dependent on on-the-air personalities. Easy Listening and Golden Oldies formats, on the other hand, mostly rely on prepackaged (canned) programming provided by syndicators and utilize automation systems to varying degrees. Furthermore, most music programs require high-fidelity stereo sound and as a result are considered to be FM formats. News/Talk and Nostalgia (because such music usually predates stereo processing) are more suitable for AM broadcasting. Nonmusic formats are beginning to appear on FM, however, and AM's adaptation to stereo is providing some impetus to shift music programming in AM stations as well (Keith and Krause 1989).

RADIO BROADCASTING AND ALTERNATIVE INSTITUTIONAL FRAMEWORKS

The American system of radio broadcasting represents a peculiar combination of competitive private enterprise and government franchise. The industry is a network of complex transactions not only between radio stations and listeners but networks, advertisers, advertising agencies, talent agents, performers, manufacturers, rating agencies, and, of course, the state, which acts as a regulator of the transactions between parties. The present structure of the industry and its evolution, however, cannot be understood without a clear knowledge of its technological components and the institutional infrastructure that were necessary for its utilization.

The idea of using electromagnetic energy to communicate through space without the aid of wires was a product of nineteenth-century scientific thinking. The first two decades of the twentieth century had witnessed the major broadcasting innovations as well as the experimentations in their institutional framework. The Dutch and Canadians started radio broadcasting in 1919 and were followed by the United States in the fall of 1920 with the opening of the first commercial station (KDKA) in Pittsburgh. Regular broadcasting in the USSR began in 1922, and at the end of the 1920s, some forty countries had started their regular broadcasting operations. By the 1960s, nearly all nations had radio.

From its inception, radio broadcasting had to address critical issues associated with three historically related but analytically distinct components of broadcasting: the manufacture of radio receivers and transmitters; the production and broadcasting of radio programs; and the radio spectrum. From the beginning, each of these elements created unique coordination problems for the participants of the industry. Each country addressed these issues differently depending on their sociopolitical conditions.

Technologically speaking, radio broadcasting consists of radio signals (e.g., programs), the radio spectrum, and the broadcasting apparatus, including transmitters and receivers. In economic terms, radio signals that carry programs such as music are public goods. They have the characteristics of nonrival consumption (the addition of one more radio receiver does not reduce the quality of signals received by others) and nonexclusivity (anyone who has a radio can receive the signals). As any public good, radio signals are prone to free-rider problems, and consequently, the possibility of underproduction (Samuelson, 1955; Cornes and Sandler, 1986). Thus there was a continuous search for alternative financing mechanisms for broadcasting.

The radio spectrum, or the range of frequencies of electromagnetic waves through which the radio signals are carried, is usually defined as a common property good (Olson 1965). From a strictly economic perspective, users of such resources lack incentives to refrain from overuse, which would lead to the depletion, congestion, or economic inefficiency unless public control or joint cooperation is established (i.e., the problem of commons). In the case of radio, too many radio stations would lead to interference and hence lower quality of signals. This is exactly the opposite of the underproduction problem for the availability of radio signals.

The final element of the radio industry, broadcasting apparatus, has always been private goods protected by patent rights. For the patent holders and manufacturers, the overarching concern was not free-riders or overuse but the protection of their monopoly power over the production and use of radio apparatus. As a complex technology, the production and use of these devices required coordination among a very diverse group of individuals and companies that had exclusive rights to the technology. Even today, only few countries have the industrial base to manufacture major electronic components such as transmitters. The twenty-five leading manufacturers are found only in six countries (U.S., Japan, France, Netherlands, U.K., and Germany) (Head 1985). The question of who should have the right to own and operate the radio transmitters, however, has always been a source of dispute and government intervention.

Every country had to devise different broadcasting systems that combined these three aspects of broadcasting ranging from total government ownership to ownership by associations of listeners. For example, by the end of 1930s, several major alternative forms had been instituted: ownership and operation by the state (Italy, USSR, Turkey), technical operation by the state and program production by a state-controlled society (Sweden and Switzerland), ownership and operation by an independent public corporation under government franchise (United Kingdom), ownership and operation by an association of listeners (Netherlands), ownership and operation by the government plus ownership of receiving sets themselves that were rented out to listeners and were maintained by the government (Iceland) (Waller 1946). These alternative institutional frameworks reflect the variety of technologically feasible forms of organizing the fundamental interdependency between the broadcasters and listeners.

Today, there are basically four major systems of organizing radio broadcasting. One is total government monopoly in which broadcasting is under direct state control as a national institution, or government department. According to *UNESCO Statistical Yearbook* (1979), about 49 percent of all countries utilize such an ownership system. The second most common system is the ownership by a public corporation that enjoys a certain degree of operational independence, e.g., British Broadcasting Corporation (BBC) (22%). In both systems broadcasting is organized on a noncommercial basis and is largely financed through license fees and/or government subsidies. The third system (20%) is where broadcasting is carried out by profit or not-for profit entities entirely financed by income from advertising and/or donations. The last category is the hybrid or mixed system that combines two or more types of ownership (10%). Australia, Canada, and Japan are the most influential representatives of this system (Head 1985).

The dominant trend in the world toward these hybrid systems is partly due to the inroads by pirate stations that appeal to often neglected but commercially significant segments of the population such as teenagers. Early pirate stations started with the appearance of ship-borne stations operating in international waters in 1958 off the coasts of Britain, Belgium, Holland, France, Germany, and Italy. These stations were heavily influenced by American program formats, sales methods, and promotional techniques. Given the continuous popularity of pirates, most states have found it necessary to change their legal statutes and liberalize their systems.

Compared to these developments in other countries, broadcasting in the United States has always been a privately owned and commercially supported activity. Still, the integration of the three elements of broadcasting—spectrum, programs, and radio apparatus—required some degree of government intervention and regulation.

At the turn of the century, the radio spectrum as a new technological resource had no established institutional mechanisms for its use and allocation. A few years after the introduction of scheduled radio broadcasting in the 1920s, many governments began enacting statutory controls. These laws had four basic goals: to prevent technical interference among stations; to conserve channels because of spectrum scarcity; to treat the spectrum as a valuable national resource that should serve everyone; and to prevent the so-called misuse of broadcasting to influence the society. All these reasons have regularly been used by governments to legitimate their regulatory efforts.

For similar reasons, the radio spectrum was defined as a common property resource in the United States. It is interesting that even though the use of radio spectrum is a limited resource, transferable, and exclusive, its allocation among users through a market mechanism was never considered (Coase 1959). A central administrative system operated by the federal government under the general guidelines of "public interest, convenience, or necessity" has always been the standard justification used for its allocation (Levin 1971).

Even though the radio as a means of point-to-point communication (e.g., ship to shore) was around since the turn of the century, its phenomenal growth in the United States required a new definition of its nature. As all other leading countries, the United States adopted its first major broadcasting statutes between 1925 and 1935. The Radio Act of 1927, though not the first to be enacted, was the most comprehensive of these early statutes. It created a federal agency to allocate frequencies, license stations, and to generally regulate all forms of radio communication. The Communication Act of 1934 brought together under one statute the federal laws governing both interstate and foreign communication by both wire and radio (Head 1985). The 1934 act is the oldest major broadcasting statute in the world. Most other countries, on the other hand, found it necessary to make major revisions in their statutes first with the advent of TV in the 1960s and later with the advent of new technologies in the 1980s. Currently most nations are in the process of developing regulations integrating cable TV, satellite broadcasting, videotext, and other new technologies.

With respect to the broadcasting apparatus, the overriding concern for the established players of the communication industry has always been the control of key patents. At the beginning, for the key patent holders, radio was essentially perceived as a means of rapid, long-distance, wireless, point-to-point communication for international and maritime message transmission rather than an instrument of mass communication (Sterling and Kittross, 1978, p. 46). The most critical question for the major patent holders was the coordination of exchange relationships between the manufacturers and broadcasters. Because patents for technical innovations were held by many individuals and companies, amateur radio operators were able to pirate these innovations and build their own sets and equipment. They could get the few items that were hard to produce at home from small manufacturers who were rather lax about paying royalties. In 1921, these problems were solved by a patent pooling agreement between the major patent holders (RCA, GE, AT&T, and later Westinghouse).

The final element of broadcasting, programming (or broadcast signals) as a common good available to anyone who owned a receiver, necessitated finding answers to such practical problems as how broadcasting could be transacted, and what the value of such transactions could be. The organization of this fundamental interdependence between the radio stations and their listeners have required new solutions. The radio broadcasting industry all over the world developed a variety of conventions, or regulations, to solve these practical problems—who can produce broadcasting programs, how the industry can be financed, or how programs can be evaluated.

In contrast to the financing system selected in the United States, most of the European countries have been dependent on receiver license fees for their revenues. With the introduction of transistors in the late 1950s, however, radio licensing became impossible to administer efficiently and they had to drop radio licensing altogether or combine it with TV licensing. Such difficulties resulted in the acceptance of limited advertising as a source of supplemental income worldwide. Financing, however, is only one aspect of programming. There are a myriad of regulations and conventions developed that help coordinate the production of programs (their content, language, schedule lengths, balance among program types), their distribution (networks, relay stations, satellites), and ownership of stations (citizenship requirements, ceiling on ownership, cross-media ownership).

As the following historical account attempts to show, the growth of any organizational population depends on its ability to establish munificent relationships with other populations of organizations in their environment. Moreover, the variety of organizational forms within a population is limited by the extent of its varied transactions with other populations in a community of organizations. This is especially true for a new industry such as radio broadcasting. The evolution of broadcasting demonstrates that the growth of the industry and the variety of organizational forms it introduced was mainly achieved by the establishment of new economic transactions with other established players in related domains. As the population ecology literature argues, every new organizational form needs institutionalized practices that support these economic relations. These institutional practices, however, are not static but evolve with the invention of new practices and the introduction of new participants as a result of growing division of labor in the industry. As presented in this chapter, the institutionalized practices at each stage of the radio broadcasting industry's history were mainly associated with the nature of economic transactions among diverse participants in the industry.

THE EVOLUTION OF COMMERCIAL BROADCASTING IN THE UNITED STATES

The following historical account of the radio broadcasting industry covers the period from its origin in the early 1920s to its state of maturity at the end of the 1980s. Although there are several alternative ways of identifying its critical phases, we select four major periods: 1920–34, which covers the beginning of the industry and its commercialization; 1935–49, the so-called Golden Age of Radio, which covers the period of growth especially in networks; 1950–65, which covers the development of local independent stations and the decline of national networks; and 1966–90, which covers radio's mature but also most revolutionary period.

The evolution of broadcasting from a public good to a privately owned and commercially supported activity in the United States, was a product of a unique organization that coordinated the economic cycle of broadcast-related transactions between the listeners and stations. The historical account presented reflects the way these transactions evolved through the development of new practices and their institutionalization within a competitive environment.

The Age of Manufacturers (1920–34)

Three interrelated practical concerns dominated the early experimentation in the industry and the eventual establishment of critical institutions that formed its foundation: How should the broadcasting (the programs and the facilities to air these programs, i.e., stations) be financed? Who should produce these programs? How should they be distributed or made available to the listening public?

At the beginning, however, none of these problems were actually relevant for the established players in the industry. The founders of the Radio Corporation of America (RCA) considered "radio" as radiotelegraphy. Their patent pooling agreements were designed to manufacture, install, and sell radio apparatus and to establish worldwide radiotelegraphy services. Their competitors were also well defined: the intercontinental cable networks for point-to-point private communication. They continued to think of radio largely in terms of tolls collected for messages from specific senders to specific receivers and as engineering and manufacturing activities associated with it.

At the same time, however, thousands of radio enthusiasts, many of them high school students, began building their own makeshift home receivers. The market for parts, wires, earphones, crystals, and blueprints skyrocketed. The American public spent $60 million on home sets during 1922 and $136 million in 1923 (Landry 1946). The same amateur enthusiasm was also evident in the increase of the number of radio stations. Even though most were short-lived, their numbers increased from 382 in 1922 to 572 in 1923.

The idea of selling radios through broadcasting was first adopted by Westinghouse. Even though small parts manufacturers were the early initiators of this practice, Westinghouse, which had invested extensively in the production of radio equipment for military purposes during the First World War, was left with huge idle capacity after the war. Furthermore, as the last participant of the patent pooling agreements, its competitive position in the international communications market was not strong. The solution it discovered was to establish a station (KDKA) in Pittsburgh, broadcast on a regular daily schedule, and give buyers of receivers the assurance of continuing service.

Others followed the same practice. The new stations were mainly licensed to radio and parts manufacturers, or retail outlets that wanted to stimulate the sale of radio sets, parts, tubes, and batteries. For instance, in 1923, out of 476 radio stations whose ownership is known, 324 were operated either by radio manufacturers (47%) or by commercial establishments such as department stores, arts dealers, jewelry or music stores (20%) (Banning 1946). The rest were mostly educational or amateur stations. At this time there was also a geometric increase in the number of radio manufacturers. During the peak period of 1923–26, there were 748 manufacturing establishments. However, only 72 of them lasted until 1927, and at the of 1934, only 18 were still operating (Eoyang 1936).

Thus, the initial organization of the industry was quite simple. Radio stations were operated either by the radio manufacturers or retailers to increase the sales of receivers, or by newspapers or department stores to increase the visibility of their services.

Because radio manufacturers supported radio broadcasting in order to sell their products, major producers such as Westinghouse, GE, and RCA all built stations without worrying about their financing. The increase in broadcasting costs, however, eventually raised the question of how to finance these operations. In 1923, *Radio Broadcast* magazine initiated a public debate on the possibility that the radio manufacturers would have less interest in bearing these costs after the radio-buying boom subsided. As Figure 15-1 shows, the number of radio stations continued to increase without any agreed-upon financing scheme.

Several different schemes of financing were being tested during this time. One was purely philanthropic. Universities particularly gained entrance to the medium through endowment of stations by public citizens (e.g., Alabama Polytechnic Institute, Michigan State College, Georgia School of Technology). In some cases, these donors operated their own stations (WMAF at Dartmouth, MA.) Another alternative was radio clubs, which relied on donations from listeners. WHB at Kansas City, for instance, initiated the idea of an "invisible

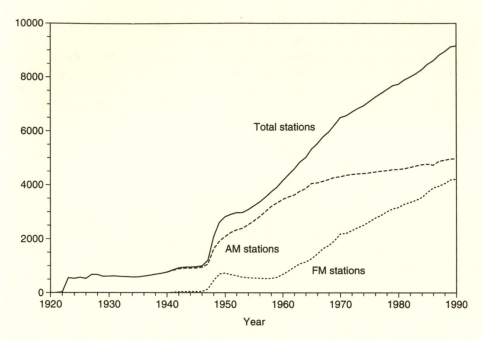

Figure 15–1 Density of AM and FM radio stations. (*Source:* Adapted from Leblebici et al. 1991. Copyright © by Cornell University. Used by permission.)

theater" to which radio fans bought tickets. The other dominant players, however, preferred public financing. During 1925, RCA proposed the idea of Broadcasting Foundation of America in which the big radio manufacturers would be contributing subscribers. The least supported alternatives were municipal financing, financing by states, or a common fund controlled by an elected board (tried by AT&T), and advertising (Barnouw 1966).

The idea of self-financing radio, however, was brought home by the sellers of questionable commodities and services ranging from fortunes in real estate to hair-growth products to fortune-tellers who could no longer persuade most print media to accept their advertising. Prominent in this respect was "Doctor" J. R. Brinkley, who established KFKB in Milford, Kansas, to develop trade in the infamous goat-gland male sexual rejuvenation operations, of which he performed thousands to revitalize elderly gentlemen for a fee of $750. Success of these schemes made it clear to all participants that the combination of a radio personality and a wavelength was financially feasible. The Annual Radio Conference (1922–25), initiated by the Department of Commerce, attempted to develop some form of self-regulation on such direct sales but eventually helped develop the concept of indirect advertising. This new institutional framework, combined with the power of advertising, segregated the industry into three groups: manufacturing, broadcasting, and telephone.

Once advertising became a legitimate mode of financing broadcasting, the relationship between the stations and their financial supporters was open to modification. Advertisers, who earlier needed to operate their own stations in

order to develop goodwill among the purchasing public, supported broadcasting by sponsoring individual programs. The first group of sponsors were the
national manufacturers of branded, packaged consumer goods. These advertisers, who had traditionally relied on the advertising agencies to write copy and
obtain space in print media, initiated the same practice in broadcasting.
Through their advertising agencies, they paid for the production and broadcasting of their sponsored programs (Palmolive hour, Lucky-strike hour, Ever-
ready hour).

The selection and production of programs quickly became the function of the
advertising agencies, which decided both the content and the distribution of
sponsored programs, transforming these agencies into the most powerful players of the broadcasting industry. By 1931, the agencies had taken on program
selection, casting, directing, scheduling, and other production aspects. Thus
the two fundamental issues faced by the broadcasting industry at the beginning
of the 1920s—the financing and production of programs—were resolved by
making radio programs the basic units of transaction that were financed by
advertisers, produced by advertising agencies, distributed by networks, and
broadcasted by the stations.

Parallel to these developments, the problem of program distribution was
solved through the creation of broadcasting networks. The idea of connecting
two or more stations for simultaneous broadcast of programs existed from the
start of broadcasting. In 1923, Col. E. H. Green, who operated WMAF for his
amusement and had no facilities for or interest in programming, persuaded
AT&T station WEAF to feed him its programs by telephone wire for his listeners. The breakup of the patent pooling agreement and the resulting creation
of National Broadcasting Corporation (NBC) firmly established the idea of a
network of cooperating stations. In this way, a given message could reach a far
larger audience at a more reasonable cost. But this was not the only technologically feasible alternative. One possible solution was to form several very powerful stations to cover most of the United States. Transcription was yet another
possibility. Transcribed programs repeated, potentially at least, a real alternative to network distribution of "live" programs.

When radio began, the phonograph had been in use for forty years and specialized discs for broadcast use were available. With successive refinements in
recording techniques, transcription was both economically and technically as
good as live broadcasting. It also provided flexibility for stations in scheduling
and accepting spot advertising. Neither transcription nor the installation of
powerful stations, however, became as popular or as important as the networks
in this early period. Replacing live programs with transcribed ones was unacceptable because of the general belief that airing transcribed programs or phonograph records would not be acceptable to the listening public. The networks
constantly maintained this belief and openly restricted the use of recording on
network time through self-regulation. Similarly, the record producers, recording agents, and the artists themselves considered such an alternative economically unacceptable because of its presumed negative impact on record sales.
In fact, in 1922, the secretary of commerce had denounced the large stations
using records and required stations to announce explicitly when their programs

were recorded. As a result, the ever-increasing cost of live programs made the establishment of national and regional networks the acceptable choice for all the parties concerned.

Until the end of the 1920s, one critical element of this cycle of transactions was missing. There was no accepted scheme by which the economic value of broadcasting to the advertisers could be determined. This was especially crucial once the industry moved away from creating demand for receivers to creating demand for advertisers' products. Early on, the stations purely relied on the voluntary response of the amateur listeners. The listeners called, sent fan mail, or mailed in specially designed postcards distributed by the radio retailers.

Measuring the success of sponsored programs was the responsibility of the advertisers. They provided free samples to those who wrote in; they developed contests; or they made the payment to the stations contingent upon the number of inquiries they received. These patchwork arrangements were finally resolved through a national program rating system. The first national rating service was organized by the Association of National Advertisers (Cooperative Analysis of Broadcasting, also called Crosley ratings) in 1929. The service mostly benefitted advertising agencies but was paid for largely by the networks and stations. Most stations, which were content to solicit reactions to programs through incoming mail, were pressured by the advertisers to conduct audience research. As the emphasis of broadcast advertising shifted from selling to persuading mass audiences, ratings further became the explicit focal point around which the exchange relations among all interested parties were organized (Hurwitz 1983).

Figure 15-2 shows the proportions of three different types of advertising—network, national spot, and local advertising—to total radio advertising revenues. With the advent of network broadcasting, major financial support for radio was provided by the networks until the end of the 1940s.

During the early 1920s, radio manufacturers were usually the ones who supported broadcasting and used it for selling radios. At the end of this period, however, we observe expansion and diversification. New transactional linkages between the critical participants revolutionized the division of labor in the industry during the 1930s. These linkages were now specialized around the programming activities either providing input for programs (e.g., talent agencies, independent producers), facilitating their distribution (networks, transcription syndicates), or determining the value of programs (rating agencies). In other words, the legitimacy of radio as an economically viable activity was finally institutionalized.

Three major institutionalized beliefs formed the foundation for the new organization of the industry during this period: (1) the number of radio stations are limited by technology because of long-distance interference; (2) live programming is the essence of radio; and (3) only networks could help finance expensive programming by spreading costs over many stations. The ultimate outcome of these beliefs was the segregation of radio broadcasting industry into network and independent radio stations. Networks and their affiliated stations dominated the industry for the next two decades as the most powerful forms

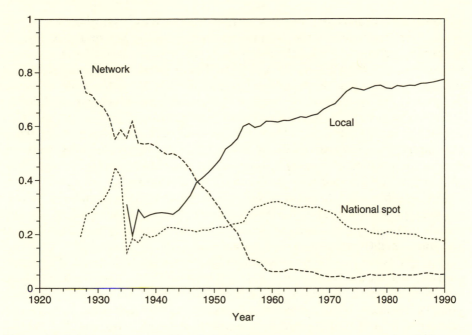

Figure 15–2 Network spot, and local advertising revenues as percentage of total. (*Source:* Adapted from Leblebici et al. 1991. Copyright © by Cornell University. Used by permission.)

of organizing. Still, the vestiges of the early radio survived in locations not deemed profitable by the networks. These independent stations, not affiliated with any network, relied altogether on phonograph recordings and transcriptions for entertainment, and were financed by spot announcements alone.

The Age of Radio Networks (1935–50)

This period, sometimes called the Golden Age of Radio, was dominated by the national networks and their financial power. The early network idea developed by AT&T did not involve programs, but it became clear early on that network-level programming was necessary to sustain listenership. Networks instituted the provision of two types of programs—commercial and sustaining—that formed the foundation of the exchange relationship between them and their affiliated stations. Commercial programs were sponsored and paid for by the advertiser; the sustaining programs were produced and made available to the affiliates by the networks.

The exchange of these programs required the establishment of some mechanism to maintain the relationship between the networks and the affiliates. Different contractual agreements were possible and probably all were tried. While the details of the contracts varied, two basic arrangements became the most popular. NBC, and later CBS, offered their affiliate stations a package of both nationally sponsored and sustaining programs in return for the station time. The Mutual Broadcasting System (MBS) was the only commercial network that was organized along radically different lines from NBC or CBS. It was an organization owned by the member stations themselves. The commercial programs were produced by the originating stations, or by the sponsors, and the sustaining programs were selected from among those put on by the stations associated with the network (FCC, 1941). The network was in a sense a clearing agency providing the members, at least in theory, with a wide choice of programs. This cooperative arrangement, however, never became as stable, or as profitable, as the commercial network arrangement.

Once programs rather than broadcasting itself became the medium by which the industry was organized, the focus of attention shifted to the variety and national popularity of programs. Such a focus made two linkages particularly problematic for the parties concerned: (1) the relationship between the networks and their affiliates, whose survival depended on the popularity of their network programs; and (2) the relationship between the advertising agencies and the networks, who were dependent on the advertising agencies for the production of highly rated sponsored programs.

During this period, the major commercial networks, NBC and CBS, formalized and standardized their relations with their affiliates. They realized that as networks they had no control over either the program production or its scheduling independent of the advertising agencies. At the beginning, NBC used to reimburse its affiliated stations for sponsored network programs that they accepted and NBC charged the affiliates for its sustaining programs they broadcasted. The acceptance of network programs was a matter of the affiliates' decision.

In place of this unstable patchwork arrangement, CBS developed a simpler but more formalized contract. It made the entire sustaining programs free to affiliates without any obligation on the part of the affiliates to use any of these programs. In exchange, it acquired the option to use any part of the affiliates' schedules. Therefore, CBS could assign time to a network sponsor without any uncertainty about clearance from its member stations.

In addition to optioning all of the affiliates' best-time, long-term affiliation contracts, exclusive access to affiliates' stations assured the much desired flexibility and stability needed by the networks. Despite these new limitations, most stations found it necessary and desirable to belong to one of the networks. For instance, as Figure 15-3 shows, 95 percent of all commercial radio stations in 1945 were affiliated with one of the national commercial networks. The success of an individual station now depended entirely on the ratings of its network programs.

In the meantime, large metropolitan independent stations (such as WOR, Newark; WLW, Cincinnati; WMAQ, Chicago) found an alternative way to maintain their competitive edge through spot advertising. The practice of spot announcements (inserted between transcribed programs) both for the national and regional advertisers required no expensive programming effort from the advertisers. Some of the new enterprising advertising agencies began to discover that important local markets remained outside the range of network influence. In response to this demand, a new specialized service gained prominence—station representatives and time brokers—that was designed to furnish a point of contact between the agencies and stations.

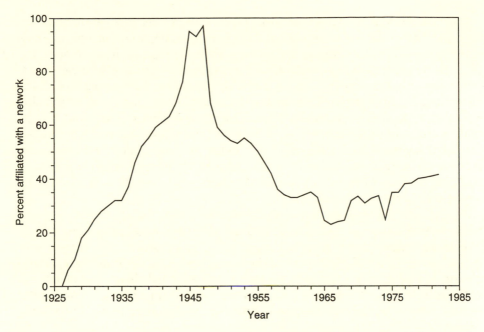

Figure 15–3 Network-affiliated radio stations. (*Source:* Adapted from Leblebici et al. 1991. Copyright © by Cornell University. Used by permission.)

Against the continuous discouragements from the national networks, recorded programs and spot advertising became more available because of the popularity of these programs. Some of these independent stations were later bought by the networks and eventually reduced the networks' resistance to spot advertising. As Figure 15-2 shows, the revenues generated from national spot and local advertising grew equally in this period.

Emphasis on programs as the medium of transaction also influenced the relationship between the advertising agencies and the networks. Instead of solely depending on the advertising agencies for the production of successful programs, networks started to experiment with producing, scheduling, and selling their own programs following the practices developed by the independent stations. Networks discovered that the sustaining programs, which usually meant broadcasting orchestra music during unsold periods to fulfill obligations to their affiliates, could be used to experiment with new programs.

At the end of the 1940s, each network had created new positions in their organizations for network programming. The success of these new programs made it possible for networks to produce and schedule their own programs for which they could sell advertising time (spot announcements) instead of looking for sponsored programs produced by the advertising agencies. These new arrangements extended the networks' domination to other organizations that were necessary for programming such as talent agencies. Such controls continuously increased the tendency toward centralized programming but at the same time increased the costs of programming for the networks.

The Golden Age of Radio was marked with stability because of the dominating presence of the national networks. The major commercial networks were able to maintain their power and control the entrance of new competition through internalization of programming activities. Transactions between parties in the industry were now based not on programs but advertising time. Such an arrangement produced the intended outcome of lesser control of advertising agencies as well as some major unintended consequences. The trend toward more variety in programming led to competition among networks for highly rated but increasingly expensive programming and consequently the development of cheaper music and quiz shows. As long as these alternative programs had high national ratings, they attracted advertisers to buy time without being a sponsor for the whole program.

While most network shows were still live programs, ABC, the newest network, which could not find enough national sponsors to cover the cost of programming, began to use recorded programs. The recorded and cheaper programs, however, similarly expanded the resources available to individual radio stations to develop a variety of programs and reduced their dependency on national networks. These new practices not only changed the exchange relationships between the existing parties but also the definition of what was being exchanged.

The Age of Independent Radio Stations (1950–65)
The next period covered in this study marks the end of the network era and the rebirth of independent stations. Two exogenous pressures played a significant role in accelerating this transformation: an increase in the number of radio stations as a result of changes in FCC regulations, and the expansion of TV as another medium of mass communication.

For many observers of the industry, these new developments meant the end of radio. Radio jokes abounded in the early 1950s: one cartoon showed a young boy dusting off a radio in the attic and asking his father, "What's that?" (Fornatale and Mills 1980). The general exodus of staff from networks contributed to this belief. But the turnover actually opened the door to a new generation of broadcasters who had nothing to unlearn.

During the Second World War, there were economic and regulatory restrictions on the establishment of new, particularly FM, stations. But the returning young veterans, especially those who gained technical knowledge in broadcasting during the war, applied for licensing. Under pressure, the FCC relaxed its technical standards to allow more local stations serving local needs by reversing its long-held policy of serving rural areas through powerful clear-channel stations. As a result, the number of AM stations increased from about 940 in 1945 to more than 2,350 at the end of 1952 (Figure 15-1). Because of this policy shift, the effective range of many stations was reduced and led the growth of smaller stations in smaller markets. Small towns that used to rely on distant stations now had their own local radio (Sterling and Kittross 1978).

The experimentation with TV had been going on since 1935. In fact, radio and TV were born in the same era. With the outbreak of the war, licensing, experimentation, and commercialization of TV were stopped. After the war, the economic strength of the national networks facilitated the growth of television. By using already successful radio programs with added video, networks maintained their dominance in this new industry. Both the networks and the national advertisers supported TV at the expense of radio broadcasting.

Radio networks and their affiliates, through trial-and-error, tried to cope with these developments. They tried to simulcast audio portions of TV shows; they asked their stars to work without live orchestras and the staff of writers; they tried stereo broadcast through the use of AM and FM stations. The old concepts, such as the idea of pay radio, or completely new concepts, such as home music services (similar to cable TV), were introduced briefly without much success.

Many of the most innovative and successful experimentations, however, were taking place at small independent stations far from the media centers. Stations such as KLIF, Dallas, and KOWH, Omaha, became the new innovators. Their local announcers, who became the disc jockeys of the new radio, evolved from being anonymous regimented studio employees into a critical force who built their own on-air personality by tailoring music and other programming elements to their local listeners. To the unhappiness of unions and the joy of station managers, disc jockeys ran their own control boards, played their own turntables, and cut the broadcasting costs significantly for local stations. They developed new practices to give their stations a recognizable personality.

Localization brought with it the idea of specialization. Stations started to invent specific programming formats (e.g., top 40, middle-of-the-road, rock, country and western, all news), and thus concentrated on specific listener groups and sold time to advertisers who were specifically interested in these groups. As Table 15-1 shows, the number of new formats expanded in every decade as the stations and advertisers discovered new niches of listeners.

Another important discovery of the period was the promotion of record sales through radio. Contrary to the long-established fears of record companies, music publishers, and concert promoters, experiments by independent record companies (particularly those in rock 'n' roll music) with local independent stations showed how critical the airplay was to promoting sales. The new relationship was mutually beneficial: by providing the latest hits, record companies kept the operating costs low for the stations; and the stations, in turn, provided free publicity.

The success of local stations began to attract both the regional and national advertisers who had defected to TV. As Figure 15-2 shows, during this period the local and national spot advertising became more critical than network-sponsored advertising in financing broadcasting and it further eroded the networks' power. The networks eventually began adopting these new practices. First the regional networks and later national networks started to tailor their activities to specialized station formats. For instance, ABC replaced its old network with four separate specialized networks—entertainment, information, contemporary, and American FM. These new practices, however, were more suitable for local audiences whose taste were familiar to deejays. With networks no longer providing income, their affiliates first dropped sustaining programs and then

Table 15–1 The introduction of new formats at different decades

Before 1950	1950s	1960s	1970s	1980s
Classical	Middle-of-the-Road	News	Adult Contemporary	Arena Rock
Country	Top 40	Talk	Album-oriented Rock	Hot Adult
Hit Parade	Beautiful Music	News/Talk	Easy Listening	Contemporary Hit
Religious		Progressive	Contemporary Country	Urban Contemporary
Black		Acid/Psychedelic	Urban Country	New Age
Hispanic		Jazz	Mellow Rock	Eclectic-oriented Rock
		All Request	Disco	All Sports
		Oldies	Nostalgia	All Motivation
		Diversified	British Rock	All Comedy
			New Wave	All Beatles
			Public Radio	Classic Hits
				Classic Rock
				Male Adult Contemporary

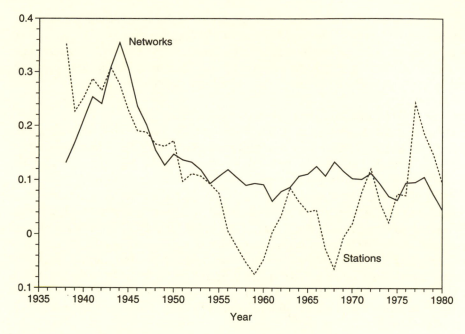

Figure 15–4 Average profit ratios of networks and stations. (*Source:* Author's analysis.)

most of the remaining sponsored programs. Many affiliates no longer cleared time for network shows. At the end of this period the percentage of network-affiliated stations dropped to 32 percent compared to 95 percent in 1945 (see Figure 15-3).

Contrary to the general belief in the industry that TV would make radio obsolete, the new arrangements at the station level cut the operating costs drastically and made local broadcasting a feasible economic activity even without the support of networks. Local advertising became the dominant source of revenue and the critical role of national advertising disappeared. As a result, even though roughly one third of AM and most of FM stations were losing money, the number of stations continued to increase dramatically. As Figure 15-4 shows, the impact of increased competition was obvious and this is the first time the profitability of radio in general declined with an accelerated speed.

During the network era, programming sought to provide a bit of everything to everyone in order to develop national audiences. In this new era of local broadcasting, however, advertisers now sought a specific audience segment for a specific product. What was now exchanged between the advertisers and the stations was a promise to expose those mini-audiences to specific commercial messages. Radio stations have come to see their role as delivering a specific local market segment to their advertisers.

These new transactional arrangements eliminated the fundamental differences between network-affiliated and independent radio stations. National mass audiences were now replaced with segmented special mini-audiences in local markets. The old institutionalized beliefs were no longer relevant within this organization of the industry. The supposed technological limitation (interference among stations) for the number of stations was no longer true as long as the audiences lived within a close proximity to the stations. The economic necessity of networks with their live programs disappeared with the introduction of less expensive but equally effective local program formats.

The Age of FM Radio and Deregulations (1966–90)
The last and contemporary period of radio covered here starts with an evolutionary pattern but ends with a revolutionary character. The major impetus for this accelerated change was the introduction of new technologies and the change in the regulatory environment.

From the industry's beginning, the radio broadcasting regulations were framed within the concept of local stations. Based on the American political system of sovereign states and local electorates, the FCC always envisioned stations as serving their local population. For this end, almost every transmitter was licensed to be a separate station, the number of stations that could be owned by a single licensee was restricted, and local stations affiliated with a network were required to provide some local programming. The idea of local radio, however, was basically inconsistent with the economic character of radio.

The expansion of national networks in the 1930s clearly indicated that there were economies of scale in a system of network advertising and programming. The decline of networks and the continuous increase in the number of AM and FM stations brought back the localism to radio at the beginning of this period. This trend, however, was short-lived. At the end of this period the industry was dominated with nationwide packaged programming and a limited number of music program sources. The idea of network was now replaced with national distribution of radio formats and satellite technology as these new delivery systems were introduced. The use of satellite transponders allowed national program service firms to reach hundreds of stations, which were fully automated, without the need for expensive wired interconnections.

By the late 1980s, there were more than twenty service firms that delivered twenty-four-hour music formats across the country using the new satellite technology. For instance, Transtar Radio and Satellite Music together produced fifteen different formats for nationwide distribution (Sterling and Kittross, 1990, p. 475).

In addition to the introduction of new delivery systems, another critical technological change occurred in the radio receivers. At the beginning of the 1960s, receivers used the technology of the 1920s—the electronic tubes. The introduction of transistors and later the integrated circuits, however, changed not only the size of radio receivers but also the manufacturing economics. Most sets now had the AM and FM capability including automobile radio receivers, and their average price declined precipitously. By 1975, the number of receivers per 1,000 inhabitants in the United States increased to 1,879.2, the largest in the world (UNESCO 1979). The major beneficiary of these technological changes was the FM radio. FM, which was once considered a loser, was now the fastest-growing segment of the industry. As Figure 15-1 shows, there was a geo-metric growth in the number of FM stations during this period. Most of these new FM stations were equipped with stereo broadcasting facilities.

As the number of both AM and particularly FM radio stations increased, their specialization in programming also increased. As Table 15-1 shows, for-mats commonly used by AM and FM were now being clearly differentiated. Most of the new music formats, which required high-fidelity stereo sound, were more suitable for FM. All stations continued to fragment the existing music and talk formats in search of new audiences. Especially for stations in major markets competing with thirty to fifty stations, focusing on small but specific demographic groups became a common strategy. At the end of the 1980s, FM had increased its share of audiences from 40 percent to 70 percent. In order to survive, AM stations developed more specialized formats and focused on very specific audience niches. AM-FM distinction became the new segregating force of the industry.

The second major impetus for change in radio broadcasting came as a result of deregulations that began in the mid-1970s and accelerated during the 1980s. The public debate was chiefly between the supporters of the traditional concept of "public interest, convenience, or necessity," which required government in-tervention, and the supporters of "marketplace competition." The continuous attempts to deregulate the industry not only influenced the way new technical standards were established (by the marketplace) but also the ownership struc-ture of the industry. Until the 1980s, the FCC played an essential role in deter-mining, testing, and enforcing technical standards. This role of the commission as a national technical overseer was now strongly questioned. The concrete example of this change came about in the case of AM stereo broadcasting. AM station owners, who were hoping to counteract FM's growing success, wanted the FCC to select one of the five systems as the new technical standard. FCC decided to allow AM stereocasting but claimed that the marketplace would decide on the best system.

The same framework was also applied to regulating competition, especially for resolving the questions of ownership, mergers, and the concentration of control. The number of stations anyone entity should be able to own had been a topic of contention since the beginning of the industry. The FCC wanted to drop all ownership rules but Congress would not support such a radical change. The final compromise was to establish a new 12–12–12 rule, which meant that a single entity can now own twelve AM, twelve FM, and twelve TV stations.

The elimination of the local programming requirements (the FCC rule that required the airing of locally produced programs) furthered the transformation of radio from being strongly tied to local communities to being simply a local outlet for nationally produced formats. Such a change facilitated the view that stations are like any other businesses that can be part of a diversified portfolio. They became the means to spread the increasing cost of production for the syndicators, or satellite service firms. Still, compared to many parts of the world, American radio stayed a local phenomenon supported by local adver-tising. As an advertising medium, it has been able to maintain its share of total advertising revenues at around 7 percent since the mid-1970s. Even though this is half of its maximum share in 1945 (15%), it is a clear indication that radio continued to be a successful medium.

The major changes discussed in this section are still unfolding today. With the introduction of new technologies, and their adaptation to radio, a new organization of the industry with a new set of diverse players is taking place.

NOTE

This chapter is partly based on a study published earlier (Leblebici, Huseyin, Gerald R. Salancik, Anne Kopay, and Tom King. 1981. "Institutional Change and the Transformation of Interorganizational Fields: Organizational History of the U.S. Broadcasting Industry." *Administrative Science Quarterly* 36:333–63. In order to eliminate excessive use of references and to increase the readability of the text, all the historical sources are listed in Additional Readings. The archival sources used for the data collection are listed in the periodicals section of Additional Readings.

BIBLIOGRAPHY

Banning, William P. 1946. *Commercial Broadcasting Pioneer: The WEAF Experiment, 1922–1926*. Cambridge, MA: Harvard University Press.

Barnouw, Erik. 1966. *A Tower of Babel: A History of Broadcasting in the U.S. to 1933*. New York: Oxford University Press.

Coase, Ronald H. 1959. "The Federal Communications Commission." *Journal of Law and Economics* 2:1–40.

Cornes, Richard, and Todd Sandler. 1986. *The Theory of Externalities, Public Goods,and Club Goods*. Cambridge, MA: Cambridge University Press.

Eoyang, Thomas T. 1936. *An Economic Study of the Radio Industry in the United States of America*. New York: Columbia University Press.

Federal Communications Commission. 1941. *Report on Chain Broadcasting*. Washington, DC: Government Printing Office.

Fornatale, Peter, and Joshua E. Mills. 1980. *Radio in the Television Age*. Woodstock, NY: Overlook Press.

Head, Sydney W. 1985. *World Broadcasting Systems: A Comparative Analysis*. Belmont, CA: Wedsworth Publishing.

Hurwitz, Donald L. 1983. "Broadcast Ratings: The Size and Development of Commercial Audience Research in American Broadcasting." Unpublished Ph.D. dissertation, University of Illinois.

Keith, Michael C., and Joseph M. Krause. 1989. *The Radio Station*. Boston: Focal Press.

Kellogg, H. D. Jr. 1925. "Who Is to Pay for Broadcasting—and How." *Radio Broadcast* 5:863–6.

Landry, Robert J. 1946. *The Fascinating Radio Business*. Indianapolis: Bobbs-Merrill.

Levin, Harvey J. 1971. *The Invisible Resource: Use and Regulation of the Radio Spectrum*. Baltimore: Johns Hopkins University Press.

Olson, Mancur. 1965. *The Logic of Collective Action*. Cambridge, MA: Harvard University Press.

Radio and Records. 1987. *Radio and Records Fall 1978 Book*. New York: Radio and Records.

Samuelson, Paul A. 1955. "A Diagrammatic Exposition of a Theory of Public Expenditure." *Review of Economics and Statistics* 37:350–6.

Sterling, Christopher H., and John M. Kittross. 1978. *Stay Tuned: A Concise History of American Broadcasting*. Belmont, CA: Wadsworth.

Sterling, Christopher H., and John M. Kittross. 1990. *Stay Tuned: A Concise History of American Broadcasting,* 2nd ed. Belmont, CA: Wadsworth.

UNESCO. 1979. *Statistics on Radio and Television 1960–1976*. Paris: United Nations Educational, Scientific, and Cultural Organization.

Waller, Judith C. 1946. *The Fifth Estate*. Boston: Houghton-Mifflin.

ADDITIONAL READINGS

General Sources

Edelman, Murray. 1950. *The Licensing of Radio Services in the United States, 1927 to 1947*. Urbana, IL: University of Illinois Press.

Emery, Walter B. 1969. *National and International Systems of Broadcasting: Their History, Operation and Control*. East Lansing, MI: Michigan University Press.

Gibson, George H. 1977. *Public Broadcasting: The Role of the Federal Government, 1912–76*. New York: Praeger.

Hilliard, Robert L. (ed.). 1974. *Radio Broadcasting: An Introduction to the Sound Medium*. New York: Hastings House.

Settel, Irving. 1960. *A Pictorial History of Radio*. New York: Citadel Press.

Slate, Sam J., and Joe Cook. 1963. *It Sounds Impossible*. New York: Macmillan.

Smith, Anthony. 1973. *The Shadow in the Cave: The Broadcaster, the Audience, and the State*. Urbana, IL: University of Illinois Press.

Willis, Edgar E. 1951. *Foundations in Broadcasting*. New York: Oxford University Press.

Sources for Period 1 (1920–35)

Archer, Gleason L. 1938. *History of Radio to 1926*. New York: American Historical Society.

Archer, Gleason L. 1939. *Big Business and Radio*. New York: American Historical Society.

Arnold, Frank A. 1931. *Broadcast Advertising*. New York: Wiley.

Banning, William P. 1946. *Commercial Broadcasting Pioneer: The WEAF Experiment, 1922–1926*. Cambridge, MA: Harvard University Press.

Barnouw, Erik. 1966. *A Tower of Babel: A History of Broadcasting in the U.S. to 1933*. New York: Oxford University Press.

Codel, Martin (ed.). 1930. *Radio and Its Future*. New York: Harper.

Dunlap, Orrin E. 1951. *Dunlap's Radio and Television Almanac*. New York: Harper.

Floherty, John J. 1938. *On the Air: The Story of Radio*. New York: Doubleday, Doran.

Head, Sydney. 1956. *Broadcasting in America: A Survey of Radio and Television*. Boston: Houghton-Mifflin.

Herron, Edward A. 1969. *Miracle of the Air Waves: A History of Radio*. New York: Julian Messner.

Hettinger, Herman S. 1933. A Decade of Radio Advertising. Chicago: University of Chicago Press.

Jome, Hiram. 1925. *Economics of Radio Industry*. Chicago: A. W. Shaw.

Landry, Robert S. 1942. *Who, What, Why Is Radio?* New York: George W. Stewart.

Lichty, Lawrence W., and Malachi C. Topping. 1975. *American Broadcasting: A Source Book on the History of Radio and Television*. New York: Hastings House.

Lumley, Frederick H. 1934. *Measurement in Radio*. Columbus, OH: Ohio State University Press.

Rothafel, Samuel L., and Raymond F. Yates. 1925. *Broadcasting: Its New Day*. New York: Century.

Schubert, Paul. 1928. *The Electric Word: The Rise of Radio*. New York: Macmillan.

Shurick, E. P. 1946. *The First Quarter Century of American Broadcasting*. Kansas City, MO: Midland.

Weeks, Lewis E. 1962. "Order Out of Chaos: The Formative Years of American Broadcasting." Unpublished Ph.D. dissertation, Michigan State University.

Sources for Period 2 (1935–50)

Barnouw, Erik. 1968. *The Golden Web: A History of Broadcasting in the U.S. 1933–1953*. New York: Oxford University Press.

Eoyang, Thomas T. 1936. *An Economic Study of the Radio Industry in the United States of America*. New York: Columbia University Press.

Floherty, John J. 1944. *Behind the Microphone*. Philadelphia: J. B. Lippincott.

Landry, Robert J. 1946. *The Fascinating Radio Business*. Indianapolis: Bobbs-Merrill.

Midgley, Ned. 1948. *The Advertising and Business Side of Radio*. New York: Prentice-Hall.

Robinson, Thomas P. 1943. *Radio Networks and the Federal Government*. New York: Columbia University Press.

Rose, C. B., Jr. 1940. *National Policy for Radio Broadcasting*. New York: Harper.

Waller, Judith C. 1946. *The Fifth Estate*. Boston: Houghton-Mifflin.

While, Llewellyn. 1947. *The American Radio*. Chicago: University of Chicago Press.

Wolfe, Charles H., and Frank LaClave. 1949. *Modern Radio Advertising*. New York: Printers' Ink Publishing.

Sources for Period 3 (1950–65)

Federal Communication Commission. 1958. *Network Broadcasting*. U.S. House of Representatives Report 1297, 85th Congress, 2nd Session. Washington, DC: Government Printing Office.

Fornatale, Peter, and Joshua E. Mills. 1980. *Radio in the Television Age*. Woodstock, NY: Overlook Press.

Gross, Ben. 1954. *I Looked and I Listened: Informal Recollections of Radio and TV*. New York: Random House.

Passman, Arnold. 1971. *The Deejays*. New York: Macmillan.

Poyntz, Tyler (ed.). 1961. *Television and Radio*. New York: H. W. Wilson.

Sterling, Christopher H. 1975. "Trends in Daily Newspaper and Broadcast Ownership, 1922–1970." *Journalism Quarterly* 46:227–36.

Sources for Period 4 (1966–90)

Barnouw, Erick. 1970. *The Image Empire: A History of Broadcasting in the U.S. from 1953*. New York: Oxford University Press.

Heighton, Elizabeth, and D. R. Cunningham. 1984. *Advertising in the Broadcast Media*. Belmont, CA: Wadsworth.

Johnson, Joseph S., and K. Jones. 1978. *Modern Radio Station Practices*. Belmont, CA: Wadsworth.

Le Duc, Don R. 1987. *Beyond Broadcasting: Patterns in Policy and Law*. New York: Longman.

Levin, Murray B. 1987. *Talk Radio and the American Dream*. Lexington, MA: Lexington Books.

Singleton, Roy A. 1986. *Telecommunications in the Information Age*, 2nd ed. Cambridge, MA: Ballinger.

Sterling, Christopher H. 1984. *Electronic Media: A Guide to Trends in Broadcasting and Newer Technologies, 1920–1983*. New York: Praeger.

Sterling, Christopher H., and T. R. Haight. 1978. *The Mass Media: Aspen Guide to Communications Industry Trends*. New York: Praeger.

Vogel, Harold L. 1986. *Entertainment Industry Economics: A Guide for Financial Analysis*. New York: Cambridge University Press.

Williams, Frederick. 1989. *The New Communications*. Belmont, CA: Wadsworth.

PERIODICAL PUBLICATIONS USED FOR DATA COLLECTION

Broadcasting (later, *Mass Media*). 1931–88. Washington DC: Broadcasting Publications.

Broadcasting Yearbook. 1939–89. Washington DC: Broadcasting Publications.

Broadcasting-Telecasting Yearbook. 1945–65. Washington DC: Broadcasting Publications.

Department of Commerce. 1927–75. *Historical Statistics of the U.S.* Washington DC: Government Printing Office.

Federal Communications Commission. 1938–80. *AM and FM Broadcast Financial Data*. Washington DC: Government Printing Office.

Federal Communications Commission. 1935–88. *Annual Report*. Washington DC: Government Printing Office.

Federal Radio Commission. 1927–33. *Annual Report*. Washington DC: Government Printing Office.

Federal Trade Commission. 1924–26. *Reports*. Washington DC: Government Printing Office.

National Association of Broadcasters. 1955–88. *Radio Financial Report*. Washington, DC: NAB.

Radio Annual. 1938–45. New York: Radio-Television Daily.

Radio Broadcast. 1922–30. Garden City, NY: Doubleday.

U.S. Department of Commerce. 1920–34. *Radio Service Bulletin*. Washington DC: Government Printing Office.

Yearbook of Radio and Television. 1946–80. New York: Radio-Television Daily.

16

Biotechnology Firms

ALLAN RYAN, JOHN FREEMAN, AND RALPH HYBELS

As the twentieth century dawned, scientists were just beginning to penetrate the secrets of the atom. By the time the century was half over, physicians had solved many of these secrets and devised numerous applications, including the atomic bomb. Nuclear physicists were the iconoclasts of the first half of the century. They seemed to subvert what was known about the physical world, even questioning basic notions such as the immutability of matter.

In the second half of the century, molecular biologists would repeat the creative destruction previously wrought by physicists. While physicists had forced a reconstruction of modern man's view of matter, biologists would force their contemporaries to rethink the most fundamental biotic processes. The strength of this challenge first became apparent in the 1950s as scientists such as Watson and Crick began to understand the structure and role of DNA (deoxyribonucleic acid). At the crucial moment, when they realized that they had solved the theoretical puzzle, Crick called his wife to tell her that he had discovered the secret of life (Watson 1968).

As the twentieth century draws to its close, molecular biologists and biochemists have entered the inner sanctum of the cell, and the age of biotechnology is upon us. As with nuclear physics before it, the implications of biotechnology are so pervasive that its activities are the focus not only of scientific but also of philosophical debate and controversy. Views of biotechnology fall between two poles. In one, biotechnology is presented as the gateway to a future of possibilities unlimited by the variety provided by nature. In the other, biotechnology is denounced as a Pandora's box that signals an end rather than a new beginning. Man can now create new life-forms whose behavior may not prove benevolent. Furthermore, moral understanding and consensus lags human capability. Whether people ought to apply technology in various ways is as important an issue as whether technology can be applied in these ways. While biotechnology has been shaped by its social context, it has also been changing the very context in which it has been developing.

Biotechnology does not conform to any of the usual definitions of an industry. The majority of American biotechnology companies were created to develop therapeutic and diagnostic pharmaceuticals. These companies can thus be viewed as part of the pharmaceutical industry, but biotechnology is more than a new wrinkle in pharmaceutical production. The biotechnology sector also includes a wide range of companies that have nothing to do with medicine. There are, for example, companies in agriculture that are modifying and securing patents on plants. Waste treatment of pollutants, sometimes called bioremediation, is increasingly employing genetically altered bacteria. Some firms use biotechnology to develop biopesticides. Others use it for animal breeding. In addition, the companies supplying equipment, raw materials, and software to the biotechnology marketplace are themselves often categorized as biotechnology companies. Because of this diversity of commercial foci, Standard Industrial Classification (SIC) codes cannot be used to define the population of biotechnology companies.

The common thread requiring analysis of these organizations as a group is not that they compete in the same product markets but rather that they employ technologies that involve direct manipulation of genetic materials. These technologies are derived from still-developing basic science. Because many biotechnology firms are engaged in advancing this basic science, profitable commercial outcomes of their research are little more than promises and prospects that have yet to be realized.

To secure investment capital, these firms need the prestige of leading scientists. The scientists, in turn, often maintain their affiliations with universities and not-for-profit laboratories. Thus, it is best to consider the biotechnology arena as an evolving *community of organizations* that includes freestanding entrepreneurial biotechnology specialists (called dedicated biotechnology companies), large diversified corporations, financial institutions, government agencies, and research organizations such as hospitals and government laboratories. The web of interdependencies reflected in strategic alliances joins this collectivity in a structure that is best described as a social network (Barley, Freeman, Hybels 1992).

One might wonder why this community exists at all. Why have this variety of specialized participants? One could imagine the commercialization of basic science being carried out by large diversified companies with biotechnology divisions. Indeed, some members of the community fit this description. So why do we see the others? This is another way of asking the key question of this group of chapters: How do segregating processes lead to distinct organizational forms? We begin to fashion an answer by examining the history of the technology itself.

TECHNICAL BREAKTHROUGHS

Since people began to farm with domesticated livestock, they have bred animals, hybridized plants, and used fermented silage and beverages. In the usual application of the term, however, biotechnology is linked to the utilization of several technical breakthroughs that enabled scientists to make predictable and controllable interventions in cellular and subcellular processes, directly manipulating genetic materials. Most histories view the creation of hybridomas and the development of recombinant DNA (rDNA) as the key discoveries.

The team of Cesar Milstein and Georges Köhler created hybridomas in 1975. Working in their lab at the Medical Research Council's Laboratory of Molecular Biology in Cambridge, England, Milstein and Köhler created hybrid cells that had two critical properties: the ability to reproduce in vitro (i.e., in a medium outside a living organism) and the ability to produce quantities of specific antibodies. Milstein and Köhler fused a specific kind of tumor cell, a myeloma, that could easily be maintained in a test tube environment, with a specific kind of cell referred to as a B lymphocyte that had been pretreated so as to stimulate the production of a specific antibody of interest. In a sense, the resultant cell mass, the *hybridoma,* became a cellular factory for the targeted antibody referred to as a monoclonal antibody (MAb).

The other seminal development in biotechnology arose out of the collaboration of Herbert Boyer of the University of California at San Francisco and Stanley N. Cohen of Stanford University. Around 1973, Boyer was investigating the properties of restriction enzymes that had the property of being able to cut DNA at known spots. At the same time, Cohen was studying the properties of plasmids, which are rings of DNA found outside of chromosomes. By combining forces, Boyer and Cohen were able to devise a recipe for inserting several different kinds of genes into the bacterium *Escherichia coli,* thereby altering its genetic structure. In simple terms, restriction enzymes provided the means for judiciously slicing DNA, and plasmids provided the raw materials for attaching new DNA to the sliced ends, hence, recombinant DNA (rDNA). A key aspect of their technology was that once the bacterium had been modified it retained the ability to reproduce. When it did so, the modified DNA was faithfully replicated.

PATENTS

Both the Milstein and Köhler and Boyer and Cohen discoveries occurred at the border between basic and applied science. The fact that they both opened up avenues for the reproduction of biological substances or the replication of genetic characteristics raised the possibility of direct commercial application of their discoveries. In the case of hybridomas, Milstein recognized the commercial possibilities and wrote a note to the Medical Research Council suggesting that patent protection might be appropriate. Milstein's suggestion was ignored.

In the case of Boyer and Cohen's work, the director of Stanford's technology transfer program suggested pursuing a patent. In 1974, just before the legal right to do so lapsed, Stanford, on behalf of itself and the University of California at San Francisco, filed a patent application for the Boyer and Cohen process. Although Boyer and Cohen renounced their own rights to the patent, they were exposed to considerable personal attack when at a conference in 1976, it became common knowledge that they had cooperated in an effort to patent what was seen as a basic technology. The fact that Boyer and Cohen have not received a Nobel prize for their efforts is sometimes attributed to their participation in this patenting effort and their subsequent involvement in some of the more prominent biotechnology start-up companies. In contrast, Milstein and Köhler shared a Nobel in 1984.

At the time of the original Boyer and Cohen patent application, the status of attempts to patent life-formats and procedures relating to the modification of life-forms was already a controversial legal point. In 1972, Ananda Chakrabarty, a scientist working for General Electric (later, the University of Illinois), had used certain techniques to force genetic modification of a *Pseudomonas* bacterium that enhanced its ability to break down oil. The resultant bacterium was seen as a possible treatment for oil slicks and other oil pollution. At the time, the Patent and Trademark Office accepted the patent application insofar as it covered the means of producing the organism and the means of dispersing it, but rejected patent coverage of the organism itself.

As the claim progressed through various stages of appeal, the major issue related to the Chakrabarty patent came to be whether living things could be patented. On June 16, 1980, the U.S. Supreme Court ruled five to four *(Diamond v. Chakrabarty)* in favor of granting patent protection to living things. According to the Burger Court, the intent of Congress had been to extend patent protection to "anything under the sun that is made by man."

The Chakrabarty decision was considered a landmark for the development of commercial biotechnology. Before the end of 1980, the ruling in favor of the Chakrabarty patent was followed by the approval of the second reformulation of the basic Cohen and Boyer patent covering the rDNA process. The December 2, 1980, patent entitled "Process for Producing Biologically Functional Molecular Chimeras" was granted to "Cohen et al." As the assignee for this and two later patents that are sometimes collectively referred to as the Boyer-Cohen program, Stanford collected approximately $17 million in 1991 and "is expected to make $150 million by the time it expires in 1997" *(Boston Business Journal,* March 8, 1992).

Stanford's ability to patent work that had been funded from public coffers was only possible because specific agreements with the National Institutes of Health (NIH) allowed it to do so. In 1980, however, Congress passed the Patent and Trademark Amendments Act of 1980, which provided blanket provisions under which universities could pursue patent protection for work funded by government agencies.

Together, Chakrabarty, Boyer and Cohen, and the Trademarks Amendment Act of 1980 represented a watershed in the commercialization of biotechnology. Before 1980, the lack of precedent and a prevailing reticence among scientists to appear too strongly tied to commercial concerns conspired to restrict patenting activities of universities. After 1980, many of these constraints were lifted or were greatly diminished. On a more general basis, it became apparent to commercial (and university) interests that research conducted in biotechnology now had the potential to be protected by patent, and the financial risks associated with developing products in this area were substantially reduced.

Equally important for our purposes here is the fact that coordinated action by various kinds of organizations was required to combine the financial incentives, scientific knowledge, and organizational resources necessary to transfer the technology from scientific laboratories into the commercial arena. The institutional structures set up to protect rights to intellectual property set the stage for a segregating process in which such organizational forms as universities, venture capital firms, law firms, government agencies, and specialist biotechnology companies combined efforts. Protecting the interests of specialized organizations removed one of the major reasons for organizing in a single, generalized form.

According to a survey conducted by the House Science and Technology and Oversight Subcommittee, patent applications involving human biologicals filed by universities and medical research institutions increased over 300 percent from 1980 to 1984 compared to the preceding five-year period (U.S. Congress, Office of Technology Assessment 1987). According to the same source, this type of patent constituted 22 percent of university and research hospital patenting over this period. The study also notes that 49 percent of all medical institutions have participated in this patenting process.

The greater security for intellectual assets afforded by these developments in patent law has provided the basis for a wide variety of strategic alliances among members of the organizational community in U.S. biotechnology. Biotechnology firms need funding to support their research activities, but often they have no products generating profits. Because they have no profits from operations, it is difficult to raise capital. One way to generate funds is by selling off intellectual property currently being developed. Essentially, the firms sell futures contracts on products yet to be developed. The uncertainties involved are obvious and would probably be unacceptable to investors.

If a firm has a strong patent position on products it is developing, other firms often are willing to exchange funding for the rights to market or manufacture the product when it is through development. At a less concrete level, well-established firms often are willing to underwrite part of the research and development cost in order to keep abreast of rapid developments in a subfield and to develop a relationship with a biotechnology firm that may subsequently yield commercial rights to a new process or product. Patents underlie many of the patterns of alliance formation that reflect the interdependencies and mutual support structures that make the community of biotechnology organizations viable.

THE ACADEMIC MIGRATION
TO COMMERCIAL BIOTECHNOLOGY

By the time the fundamental decisions of 1980 had been rendered, the precedent for academic biologists and biochemists expanding their connections with outside commercial enterprises had already been set. In 1971, Cetus had been founded to exploit the commercial potential of molecular biology. By 1977,

Cetus already had two directors or advisors who had won Nobel prizes (Joshua Lederberg and Ronald Glaser). Stanley Cohen had also signed on as an advisor to Cetus. In 1976, Herbert Boyer had joined with a former venture capitalist, Robert Swanson, to form Genentech. Harvard's Warner Gilbert and the University of Zurich's Charles Weissmann formed Biogen in 1978 as the first multinational biotechnology firm. In 1980, Gilbert would share the Nobel prize in chemistry and Weissman would become the first scientist to succeed in making bacteria produce facsimiles of human interferon. In short, by the end of the 1970s, many of the finest scientific minds in the world were also some of the first biotechnology entrepreneurs.

The activities of scientists such as Glaser, Cohen, Boyer, Gilbert, and Weissman gave proof to the observation that a new relationship was developing between academic biology and industry. By 1980, there was already widespread recognition of the fact that the bulk of the expertise that would be required to translate the advances of biotechnology into the commercial marketplace resided in research universities and other research-based, nonprofit institutions. Commercial interests were already devising a variety of means for tapping into these critical resources. Directly involving academics in biotechnology start-up companies was only one of these means. But these scientists often wished to retain links to academe. Even for them, the risk of obsolescence was great. Therefore, many of them retained academic appointments while holding equity interests in commercial ventures. Universities and various kinds of not-for-profit laboratories continued to play an important role in the development of biotechnology.

The formation of new business based on biotechnology provides a fairly clear measure of the rate at which biotechnology was attracting commercial interest. Records of such entries are well documented, in part due to the fact that biotechnology was being assiduously tracked by government, by interest groups, and by members of the investment community. The pace at which established companies began to conduct genetic and biotechnology research on their own account is both harder to measure and harder to interpret.

INVOLVEMENT OF ESTABLISHED COMPANIES

In 1977, a *Business Week* (January 17, 1977) article about Cetus, one of the first biotechnology start-ups, made the observation that most major pharmaceutical houses and many major chemical companies had already started to make direct and indirect investments in biotechnology. With few exceptions, however, information on the extent, exact timing, and nature of this early investment is limited. It is clear, however, that by the time Stanford's initial licensing deadline for the Cohen-Boyer patent had passed at the end of 1981, seventy-two corporations from nine countries had paid $1.44 million (McGraw-Hill's *Biotechnology Newswatch,* December 21, 1981) for the rights to use this basic genetic engineering technology.

Counted among these initial licensees were giant American chemical, agricultural, and food corporations such as Nabisco/Standard Brands, Allied Corporation, American Cyanamid, Corning Glass, E. I. duPont, and Texaco. Predictably, the majority of the major pharmaceutical houses were also among the licensees. Of course, some of these early licensees may not have been very active in rDNA research at the time and may have paid for licenses primarily as a means for securing an option to pursue potentially profitable technology.

A factor limiting the use of biotechnology within large chemical and pharmaceutical companies was their lack of strength in the science on which the technology was based. The well-established companies were dominated by people whose training was in chemistry. Chemists discover the uses of new compounds by a trial-and-error process. Frequently, chemists working for pharmaceutical firms start with the compound and then search for a disease it might be used in treating. Biotechnology begins with the disease. The drug is synthesized to treat that disease. This difference between the focused method of the biologist and the trial-and-error method of the chemist makes managers trained in the latter discipline skeptical of the potential of the alternative method. Furthermore, the level of medical understanding required for success of the biotechnological approach is much higher.

Study of the biotechnology research efforts of large corporations is based largely on the self-reports of such corporations. But researchers interested in studying large company involvement in biotechnology also have been able to rely on observable and verifiable actions taken by such companies. These actions include founding new subsidiaries or divisions devoted to biotechnology, technology licensing, research agreements, and contracts signed with universities and research centers; applications for approval of experiments (from the Recombinant Advisory Committee, for example); and various agreements with the biotechnology start-ups. A number of researchers have studied the pattern of ties to dedicated biotechnology firms in order to gauge both the level and focus of diversified corporations' strategic intents vis-à-vis biotechnology.

Without question, large companies were crucial players in the early development of biotechnology. The first rDNA-derived therapeutic pharmaceutical product was marketed by Eli Lilly. Many of the first diagnostic products based on monoclonal antibodies were marketed by Syntex (a manufacturer of birth control pills). Throughout the 1970s, small biotechnology firms such as Cetus and Genentech relied on large companies not only for research contracts but also for investment capital. Indeed, in the area of agricultural biotechnology, companies such as Monsanto have been dominant investors since the very inception of the technologies. By 1990, Monsanto's cumulative investment in agricultural biotechnology was on the order of $800 million (*New York Times,* 1990). Even in Monsanto's case, its work in developing bovine somatotropin, a growth hormone that stimulates the production of milk in dairy cattle, found its start in work conducted by Genentech.

While large diversified corporations had resources that expensive biotechnology research and development required, they also had disadvantages that kept them from simply taking over the promising technology, a process that might have served to exclude the other forms from the burgeoning organizational community.

THE APPARENT DOMINANCE
OF THE BIOTECHNOLOGY START-UP

While some Fortune 500 firms have shown consistent interest in biotechnology, much of the productive activity in American commercial biotechnology has occurred outside the confines of giant corporations. Indeed, it could be said that biotechnology is a young company's game. Since the inception of biotechnology, many large pharmaceutical, chemical, agriculture, and food companies have been active investors and researchers. Indeed, many large companies have established subsidiaries or divisions devoted to biotechnology. Their numbers, however, have been dwarfed by the number of start-up companies devoted to commercializing biotechnology, as can be seen in Figure 16-1. New companies have achieved not only numerical dominance but there is considerable evidence that the commercial success of the biotechnology-based start-ups has so far outstripped the contributions of better-established firms.

One has to ask why this should be so. How can small, entrepreneurial firms outperform giants such as Johnson and Johnson, duPont, and Eastman Kodak? There are two general answers. First, the people running the specialist firms know the technology intimately and are committed to it. Research in this field is often their life's work. They understand the risks but also can grasp the possibilities. In contrast, top management of the larger, diversified companies rarely includes molecular biologists. Even when these managers are scientists, they generally are from branches of science only remotely involved in biotech-

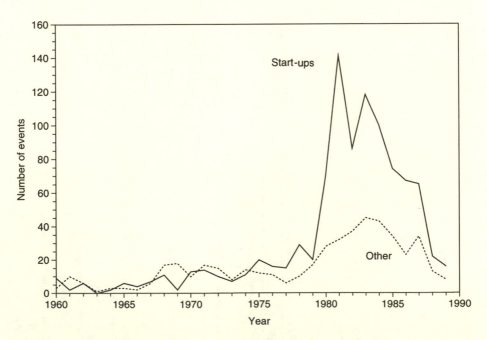

Figure 16–1 Biotechnology entries by year. (*Source:* Authors' analysis.)

Table 16–1 Biotechnology-generated human therapeutics products

Brand	Market Co.	Original Co.	Condition	FDA approval
Human Insulin rDNA Origin				
Humulin	Eli-Lilly	Genentech	Diabetes	29-Oct-82
Erythropoietin Alpha				
Epogen	Amgen	Amgen	Dialysis anemia	01-Jun-89
Procrit	Ortho Biotech	Amgen	AIDs-related & predialysis anemia	31-Dec-90
Granulocyte Factors				
Neupogen	Amgen	Amgen	Chemotherapy white blood cell dest.	20-Feb-91
Leukine	Immunex/Hoechst	Immunex	Post transplant bone marrow infect.	05-Mar-91
Human Growth Hormone rDNA Origin				
Humatrope	Eli-Lilly	Amgen	Growth deficiency in children	08-Mar-87
Protropin	Genentech	Genentech	Growth deficiency in children	18-Oct-85
Interferon Gamma 1-B				
Actimmune	Genentech	Genentech	Granulomatous disease	21-Dec-90
Tissue Plasminogen Activator, t-PA				
Activase	Genentech	Genentech	Heart attacks	13-Nov-87
Activase	Genentech	Genentech	Pulmonary embolism	06-Jun-90

Alpha Interferon				
Roferon-A	Hoff-LaRoche	Genentech	Hairy cell leukemia	04-Jun-86
Intron A	Schering-Plough	Biogen	Hairy cell leukemia	04-Jun-86
Intron A	Schering-Plough	Biogen	Genital warts	06-Jun-88
Intron A	Schering-Plough	Biogen	Aids related Kaposi's sarcoma	21-Nov-88
Intron A	Schering-Plough	Biogen	Hepatitis C	26-Feb-91
Roferon-A	Hoff-LaRoche	Genentech	Aids related Kaposi's sarcoma	21-Nov-88
Intron A	Schering-Plough	Biogen	Hepatitis B	13-Jul-92
Haemophilus B Conjugate Vaccine				
Hib Titer	Praxis Biol	Praxis Biol	Haemophilus-B (children)	22-Dec-88
PedvaxHIB	Merck	Merck	Haemophilus-B (children)	12-Feb-90
Hib Titer	Lederle	Praxis Biol	Haemophilus-B (infants)	04-Oct-90
Hepatitis B Vaccine (Recombinant MSD)				
RecombivaxHIB	Merck	Chiron	Hepatitis B prevention	23-Jul-86
Engerix-B	Smithkline Beech	Biogen	Hepatitis B prevention	28-Aug-89
Anti T-Cell MAB				
Orthoclone	Ortho Bio	Ortho Bio	Kidney transplant rejection	19-Jun-86
Interleukin-2				
Proleukin	Chiron	Cetus	Renal cancer	05-May-92
Bovine Pegademase				
Adagen	Enzon	Enzon	Combined immunodeficiency disease	23-Mar-90

nology. It is difficult for such people to evaluate the results of forays into bio-technology.

The second reason is that biotechnology is developing on so many fronts at such a rapid pace that it is extremely difficult for even the largest firms to support research activities in all of them simultaneously. A giant can tolerate only so much risk, especially when other, less risky parts of the corporation are hungry for capital as well. Rather than build and support research teams in each of these application areas, the large firms find it easier to manage a more remote involvement. Such firms can spend modest amounts of money to monitor a large number of developing areas and have some role in the commercialization of the most promising areas. Building alliances with pure-play biotechnology firms is a way to limit financial risk.

The relative impact of start-ups versus large, established companies is illustrated by the sources of the biotechnology-based products that have appeared in the therapeutic pharmaceutical sector. Table 16-1 provides ample evidence of the dominant role biotechnology start-ups have played in technical innovation. Of the twelve broad classes of biotechnically derived therapeutic substances approved by the Food and Drug Administration (FDA) from 1982 through 1992, only one (orthoclone-CD3) emanated exclusively from the laboratories of a large pharmaceutical house. Indeed, of the twenty-five approvals of eighteen trademarked substances, all but two could be traced back to work originally conducted by biotechnology start-ups.

THE MARKET IMPACT OF BIOTECHNOLOGY
IN PHARMACEUTICALS

While the biotechnology firms proved their ability to develop products throughout the 1980s, the growing number of biotechnology drug approvals did little to establish biotechnology firms as direct forces in the pharmaceutical market. There were two reasons for this. First, pharmaceutical houses were marketing many of the most successful products of biotechnology firm research. Second, the regulatory approval process overseen in the United States by the FDA was slow and incremental. Under the regulatory system, biotechnology drugs of potentially wide application were being approved for use on a disease-by-disease basis. For example, alpha-interferon received separate approvals for five conditions over a space of six years. Because of the rarity of some diseases for which approvals were granted, the market penetration of biotechnology-derived pharmaceuticals was slow.

When pharmaceutical companies introduce a new product in the United States (and in most other economically advanced countries), the drug must be shown to be both safe and effective before it can be sold. This requires a series of studies moving from laboratory research on substances such as tissue samples, through clinical field trials, where the new product is used on people. With each step, the process grows more expensive. The risks of failure rise. Finally, in the United States this evidence is presented before the FDA. Both the timing of the presentation and the manner in which evidence is presented are guided by artful management skills that neophytes usually lack (Hirsch 1975). So alliances are often sought to provide the funding for these tests and also for help in gaining the vital approvals. As costs mount, risks of falling short of full approval often amount to betting the company. Weak firms often never get to this point. Being able to bet the company on a roll of the regulatory dice is a privilege accorded only the best companies—those with the best scientific talent and the most adept management. Even after approval, the product still has to prevail in the marketplace for the firm to recoup its investment. Sometimes this does not happen.

Genentech became the first biotechnology company to begin the transition from research boutique to full-fledged biopharmaceutical company in 1985. In that year, the first biotechnology drug was both developed and marketed by a biotechnology firm, rDNA-originated human growth hormone (Protropin). Genentech was poised for a change of character.

For months prior to the Protropin launch, Genentech had been quietly laying the groundwork for the creation and activation of a dedicated sales force to sell the drug. Protropin's approval served as the signal to activate the strategy (Hamilton 1986). Over the course of the next five years this marketing strategy was repeated not only for Genentech's other star drug, Activase (tPA used to dissolve blood clots after heart attacks), which was approved in 1987, but was also utilized by Amgen when it introduced its first two products. When Amgen introduced its drugs Epogen in 1989 and Neupogen in 1991, it retained the majority of U.S. marketing rights and built a targeted sales force. Figure 16-2 provides evidence that it is possible for a company to penetrate a market quickly when the demand is present for the product. However, all four of the drugs shown were destined for specialized niches that made targeted marketing and sales to select medical specialties and hospitals.

Aside from the history of the sales growth of the successful biotechnology products presented in Figure 16-2, other important things were happening to the firms that introduced the products. Genentech was 60 percent acquired by the Swiss pharmaceutical company, Hoffmann-LaRoche in 1990, and, in January 1992, Amgen became the first biotechnology company to join the Fortune 500. The major marketing successes of the two preeminent pharmaceutically oriented biotechnology firms thus served as precursors in one case to surrender independence and in the other to become one of the independent forces shaping the biotechnology market. In order to help in understanding these events, consider the stories of some of the new biotechnology companies, with a special focus on the history of Genentech.

THE BIOTECHNOLOGY PIONEERS

Among the pioneering biotechnology companies were Cetus, Genentech, Agrigenetics, Biogen, Genex, Hybritech, and Centocor. Of this group, Agrigenetics was acquired by Lubrizol in 1985, Hybritech was acquired by Eli Lilly in 1986, Genentech was acquired by Roche in 1990, and Cetus was acquired by Chiron in 1991. At various stages in their histories each of these companies experi-

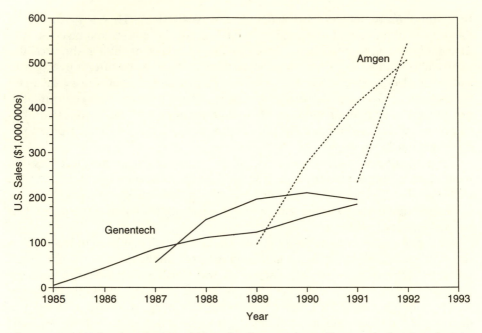

Figure 16–2 U.S. sales of selected biotechnology products. (*Source:* Authors' analysis.)

enced difficulties, but none could be categorized as a failure. In fact, most observers would count these among the success stories of commercial biotechnology.

As can be seen in Figure 16-3, the number of biotechnology firms that have dissolved in one way or another has been steadily increasing. However, it is deceptive to characterize this trend as evidence of an increasing number of true business failures. Biotechnology companies disappear in a variety of ways. In absolute numbers, failures of firms are rare. We can see from Table 16-2 that bankruptcy is a very rare phenomenon in biotechnology; acquisitions are more common. The "Acquired" row in Table 16-2 includes acquisitions of organizations that continued to operate after the acquisition. Subsumed within the "Died" row, however, are acquisitions that resulted in the disappearance of the organization as a distinct entity. The most reasonable explanation for the lack of outright failures in biotechnology is that because the assets of these organizations are mostly intellectual there is little to sell at auction. Creditors will receive more if other companies buy out a dedicated biotechnology firm than they would receive if it were to dissolve.

By the time Genentech was acquired, it had achieved preeminence in American biotechnology. As mentioned, Genentech had been responsible for the first rDNA-produced therapeutic agent (human insulin). With the launch of its rDNA–human growth hormone, Protropin, in 1985, it became the first biotechnology firm to bring a therapeutic pharmaceutical product from discovery, through regulatory approvals, to market by its own sales force. Even in its

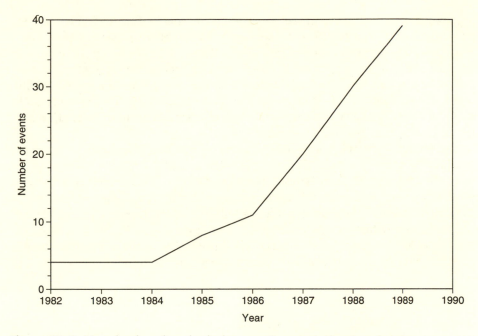

Figure 16–3 Biotechnology firm deaths by year. (*Source:* Authors' analysis.)

earliest years, Genentech was much more than a research boutique. It was a groundbreaker and, as such, it became a symbol for all of biotechnology. To a certain extent, knowing Genentech's history is to understand the history of commercial biotechnology in general.

Since the beginning of the 1980s, Genentech was the stuff of legends and the darling of the financial community. When it went public on October 14, 1980, its stock rose from an opening price of $35 to $89 in a matter of twenty minutes. This precipitous price run-up is said to have set a record for the quickest increase in stock price of an initial public offering in the history of American finance.

The central role that Genentech played in the commercialization of biotechnology is established by reference back to Table 16-1. Of the twenty-four FDA drug approvals for biotechnology-derived therapeutics, seven (for five separate

Table 16–2 Frequency of types of ending events for biotechnology firms

Ending event	Frequency
Acquired	118
Bankruptcy	3
Changed name	77
Died	122
Merged	24
Other	3
Set free	11

substances) have been granted to products associated with Genentech research. Since the early 1980s, Genentech also established itself as the largest biotechnology employer among new firms. Throughout its history, Genentech has served both as a symbol of biotechnology and as an exemplar for new businesses to emulate. As such, Genentech has served to educate the public and to disseminate information about the sector as a whole. The fortunes made by Genentech founders and early investors also served as an example that motivated both scientists and financiers.

The means by which a new idea is financed and made concrete in the form of a new product or service is a complex function of seemingly chance events (including the unique contributions of visionaries or risk-seeking investors), the structure of the market for which the innovation is destined, the public perception of the technology, and the shifting features of the broad economy. In addition, the early history and experience of companies and individuals attempting to exploit emerging technologies can serve to shape the very environment in which similar innovations must compete for capital and legitimacy.

THE DEVELOPMENT OF THE VIEW
OF BIOTECHNOLOGY AS A HAZARD

In 1974 and 1975, the focus of media-related coverage of biotechnology was on its hazards. In the aftermath of publicity and controversy associated with his plans to use a cancer-causing virus as a means of inserting new genetic material into a bacterium, Stanford University scientist Paul Berg organized a moratorium on certain types of genetic experimentation that were held to be especially dangerous. Some of the most distinguished researchers of the time were signatories to the July 1974 letter that instigated the voluntary moratorium.

As the impact of the voluntary moratorium took hold, the world's attention focused on the Asilomar Center in Pacific Grove, California. From February 24–27, 1975, Berg and most of the world's (and certainly America's) major names in molecular biology and biochemistry gathered to debate and to devise a system of guidelines for scientific experimentation in genetic technologies. It was hoped that proper procedures and regulation would reduce or eliminate the danger of the accidental creation of renegade viruses and other biological hazards. Asilomar was more than a scientific conference. It was also a media event. The fact that one of the more famous accounts of the proceedings was run in *Rolling Stone* magazine serves to illustrate Asilomar's impact on popular culture and public perception of biotechnology. Ultimately, these fears were allayed and research continued.

In Europe, these concerns were at least as serious. The Greens party in West Germany mobilized resistance, which was as much a moral issue concerned with the limits of human intervention in life processes, as a concern for potential damage from errors in research or manufacturing. Public suspicion of biotechnology in Europe has led many European chemical and pharmaceutical firms to establish research laboratories in the United States and to develop research, development, and other alliances with American firms. Legitimacy problems threatened to stifle the organizations seeking to develop biotechnology. However, diversity of organizational forms in the U.S. community produced ways of getting around these legitimacy problems.

RISK TOLERANCE OF SMALL COMPANIES

In the presence of significant liability hazards, smallness accords a firm competitive advantages in conducting research in potentially hazardous technologies (see Barney, Edwards, and Ringleb 1992). A small asset base means there is little to lose. At the very least, tort risks increase the incentives for large companies to conduct research through the veil of legally distinct subsidiaries and joint ventures (witness Dow-Corning's experience with breast implants where the joint-venture structure insulated Dow and Corning from direct liability hazards).

Asilomar focused public attention and fears on the emerging technologies of biotechnology. Perhaps Asilomar also served to caution large cash- or asset-rich companies from taking the lead roles in investigating and developing the commercial opportunities these technologies represented. For large companies the challenge presented by biotechnology was to balance the risk of conducting potentially hazardous research internally against the risk of missing out on maintaining long-term competitive capabilities. But by 1984, a vice-president of Hoffmann-LaRoche was quoted as saying of biotechnology: "It is risky not to be in the business" (*Business Week,* 1984). By that time the relaxation of voluntary guidelines for oversight of genetic engineering experiments and the absence of major laboratory disasters had perhaps also reduced industry misgivings.

While the voluntary moratorium on genetic engineering proved to be temporary, as did the most onerous guidelines governing experimentation, activists against biotechnology have had a considerable and enduring impact on the development of agricultural biotechnology. The leading exponent of the antibiotechnology movement has been Jeremy Rifkin, an activist who first rose to prominence after disrupting a 1977 National Academy of Sciences session dealing with rDNA science policy (Krimsky 1991, p. 109). In the intervening years, Rifkin and his colleagues have had little impact on either diagnostic or therapeutic pharmaceuticals.

It is difficult to secure widespread public support for halting medical research that holds promise to alleviate human suffering through either therapeutic intervention or detection. In the case of agriculture, however, emotions are more easily roused in opposition to innovation. Although Rifkin has often been criticized as a modern-day Luddite, he has proven adept at forming coalitions of farmers, environmentalists,, and other groups in common cause. The most effective tactic of opposition has been filing lawsuits.

PATTERNS OF INVESTMENT

Fiduciary Responsibilities and High-Risk Investment

April 25, 1978, could be seen as one of the red letter days in the development of biotechnology. It was not a day when a famous patent was granted or a scientific discovery was announced. Rather, it was the day that the Department of Labor released a proposed regulation regarding its oversight of pension fund investment in the United States. The ruling concerned guidelines for interpreting the Employment Retirement Income Security Act (ERISA)—the Prudent Man Rule. When invoked in the context of ERISA, this rule threatened to hold managers of funds personally liable if imprudent investments damaged a fund's financial position. Since no interpretive guidelines were included in the pension fund legislation, pension trusts were effectively confined to investments that were most damaged by inflation in the 1970: bonds and high-dividend blue-chip stocks. Thus virtually none of this vast store of money in pension funds was available to fund small companies that promised to be the fuel of future economic expansion.

After 1978, however, the Prudent Man Rule was applied to the entire portfolio of investments. High-yield investments that bore a corresponding higher risk could be balanced by more secure investments. With this change, the gate through which a huge volume of capital was to flow was lifted. The direction of this flow increasingly favored the new wave of technology engendered by the surge of scientific discovery in biology. An important link between organizations managing funds and organizations specializing in biotechnology development was forged.

Venture Capital

Since small stock investments had taken a beating in the late 1960s and early 1970s, the prudence of investing in new and small businesses was open to question. The uncertainty associated with the treatment of such investment restricted funds available to the venture capital industry. In an article in the *Washington Post* (1979), Nancy L. Ross wrote:

> Risk capital needed to finance nascent businesses—the Xeroxes of tomorrow, as they are often called, dried up. It is believed that the new prudence standard will act as a pump primer. According to Stanley E. Pratt, publisher of *Venture Capital,* the amount of money available remained virtually static at about $3 billion for a decade. "Then last year the dam broke," he said. While the principal impetus was lowering the capital gains tax, Pratt said, the 15 to 20 percent returns realized by some venture capitalists also attracted some investors. A billion new dollars in commitments has been received in the past 18 months by organized venture capital groups; pension funds, which began to jump in during the final quarter of last year, placed $50 million. Pratt said the groups are now busy raising $300 million, a far greater share of which is expected to come from pension funds. "If we could get just one percent of their ($550 billion plus) assets, we could double our capital base," sighed Pratt.

While changes in tax law and the privations of inflation were forcing investors in the late 1970s to look toward venture capital investment opportunities, this avenue of investment would have been off-limits to pension fund investors had they not been freed up by the ERISA guidelines.

Given the prominent successes of venture capitalists in the semiconductor and computer markets (e.g., Intel, Digital Equipment), at least part of this pension fund money of "institutional investors" was given over to the management of both new and established venture capital funds. The late 1970s and early 1980s were the boom years of venture capital. As is evident in Figure 16-1, a good portion of this capital found its way into financing the early efforts of a number of biotechnology start-ups. The ERISA interpretation allowed pension fund investment in American venture capital funds to rise to 33 percent (*Annual Review of Venture Capital* 1985) of total venture capital commitments by 1982 (with another 21% provided by insurance companies and endowments and foundations). The new interpretation guidelines also freed pension funds and similar fiduciary funds to participate in direct stock market financing of biotechnology firms that started to develop in 1980.

Public Offerings and the Market for Small Firm Equities

The 1970s also saw the over-the-counter stock market mature and grow more efficient. In 1971, the National Association of Securities Dealers introduced a computerized stock quotation system called the NASD Automated Quotations System (NASDAQ). Although the 1970s were drought years for financing new or young business ventures with public equity by selling stock to the public via Initial Public Offerings (IPOs), by the early 1980s NASDAQ was well equipped to provide a postsale market for small and growing companies when this market reemerged.

The number and dollar volume of IPOs began to grow in the closing years of the 1970s. With this growth came expanded opportunities and incentives for new business formation in growth industries such as biotechnology. In many ways the startling success of Genentech's IPO on October 14, 1980, signaled that a new age had begun for biologically sophisticated start-up companies. The success of the Genentech IPO also reinforced the attractiveness of the biotechnology sector for venture capital investment, since an IPO is the preferred "exit strategy" for most venture capitalists.

VENDIBLE EXPERTISE

Genentech's progression from idea, to start-up, to stock market star was carefully orchestrated by financiers, but the development of the company also tracked the development of its science. This was not to be the case for many of the "instant" biotechnology companies that would follow its lead. Perhaps the most important example that Genentech set was not how to run a business or how to develop new products but rather how to sell an idea to investors. Unlike Genentech, not all start-ups were to follow the Silicon Valley template of locating near their financiers and being well advanced on a program of research before significant sums of money were solicited from the public. One of the best-known examples of an instant biotechnology company is Genetic Systems.

According to the legend (Kleinfield 1983; Saunders 1983), David Blech, a twenty-four-year-old stockbroker/musician, and his brother Isaac, a thirty-year-old advertising copywriter, formed Genetic Systems Corporation in November 1980 on the basis of a magazine article about monoclonal antibodies. Their motivation was provided by the example of the Genentech IPO. Within months of devising the original idea of creating a company based on monoclonal antibodies, the brothers had incorporated a company, recruited one of the field's top scientists (Robert Nowinsky) to act as a founding father, and raised over $4 million in venture capital. Eight months after incorporating Genetic Systems, the brothers Blech launched a successful IPO that raised an additional $6 million. The Blechs' initial cash investment of approximately $200,000 now had a paper value of between $12 million and $24 million. Genetic Systems soon helped establish Seattle as a significant center for the commercialization of biotechnology.

Genetic Systems was destined not only to serve as the example of an instant biotechnology company but as one of the earliest cases of a biotechnology start-up purchased by a major corporation that paid a premium price to establish a direct foothold in biotechnology. Thus when Genetic Systems was acquired by Bristol-Myers in 1986 for $294 million, its example became even more compelling.

The success of Genetic Systems established a strategy that begged for replication. In the years that have passed since the Blech brothers founded Genetic Systems, they have used similar techniques in the other biotechnology start-ups in which they have participated. They select an attractive technological niche, recruit first-rate scientific talent knowledgeable in the technology, recruit credible management, ensure that significant start-up capital is made available, and bring the company public with blinding speed. The Blechs have specialized in marketing biotechnology companies to investors when the company is still "pure organization" and little more than a legal structure of personnel contracts, a stated technology niche, and private financial backing sufficient to demonstrate that the company means business. As an example, Nova Pharmaceutical went public before the company even had a lab.

Well-publicized successes in biotechnology investment have often generated more investment in start-ups. Biotechnology is a field where a good deal of the managerial talent has been devoted to enterprise formation and to securing early-stage financing. With a fortune estimated to be on the order of $295 million, Blech has been able to use personal resources to rescue several companies from cash-flow crunches. Rescue operations in which he has been involved include Pharmatec, Ecogen, Liposome Technology, and Neorx. Thus, the Blechs' activities maybe viewed as an early warning system of developing opportunities and industry trends.

One question that the history of biotechnology raises is the relationship between innovation and organizational structure. When funding for new ventures is readily available, the history of biotechnology suggests that the most creative and valuable talent will leave rather than remain employees in large corporations where rewards are highly linked to positions in hierarchies. All of biotechnology's success stories have illustrated this principle.

First biotechnology start-ups stole scientific talent from universities and executive talent from the pharmaceutical and chemical companies. Over the past few years, however, the stories of prominent departures have been from large biotechnology firms to small biotechnology firms. Thus 1990 saw the former Amgen chairman join with Genetic Systems founder Robert Nowinsky to found Icos, with Blech financing. In 1992 Nowinski would join with former Baxter International president Wilbur Gantz to found Pathogenesis, also with Blech financing. After the Roche takeover of Genentech, it too began to lose important personnel. The most serious was the loss of David Goeddel, leader of Genentech's development of human insulin, human growth hormone, and TPA, who left to found Tularik.

STRATEGIC ALLIANCES

Dedicated biotechnology companies have proliferated rapidly in large measure because of the support of a diverse set of other organizations that provide funds, technology, human resources, market access, and even feed stocks and other materials. Typically these relationships involve a kind of partnership in which the other firm expects access to the technology being developed by the biotechnology firm. In Table 16-3, we present the frequencies with which the various kinds of alliances are found in the biotechnology community.

By far the most common relationship is an equity investment. The firms most likely to provide capital in exchange for equity are, of course, financial institutions such as banks or venture capital funds. In addition, however, there are pension funds, university endowments, and foundations, as well as for-profit diversified corporations. The next two most common kinds of agreements involve the direct exchange of funding for technology. Marketing agreements usually involve a product that is ready for sale, and they are frequently geo-

Table 16–3 Frequency of forms of alliances in the biotechnology industry

Type of alliance	Frequency
Equity investment	1983
Marketing agreement	1355
Licensing agreement	1029
Development	1017
Research	691
Research & development	609
Joint venture	327
Manufacturing agreement	272
Grant	273
Supply agreement	177
Other	304

Table 16–4 Countries where firms are headquartered

Country	Number	Percent
United States	2,094	65.8
Japan	219	6.9
United Kingdom	219	6.9
Canada	114	3.6
France	86	2.7
Germany	51	1.6
Sweden	49	1.5
Australia	46	1.4
Netherlands	42	1.3
Italy	42	1.3
Other	223	7.5
Unknown	691	—

graphically specific. One might negotiate such an agreement with a Japanese company, for example, in order to secure access to the Japanese market. Licensing agreements often involve a flow of technology in the other direction. That is, the dedicated biotechnology firm secures from a university or government laboratory the rights to develop a promising lead.

Ties between companies for development, research, or both research and development involve the creation of new technology but vary in the specificity of the final product. This is important because in the United States research shows up in accounting systems as an expense to be charged against income while product development is amortized over a period of time and charged against expected revenues from the project under development.

Joint ventures and manufacturing agreements are strategically important but less common. They usually are formed only when a product is ready to go into production. Small dedicated biotechnology companies often lack the capital for vertical integration, and they seek allies to help get their products into the marketplace. Grants usually flow from government agencies or not-for-profit organizations to biotechnology firms. Supply agreements usually involve some hard-to-find raw material such as a particular kind of organism used in research.

The diversity of these agreements serves to support the strength of the biotechnology community. Organizations from around the world provide resources for each other, allowing a constantly shifting structure to keep up with rapid technical change and the swift creation of new, sometimes enormous markets.

Of the 3,876 organizations that we have observed as having some involvement in the biotechnology community, the majority are headquartered in the United States, as can be seen in Table 16-4. This is to be expected, of course, since we are discussing the U.S. community. However, many partners in strategic alliances are located in Japan and Europe.

As can be seen in Table 16-5, there is an important distinction between the Europeans and Japanese in their manner of involvement in U.S. biotechnology. Japanese companies are more likely than European companies to seek partners in mature technologies—those with products in the market or ready to go to market. They are less likely to take equity positions in American biotechnology

Table 16–5 Japanese and European share of alliances in the biotechnology industry (by percent)

Type of alliance	Europe	Japan
Equity investment	13	6
Licensing agreement	17	13
Development	15	13
Research	14	5
Manufacturing agreement	17	15
Supply agreement	18	4
Total	16	11

firms. The rarity of Japanese equity investments is all the more striking because equity ties are the most common form of alliance.

Japanese firms are almost as likely to be involved in development agreements as are the Europeans, but much less likely to participate in research agreements. Similarly, European companies often negotiate supply agreements with American firms, but the Japanese rarely do so. What accounts for these tendencies?

An answer can be found in the scientific strengths of European societies as compared to Japan. Many of the fundamental scientific discoveries that formed the basis for the emergence of biotechnology were made in Europe. Watson and Crick developed their double helix model of DNA at Cambridge University. Important scientific institutions are found in France, Germany, and Switzerland. All of these countries have major firms in chemicals and pharmaceuticals. Japan's universities turn out large numbers of engineers, but only a small number of Ph.D. scientists in areas related to biotechnology. Their industrial strengths are not in chemicals or pharmaceuticals. In fact, their main biotechnology strength is in fermentation, which is important primarily in large-scale manufacturing. This competitive advantage encourages Japanese companies to concentrate on ties to American firms for technologies ready for market.

The American community of diverse organizational forms is not found elsewhere in the world. Participation in U.S. biotechnology involves a selection process in which foreign firms plug into the community structure selectively. On one hand, this makes it difficult for them to develop a competitive structure in their own countries—they do not develop all the necessary capabilities indigenously. On the other hand, it permits the American community to take advantage of capabilities of foreign firms opportunistically, without carefully orchestrating the details of the development process.

CONCLUSION

This chapter has presented an overview of the major issues and trends involved in the development of the U.S. biotechnology organizational community as we know it today. As such, it has been largely descriptive. We have integrated information from a wide variety of sources to provide a detailed context for the study of organizations in biotechnology at a population level of analysis. Nonetheless, some key points have emerged that may suggest wider trends in contemporary industry.

The most striking observation drawn from research on biotechnology organizations is also the most obvious—that a population of small entrepreneurial science-based firms may remain viable and indeed flourish for over a decade while engaged more in research than in product development. An important task for organizational research, then, is to explain the proliferation and persistence of the dedicated biotechnology firm as an organizational form. The material presented here in digest format provides a survey of the key factors in the institutional environment that coincided to produce ideal conditions for firm foundings and initial public offerings.

In the legal arena, key patent decisions laid the groundwork for the rapid transfer of microbiology and biochemistry into commercial enterprise. Changes in the interpretation of the Prudent Man Rule and the hegemony of portfolio theory ensured the availability of venture capital. Finally, a burgeoning of activity in small public stock offerings provided fuel for the entire enterprise. These legal and economic factors were essential to the establishment of a population of dedicated biotechnology firms.

Perhaps the most important factor has been the strategic orientation of large established corporations to the proliferation of start-ups. Partly because of the threat of lawsuits or public recrimination, most diversified corporations have engaged in biotechnology primarily through strategic alliances. These alliances have in turn become the lifeblood of many biotechnology start-ups.

Finally, the history of biotechnology reveals how pervasive is the influence of key initial organizations, the "founding fathers" of the field. The story of Genentech, for example, was widely circulated, providing a template for the foundings of many other biotechnology firms. One such firm, Genetic Systems, has provided in turn a schema for the formation of many more, especially by demonstrating the potential for astronomical returns to nonscientists who organize new biotechnology enterprises.

What are the organizational lessons we can learn from biotechnology? As businesses are driven toward cooperative patterns in which change and complexity create uncertainty, large organizations can be expected to develop coping strategies that compartmentalize varieties of uncertainty, organizing them externally where they can be kept at arm's length. Rapidly developing technology, with large markets appearing sporadically, offers opportunity for entrepreneurs because existing companies are often too slow to move. Entrepreneurs who know the technology intimately see those opportunities before outsiders do. So existing organizations externalize the uncertainties associated with rapidly changing technology by encouraging the proliferation of small, entrepreneurial dedicated biotechnology firms. They maintain contact through strategic alliances. Ultimately, these alliances provide the information necessary to select targets for takeovers via acquisition. The information may pertain to the ultimate takeover target, but less obviously, it provides context from which to judge the potential of other dedicated biotechnology firms.

An essential characteristic of this system is protection of intellectual property. Without this protection, large, illiquid investments in biotechnology make little sense. Protection of intellectual property allows contracting, in the form of strategic alliances, to be used to replace or at least supplement direct equity investment on one hand and debt financing on the other. The pattern of alliances serves as a mechanism for the distribution of intellectual property across organizational boundaries. Information is transferred from dedicated biotechnology firms to large corporations in exchange for money. Large corporations also receive intellectual property rights in exchange for funding biotechnology research at not-for-profit research institutes, laboratories, universities, and hospitals. Thus, technology is transferred among organizations not through bureaucratic programs but through multiorganizational structures that have emerged from a myriad of relationships among independent organizations. The community grows, flourishes, and evolves as the technology develops.

BIBLIOGRAPHY

Annual Review of Venture Capital. Wellesley Hills, MA: Venture Economics, Inc. A yearly report describing trends in the venture capital community.

Barley, Stephen R., John H. Freeman, and Ralph C. Hybels. 1992. "Strategic Alliances in Commercial Biotechnology." In Nitin Nohria and Robert G. Eccles (eds.), *Networks and Organizations*. Boston: Harvard Business School Press, pp. 311–47. Describes preliminary results of a large project in organizational studies focusing on networks of strategic alliances in biotechnology.

Barney, Jay B., Frances L. Edwards, and Al H. Ringleb. 1992. "Organizational Responses to Legal Liability: Employee Exposure to Hazardous Materials, Vertical Integration, and Small Firm Production." *Academy of Management Journal* 35:328–49. Study of organizational policies for dealing with the risk of litigation related to workplace hazards. Shows that vertical integration is less likely in industries with higher risks.

Boston Business Journal. 1972. "There's Gold in Them Thar Laboratories." June 8, p. 1. Journalistic discussion of the transfer of biotechnology from academia to industry. Focused primarily on Massachusetts, but also discusses the Stanford technology transfer program as a model for others.

Burrill, G. Steven, and Kenneth B. Lee, Jr. 1993. *Biotech 93: Accelerating Commercialization*. San Francisco: Ernst & Young. The seventh annual report on biotechnology published by the Ernst & Young consulting group. One of the primary sources of business-oriented information about the field. Includes the results of an annual survey of decision makers in biotechnology. The current report is available from Ernst & Young for no charge.

Business Week. 1977. "Set for Biology's New Revolution." January 17, p. 76. An early examination in the business press of Cetus Corporation.

Business Week. 1984. "Biotech Comes of Age." January 23, p. 84–94. Reviews the commercial results of biotechnology research as of that date.

Cahill, Scott, Richard Caligaris, and David Williams. 1992. "Have Pharmaceutical Companies Missed the Boat on Biotechnology?" *Medical Marketing and Media*, January, pp. 28–38. Suggests that it is now generally too late for pharmaceutical companies to take advantage of opportunities to enter biotechnology by either acquiring biotechnology firms or negotiating marketing rights.

Dodgson, Mark. 1991. *The Management of Technological Learning: Lessons from a Biotechnology Company.* New York: Walter de Gruyter. A case study of Celltech, Ltd., one of Europe's leading biotechnology firms. Long on detail, but short on contributions to the theory of organizational learning.

Fildes, Robert A. 1990. "Strategic Challenges in Commercializing Biotechnology." *California Management Review,* Spring, pp. 63–72. The internal strategic challenges facing the managers of biotechnology companies include managing technical excellence, maintaining commercial focus, selecting realistic business targets, and the timely acquisition of downstream capabilities. The external strategic challenges include obtaining sufficient capital in volatile markets, competing with Europeans and Japanese, and managing relations with regulatory agencies.

Hamilton, Joan O'C. 1986. "Biotech's First Superstar." *Business Weekly,* April 14, p. 68. Discussion of business strategies at Genentech.

Hamilton, William F., Joaquim Vila, and Mark D. Dibner. 1990. "Patterns of Strategic Choice in Emerging Firms: Positioning for Innovation in Biotechnology." *California Management Review,* Spring, pp. 73–86. Discusses various strategic orientations of biotechnology firms in context of "competence-destroying" technological change. Motivated by two research questions: "To what extent does the relative commitment of emerging firms to commercial activities increase over time in relation to technical activities?" and "Can distinctly different patterns of strategic choice be identified among emerging firms seeking to exploit a common technological discontinuity?" With data from a survey of top managers of biotechnology firms the authors found that new biotechnology firms steadily shifted their focus over the first several years from science to commercial activities. Identifies several strategic types, ranging from firms that are "technology-driven/externally oriented" to those that are "market-driven/internally oriented."

Hirsch, Paul. 1975. "Organizational Effectiveness and the Institutional Environment." *Administrative Science Quarterly* 20:327–44. A comparison of the music recording and pharmaceuticals industries with emphasis on their relative competitive structures.

Kenney, Martin. 1986. *Bio-technology: The University-Industrial Complex.* New Haven, CT: Yale University Press. A history of the biotechnology field, focusing especially on the links between academic microbiology and biotechnology startups. Also examines the roles of venture capital and large multinational corporations. Concludes with a discussion of the likely impact of biotechnology on agriculture.

Kleinfield, N. R. 1983. "Birth of a Health-care Concern." *New York Times,* July 11, p. D1. A brief report on the origins of Genetic Systems Corporation.

Krimsky, Sheldon. 1991. *Biotechnics and Society: The Rise of Industrial Genetics.* New York: Praeger. A history of the field of biotechnology, focusing on the public debate surrounding its perceived risks.

McGraw-Hill's Biotechnology Newswatch. 1981. "72 Firms in 9 Countries Buy Licensing Rights to Cohen-Boyer Basic Patent." December 21, p. 4. Lists licensors of the basic rDNA patent from Stanford.

Ono, R. Dana. 1991. *The Business of Biotechnology: From the Bench to the Street.* Boston: Butterworth-Heinemann. Nineteen chapters by various authors treating many issues arising from the commercialization of biotechnology. These include the transfer of knowledge and commercial rights from universities to industry, how stock in biotechnology firms is promoted to investors, how and why alliances are formed, and the impact on the U.S. field of biotechnology efforts in Europe and Japan.

Pisano, Gary P. 1990. "The R&D Boundaries of the Firm: An Empirical Analysis." *Administrative Science Quarterly* 35:153–76. Examines "make-or-buy" decision in a study of ninety-two R&D projects sponsored by pharmaceutical companies from a transactions-cost perspective. Results indicate that "small-numbers bargaining" problems lead established companies to avoid contracting out certain research projects. Pharmaceutical companies were more likely to have sponsored research internally in product areas where few biotechnology firms operated.

Ross, Nancy L. 1979. "New Law Gives Money Managers Breathing Space." *Washington Post,* July 15, p. G4. A discussion of the projected impact of changes in the interpretation of the Prudent Man Rule on institutional investment policies regarding venture capital.

Saunders, Laura. 1983. "I Can Do That." *Forbes,* July 18, p. 36. A brief report on the origins of Genetic Systems Corporation.

Schneider, Keith. 1990. "Betting the Farm on Biotech." *New York Times Magazine,* June 10, pp. 26–39. A thorough review of Monsanto's efforts in agricultural biotechnology.

Shan, Wijian, Jitendra V. Singh, and Terry L. Amburgey. 1991. "Modeling the Creation of New Biotechnology Firms, 1973–1987." *Academy of Management Proceedings,* pp. 78–82. The authors model founding rates of new biotechnology firms as a function of factors drawn from institutional, resource dependence, and population ecology theories. Results support the first two perspectives. However, received wisdom from population ecology is contradicted by evidence that population density had a negative effect on foundings in the early years of the field, and a positive effect in later years.

Teitelman, Robert. 1989. *Gene Dreams: Wall Street, Academia, and the Rise of Biotechnology.* New York: Basic Books. Given the recent performance of biotechnology stocks, this book appears dated because of its relatively gloomy forecast for small biotechnology firms' prospects. Nonetheless, it is a well-researched journalistic account that presents a refreshingly skeptical view of the relationship between Wall Street financiers and the commercialization of biotechnology. The story of Genetic Systems is treated in special depth.

U.S. Congress, Office of Technology Assessment. *New Developments in Biotechnology: Ownership of Human Tissues and Cells.* OTA-BA-337. March 1987. One of several reports by the OTA on issues related to the biotechnology field. These reports are an excellent source of information for organizational studies of biotechnology.

Watson, James D. 1968. *The Double Helix.* New York: Atheneum Publishers. An engaging narrative about the discovery of DNA, written by one of the key players.

Wirtschafter, Jacob. 1990. "High-flying U.S. Investor Raises Stake in Israel Biotech Company." *Jerusalem Post,* May 1. Report on the involvement of David Blech in Biotechnology General.

CONCLUDING NOTES

In introducing this book we promised a different glimpse of industry—one informed by organizational theory and gleaned from the organizational histories of production activities. We paid special attention to organizational ecology. This theory of organizations seeks to explain long-term organizational change by examining selective patterns of organizational founding, growth, decline, and failure. Chapter authors examined the histories of various industries through this lens.

In concluding, we reflect on the materials covered in the chapters on industries and reconnect them to theoretical and managerial concerns. In other words, we seek to review briefly what we have learned from the chapters at a general level and to place it in broad perspective. The discussion is organized around three general topics: organizational structures, selection processes, and strategy and organizational design.

STRUCTURES

Perhaps the most striking feature of the industries we have examined is their *abundance and diversity* of organizations. In most industries, literally thousands of organizations have operated at one time or another. Such abundance permits great diversity of structures. The populations we have examined are made up of organizations of very different sizes, with many different types of structures, and with strategies ranging from extreme specialism to broad generalism.

The great abundance and diversity of organizations and organizational structures should not be surprising for industries such as microcomputer manufacture and biotechnology, whose diversity is regularly regaled in the contemporary press. However, we doubt that the earlier diversity of industries such as telephone service, railroads, and automobile manufacture is widely understood or appreciated.

Consider, for instance, the automobile industry. Some critics of organizational ecology had pointed to it as an industry where explanation based on selection processes seemed implausible, because in the 1980s they saw only three large American firms: General Motors, Ford, and Chrysler. A look below the surface showed many more firms, as many as 100, all producing automobiles for specialized or anticipated future markets. It is easy to ridicule a comparison of any one of these firms with GM. Perhaps none will grow to rival its giant competitor. But consider an example from another industry: computing. Only a few years ago, IBM stood as the unchallenged master of the industry. Firms like Microsoft and Apple Computer were ridiculously smaller and less powerful than IBM. However, fifteen-year-old Microsoft is worth more in terms of stock market valuations than IBM (and General Motors, for that matter) as we write this chapter. If such a reversal can happen in one core industry, why not another? A sudden breakthrough in technology or a radical change in market conditions could allow one or more marginal firms to become the major players in the industry.

Even more enlightening is the abundance and diversity of automobile producers in the full historical record, traced to origin of the industry. By our count, over 2,200 firms participated in this industry. Another 3,300 groups of actors attempted to enter the industry but never succeeded in ramping-up production. The variety of autos produced by early entrepreneurs stimulates the imagination. Steam and electric engines are well known; autos with six wheels or airplane propellers are not.

What are we to make of such diversity? Most organization theory makes nothing of it, sweeping it under the rug and ignoring it. In ecological theory, however, organizational diversity takes center stage. The ecological orienting question, "Why are there so many different kinds of organizations?" encourages one to focus on diversity as a key to understanding the larger social and economic conditions that shape industry. It sensitizes one to the similarity of processes that drive different organizational populations. It also directs attention away from the fates of individual organizations and the actions of their leaders. Each of these redirections assists in developing a more sociological understanding of organizations and industry, one that does not assume every action and outcome observed is economically rational.

SELECTION PROCESSES

We have examined many different industries in which diverse factors operate. In seeking to make sense of this variety, we have emphasized a few processes that shape selection and evolution in the world of organizations. In particular, we organized the book around four types of organizational evolutionary processes: environmental selection, density-dependent evolution, resource partitioning, and segregation. We adopted this structure not only to feature these important evolutionary processes but also to illustrate the different ways each might get played out.

Environmental selection theory uses a general framework to explain the rise and fall of organizational forms based on environmental and other resources. The chapter by Philip Anderson on the microcomputer industry shows how technology and consumer market resources shape an organizational population. A very different view of environmental selection is given by Frank Dobbin in his discussion of railroads, where public policy is the central environmental factor. An even different notion is provided by Judith Blau in her account of art museums. Here culture and ideology drive the selection process.

Density dependence describes the empirical implications of a specific ecological theory of evolution driven by legitimation and competition. Labor unions, credit unions, health maintenance organizations, newspapers, and automobile manufacturers are among the many organizational populations known to evolve according to the predictions of this theory. However, as the chapters on these industries by David Barron, David Strang, and ourselves show, there is still much variation in the ways organizations within an industry proliferate over time. Understanding these differences and assessing them in terms of the strength of density dependence is a task for comparative organizational analysis.

The other specific theory of organizational ecology we reviewed is resource partitioning. This theory accounts for the rise of specialist organizations in concentrated markets, a situation many consider paradoxical. Both beer brewing and medical diagnostic image manufacture show signs of resource partitioning. For brewing, a single specialist segment composed of two organizational forms (brewpubs and microbreweries) has emerged according to Swaminathan and Carroll. For diagnostic imaging, a series of specialist segments has appeared, by Will Mitchell's account.

Organizational populations segregate on many dimensions and the industries we reviewed illustrate the range of segregating mechanisms. William Barnett's discussion of the early telephone industry focuses on constraints imposed by law and the interactions of different organizational forms. In examining investment banks, Joel Podolny identifies status-oriented boundaries segregating the various firms. Huseyin Leblebici's review of the radio broadcast industry points to the networks and bank types as factors isolating groups of firms. Allan Ryan, John Freeman, and Ralph Hybels discuss how product market orientation segmented biotechnology firms into homogeneous subgroups.

The four organizational population processes thus are broadly applicable. Understanding these processes helps one to predict how industries might unfold over time.

STRATEGY AND ORGANIZATIONAL DESIGN

A recent textbook on organizational theory claims that organizational ecology has no strategic implications for managers. The author does not fully explain the reasoning behind his proclamation but, given that we have heard others state similar views, we conclude by making a few comments on strategy and organization design.

Principles of organizational design are formulated to solve three basic problems of managing organizations: (1) control of behavior within the organization; (2) coordination of activities within the organization; and (3) matching of the organization with its environment. There are, of course, many ways to solve

these problems and theoretical perspectives such as contingency theory, resource dependence theory, transaction cost theory, and institutional theory differ in both the problems they primarily address and the specific solutions they
propose. The goal of an organization designer is not just to choose a theory
that works in that it solves the problem, but to choose the least costly or most
efficient of workable solutions available. In the modern world, many performance differences of organizations hinge on this choice—personnel and other
resources are often less important than is efficient organizational structure.

The many specific theories of organizational design address a common set of
choices in structure that need to be made for every organization. These choices
can be considered principles around which the design is organized. The essential prescriptive material found in textbooks usually covers the following principles:

1. *Grouping principle*: Design formal organizational structures to group
   together interdependent activities that require the greatest effort and
   most time to accomplish. In its most general form, this principle includes questions of where to draw organizational boundaries.
2. *Culture principle*: Substitute informal organizational structures for formal structures when this does not undermine strategic goals.
3. *Strategy principle*: Set a clear direction for the organization's intended
   future; articulate it in an abstract way that allows members to drive
   and understand operating guidance at even the lowest level of the organization.
4. *Environmental principle*: Design structures that map onto important
   environmental dimensions in a way that provides for fast and reliable
   flows of information, services, and products across organizational
   boundaries.
5. *Legitimation principle*: Set up structures that signify conformity with
   prevailing environmental laws and institutional rules, even when these
   structures have no immediately apparent means-ends like connection
   with the organization's tasks.

Ecological theorists do not subscribe to a single principle of organizational
design—in fact, their approach is compatible with many different specific design theories. For instance, one could attempt to explain the rise and fall of
various organizational forms from transaction cost minimization or cultural isomorphism.

Ecological theories also have implications for various specific theories of
organizational design. Those we have examined in this book focus mainly on
predictions about generalism-specialism.

The antipathy to organizational ecology in some design circles most likely
stems from the theory's strong stance on inertia. Often, the ecological theory
of inertia is interpreted as meaning that organizations never change. As we
have taken pains to explain, that interpretation is wrong—ecological theory
only holds that successful planned change is very difficult to effect, a view held

by many managers and executives. Moreover, it is consistent with an emerging sixth principle of organizational design:

6. *Inertia principle*: When attempting strategic redirection or major transformation, establish new and isolated structures rather than attempt to change existing structures embracing old patterns.

Finally, we note that whatever its current implications for organizational design, it is difficult to believe that organizational ecology will not become increasingly valuable to managers. As the organizational world continues to change rapidly and new forms of organization replace old ones, understanding the processes that drive these changes can only help managers anticipate and prepare for them. If the processes suggest that organizational adaptation is difficult, then managers should know that.

SUBJECT INDEX

ORGANIZATION INDEX